DISCOVERED COUNTRY

DISCOVERED COUNTRY

Tourism and Survival in the American West

edited by
Scott Norris

Stone Ladder Press
Albuquerque, New Mexico

Some of the essays in this book originally appeared in other publications. The following are reprinted with the permission of the author and the original publisher:

From *High Country News*: "Aspen: A Colonial Power with Angst," "A Passive Town in Utah Awaits Its Fate," and "New West Blues"

From *Northern Lights*: "Communiqué from the Vortex of Gravity Sports," "The Meadow at the Corner of Your Eye," and "Tourism Trap"

From *Wilderness* magazine: "Mountain Passages" and an earlier version of "Careless Love"

From the *Santa Fe Reporter*: "Romancing Mora" and "What Price Tourism?"

From the *Journal of Anthropological Research*: "Art, Tourism, and Race Relations in Taos."

Grateful acknowledgment is made for permission to reproduce the following:

A slightly different version of "Mudwomen and Whitemen" was originally published in the book *Gender and Material Culture* (Winterthur Publications).

Earlier versions of "Swiss Wilderness" appeared in *The Gettysburg Review* and in *The Four-Cornered Falcon: Essays on the Interior West and the Natural Scene* (Johns Hopkins University Press, 1993).

"The View from the Road" is excerpted from a longer chapter of the same name in *The Culture of Nature: North American Landscape from Disney to the Exxon Valdez* (Blackwell Publishers, 1992).

First edition August 1994
ISBN 0-9637623-0-3
Library of Congress Catalog Card Number 94-66179

Cover photograph: *Tours* (sign above expired gold dredge on the Yankee Creek, central Idaho) by Courtney White
Cover design by Michael Reed
Typography and production by Prototype, Albuquerque, NM

Stone Ladder Press
P.O. Box 82577
Albuquerque, NM 87198

Contents

Preface

Scott Norris

*I*n putting this collection together, I found that the idea of "a book of critical writings on tourism in the West" made perfect sense to some people but drew only blank stares from others. There are those for whom tourism is a problem, at least on some level, and those for whom it is not . . . at least not yet. The word *tourism* itself may bring to mind pleasant images of vacationers enjoying themselves in picturesque or exotic surroundings, or it may suggest a very different kind of scene: communities overwhelmed by hoards of visitors and a sprawling service sector infrastructure built to accommodate them. How a person views tourism depends largely on his or her experience. Most Americans have been tourists. Fewer have seen their own lives and surroundings become slowly objectified, transformed by an essentially ungoverned economic response to the needs and desires (comfort, pleasure, experience, understanding) of people from some other place. But in the American West, as in much of the rest of the world, this ratio is rapidly changing.

This is not to suggest that, for the places travel agents call "destinations" and sociologists call "host communities," the effects of tourism are all negative. It has been common, however, for tourism to be promoted as a low-impact, sustainable industry with few serious social or environmental costs. That such a view is naive is apparent to anyone who has ever peered behind a high-rise facade in a resort city like Cancun, anyone who understands what *aspenification* means. Tourism is a global industry—current trends indicate it is fast becoming *the* global industry—and its impacts must be considered as a function of its enormity. As a worldwide enterprise based on the packaging and selling of *place*, tourism will play a major role in shaping, for good or ill, the physical, social, and psychological geographies of the year 2000 and the coming century. In some places and in some contexts its role may be positive. It remains to be seen, for example, whether "ecotourism" can in the long run fulfill its promise of promoting both economic development and ecosystem preservation; but as we enter a period of catastrophic decline in global biodiversity, the potential benefits of this kind of tourism should certainly not be discounted.

For most of the writers in this book, the "tourism problem" is really a set of problems that seems to emerge whenever tourism becomes a significant economic and social force in a region or community. "Tourism" in this expanded sense includes or implies a number of issues: the often abrupt and unplanned development of service industries and of a low-wage economy based on these industries; seasonal or permanent increases in population that exceed the carrying capacity of community infrastructure, resulting in environmental damage and social displacement; overuse and degradation of even "protected" natural areas and scenic resources; the commodification and commercialization of local history, culture, and ethnicity; and the rapid growth, inflation, and gentrification brought about not just by the flow of visitors but also by what anthropologist Sylvia Rodriguez (following Lawrence Moss) terms "amenity migrants"—former tourists who move to, or buy second homes in, their favorite vacation site. All of these problems and others can be found to differing degrees in different locations throughout the West.

I first became interested in tourism as a social phenomenon in 1990. At the time I was a graduate student in cultural anthropology at the University of New Mexico and a manager of an Albuquerque bookstore specializing in regional and environmental issues. I became intrigued by the extent to which tourism was (and is) being critically discussed and debated in quite different ways by two largely separate groups of people. One group consists of academics—anthropologists, sociologists, cultural theorists of various sorts—who study tourism and the transformations it brings about as illustrative of various larger theoretical issues regarding social relations in modern society, the hegemonic appropriation of cultural difference, and postmodernity. A benchmark and frequent reference in this field of "tourism studies" is Dean MacCannell's book *The Tourist*, first published in 1976.

In the American West tourism is also being discussed in more immediate and pragmatic terms by regional writers and journalists, environmentalists, community activists and others. This discussion is going on wherever tourism and related development are changing the character of local communities and surrounding landscapes. It can be followed in the editorial columns (and sometimes the front pages) of small-town newspapers throughout the West, in the environmental media, and in regional publications such as *High Country News*. Some see tourism as a sustainable economic base for a region in desperate need of alternatives to the unpredictable cycles and heavy environmental costs of extractive industry. Others see conversion to a tourist economy as a kind of devil's bargain, a selling of place, history, and cultural identity in exchange for seasonal, low-wage employment in an increasingly urbanized, economically stratified, and corporate-dominated social environment. Although tourism is the focus of discussion, the wider issue is survival—of towns and peoples, of ways of life, of "the West."

This book could easily have become two—a collection of academic papers on the one hand, an anthology of New West essays on the other. Such volumes already exist, in good number. My explicit goal here was to bring together a representative sampling of the *entire* critical discourse on tourism in the West. Thus, in addition to being a book about tourism, this collection is also intended as something of an experiment in textual composition. It is at least a gesture toward bridging the gap that (I think needlessly) distances critical social theory from on-the-ground political, ethical, and aesthetic concerns, and that tends to cause academic and non-academic writers (and their respective readers) to ignore or disvalue the others' insights and concerns. My hope is that followers of the theoretical work on tourism can gain some new insights from a close reading of some of the journalistic accounts and personal reflections contained in Section One of this collection, and that general readers with an interest in these issues can benefit from a look at what the anthropologists and sociologists are up to.

The collection begins with an historical overview of tourism in North America, reprinted from Alexander Wilson's fine book *The Culture of Nature*. Section One includes a series of articles and essays detailing the impacts of tourism on different Western communities in different stages of transition to, or development of, a tourism-based economy. These journalistic pieces are best viewed as neither up-to-date nor dated; they are snapshots in time, profiles of communities in particular moments of change— e.g., Moab 1991. This section also contains some more philosophical meditations on how tourism shapes our understanding and experience of the natural world, and of each other. Most of these pieces take a cautionary or critical perspective toward the idea that tourism and related development represent a sustainable economic future for Western communities. A number of the pieces in this section have been previously published elsewhere; some have been revised or updated. The essays by Donald Snow, Linda Hasselstrom, William Corcoran, and John Nichols appear here for the first time. Courtney White's photographs, which comprise Section Two, provide commentary in a different form.

The five papers contained in Section Three have a common theme: how tourism and tourist-driven economies (such as the Southwestern Indian arts market) tend to result in the commodification (meaning literally, "the making into a market commodity") of indigenous culture and ethnicity. This is viewed as a deleterious process that involves the appropriation (by outsiders) of elements of the indigenous culture and the fixation of value in certain kinds of cultural production that can be labeled and marketed as "authentic" or "traditional." Three of these papers are reprints; Dean MacCannell's investigation into the use and abuse of "tradition" with respect to native arts and Mark Neumann's account of the commercialization of nature and culture at the Grand Canyon are published here for the first time. The book finally returns to the vernacular with an original Charles Bowden essay that stands as a counterpoint to everything else—a profile of life in a small Arizona town that has rejected every opportunity to earn a place on the map of the New West.

I'd like to thank everyone who submitted material and all the publishers who responded to my inquiries concerning reprints. Special thanks go to Ed and Betsy Marston at *High Country News* and to Don Snow at *Northern Lights* for permission to reprint several pieces. Marta Weigle and Sylvia Rodriguez provided advice and encouragement during the initial stages of this project. I'm also grateful for the unflagging support of John Randall and everyone at Salt of the Earth Books. Finally thanks to Michael Reed, without whose first-rate editorial and production work this project could never have been completed.

Introduction

The View from the Road
Recreation and Tourism

Alexander Wilson

Modern tourism was born out of the application of social policies which led to industrial workers obtaining annual paid holidays, and at the same time found its expression through the recognition of the basic human right to rest and leisure.
—United Nations declaration on tourism, 1980

*I*n the mid-1980s, I took a railway trip from Toronto to Vancouver. The train, called The Canadian, was old and tatty and filled with grumpy American travelers who were in the country by default—Canada was a tourist destination without terrorists. But no tourist experience comes without its own logic, its own way of organizing the landscape and our sense of it. The train carried us to Vancouver, all right, but on the way it stirred us to pay belated though still sincere homage to the Canadian landscape.

The dining car was the most intact remnant of this vestigial nationalism. Called the Queen Alexandra, it was a royal blue ode to prairie songbirds and prairie hospitality, with wonderful etched glass dividers and stars on the ceiling. Here was a colonial nostalgia whose restraint and innocence spoke of the early 1950s, yet it was overlaid with the ruthless corporate reality of our own day: mass-produced meals and packaged travelers who probably wanted to go to Greece but ended up in Saskatchewan.

Out the window, as always, the vast land itself flitted by, so familiar from the postcards but silent and untouchable from inside our glass cases. I remember wanting to get off the train at every point and lie in the sweet summer fields. While it's nice to think that my image of those fields came from within, from the memory of authentic, animated, *real* space, I know that it is also part of the repertoire of images of nature that tourist culture produces in great number and variety, and that in some ways are indistinguishable from nature itself.

Tourism organizes our experience of the world and its many aggregate cultures and landscapes. In the past fifty years or so it has become a global phenomenon involving millions of people. It is also a big and growing industry—and the principal one for the economies of many countries and regions in the Third World. It may also be the largest industry in North America by the turn of the twenty-first century. The history of tourism is a confusing one, because no one knows quite what it is or when it started. What we can say is that its history parallels that of modern industrial society. While people traveled for pleasure before that time, and the wealthy classes of imperial Rome or China had holiday villas in the country, modern mass tourism represents a vastly different way of moving through the world. It has created a whole range of new landscapes: motel strips and campgrounds, airports, beach compounds, amusement parks, and convention centers. It has promoted the growth of a managerial class whose job it is to organize human desires and leisure time. It has extended the commodity form both out into the natural world and back into our imaginations. The Caribbean holiday, after all, is a mass-marketed product as well as a place. Like a tin of fruit cocktail, the promise of a holiday experience has been manufactured out of the material and ideological resources available to contemporary culture. The "destination," as they say in the business, is an integral part of the identity of the Caribbean holiday product at the same time as it's strangely irrelevant: basically, anything with sun and palm trees will do. Lastly, modern tourism is a phenomenon that is both urban and rural, and at the same time it breaks down the distinction between the two. It has vastly reorganized not only the geography of North America but also our perceptions of nature and our place in it as humans.

Tourism has more than a coincidental relationship with modern industrial society. As the 1980 United Nations declaration on tourism points out, the phenomenon is one of the byproducts of that society. Certainly one outcome of the long history of industrial capitalism has been the creation of leisure time. But leisure isn't time like any other. It's supposed to be a discretionary kind of time, different from the productive time spent at work. Leisure is a nineteenth-century idea, introduced by a culture that defined work itself as a separate sphere of life, an activity that had its own politics and increasingly its own place in the landscape. In the nineteenth century, work was still a redemptive activity. But work has changed, and so has the politics of labor. Because new technologies have eliminated certain kinds of work and made much of what's left meaningless, leisure time is increasingly the time, and creates the space, where we look for meaning in our lives. A lot of social institutions are now organized around buying, eating, or sightseeing rather than around the social bonds built through labor. It isn't always this way, of course. People also use leisure time to engage in other kinds of activities altogether: to build local cultures and communities—or simply to work in the garden.

These shifts in the nature of work and leisure are also part of the history of tourism. By the mid-twentieth century, technological change in North American industry had created considerable wealth. The response of most Canadian and U.S. workers, however, was not to gain more control over the labor process—to demand shorter working hours and more time of their own, for example—but to settle for higher wages and easy credit as an entrée into the growing culture of affluence, what was usually talked about as the American way of life. The cycle of ever-increasing growth and consumption became a near universal creed. Thus, during the 1950s and 1960s, the modern utopian visions of a beneficent technology ushering in a society of ease and plenitude easily translated into mass desire for leisure commodities. Cars, trailers, motorboats, camping equipment, home appliances, vacation cottages, televisions—in other words, people sought out shopping centers, superstores, and everything inside them. These were the forms that leisure and tourism had taken on this continent by the middle of the present century.

The links between tourism and contemporary society are not only economic. Tourism has all along had a particular role to play in our experience of modernity. By circulating through the material and natural world, we juxtapose the many contradictions of our everyday lives and try to make them whole. When I recall my experience of the train that summer, I begin with images of dead queens and terrorists and grain elevators; then I remember the microwaved Pacific Salmon Almandine in the Rockies, the gleaming bank towers in Calgary, and a man fishing from a boat in the Precambrian Shield at sunset (the Korean monk in the next seat took a snapshot of him). Sometimes I read while all this was going on, and sometimes I listened to music I'd brought along. That train trip, and its many small pleasures and disruptions, somehow coalesce for me into orderly but still ambivalent images of life in Canada in the late twentieth century.

This ambivalence characterizes much of what's called modern life, and as modernity gets updated we must keep sightseeing just so we can understand our place in it. Our cultures, our landscapes, our social institutions are continually demolished and rebuilt. Each new moment of modernity promises to heal the wounds it continues to inflict, while at the same time encouraging us to imagine an open future. We tour the disparate surfaces of everyday life as a way of involving ourselves in them, as a way of reintegrating a fragmented world. Tourism is thus a thoroughly modern phenomenon. Its institutions—package cruises, museums and amusement parks, self-guided nature trails and visits to a shrine to the Virgin Mary, the grave of Wild Bill Hickok, or the site where a president was assassinated—continually differentiate and reorganize our experience of the world. One way they do this is by naming the modern and separating it off from the premodern—or the merely old-fashioned, which in contemporary culture often amounts to the same thing. Thus the tattered VIA Rail cars that hurtled us across the continent that summer were "outdated," as our U.S. visitors pointed out more than once, while Calgary was somehow "new," or in any case, different from that. The outdated is sometimes demolished (as much of it has been in Calgary) and sometimes preserved as a reference point for us, an "authentic" curiosity that reminds us of the victory of the modern over the ever-receding past.

Tourism locates us in space as well as time. It has redefined the land in terms of leisure. It began to do this at a moment when most North Americans were being wrenched from traditional relations with the land. It's no accident that industrial agriculture, the spread of suburbs, and the growth of mass tourism all coincided in the mid-twentieth century.

The Roots of Nature Tourism

Nature has figured large in leisure activities since the mid-nineteenth century and the history of nature tourism provides a good sense of the history of relations between humans and the natural world over the past 150 years. It also reveals how tourism *organizes* those relations.

Nature tourism is simply the temporary migration of people to what they understand to be a different and usually more "pure" environment. It's going out to nature for its own sake, and it's all of the ways we talk about that experience. The modern history of nature tourism is a history of altered landforms and changed ideas and experiences of the non-human. Broadly speaking, it involves a shift from a pastoral approach to nature to a consumer approach. This in itself is a huge and significant transition.

In the 1850s and 1860s, the parks movement got underway in the large cities of the United States and Canada. It grew out of a widespread dissatisfaction with industrial culture and its momentous effects on the landscape. This dissatisfaction was not a new sentiment in its time. The myth of nature as a lost garden permeates both the Greek and Hebraic roots of Western culture. In the nineteenth-century version of that myth, in the age of what would be called the Industrial Revolution, popular nostalgia for nature overlapped in key ways with the culture of Romanticism. Cities grew quickly, becoming crowded and polluted. Many people began to see nature as the tonic for an unhealthy urban life. In the 1850s in the United States, and somewhat later in Canada, amateur horticultural and urban reform organizations built small parks to "improve" urban life. These parks were to have a moral as well as physical function: healthy open spaces, reformers thought, would alleviate the cities' many social and physical ills. The parks movement was followed by the playgrounds movement in the last years of the century, and like the parks movement the playgrounds movement was originally a citizens' initiative, in this case largely organized by women's groups. Typically, a neighborhood improvement association organized itself to save a vacant lot from development; the undeveloped urban land was versatile and could be devoted to play of all kinds. In the long term, the social goal of the playgrounds movement was to convince the public of the beneficial aspects of play and games and see that "supervised" recreation of all types was provided for in schools and neighborhoods. By the last years of the nineteenth century, parks in both Boston and Montreal had sand gardens for infants, ball fields and instruction in games, folk dancing, first aid, and storytelling. Outdoor organizations like the Camp Fire Girls and the YMCA date from this period.

These movements had two effects that interest us here. One was the new possibility of thinking about recreation as an activity apart from our other everyday tasks. Recreation assumed its own schedule and its own locations in the landscape. It had become a form of leisure. In the contemporary literature of the tourist industry, this is talked about as an increase in demand for outdoor experiences. At first these new activities were organized around the dominant social institutions of their day, like schools and churches, and in fact the collectivization of recreation was closely related to the collectivization of work and the formation of unions.

The other effect of these movements was a general reawakening of interest in the natural world. To be sure, it was at first a natural world shaped by the shears and spades of urban culture, for nature appreciation directly coincided with urbanization and industrialization. By the late nineteenth century, almost half of North Americans lived in cities. It was not until then—the moment that in the United States is called "the closing of the frontier" and in Canada "the opening of the West"—that wilderness itself assumed value in popular culture. In the United States, progress was measured by how far nature—and the aboriginal peoples who were often understood to be part of it—had been pushed back, and the feeling at the close of the nineteenth century, at least in the United States, was that the job was nearly done. It became possible to argue then that the wilderness had to be preserved. In Canada, where nature was not so easily pushed back, the wilderness ethic did not gain currency as quickly as in the United States.

The love of nature flourishes best in cultures with highly developed technologies, for nature is the one place we can both indulge our dreams of mastery over the earth and seek some kind of contact with the origins of life—an experience we don't usually allow urban settings to provide. Since at least the witch burnings of the sixteenth century, people of European origin have regarded nature as separate from human civilization, which makes it possible to argue for its protection. The native peoples of North America have never shared these attitudes. For them, the natural world is not a refuge—the "other" to an urban industrial civilization—but a place that is sacred in and of itself. In native cosmologies, human cultures are compatible with natural systems, and it is a human responsibility to keep things that way.

Recreational Resources

By the 1870s and 1880s, wealthy city dwellers were taking curative holidays at Rocky Mountain spas and seaside resorts. At the same time, the recreational activities available to the growing middle class were also edging out of the city. Hunting and fishing and canoeing had evolved into sports, and the urban dwellers now flocking to the country on holidays encouraged this trend. Church and youth organizations established outdoor education programs as part of their regular activities. It was out of this general social matrix that the Woodcraft Indians, Boy Scouts, national parks, and modern conservation movements emerged.

Transportation technology was also key. Town squares and commons, for example, are old phenomena in North American cities, but public parks *per se* didn't show up until people could get to them on public transit. By the late nineteenth century, railroads allowed the growth of suburbs on the edges of cities and provided access to beaches and lakes well outside city boundaries. After World War I, the car propelled recreation out of the cities for large numbers of the middle class. By the 1950s, these trends had all magnified, and country and city now bear a very different physical and philosophical relation to one another.

This general rekindling of interest in nature and the new possibilities of access to it had effects that we still feel today. As more and more people traveled to the natural areas of the continent for a "change of scene," the areas themselves ceased to be thought of solely as sanctuaries from the ills of civilization. Instead, they were now often talked about as "outdoor recreation resources"—a jargon that came out of the popular movements to preserve the parks and forests of North America for the future. The language underscored the new ways rural spaces were appended to urban cultures and to the expanding North American economy. Recreational nature became a place of leisure on weekends and summer holidays; it became attached to the schedules and personal geographies of an urban society.

Several things happened during the years following World War II. In the first place, most North Americans had a lot more money. The war had inflated the economy, and while women were unceremoniously escorted back from factories to the hearths where they were now supposed to marshal the new armies of consumerism, men for the most part were able to move into regular employment. Many people had savings from the war, government grants were available and, if nothing else, credit was easy to arrange. (Diners Club and American Express credit cards both appeared in the early 1950s.) After a long period of austerity, the 1950s was a time of exploding affluence. Families were larger and now usually included one car if not two. Leisure time was organized into discrete activities matched to the products of a leisure industry. Outdoor recreation had become a mass phenomenon. For holidays, people often went on automobile trips along new roads that reached far into the natural areas of the continent. There was a new mass market for recreational services and commodities: motels and drive-ins, both of which were around well before World War II, sprang up in large numbers along highway strips and at interchanges. Shops and chain-store catalogues were filled with outdoor equipment of every kind.

There were exceptions to this general trend. For one thing, the idea of nature as an untrammeled refuge is most attractive to cultures situated at some distance from the rural world, and whose values tend to rest on a rigid distinction between the human and the non-human. Utopias, after all, are culturally specific. Thus the non-European peoples of this continent, particularly African-Americans and Amerindians, have traditionally regarded the idea of vast nature reserves with some skepticism and bewilderment. Moreover, both of these peoples have associations with the North American soil—associations as painful as they are deep. Black slaves were imprisoned on the harsh plantations of the South, and freedom historically meant flight to the northern cities. Latinos have had a similar history in the industrial plantations of the modern sunbelt and in Puerto Rico.

Native people, on the other hand, have been explained away as savages almost to the present day. Their ancient kinship with the animals of North America has often been turned into a slur. In the early years of the U.S. national parks, especially in the Southwest, native families were simply part of the scenery; their production of handicrafts was a popular attraction for the white tourists who were herded through Indian households as if those homes were museums. Non-white people have enjoyed very little of the immense wealth that has saturated Canadian and U.S. societies since the Second World War. For all of these reasons, the postwar boom in recreation took place largely without the direct participation of non-whites—a fact usually ignored in the professional literature on the subject.

Regardless of who participated, the rapid development of a recreational infrastructure brought about a new set of relations between humans and everything we call nature. While the places visited might all have existed before, people experienced them in new ways. Nature tourism catalogued the natural world and created its own spaces out there among the trees, lakes, and rocks. It sold us nature-related products, and indeed it began to sell us natural space and experiences too. All of these activities served to fragment the land: here we have a sunbathing beach, over there a nature trail for the blind, further along there's an RV (recreational vehicle) campground or a petting zoo or a "singles' crosscountry weekend." Nature tourism differentiates our experiences of the natural world, with several consequences. The most obvious is that this differentiation makes it easier to package and sell nature as a product. It also means more people can enjoy natural areas. It means that it's now more difficult to experience nature as a whole, as the total environment that for centuries and centuries has been our *home*—which is, after all, a very different kind of space from a "recreation resource."

The Car and the Road

By the 1920s, the car had become a popular means of transport, and with the beginnings of a highway infrastructure, intercity travel increased dramatically. Between the two world wars, the construction of surfaced roads increased fourfold. Even during the Depression of the 1930s, large-scale road construction continued unabated, often as a part of government relief programs. By the mid-1950s, multi-lane parkways and freeways had been built to expedite traffic from city to suburb and city to city; and the car had insinuated itself into the daily habits and desires of millions of North Americans.

While the population of North America has roughly doubled in the past fifty years, highway travel has increased almost tenfold. The private car accounts for more than 80 percent of all travel—75 percent of all tourist travel—in North America. These trends—from highway construction to car acquisition and use—have remained relatively constant for the last five decades. They are a good indication of how the automobile became the keystone of the postwar North American economy. These changes didn't happen by themselves of course; several U.S. corporations, most notably General Motors, practiced ruthless marketing strategies that would ultimately ensure the car its central place in North American culture. This meant designing cars with what's now called planned obsolescence and making them the only choice for millions of commuting workers. The control over choice was achieved partly by buying up and eliminating mass-transit companies.

This is a well-known history, with consequences that most people understand. But what does it mean in terms of the landscape and our relation to it? In the first place, the car and the modern highway bring with them a different ordering of space. Before the car, most roads took care of all manner of traffic. But once the car was in general use, traffic had to be functionally separated: trucks and cars from pedestrians and bicycles, local and feeder traffic from intercity travel. Expressways, for example, are usually set off on a different grade from surrounding land, and access to them is strictly controlled—changes that imply a rationalization of space. Certain roads come to have certain purposes: some are for whisking travelers and goods past places (whether urban or rural) as quickly as possible. In this case, the landscape you move through is subordinate to your destination. Other roads, such as the nature parkways begun in the 1930s, bar commercial traffic and in the design of their curves and rest areas instruct drivers about how best to appreciate the scenery out the window. In both cases, the car further divides the landscape, and our experience of it, into discrete zones. It promotes some landscapes and discourages others.

In the 1950s, new road-building technologies carried more people than ever before out of the cities to play in the country. In 1944, the U.S. Congress passed the Defense Highway Act, which authorized the construction of a massive national network of roads that would supposedly allow for movement of troops and materiel in case of foreign attack. In Canada, the Alaska Highway, authorized in 1948, had similar military beginnings. In 1956, U.S. workers began construction on the Interstate Highway System, aided by revenues from a gasoline tax. The tax, in fact, could only be spent on highway construction for the first sixteen years. The highways encouraged car acquisition and use, the cars in turn consumed more gas, and the tax on the gas ensured the construction of more highways. The interstate highways, completed in the mid-1980s, amounted to a massive government subsidy to the auto industry and its many dependents, including tourism.

Tourism grew by about 10 percent annually during the 1950s and 1960s, and it was largely a tourism organized around the car and the highway. Pleasure driving had become the most popular form of outdoor recreation, and for many people older forms of outdoor activities—camping, for example—became an adjunct of car travel. Car and camping technologies merged. The new highways were thus not only a measure of the culture's technological prowess, but they were also fully integrated into the cultural economy. They were talked about as though they had an important democratizing role: the idea was that modern highways allowed more people to appreciate the wonders of nature.

The car also made possible the establishment of a vacation-home industry during the 1950s and 1960s. This changed the physiography of resorts in interesting ways. It used to be—and here we might recall the great nineteenth-century spas—that resorts were typed according to the natural features of the landscape they were part of. So there were mountain resorts like Banff, there were spas, ski resorts, seaside resorts, and so on. Once mass second-home building got under way in the late 1950s, resorts lost many of their ties to locale. The most obvious effect of the car on nature tourism was a large-scale diffusion of recreation across the landscape. Holidaygoers no longer took rest cures at one place, but sought out ever more distant and "unspoiled" recesses in their cars. When A-frame and other prefab homes replaced resorts in many people's itineraries, there was a proliferation of tourist sites, and consequently the experience of nature became more private for many people. By the mid-1960s, the resorts themselves had changed in character: either they went out of business or they adapted to the demands of a new and different clientele. Today, traveling families have been replaced by conventiongoers and corporate head officers attending marketing seminars. These clients expect familiar surroundings—amenities, they're called—that are not specific to locale.

As the growth of rural tourism proceeded, the geographical focus shifted from natural features of the landscape to artificial ones such as golf courses or African animal–safari parks. The reasons for this are complex, but they had mostly to do with the need for the industry to differentiate its products to serve a rapidly expanding market. Marine parks and Santa's Villages, whether in California or Kansas, were like so many interchangeable brands of cigarettes or pain relievers, each with its target audience. Thus scenic legitimacy came to rest partly on the marketing strategies of the tourist industry, as well as on the vagaries of land speculation. All of these changes led to new fields of study, including tourist motivational assessment and scenery evaluation, which by the 1960s had become the subject of intense scrutiny within the industry.

Where the landscape itself was adaptable to this new industrial situation, so much the better. For example, in the forest-lake complex of much of the north-central area of the North American continent, the aesthetic values already in place coalesced with the demands of a growth industry. The two most desirable features of a woodland cottage site are the illusion of solitude and the view out over water. In the sinuous lake and river country of the Great Lakes–St. Lawrence watershed, the land is relatively flat and yet densely vegetated. There are no sweeping vistas, so the aesthetics of this landscape in its more or less wild state is built on experiencing nature in its details. The activities that make sense here are intimate, even private, like canoeing or mushrooming. Yet the geography allows for great numbers of people to have this experience of the immanent frontier all at the same time. When you add the automobile and the express highway to this equation, you end up with a well-populated region of the continent colonizing large portions of the remaining bush with millions of second homes, each with its private road and intimate view.

The car is not the only vehicle that roamed the new highways of the 1950s. A related technology, the trailer, has had a profound effect on the way we move across and inhabit this continent. Originally—in the early 1930s—trailers were a kind of house on wheels, like a covered wagon for vacationers or itinerant workers. Now they're called mobile homes and they've become the predominant form of prefabricated housing. They are permanent features of the landscape, as the evolution of their town names indicates: from trailer camps to trailer parks to mobile home estates. In the U.S. Southwest, these communities are simply called parks, and the trailers themselves are called park models. Temporary dwellings—which are an ancient phenomenon—imply a kind of freedom and have thus found a special place in the North American ideological landscape. This phenomenon is usually expressed as freedom from ties to place, to family, and to job; freedom to move across this land as we want and to make new connections with it. For people who work at migratory or temporary jobs—and today this includes work in sales or mid-management as well as on farms—moving from one place to another is often a necessity. It's as if physical mobility is standing in for the dream of social mobility that North American society has been unable to deliver. Camping is one form of this refusal of station; so is desert retirement in a mobile home.

In any case, the trailer is now something people use to tour nature (among other places) and dwell there temporarily. In fact, technologies like the trailer, and the cultures that surround them, construct nature as a place of freedom and repose. As our technical mastery over nature has progressed, the idea of nature as freedom has flourished—an idea that would be meaningless in a time or culture other than this one.

Other transportation technologies have been developed since the Second World War, and all of them have helped to transform the landscape and our perceptions of it in some way. Most fall under the name of recreational vehicle (RV), and they include the snowmobile, the off-road vehicle (ORV), the van, the camper, and so on. Many of these technologies have insinuated themselves into everyday North American life, and the social activities of clubs and vacation caravans are now often planned around them. Indeed, a new kind of campground has been designed for people who travel with recreational vehicles.

The trucking industry was also born in the postwar years—often as a result of the car companies' marketing strategies—and it too has had a curious effect on how our culture perceives nature. Before continuous streams of trucks plied highways of every size, trains carried most freight, including foodstuffs. Refrigerated train cars were first put to use in the late 1920s. As John Steinbeck's novel *East of Eden* documents with some bitterness, refrigeration allowed produce from warmer parts of the continent, such as Florida and California, to be shipped to large markets in the cooler regions. Like the car, however, the transport truck is a more versatile, if less efficient, technology than the train. It was able to get right into the fields and collect the avocados and grapefruit soon after they were picked. This development coincided with two others of equal import. Postwar agricultural research bred fruits and vegetables to be part of an industrial process—they could be mechanically picked, were resistant to biocides, and took well to shipping. This led to great increases in farm productivity during the 1950s. At the same time the transportation industry was consolidating itself: trucking firms began to be vertically integrated with food growers, processors, and retailers.

This is a complex tangle of changes, and there were a number of consequences. One was the replacement of local and regional market gardeners by large, often corporate, growers in the new agricultural zones of the sunbelt. They in turn introduced vast amounts of biocides, with ecological effects that in many cases remain unknown today. The industrialization of agriculture—which included the development of supermarkets— also led to a homogenization of the seasons as summer produce (or some semblance of it) began to appear in winter as well. This in turn led to a very different relation between the culture and the geography and climate of North America. The land began to look and feel different. As models of domination began to flourish in North American cultures in the 1950s—and the industrialization of agriculture was mirrored by the U.S. military policy of the time—it became possible to think of nature as a servant, or a well-loved pet. It also became possible to think of nature as a victim—a sentiment that underlay much of the thinking of the environmentalist movement in its earliest years.

The car also had a more instrumental effect on the landscape. Most obviously, it brought massive environmental change in the form of roads, traffic, and deteriorating air quality. These all have had their own secondary and tertiary effects, most of them bad if not catastrophic. But much less discussed are the aesthetic and psychological changes the car has brought to landforms and our perception of them.

Once the roads were full of cars, there had to be a physical infrastructure to service them. Thus we get the creation of the strip: gas stations, roadside motels and drive-ins, coffee shops, muffler franchises. These came with their own logic. Highway businesses had to design their buildings and advertising to attract motorists. Recognition from the road became paramount, and this led to the spread of the franchise business and use of standardized images and eventually logos in advertising, both on and off site. Consider the repetitive architecture of chains like Howard Johnson's or the Holiday Inn, or indeed of national parks. Tourist services had to be built on a scale compatible with the automobile. Large signs and facades and small cheaply constructed buildings were the lessons learned from Las Vegas. Motorized access and parking lots became necessary adjuncts to every new building, whether souvenir shop or campground office. These in turn were often "naturalized" by planting gardens around them, and work like this became the bread and butter of the newly prosperous profession of landscape architecture. A roadside coffee shop or gas station was transformed into an oasis in the midst of the created deserts of parking lot and highway. Similarly, driveways and garages—and the reappropriated ranch architectures they complemented—contributed to the sprawling character of postwar urban design. More recent architectures like shopping malls turn inward from their parking lots, toward the retreats of indoor garden. The roadside environments of just thirty years ago are now largely in decay.

The car imposed a horizontal quality on the landscape (as well as architecture). The faster we drive, the flatter the earth looks: overpasses and cloverleaf interchanges are almost two-dimensional when seen from the car window. They are events in automotive time. As highway and tourist space has become more homogenized—like the universal space of modern communications—distance is experienced as an abstraction: suburbs lie "minutes from downtown," and the miles per gallon we achieve getting to them quantify field and stream. Compare this experience of the landscape with that suggested by aerial photography, which wasn't really accessible to people outside the military until the 1960s. Seen from a plane window the landscape flattens out to something like a map: it is a landscape of fact (or, to the military, of secrets). With more advanced satellite photography, the landscape has been inscribed with representations of resources—healthy crops, or deposits of subsurface minerals, or Cuban missile bases. The image of the Earth from space, and its Whole Earth counterpart, are extensions of this impulse to picture the planet as a resource. But in the 1950s, travelers weren't yet able to perceive this factual landscape. What we saw out the window of the speeding car—the Futurists were right after all, it is one of the great experiences of modern life—was the future itself. Consider the thrill of entering New York along the Henry Hudson Parkway or Vancouver crossing the Lion's Gate Bridge. The speeding car is a metaphor for progress. It is always moving ahead—although the effect is the opposite, as if the landscape were moving past us, into the inconsequential shadows of history. In this very limited respect, time has replaced space as the predominant way our experience of the world is organized.

The car itself was increasingly laden with technology in the postwar years, and some of these devices accentuated the kinds of changes underway. Air conditioning was the most obvious. It began to be sold as a feature of a few luxury cars in the mid-1950s and soon became a sign of status, especially in climates where it was unnecessary. Of course, as more asphalt was laid down and more engines circulated, roadside temperatures rose, and air conditioning often did become a necessity even in temperate climates. High-speed cars also encouraged the use of air conditioning.

In a car or a building, air conditioning allowed the illusion of human control over environment. This was made possible by the "magic" of what was understood to be a benign technology. Of more interest to us here is the aesthetic effect of air conditioning on the natural world. Nature was now even more something to be appreciated by the eyes alone. Never mind the dust and heat or the snow, nature was now accessible year-round and under any circumstances. There were no longer any contingencies—just the purely visual experience that lay outside the picture window. The other senses were pushed further to the margins of human experience as nature came to play a role in human culture that was at once more restricted and infinitely expanded.

Although car travel is largely an *individual* activity, this is not to say that people usually drive alone, although for commuters and truckers that tends to be the case. It's more that driving is a private exercise, whether done alone or with company. It is a technology that fits well with the North American psyche, and Detroit has done its best to manipulate this. The individual hero on the road, pushing back the frontiers and discovering this land for "himself": this myth has a long and bloody history, particularly in American culture, and the car continues to play a part in it. It's hard to imagine a technology that better discourages communal activity and an egalitarian experience of the non-human world. After all, the private car and the nuclear family have a parallel history. They are both founded on an act of exclusion. Within is radically different from without. The family and the car—and the family car—are bounded entities that discourage unregulated exchange.

The mobility the car has brought to North American society has contributed greatly to the restructuring of the traditional nuclear family. Its privatizing functions have been splintered by cultural practices like hitchhiking or drive-in movies. The car has also given kids the freedom to get out, put some miles between themselves and the home. It has carried many North Americans, myself included, far away from the consumer culture that engendered it, and into closer contact with the natural world.

Conserve—and Develop

Like tourism and cars, the histories of tourism and conservationism are closely connected. The conservation movement in North America began in the late nineteenth century as a moral crusade to conserve "wilderness"—places supposedly uncontaminated by the physical traces of humanity, meaning people of European origin. As an expanding industrial infrastructure began to extract more and more raw materials from the land, the movement demanded regulation and protection of wild areas for non-industrial uses. In hindsight, those non-industrial uses have by and large turned out to be tourism.

By the early twentieth century, both the Canadian and U.S. governments had adopted conservation strategies as part of what they understood to be the efficient management of natural resources. At first many people saw this project as incompatible with the protection of wild lands for aesthetic reasons. But in time—and the watershed years were the tenure of Gifford Pinchot at the newly created U.S. Forest Service during the Theodore Roosevelt administration—the consensus, at least among the elite sectors of the population, was that tourist development and resource exploitation could be complementary. In Canada, tourist development and mining were part of the mandate of the national parks from the beginning: the government created Banff National Park as an agreed-upon part of the development portfolio of the Canadian Pacific railroad.

Like all social movements, nature conservationism has had both reactionary and radical moments. In general, the state has adopted conservation measures consistent with its own interests, including the "wise use" of timber, water, grazing, mineral, and, later, recreation resources in the more remote parts of the continent. Conservationism became a matter of resource management—an expedient measure ensuring the greatest return on investment for what is usually called the foreseeable future. There are several other strains of conservationism historically, and all of them have grown up alongside tourism when they haven't actually promoted it. The principal ones include: animal welfare, an anti-cruelty movement that originated in England in the nineteenth century; nature appreciation, an offshoot of art appreciation with roots in the same era; biological conservationism, which seeks the protection of endangered species of plants and animals from land development of all kinds; and preservationism, which argues for setting aside nature in reserves, protected "for all time" from human manipulation, places that will function as a eulogy for what industrial civilization has destroyed.

Today the outlines of this history are hotly debated within the environmental movement, which inherited conservationism from its various constituencies. The organizers, spokespeople, and gurus of the early movement—Henry David Thoreau, John Muir, Ernest Thompson Seton, Rosalie Edge, James Harkin, Grey Owl, Aldo Leopold, and Rachel Carson, among many others, are also the subjects of considerable debate, alternatively claimed and rejected by the various streams of contemporary ecological thought.

What we can say about these early nature philosophies—aside from the fact that they have been largely ineffective even on their own terms—is that they are reductionist. They invariably understand nature to be good and civilization—or, in the formulation of deep ecology, humans—bad. This is hardly the basis for a politics of social change.

While conservation politics and nature tourism nourished one another, the growth of a tourist industry was contingent upon a substantial contribution by the state. Early recreation advocates had campaigned for government involvement in initiating and promoting outdoor activities, and governments began making this commitment around the time of the First World War. Governments at all levels started to acquire park land, build recreational facilities, draw up wildlife regulations, and write resource-management policies. They zoned cabin and cottage lands to control development, supervised boating activities, inventoried land, drew up maps, and in general began to divide up the continent according to how humans used it: resource extraction, farming, recreation, wilderness, and so on. In 1924, the U.S. government held its first National Conference on Outdoor Recreation in Washington, D.C. Many Canadians attended.

In the United States, the years of the New Deal saw the development of recreation facilities everywhere. The Civilian Conservation Corps and the Works Progress Administration embarked on a massive program to build a national public landscape. They organized unemployed workers into what was basically a military life. Crews of one hundred men and more constructed parkways, playgrounds, rose gardens, campgrounds, arboretums, parks, and lodges, as well as roads, bridges, and public buildings. The landscape work was sturdy, and much of it remains today. Its rough and earnest design reveals the moral underpinnings of the formative years of the recreation movement: these were environments meant to build character through hard work and wholesome play. Work camps organized by the Canadian government during the same years carried out similar projects, although on a much smaller and less ambitious scale.

The Tourist Industry

There were other exemplary landscapes. In the 1930s, the Tennessee Valley Authority (TVA) began to build immense reservoirs in the southern Appalachians. The TVA justified these projects by referring to increases in population and energy consumption and to the need for large-scale public recreation sites. But the reservoirs were also a chance to put the new techniques of flood control, hydrogeneration, and irrigation into operation.

During the same period, the Civilian Conservation Corps built summer camps for inner city kids—one of them, Camp David in Maryland, is now the weekend retreat of U.S. presidents. The National Park Service promoted these camps to the tourist industry as Recreation Demonstration Areas. In 1936, Congress passed the Park, Parkway and Recreation Area Act, which provided funds for much new construction.

All of these projects involved creating new spaces and new organizations to manage those spaces. As the tourist industry became more sophisticated, designers made sure that travel became a part of the landscape itself. Scenic car routes, photo opportunities, campground layouts—these built spaces have become part of our experience of nature. Thus the booming recreation and tourist organizations of mid-century—which would include older groups like the Boy Scouts, the Girl Guides, and the YMCA as well as professional organizations like the National Recreation Association, the Canadian Association for Health, Physical Education and Recreation, and self-organized clubs for canoeists, trailer owners, gardeners, bird watchers, and fly fishers—produced new landscapes, and new aesthetics of nature.

It is the mission of any bureaucracy to shape its project according to the internal needs of the organization. Promotional strategies tend to influence our experience of the places and activities they advertise. So do development schemes to maximize public use. Natural beauty, for example, was inevitably quantified as a result of applying bureaucratic and industrial models to the landscape. Industry consultants encouraged landowners considering tourist development to list the "natural attractions" of their sites: was there a marketable topography such as a seashore or trout stream? Were there unusual geological formations, or perhaps Indian ruins? "Scenic value" soon came to be a monetary concept as well as an aesthetic one. All of these developments contributed to the institutionalization of tourism. Sightseeing was no longer an individual activity, at least not in the eyes of those in the business. It was the organized mass consumption of familiar landscapes. Facilities had to be standardized and the "tourist object"—in this case an idea of nature—transformed into recognizable terms. As we'll see, this involved the creation of many new landscapes.

Although much private recreational resource development got started with state assistance—and the state still heavily subsidizes the tourist industry, when you take into account the public funds spent on facilities like convention centers, corporate sports stadiums, and the infrastructures that support them—by the 1950s, private tourist development began to outstrip government initiatives. The governments of the day produced publications that outlined how to construct private campgrounds or design summer camps for kids. Other pamphlets suggested hunting policies for industrial landowners or encouraged farmers and ranchers to add recreational enterprises to their existing operations. Most U.S. agencies made money available for either public or private development of these facilities. These agencies were often concurrently working on improved resource exploitation strategies; as we've seen, tourism and resource management have gone hand in hand for most of this century (although not without many problems). This relationship was made official in the multiple-use policy adopted by most government agencies throughout the continent in the late 1950s.

Tourism involves a massive conceptual reorganization of the landscape. Lands once productive in a traditional industrial or agricultural sense were reclassified as recreational zones. Marginal cattle-raising operations, for example, got turned into fishing camps or dude ranches; dairy farms became tourist farms or bed-and-breakfasts; in more recent years, agricultural lands near cities have been turned into sod farms, golf courses, and theme parks. One of the historical functions of tourism, then, is to be a kind of parasite feeding off sectors of the economy that seem to have become superfluous.

Nature tourism grew enormously in the postwar years, and as in other parts of the economy, the industry had to run to keep up with it. For most middle-class North Americans, car holidays had become the norm. By 1960, 75 percent of U.S. families owned at least one car, and these now brightly colored vehicles filled the new highways on weekends and during the summer months. A mass market developed for recreational services and commodities; by the late 1950s, annual sales in this sector had reached $5 billion in the United States. Shops and chain store catalogues were suddenly full of outdoor equipment of every kind, much of it making use of the new plastics being pioneered by the petrochemical industry. Among the most significant commodities were the lighter, more easy to use cameras and, later, color film. The snapshot and color slides structure the postwar experience of nature. Color, which by the mid-1950s was common in magazine ads and movies, gave images of nature added authenticity. At the moment of the greatest estrangement between North American culture and the natural world, nature opened up as real space, luring us back with saturated reds and greens.

Governments were quick to lend additional support to the new economy. In 1958, President Eisenhower appointed the Outdoor Recreation Resources Review Commission, chaired by Laurance Rockefeller. Its mandate was to gather data on The Great Outdoors and the people using it and thereby help produce a comprehensive national policy on recreational lands. It released its twenty-seven volumes of recommendations in 1962. A similar study, the Canadian Outdoor Recreation Demand Study, released reports in 1967, 1969, and 1972. The reports from both commissions suggested that outdoor recreation, far from being a fad, was a component of the national character. The powers that be saw recreational land as critical not only for economic reasons but also because, as the ORRRC put it, "the outdoors is part of what is and was America, and it's being lost." U.S. citizens needed the outdoors more than ever, the report continued, since most people now lived in cities and suburbs rather than on farms. This was much the same as the argument of the recreation and parks movements in the late nineteenth century: people need to escape the everyday urban setting and experience a change in scenery where they would have a different relation to nature. Now these needs were felt to be even more critical. The contradictory recommendations of both Canadian and U.S. commissions were basically this: conserve what was left of natural areas, and develop them for maximum enjoyment by all.

These government commissions hired demographers, geographers, sociologists, and other consultants to come up with ways the tourist industry might adapt to the new situation; the industry in turn took up many of their recommendations in the expansionary years of the 1960s and early 1970s. The tourist industry began to take a more active role in developing both markets and destinations. In other words, where vacationers once considered a holiday in the countryside, they might now consider many different holiday experiences in many different kinds of places. In a report for the ORRRC in the early 1960s, anthropologist Margaret Mead suggested that the category "family vacation" was quickly becoming outdated. She said that planners ought to be considering what children's holidays might be and how to entertain adolescents now drifting "aimlessly" around the new suburbs. She wondered if there might not be a vacation market for single women, or "minorities," or "foreigners." And—Americans are always thinking ahead—what might be the recreation possibilities in outer space?

In some ways the culture had already made these distinctions. Men had long since had their own fishing and hunting trips, and the outdoors was still largely identified with what were widely understood to be masculine qualities. The identification of women with nature and the biological would be strictly interpreted until the 1960s: their domain was the physical and social reproduction of the species, and most of that was supposed to happen indoors. For the most part, outdoor space for women continued to be confined to the garden and places (like playgrounds) associated with childrearing.

But, in the past thirty years, as families and gender identities have splintered, so too has the social organization of recreational space. Resorts like Club Med or Leisure World cater to specific consumer profiles generated by market research. So does a place like Eco-Village in North Carolina, run by *The Mother Earth News*, a back-to-the-land magazine begun in the 1960s. Most tourist destinations now include a choice of specialized environments: picnic sites, swimming pools, souvenir shops, nature trails, hard surfaces for organized games, places of solitude. The industry had diversified outdoor sports too: ice sailing, wind surfing, jogging, skin diving, hang gliding, snowmobiling—these have all been developed to meet what the industry talks about as new recreation desires. Not all market research has resulted in the creation of new environments, however. Studies done in the mid-1960s indicated that foreign tourists, especially Europeans, were most interested in the expansive nineteenth-century landscapes celebrated in Western movies. These are the spaces embalmed in the national parks of the West. This desire for the primitive—which has always included aboriginal cultures, however they're constructed in the public imagination—has become more pronounced in recent years.

The boom in nature tourism of the 1960s brought to a head some of the contradictions inherent in public policies that encouraged both nature conservation and tourist development. Debates around this issue were common in the early years of the modern environmentalist movement. For some, the debate was resolved by the creation of another legal category of land. In the United States, the Wilderness Act of 1964 gave wide statutory protection to designated roadless areas that were over 2,025 hectares in size. The government usually continued to honor prior resource-extraction rights and activities on these lands, which has neutralized the law's effect in many areas of the U.S. West. Both the U.S. and Canadian governments passed similar legislation in the 1960s, naming endangered animal species and setting out national environmental policies.

But a review of the environmental legislation of the past twenty years—which would require a book in itself—doesn't begin to address the deeper cultural changes that were underway during that time. Public attitudes toward nature—or the environment, as it has come to be known—have shifted considerably. Nature tourism is not what it used to be. Consider the encounter of the contemporary tourist with other animals. It used to be that animals were hunted and killed as part of the (male) tourist experience of the outdoors. While sport hunting is still practiced today, it has a deservedly bad name. *Photographing* animals has become the preferred trophy-taking activity, especially if the beasts can be "captured" on film in a wild setting. In 1977, a U.S. Forest Service report concluded that by the year 2000, "the primary use of wildlife resources will change from hunting to non-consumptive uses like photography and observation." This is what present-day "ecological safaris" are about. The photograph documents a vanishing species at the same time that it authenticates the nature experience. The animals are temporarily "preserved" on film for the enjoyment of the maximum number of sightseers, including the reluctant friends who end up viewing the vacation slides and movies.

In the 1970s, the expansionary days of the tourist industry began to wane. But by that time the industry had consolidated itself. Alternating cycles of overexpansion and crisis favored large operators. Almost gone were the mom-and-pop motels and the family riding stables that had done so well during the days of the circuit tour by auto. The prestige products were now capital intensive—multifaceted "destinations" like Disney World became the industry model. Tourism was no longer so much about service provision as it was about the mass production and management of sightseeing experiences.

The growth of the tourist industry had produced an enormous infrastructure. Professional planners and bureaucrats, advertising consultants, graphic designers, and cost-benefit analysts were all a seemingly necessary part of the industry, turned out by faculties of leisure studies and courses in hospitality management. The industry had vertically integrated agents, tour operators, carriers, and destinations. Its publicity and marketing had become highly sophisticated, using strategies such as demographics and psychographics invented by Madison Avenue in the 1960s. The mass-marketed package tour sold the tourist experience as a single commodity, concentrating activity in a smaller number of well-produced locales. These "place-product packages," as they're known in the industry, aim for total design of buildings, landscape, services, signage, and spin-off products. In the well-managed business, these tourist sites become industrial plants whose goods are aesthetic experiences and hospitality services. All of these strategies have made good use of the photographic image, now an integral part of most people's experience of the outdoors.

Research in leisure studies has been responsible for many of these changes. In the 1960s, social scientists and management consultants produced volumes of studies related to tourism. Favorite topics of the day were destination perception and scenery evaluation. A good place to look for some of this work is the *Journal of Leisure Research*, published in the United States by the National Recreation and Park Association. The first issue, published in the winter of 1969, featured an article on how to develop a model for testing people's landscape preferences. By quantifying responses to photographs of different landscapes, park and recreation planners could determine which "landscape features" should be purchased, developed, or preserved. The industry could then locate a scenic road or hiking trail, for example, in a way that would maximize visitor pleasure. Subsequent issues of the journal have pursued this research logic: one article draws up a typology of campers according to motivating factors; another talks about measuring eye pupillary response to landscapes—when they see a trout stream, for example, do male eyes dilate more than female eyes?

Other research has aided the administration of natural lands and control over the organisms within them. U.S. government studies have recommended certification of wilderness users, the use of robots for park maintenance, and the captive rearing of endangered species "rather than rely[ing] on natural reproduction." Thanks to researchers, we now know the maximum noise levels for optimum human enjoyment of national parks. They've also come up with statistics on the carrying capacities of ecosystems, which presumably help determine the maximum human presence those areas will tolerate. They have studied the further penetration of technology into recreation areas: the possible development of personal hovercraft and helicopters, as well as jet-powered backpacks. Scientists have invented remote sensing devices that monitor animal migrations in some areas and could be used to monitor park use by humans as well.

All this work has implications for the experience of nature, especially when we consider that the mass media, and the vast numbers of images they produce, are part of the modern environment. For example, contemporary tourist research indicates "pre-trip anticipation" is one of the key determinants of a tourist's satisfaction with a holiday destination. The images of the holiday produced by the industry must entice the potential traveler, but at the same time they must preclude the cultivation of false expectations. Obviously, not just any picture of Lake Louise will do.

Tourism: From the Recreational to the Social

Today, recreational opportunities, as they're called, are produced almost exclusively by government agencies or transnational corporations—at least at the level of investment. Development decisions are taken in the board rooms of the metropolis and rarely take into account the nature of local communities or working landscapes. Because tourism is largely about the experience of difference—whether it's cultural or geographical—the industry has played an important role in the globalization of Western industrial culture.

This leads to fascinating paradoxes. Industrial logic demands standardization, yet we've come to define natural settings in part by their uniqueness. The result has been an increasing *production* of natural attractions. For a long time now our culture of nature has typed certain topographies and climates—mountains, coastlines, islands, exotic or fragile ecosystems—as special places. But inevitably, even in culturally valorized scenic places, certain elements have to be rearranged to meet tourist expectations. In the game preserves of East Africa, for example, the elephants and lions must be visible and uncontained when the sightseers go by in their tour buses, and preferably the beasts will be eating other animals. But we don't want other buses full of tourists angling for good photos crowding the scene and causing a distraction. Native human communities, moreover, might or might not be an acceptable component of the safari experience. If they are acceptable they're perhaps best presented in traditional, that is, archaic, dress.

Or consider the case of Prince Edward Island. It has a tourist identity as a regional, working landscape. Here, the story goes, the old values predominate: family farms, picturesque villages, benign seascapes. The cosmopolitan tourist requires authentic space: Prince Edward Island should look "distinctive," which in this case means anachronistic. Town buildings should be restored to their original state; rural vistas should conform to the standard image of a bucolic potato-growing backwater. Tacky motels and drive-ins, on the other hand, should be discouraged.

These needs have led to fascinating conflicts with the people who live on Prince Edward Island, for the elite taste of the educated tourist is often insensitive to the vernacular design of the local inhabitant. In the mid-1970s, a controversy arose over billboards and abandoned cars along the highways. Tourists found they detracted from the island's identity; islanders considered them part of their culture. Another conflict involved the traditional applications of manure on the fields. Tourist organizations lobbied to have manure use prohibited near highways—its smell was apparently not part of the repertoire of bucolic experience. Because the modern tourist has been constructed as a guest rather than a client, islanders have found it difficult to oppose these changes without breaching the hospitality norms of their culture.

Other recent developments in tourism continue the earlier trends toward diversification of the industry. Sport tourism and earthquake and disaster tourism are obvious examples. Self-catering, another trend, means that tourists provide many of their own services, such as food or accommodation, while they travel. The most common form of self-catering is to travel in an RV, fixing your own meals and making your own bed. Since you carry most of your household with you in an RV, all you require is a parking lot close to the highway with a place to dump your sewage and maybe a play area for the kids. More sophisticated RV sites have clubhouses and swimming pools, laundry facilities, video games, hot showers, and cable TV hookups at the campsite: all the conveniences of home.

Private campground chains like KOA have been a familiar part of the landscape for some time now, but franchises of time-sharing campgrounds and cabins are a more recent phenomenon. For an initial investment, often on the order of $6,000, you can buy a two-hundred-year membership in a camping club. In one club this entitles you (and your heirs!) to use the club's private campgrounds for a fee as long as the lease holds, at which time the ''vacation license'' reverts to the developer.

There are other, quite different, tourist possibilities. Social tourism is the name given to an economy in which public funds are dispersed in a way that distributes the benefits of tourism evenly across society. As it is usually practiced, however, it is a kind of subsidized tourism for the "disadvantaged." It includes large institutions like the YMCA, the Boy Scouts, and Outward Bound, as well as many smaller urban groups who offer cheap nature outings for working-class urban dwellers. Trade unions and large industrial enterprises have often participated in these activities by providing vacation villages for workers. So have religious organizations such as the PTL Club. Vacation pay is also a form of social tourism. In Switzerland, state-sponsored holiday-savings plans are available that operate on a sliding scale according to the income of the subscriber.

In 1980, a United Nations conference on World Tourism in Manila affirmed that social tourism is necessary if millions of people are to enjoy ''discovery, rest, and the beauty of the world.''

Another development is adventure tourism and its recent offshoots ecotourism and biotourism. Standard offerings in the sector of the industry are river rafting, jungle safaris, trekking, and mountain climbing. For wealthy tourists seeking more, there's skiing in Antarctica, dog sledding in the Arctic, grizzly bear viewing in Alaska, and kayaking in Greenland or Baja California. An unquenchable appetite for the exotic and ''uncharted'' distinguishes much adventure travel. This description of one outfit's 1990 trip to Irian Jaya illustrates the point:

> These jungles are the home of still uncontacted upper Asmat tribes living along the rivers and on the swamps in great treehouses, and we must travel with caution. . . .
> As the terrain, river conditions and tribal situations have many unknowns, we have allotted a good chunk of time for this exploration. This is the leading edge of adventure and we must emphasize that you must be in extremely good physical condition and ready to accept unknown hardships en route.

The World Wildlife Fund defines *ecotourism* as travel to "protected natural areas, as a means of economic gain through natural resource preservation." The economic gain spoken of accrues to the host country. Governments in Costa Rica and Kenya, for example, have recognized that tourism to natural areas brings in more money than mining, forestry, or ranching would on those same lands. Some tour companies offer working vacations: harvesting crops in Third World nations, or assisting wildlife conservation work. These tour operators make a point of educating their clients about the effects of development on natural systems. Some also donate a portion of their fees to environmental groups in host countries.

Ecotourism raises questions about how a *socially* useful tourism would work. Surely it would be designed to meet local needs. At a minimum it would mean building a sustainable local economy and providing rewarding and well-paid jobs. It might also mean working the landscape in a way that invites care and participation; unpolluted swimming places for people to go to after work, for example. Lastly, it must strengthen cultural and political bonds within and between communities. Cultural exchanges and group vacations are ways of bringing people together.

An admittedly remote example of an alternative tourism is that promoted by the Annapurna Conservation Area Project (ACAP) in west-central Nepal. The Annapurna region is home to forty thousand subsistence farmers—and the annual host to twenty-five thousand foreign tourists who come to hike in the Himalayas. The area is in ecological crisis, part of a downward spiral of malnutrition, deforestation, erosion, fuel scarcity, overgrazing, and species extinction. ACAP has set itself the task of reconciling ecological restoration with sustainable community development and low-impact tourism. Based and directed in the villages, its programs include alternative energy generation, tree planting, literacy campaigns, trail repair, health centers, cultural festivals, and wildlife inventories. ACAP charges tourists a fee to enter the area and gives them a sophisticated brochure that discusses the connections between land and life in the region. Hot showers, diet, meal times, plastics, electrification, drinking water, price haggling, shitting, and begging: the brochure traces the connections between these tourist issues and both the Annapurna ecosystem and its cultures.

French social theorist Guy Debord has called tourism "a by-product of the circulation of commodities." The mass circulation of the middle classes around the globe is a phenomenon of vast proportions—now over 400 million people a year—overseen by an industry that has extended its management techniques out into the land itself. That world is a changed one, fragmented by development, diversified by marketing strategies, and overlaid with technologies like the car and the camera. The Annapurna project is just one example of another kind of circulation of people through the world, of a tourism directed in a way that encourages connections between community and region.

Section One

New West Blues:
Reports and Reflections

Selling Out the Last Best Place

Donald Snow

*I*t is with some amusement that I now watch environmentalists of the West scurrying to distance themselves from the onslaught of tourism. Environmentalists, of course, did not invent tourism, or even its sad, green little cousin ecotourism, but many of us did leap on the tourism bandwagon as it left the station sometime, as I date it, around 1979. We were struggling with Big Issues then, as now: the future of the West, the fate of the public lands, the relationship between environmental quality and economic development. But there were some other issues we didn't want to touch, or didn't know how to: the proper role of government in promoting, or subsidizing, growth; the future of labor in an increasingly globalized economy; the sweaty hands of commerce on the world's rapidly diminishing wild lands. We promoted tourism, then lived to regret it. Our hands are dirty, and we cannot avoid our complicity in the state-supported development and promotion of this "clean industry."

This essay is a brief chronicle of how we environmentalists came to embrace the promotion of tourism in Montana, the "Last Best Place" according to one poet and about ten thousand realtors. It traces a trajectory of strategic thinking, not necessarily good thinking, but thinking that seemed to make sense at the time. I guess if there's any lesson to be learned here, it's that well-meaning people sometimes make poor decisions in the heat of the kitchen. And in Montana in the mid-1970s, the political kitchen was plenty hot.

Twenty years ago Montana stood on the brink of becoming the boiler room of the nation. With its Saudi Arabia of coal underlying the eastern third of the state, Montana was to lead the country into a new era of energy independence. Americans were determined to "produce our way" out of reliance on foreign oil, and all we had to do was scoop out that massive bounty of sub-bituminous and lignite that lay underneath the northern Great Plains states of Montana, Wyoming, and North Dakota. Steam coal for power plants, coupled with aggressive development of nuclear power, would help phase out reliance on foreign petroleum, a huge amount of which was being foolishly burned to make electricity.

Environmentalists were a rising force then. Though our movement owned roots in earlier efforts in conservation and wilderness protection, and we knew it, we also sensed that ours was something new—a nascent movement that would have profound effects on the politics and economics of the conservative western energy states. By the mid-1970s just about every state of the West had its own home-grown defenders. The Colorado Open Space Council. The Wyoming Outdoor Council and the Powder River Basin Resource Council. The Utah Wilderness Association. The Idaho Conservation League. The Dakota Resource Council. The Southwest Research and Information Center in Albuquerque. And a plethora of national environmental organizations with memberships, chapters, and sometimes staffed offices out in the field. *High Country News,* based then in Lander, Wyoming, kept tabs on it all and became the journal of record for the West's emerging environmentalism.

Here in Montana the Northern Plains Resource Council and the Environmental Information Center stood among the leaders of a dozen or so homegrown groups organized to do battle on every environmental policy front, but energy was still the big issue. We were struggling with Montana Power Company's plans to triple the size of the mammoth Colstrip power station east of Billings. We were fighting the 765-kilo-volt transmission lines planned to walk across the state from east to west, connecting us with the West Coast power grid. And we were still grinding our teeth over issues like coal slurry pipelines, mined-land reclamation, new railroads to ship coal out of well-settled ranching country, and even the advent of uranium mining, an industry Montana had never seen but one that promised to do more harm than coal executives could ever dream of.

Environmentalists stood in the thick of all these issues. We saw ourselves as the great defenders of place, and we knew that this place was special. There was a lastness about it: somehow Montana had been overlooked, spared the onslaught of urbaniza-tion and rural gentrification that had overcome every other state in the West. In those days Wyoming had a slogan that captured that same feeling: "Wyoming Is What America Was," it read, but we Montana chauvinists knew that they were wrong. We knew that, despite the hard work of Wyoming environmentalists, their state had already sold out to the mammon of the energy industry and seemed quite happy with the appearance of hundred-foot-tall draglines in ranching country. Their legislature gleefully changed Wyoming's official nickname from The Cowboy State to The Energy State. In a cynical nod to antique sensibilities, they kept the cowboy and bucking bronc on their license plates.

But not Montana. This was the one western state that had made a serious pass at stopping the energy barons at the border, coming within one legislative vote of ban-ning strip mining in 1973. This was the state that had chased the beavers of the Bureau of Reclamation out of the Yellowstone, the last big free-flowing river in the West. We had passed the toughest mined-land reclamation laws in the country, and by the late '70s we were hard about the task of designating Class One airsheds to guarantee non-degradation out in coal country. We did what we could to protect our surface waters by enacting instream flow reservations; we passed the Major Facility Siting Act, that forced developers through a costly series of regulatory hoops before they could build their vaunted power plants on the semiwild plains of eastern Montana; and we even took a feeble pass at subdivision developers, making them responsible for the environ-mental impacts of large, new housing tracts.

We had a favorite slogan, too, and though it was unofficial, we knew that many people in our state shared its sentiment: "Let's Keep Montana . . . Montana." Still a few years away from politics-by-bumper-sticker, we nevertheless plastered our news-letters liberally with our slogan. It spoke to and from a sense of place, the feeling that Montana was, as we said, a state of mind, a place like no other, a strangely undiscovered country that had somehow, miraculously, been spared the American disease of placelessness. Montana possessed no Los Angeles, or Denver, or Albuquerque, or Salt Lake, and we were trying hard to make sure that Billings—the likeliest candidate—didn't become the next black hole of American mall culture.

We shared a siege mentality back then, and we tried to infect others with it. I remember a stump speech I concocted as staff director of the state's leading environmental lobbying group. I described my childhood among the strip mines, power plants, and sulphur-choked rivers of western Pennsylvania, and I then suggested that busloads of Montana voters ought to be shipped out for educational tours to the nation's real boiler rooms in Ohio, West Virginia, and my old Pennsylvania. I wanted people to see the future: ruined rivers, dead habitat, spoiled air, single-industry economies. No one took me up on my proposal, but the dramatic effects worked well enough from behind the podium.

Not to anyone's surprise, our tactics were short-lived. Politics being what it is—a stupid process of force and equal counterforce—we soon found ourselves on the defensive. We had managed to pass a bevy of protective laws during the early 1970s, and the so-called conservatives, who in actuality were the ones most interested in the radical transformation of the Montana landscape, were quite upset with us. Not everyone wanted the protection we fought for, and besides, there was no big money in keeping Montana the place it had always been. We environmentalists were soon the objects of a virulent backlash.

The leaders of the state's many trade associations called us "aginers," meaning we were against everything. They said we were obstructionist cowards who professed the need for "careful development" when what we really wanted was no development. They said our citadel of laws and protective regulations was designed to make growth so costly and painful that investors would back away from Montana and go to North Dakota or Wyoming instead. But when we visited those places, we discovered that developers there were saying the same things about their own environmentalists. In 1979 Casper, Wyoming, sported a huge, anonymously sponsored billboard next to Interstate 25 that read simply, elegantly, "Mindless Marxist Ecologists Working for Russia." Those were the days.

So we responded. We decided to become—in the jargon du jour—"proactive." We went looking for something to be *for*, for a change. Like our old, avowed enemies in the energy and minerals businesses, we decided to become promoters. Our reasons were all quite clear and, in the odd logic of politics, they made sense at the time. Trouble was, we didn't have a clue what we were about to help unleash.

What could we be for? The answer was obvious. We would be for tourism, the clean economy. The Wally World logic of it seemed so simple and clear. Force and equal counterforce. Tourism, as we configured it, represented both an economic and a political breakthrough that could have only positive results. On the economic front, tourism would create thousands of new jobs in nonpolluting businesses. It would usher in a new era of economic diversification to replace the old one-industry economies of timber- and mining-dependent communities. Tourism offered economic resiliency, diversification, sustainability. Best of all, by its very nature it seemed to be based on the appreciation, rather than the depletion, of Montana's vaunted natural resources. But the political ramifications of it were even more appealing.

Right on the surface, tourism gave us "aginers" a sure way out of the trap of obstructionism. Our enemies could no longer say that we stood in the path of growth, because tourism represented growth, lots of growth, and best of all, a growth that seemed endlessly sustainable. But there was more. Tourism, in the minds of many, represented the gradual creation of a new electorate that would see the wisdom of a New Era in Montana and the West—an era not of natural resource exploitation, but of environmental protection; not of the West as a commodity supply depot to stuff the factories of America with energy and raw materials, but a New West of "environmental amenities"—clean air and water, long vistas, wild lands. In political terms, tourists represented the beginnings of a West *left alone*, not merely for aesthetic or ethical or spiritual reasons—all of those amounting to fairy reasons in our beefcake political culture—but for America's favorite and most enduring reason: economics. Tourism represented economic progress based on husbandry rather than exploitation.

A few environmentalists, in private, expressed economic and political reasons of their own for helping to promote tourism. They looked at their various organizational coffers and found them empty, always empty. They asked themselves who the givers were and who the next (and bigger) givers would likely be. They asked for demographics: Who were the likeliest defenders of Montana? Who could be recruited for the continuing defense? To whom does this new political wave, environmentalism, finally appeal? Well . . . to the nouveau riche of the cities, the upper middle class who have always been the core supporters of preservationist causes. Leaders of perennially impoverished environmental groups saw tourist recruitment in part as the courting of a new constituency. If we could convince the newcomers to join our cause and give money, we'd inevitably grow richer and more powerful ourselves. On both counts—economic and political—it was a pathway out of the red.

Could any harm possibly come of this? Tourists take nothing but pictures and leave nothing but footprints. Don't they? They come to Montana out of curiosity and leave with love in their hearts. Tourists, by definition, don't come to stay. Boomers, by definition, try to stay and will if they can. If they can't, they get mad, fire a few rounds on the way out, and roar off in their 4×4's for the next place to pillage. Don't they? Tourists come for the wildness, the openness, the green, glorious whole. They want water left in the rivers. They want pristine lakes and long, uninterrupted views. They want the soul's own poetry, Thoreau's tonic of the wilderness. Hell, tourists want what *we* want. Don't they? Best of all, they can be expected to support us because they, like us, want a Montana attuned to environmental protection, not to the plunder of traditional natural resource extraction. They will be the New Counterforce: political tourists! The riches they bring will convince the electorate—maybe even the conservatives, who truly love riches—that amenity protection is where it's at. Wilderness, in this view, is no longer merely the preservation of the world, *wilderness is the economic engine of the future.* Tourists! An endless flow of wallets, three feet above the pavement. A pipeline of human slurry.

Embedded in this line of strategic thought was an assumption that went unchallenged then and remains unchallenged today: that tourism as an economic enterprise represents a *replacement of*, rather than merely an addition to, earlier economies. Some of us seemed confident that, by advocating this "clean industry," we would somehow, slowly, be ridding the state of all that dirty industry—like mining, clearcutting, cattle branding. We neglected to reckon that with tourism what you really get is just *more* industry—more gasoline burned, more highways "improved," more roadkills, more second homes, more real estate price escalation, more septic tanks, more power lines, more "viewsheds" clearcut with cameras, more sneaker prints compacting native soil—with no appreciable diminishment of the industry already here. The newcomers are as powerless as the old-timers to reduce the overall impact, scale, or pace of antiquated natural resource extraction; they merely add new impact, extraction of another kind, which pays workers less.

We forgot—or perhaps didn't realize—just how pervasive and entrenched are the laws and policies that protect the traditional industries of the twentieth-century American West. Here is a brief list of those laws and policies that form the political bedrock of resource exploitation in the American West. You will notice that most of these are antiques. They are policies with firm, deep roots in the nineteenth century, yet they continue to dominate western lands, waters, and other natural resources today:

• the General Mining Law of 1872, asserting the right to mine on federal lands with no return to the Treasury;

• the Taylor Grazing Act of 1934, which ended the tragedy of the commons on the open range but cemented the nineteenth-century practice of public lands ranching through a policy favoring long-term grazing leases;

• the Doctrine of Prior Appropriation, the West's principal water-allocation policy dating back to the middle nineteenth century, which protects individual water rights in a way that virtually mandates the severe dewatering of rivers and streams;

• the Newlands Reclamation Act of 1902, which eventually led to the creation of the Bureau of Reclamation and its cheek-for-jowl competition with the Army Corps of Engineers to see who could build the greater number of pork barrel dams;

• the set of federal laws and policies that created the national forests in 1905, then gradually converted the U.S. Forest Service into an agency committed to "scientific" timber production;

• the Atomic Energy Act of 1965, which led to the burgeoning growth of a secretive nuclear weapons and energy-research complex with massive, entrenched facilities in nearly every western state. These continue to prosper today, still under largely secretive missions, despite overwhelming public opposition and myriad revelations of the egregious levels of nuclear and toxic pollution that occur at every production site.

That these entrenched policies may all be collectively despised by newcomers is itself an unproven thesis. I would guess that most recent arrivals to the West know nothing of these policies. But whether they know of them or not makes no appreciable difference. All of the 2.9 million annual visitors to Yellowstone National Park could stand in one geyser basin and collectively hiss at the massive Crown Butte gold mine now being planned two miles north of the park border, but their loathing wouldn't reduce by one whit the company's *right* to mine under the antique federal mining law.

These policies were designed one at a time to protect commercial interests, and they still work beautifully, even as those very commercial interests continue to shrink into economically insignificant minorities while the West fills with newcomers who are emphatically not-loggers, not-miners, not-ranchers, not–weapons builders. The U.S. Forest Service routinely continues to sell timber at subsidized, below-cost prices in all but one national forest in Montana, and the tourists stand alongside the natives and watch the logging trucks roll through Missoula every day of the year, removing, stick by stick, the very "amenity values" that the newcomers all came to enjoy. Given the West's ironclad commodity politics, impervious to the whims of either party, there is no evidence that these practices will stop until the supply of raw natural resources is simply depleted.

Tourism is the last force that could ever halt the plunder, because tourism itself has quickly devolved into a commodity use with an agenda of its own and, true to the real history of the West, its own fat trough of government subsidies. Day after day, in Montana and all across the West, tourism is being promoted to the citizenry as "the one bright spot on the economic horizon." In Montana that phrase has become as nauseatingly familiar as the realtors' favorite stolen line, "Last Best Place." What most of us have failed to notice in the decade and a half that we've committed to the earnest recruitment of tourists is that we environmentalists applauded and aided the early efforts to get government into the business of tourist promotion, helped approve the subsidies, and now don't have the political will to stand up against the tourism juggernaut, which has begun taking much more than it's giving.

In all of this, the subsidy issue is a real sleeper. Some say that, to the state's credit, Montana gets none of its nearly $7 million annual budget for tourism promotion from the general treasury. Every dollar comes from a motel bed tax enacted in 1987—an anomaly in a state that resolutely refuses to pass any form of a general sales tax. What the promoters fail to point out is that the bed tax did not exist until tourist promotion came along looking for a handout. Finding no sources of revenue that were acceptable to an increasingly parsimonious legislature, the tourist promoters pushed the bed tax as a painless new revenue source—painless because tourists themselves shoulder much of the burden. But the bed tax really begs the essential question of what role the state should have in the direct promotion of any industry. What the bed tax proves without doubt is how wedded Montana remains to the old Western belief that government should foot the bill for what, in an open market, would be the full burden of private development. There is no qualitative difference between tourism promotion subsidies and grazing, logging, and mineral subsidies, but because tourism promotion is still new and very popular, no one questions the wisdom of tourism subsidies or the obvious manner in which they resemble the antique public lands commodity subsidies that now make national taxpayers rail against the West's old gravy train. The bed tax may be a good idea on its own merits. It is, in any event, the only significant source of public revenue currently being taken from tourists, who, in the absence of a general sales tax, get a free ride when they spend money in Montana.

There is no question that tourism promotion is working very well. The official promoters, all of them state employees, boast of "dramatic tourism growth" since 1988 due directly to the bed tax bonanza, which is dedicated to promoting—what else?— more tourism. The program is quite aggressive, based as it is on the booster's time-honored maxim, "If a little is good, then a lot must be great!"

We market Montana now in Western Europe and the Pacific Rim. We conduct trade missions and send delegates to trade shows where, as the Travel Montana "Tourism and Film Marketing Plan" rather breathlessly announces, "Travel Montana delegates are sometimes joined by private-sector participants." Golly. We conduct overseas marketing workshops where the "main emphasis [is] on how to most effectively sell Montana." We use feature films to promote Montana and the West to the world's true archdudes, the Japanese and Koreans. *City Slickers*, a slice of Hollywood banality in which Billy Crystal finds his soul and true purpose in life by going dude ranching— dude ranching!—with a curled-lip Jack Palance, enjoyed "unprecedented success" during a recent tourist promotion in the United Kingdom and Japan. Now, as I write this, our state officials are busy hustling our beloved Ol' Montany, again in Europe and Japan, with the film version of *A River Runs Through It*. Norman Maclean must be trying to claw his way out of the grave by now. Speaking of writers, we even offer "writer familiarization trips" for "carefully selected writers." As the travel promotion annual report tells us in soft, assuring tones, these are known to the cognoscenti as "fam trips." Just so we'll know.

All of this jargon, it turns out, really matters. Tourism is now seen worldwide as an economic panacea, and tourists apparently have become discriminating consumers of places. It's a competitive jungle out there in the marketplace for tourist dollars, and so the promotional jargon that goes with the trade is of some moment.

I got my first lesson in the power of tourism sloganeering when a good friend—hell, a fishing buddy—took the job of state director of tourism back in the pre–bed tax dark ages when we were spending less than a million a year on the selling of this hamburger shaped like Montana. He told me that the state had quietly commissioned a survey to determine the effectiveness of the official state slogan, which in those days was a slogan I sort of liked: "Montana—Last of the Big-Time Splendors." Well, that slogan simply had to go, he explained. Why? Because American travelers—with their soaring rates of literacy—thought it meant that Montana would be an expensive vacation. After a long, exhaustive search for a new slogan, we became "Naturally Inviting," a sort of Seven-Up among the cola states. We, of course, had the pictures to prove it: the dazzling, blue vistas of Flathead Lake, the Rocky Mountain Front, the Chinese Wall once safely locked away in the Bob Marshall wilderness area. Never mind the deerflies, the roadkills, the grizzly bears, and all those, all those, all those clearcuts.

So, what are we getting for our $7 million worth of state government–sponsored promotion? Nothing but gravy, if you read the official reports. In 1992 we sucked $930 million out of those wallets that waft through our state. Retail sales and food service each enjoyed around $270 million in nonresident spending. Factor in the induced effects of economic activity that ripples from the initial billion-dollar blast, and you find the claim that tourism is now a $2 billion annual industry. Not bad for an economic sector that in 1978, when we were still trying very hard to keep people *out* of Montana, didn't even show up in most analyses of our economy. The state now claims that tourism maintains over eighteen thousand "direct" jobs and another fifteen thousand "secondary" jobs. Six and a half million visitors now pass through Montana every year.

The trends are all up and supposed to stay up. With more bed tax money to spend, we'll promote more visitations, and that will give us more bed tax money to spend on more promotion. The promotion program will grind on because it's very popular. Every recent poll I've seen suggests that the state's residents are overwhelmingly supportive of it. They believe that it's the Last Best Bet for an economy that they have always been told was slow, halting, sputtering, stagnant, unpredictable, booming and busting, downward spiraling, anything but healthy. In fifteen years I've never seen an official forecast of the state's economy that suggested anything other than continuing gloom and doom. Those forecasts still predict dismal economic prospects . . . except in tourism, the sprightly little Tinkerbell of our economy.

Still, Montanans' professed love of tourism—at least as they profess it to pollsters—strikes me as a clear case of cognitive dissonance. On the one hand, we hear the numbers, and they sound good. From an investments point of view, who can argue with the state's tourism promotion efforts: for a scant seven million bucks' worth of promotion—most of it paid for by the tourists themselves—we get $2 billion in direct hit plus ripple. Gee, where can I buy shares? All we have to do in exchange for this money is tolerate, so far, 6.5 million gasoline racers burning up and down the highways, ogling Flathead Lake (even as it gradually fills with coliform from all the second-home development on its shores), rushing to get to the two big ski resorts—Big Sky and Big Mountain—and leapfrogging each other on hell-bent trips to Glacier and Yellowstone national parks.

On the other hand, our little cities like Missoula and Bozeman now have shopping malls and traffic jams, and we're getting the endless strips of motels, junk food restaurants, and self-serve gas depots out along the interstates that make our towns look like every other greasy little burg everywhere else in Walt Disney's Amerika. We've got increasingly egregious pollution problems now, here in the paradise of the northern

Plains, and we have seriously outstripped the abilities of local government to handle even modest levels of new home development. Recent news in my hometown paper is that a new hydrologic study of Missoula County has found significant levels of septic contamination in *every single well* surveyed by a team of university researchers, including one well drilled 220 feet down to bedrock. Many of our schools are grossly overcrowded. Classrooms at the universities are literally falling apart from disrepair, and we rank fiftieth among the fifty states in our level of support for higher education. And yet we continue to give our $2 billion tourism industry a free ride with respect to state and local revenues. If all of that isn't stupid enough, we spend what paltry money we raise from a tourism tax right back on more tourism.

The sad fact about the so-called promotion of tourism is that it is in reality the mere promotion of Montana. Lots and lots of tourists, seeing the state's glorious summers, want to own a piece of it. Since most come from economies substantially more robust than ours—where state agency attorneys are hired for $26,000 a year and starting high school teachers commonly make $18,500—they can own a chunk of Montana for a price they can hardly believe. The growth is beginning to choke us, even as our clearcut national and private forests are choking our beloved rivers and lakes with silt. Tourism didn't create our problems with public funding, any more than environmentalists created tourism. But the business of blatantly promoting Montana in what can only be described as an international real estate bonanza will only exacerbate them. We cannot keep up with the legitimate demands made by newcomers but also can't stop waving them in. Tourism, after all, is an economic panacea, the only bright spot—remember? Being against tourism has suddenly become like being against ranching, or Christianity.

Tourism is a high-rent rendezvous with a future none of us wants, but we'll accept it if it's all we think we'll get. Ask most people in Montana what they think *they* get from tourism, and if they aren't retail business owners, they're liable to say, "A headache." But they'll still vote for it, just as they still vote for Senators Max Baucus and Conrad Burns, knowing that, despite the professed political cleft between this Nouveau Democrat and Paleo Republican, both do everything they can to maintain the historic federal subsidies to all of those industries that are—we were once told and apparently believed—soon to be obsolete.

While the tourists mill about on the streets of our fair towns, pointing aimlessly into the Big Sky that abounds, we who live here watch the day-by-day deterioration of public services, universities, federal lands, rivers and lakes, airsheds, and wildlife habitats. We are told to bow our heads before these folks from Sacramento, Cincinnati, and Seoul because they are the future. Once we believed that their ingress into Montana's perennially slumping economy was our ticket to environmental quality. Now we see that they are not better but simply more.

Despite the influx of new people, new ideas, new values, our legislature is *less environmentally inclined* than it was fifteen years ago. Our public interest movement, robust and growing during the 1970s and early '80s, is now moribund. Environmental organizations' coffers, with few exceptions, did not swell. The electorate did not suddenly turn green, and there is no evidence that it will. The inrush of enlightened newcomers didn't help with the designations of new federal wilderness areas. Indeed, we still can't pass our twelve-year-old Montana wilderness bill. Our two senators are congressional leaders in the last desperate attempts to save the West from its eventual rendezvous with the marketplace in timber, grass, and minerals; we will bow our heads and dutifully elect both again when the time comes. Trust me on this. We didn't get what we bargained for in our Faustian contract with boosterism. We simply got more, which somehow amounts to less.

We are an increasingly desperate nation, ripping up and down our homicidal highways to escape our own lives. We are fleeing crime and poor schooling, fleeing the underclass we have created, fleeing our own families. In a country of placelessness we are desperate for place, but we don't know how to treat it well when we find it. What if the poet was right—what if Montana is the Last Best Place? Well, in our fashion, we'll fix it.

Romancing Mora

Eduardo Paz-Martinez

reprinted from *Santa Fe Reporter*, July 15–21, 1992

*T*he warm winds of an early July afternoon whip through downtown Mora, clouding up the main street in yet another swirl of blowing dust openly disdaining the land, the buildings, and the people. It is a harsh scene, yet oddly, hardly anyone notices. Women on their way into the county courthouse do no more than take hand to hair; men stumble out of pickups to tug down on gimme caps before ambling into Theresa Marie's restaurant for long conversations and a potful of coffee that comes a cup at a time.

Along this isolated stretch of the rural northern New Mexico byway, it is not the summer's dust devils that much bother residents. Like other seasonal meteorological roars, winter snowfalls included, this sandstorm, too, comes and goes.

Suddenly a more excitable sort of environmental angst is capturing the attention of people who live in the Sangre de Cristo Mountains' charming Mora Valley: namely, a growing perception that, with each passing weekend, more and more people are pulling into town. When they look out the picture windows at Theresa Marie's, they see rental cars and Winnebagos on slow, sightseeing crawls.

Enigmatic Mora—rich in French and Spanish settler history that dates back to the late 1600s but saddled for the greater portion of this century with the reputation of being a poverty-stricken, backwoods region of the state—is being discovered anew.

For residents used to living the easy, uncomplicated lifestyle of the countryside, this is the best and worst bit of news. It is good in a business way for residents, such as Katie Almanzar, who along with her husband owns the Almanzar Motel.

"Weekends are really good," she says cheerfully. "It's people who say they passed through here last year and fell in love with the valley. They've come back. Others say they're from out of state and looking for land to buy."

Among those staying at the ten-room motel last week was a small group of visiting Germans on their way to Taos, who told Almanzar the local scenery reminded them of home.

Another who has welcomed the first signs of a tourist trade is Mora Valley rancher David Salman, who says positively: "Our major resource today is our beauty, the pristine environment. To try to deny that they don't exist is a fallacy. Tourism—and I mean more than just a van full of people—is coming."

That would seem to be true.

''You could say it's summer and people are on vacation,'' says native Tony Martinez, owner of the popular Cleveland Bar. ''But you could also say these people are way out of their way. I can't imagine they'd come through here on their way to the Grand Canyon or Disneyland. Do you?''

Tucked in a cupped-palm valley of the august Sangre de Cristos, snowcapped Jicarilla Peak rising majestically to the west, Mora is about ninety-five miles from Santa Fe by way of Las Vegas. The land rolls in dignified geography, painted by proud piñon, stately evergreens, and busy, clear streams. Such beauty contrasts with the residents' modest contribution—basic architecture from another era, a good chunk of it abandoned: Mora and its decaying downtown structures; neighboring Cleveland and now-closed groceries of yesteryear; Holman and its adobe churches; Chacon and its weed-filled cemetery. Beauty and remnants of history for everyone.

But for residents, tourism is, for the moment, more discernible. They see the travelers and even talk with them. Development is not as visible yet, although real estate agents say more outsiders are inquiring about Mora County properties. Still, drive up and down the valley and you see new redwood homes here and there, some dressed up with satellite dishes and gleaming metal fireplace piping.

Ask real estate agent Marcia Leyba, who lives in Grants but journeys to Mora from the western New Mexico city to do business as MJ Realty, and hear this: ''My impression is that there is a discernible increase in outsiders. It's too early to say that they are buying everything in sight, although I hear people in Mora telling me they see more and more tourists coming by. Tourism could be a good thing for them.''

But even as young and old couples from Texas and California shyly walk into Theresa Marie's for a glass of iced tea or pull into a service station for another tank of gasoline, some in Mora firmly believe these are not just tourists out to see the American West.

There are those who see these visitors as outsiders out to become neighbors. ''People with big city ways and needs,'' is Tony Martinez's read. Newcomers eager to whip out their wallets and buy in, goes the line. Already, residents note, a sprinkling of high-windowed, Santa Fe–style homes have been built on the picturesque hillsides overlooking Highway 518, which cuts through the center of Mora and its tiny neighbors of Cleveland, Holman, and Chacon.

To some extent, Martinez is right. Names to be found these days on the Mora County property tax roles include recent buyers from Los Angeles, San Jose, and Pueblo, Colorado, as well as Amarillo, Texas. Their designation as ''non-residential'' property owners does not mean that the acreage is zoned for business use as much as it means the new owners do not yet live in the county.

Taken together, the signs of activity keep growing, convincing Mora's residents that their way of life is changing. More visitors are coming, more residents are coming—and the resistance that held them off for decades is finally weakening in the face of the inevitable.

Seated behind his executive desk at the Mora Valley Clinic, Antonio Medina, a descendant of one of the community's early Hispanic settlers, isn't quite ready to side with Salman. He sees any talk of growth as loss of more than just chunks of land down by the verdant banks of the pretty Mora River. Medina, like other Hispanics in the valley, worries that a rediscovery of his homeland may lead to something bigger: newcomers without a clue of the area's past; people more interested in arts colonies than in his culture.

''I like Mora the way it is,'' Medina says firmly. ''If it's changed to something else, it will be ruined. I have a very serious problem with development that is going to exploit our natural resources for the benefit of the wealthy outsider."

So what's going on in Mora?

The exchange between Salman, a wealthy landowner who'd like to see Mora plunge into the 1990s, and Medina, who has a reputation as a defender of all things Hispanic, is legendary. The two have clashed repeatedly, always about something new and different wanting to come to the sleepy valley.

Salman, who came to Mora forty-nine years ago from Houston, sees tourism and new residents as viable vehicles for the region's needed economic growth. Medina believes tourism means fast-food eateries, chain hotels and motels, and shopping centers.

More to the point, Medina insists he does not want to see Mora become a "little Santa Fe," insisting that northern New Mexico villages "need not take an 'Old Town' image and become 'art and culture' havens and museums for non-Hispanics."

In 1979, when Salman sought to help stage the tenth anniversary of Woodstock in Mora, it was Medina who led the opposition, raising a loud voice in public forums at which he characterized the proposed rock concert as "wild desecration of our hallowed lands."

Salman lost that one, and not a sound from Country Joe & the Fish was ever heard.

In the early 1980s Medina fueled protests against construction of an Allsup's convenience store. Steadfast in their belief that the twenty-four-hour store's arrival would kill off smaller family stores, Mora residents organized to fight it, spreading posters throughout the community, the mildest of which said Allsup's Must Go.

In the end, Medina lost that one. Today Allsup's is a thriving enterprise, and the stores it replaced are notches on its gun handle.

The 1990s began with both men on opposite sides of a proposed experimental fish hatchery that appears to be on its way to Mora County. Medina and his Mora Water and Land Protective Association say the project is unnecessary. The $16 million hatchery, to include construction of a four-building compound, is expected to bring twelve to fourteen jobs to Mora. The association has vowed to seek legal action on environmental concerns the moment the federal U.S. Fish and Wildlife Service breaks ground.

Salman, on the other hand, is all for the hatchery. He argues that it is a model for the sort of new industry the community should be soliciting. He sees the hatchery not only as an aid to research but also as an eventual tourist attraction.

Medina's point is really the same one he uses to say tourism is bad for Mora: erosion of natural beauty and loss of privacy. In the case of the hatchery, whose primary mission would be production of trout, he is also concerned that it would drain yet another resource he deems precious: water.

"Water is our past, our present, and our future," Medina says. "We can't be dislocated. This is a monster water project, and I am not convinced that the government has answered all our questions."

That battle is yet to be resolved, but still another telling skirmish came after publication in the *Wall Street Journal*'s April 21, 1988, issue of a quote from Salman. His words were part of a front-page story about the three poorest counties in the United States, of which Mora was one. "The main thing," he said, "is that there is nothing here. There's no agriculture, and there's no industry. There are no resources, no oil, no minerals. There's nothing a family can get by on."

Medina laughs at the newspaper story, which, while saying Mora is a "region of haunting beauty," described it as "a place of vacant storefronts."

"I am not against economic development," Medina insists. "I want business growth from within ourselves, which means that whatever we go after is from the bottom up and from within. I am not one of those who see the arrival of fast-food joints as being progress. Tourism is seen here by a handful as a panacea, but it's the biggest lie. Tourism will not cure the ills of our elderly."

Mora is poor. No one disputes that. There are few jobs. Indeed, nearly seven of every ten residents employed in this part of western Mora County draw their paychecks from the government—county, state, or federal. Its annual per capita income of $8,194 ranks it thirty-second among New Mexico's thirty-three counties. The median family income of $8,608 is more than $5,000 below the national average. Unemployment is nearly 25 percent, a substantial portion of it in the sparsely populated valley in the western corner of the county. After the 1990 federal census, Mora County numbered only forty-two hundred people. Thus, it is not surprising that, according to government records, nearly as many residents (928) receive monthly food stamps as are unemployed.

Tough place; tough times, it would seem.

Statistics don't tell the whole story, however. Mora County remains an agrarian community, and that, too, is a big part of its history. Once, in the late 1800s, it supplied Fort Union, the largest army post in the Southwest, with livestock and grain. Earlier this century, even after the federal government shut down the army post in the early 1890s, Mora County was the acknowledged breadbasket of a younger New Mexico—providing wheat, oats, alfalfa, corn, barley, rye, potatoes, and vegetables. Indeed, multi-story stone structures that housed many of the area's mills still stand in Mora, their exteriors a portrait of weathered stone, wood, and rusted metal.

Varied reasons have been given for the industry's collapse, but central to it was a decision by the railroad companies to abandon service to Mora in the mid-1920s. ("We used to have our farmers line up for miles to get their crops aboard the trains," recalls Father Walter Cassidy.) The advent of high-tech farming—bigger spreads farming larger acreage elsewhere—coupled with modern-day trucking, also contributed to Mora's fall.

Semblances of those days can still be found, however. Visit with a handful of residents and see it at work. The house and yard may not be pretty, but out back invariably are a cow or two, some chickens, a small vegetable garden, and peach trees. This is subsistence farming, the growing and raising of food and animals for home use. It is an aspect of rural life that rarely finds inclusion in state and federal social aid programs that are more interested in how much cash you earn—or do not earn. In Mora it appears to work.

But along with the country lifestyle has come the outside microscope. Valley residents unhappily acknowledge that they have a history of being dangled at the end of negative newspaper and magazine reports.

"Drinking," says Tony Martinez. "They always write about our drinking. We don't drink any more or any less than they do in Santa Fe. Hell, I could go to Santa Fe and come back and write a real story about drinking in that town."

People drink alcohol in Mora. They admit that some of their neighbors have drinking problems. But they also laugh. They fight. They wake up early, work hard, go to bed late. They file lawsuits against family. They worry about their kids and about paying bills.

"We're really no different than any other small town anywhere else," says school board member John Romero. "But outsiders want to come here and tell us what's wrong with Mora. It's almost like a sport for people in the city."

Tourism may or may not help the area, but what it will do is bring dramatic change to a lifestyle many in Mora are not interested in losing. Things could get better in various ways, however.

A sizeable increase in population could finally bring door-to-door mail delivery. More residents and increased business activity could mean the Bank of Las Vegas would open a full-service facility instead of the branch office it currently operates in Mora. The community could get a newspaper like the *Mora County Star*, a crusading weekly that fell out of grace with several local politicians and was ultimately run out of town in the early 1980s.

The lack of a newspaper never killed off a town, but it helps substantiate resident Dan Cassidy's claim that Mora is "an insular community."

"There is a strong historical tendency to hold on to history around here," he says. "People here fear change. It's apprehension. Rumors come and go."

Additional services would in themselves boost the area's ability to entice business investment, says pro-growth advocate David Salman, who notes: "We have as much history and as beautiful scenery as Taos, but tourists hesitate because they have not been given a reason to stop."

Yet while one could quickly draft a lengthy list of things Mora does not have, it also must be said that there are many "luxuries" Mora residents have long lived without. There is no movie theater, although a video rental store does a brisk business out of a mobile home not far from Allsup's. There are no hotels. Visitors have the ten-room Almanzar Motel or the open skies. Hungry? Theresa Marie's is open during daytime hours only. Same for Hatcha's Cafe. B-Jay's ("Columbus ate here," reads its highway sign) is open whenever owner Baudy Martinez wants to open it. There is no shopping center (residents travel thirty-two miles to Las Vegas), no gift shops, and no hospital.

But some in Mora ask: Would all of these things really make the community better?

"We lived in Grants for several years, and we had everything," says Anita Lovato LaRan, who is director of Helping Hands Inc., a social service agency in town. "I mean, we had McDonald's, Baskin-Robbins, dry cleaners, movies, Holiday Inn, everything. My kids no longer watch hours and hours of television. Now they go fishing, they hike, and they play outside like kids. This is a very healthy community, and I think that's good."

So what does she think of this tourist stuff?

"I think it'll happen," she begins. "But it will be a sad time in our history. Let's be realistic, too. The state wants Mora to grow economically so that it can contribute more to tax revenues. Tourism will come, only it will not be led by people in Mora. I guess we'll fight it individually. By that I mean that if Motel 6 decides to move in next to my home, I'll fight it."

Last year Mora County contributed $755,000 in tax revenues to the state, placing it ahead of only Catron, DeBaca, and Harding counties. Taking schools, law enforcement, and administration of local government into account, the state spent more money on Mora than it got in return.

Still, Anita LaRan's exposure to tourism comes down to this: An enterprising photographer, finding her home irresistible, took his fancy camera, snapped a picture, and eventually sold it as a postcard in Santa Fe gift shops. The caption?

"He called my house 'The Red Barn,' " she remembers reading when she flipped it over. "Can you believe it? The least he could've done was stop by, knock on my door, and ask if he could use my property to make money. That, too, is tourism, I suppose."

For others, it isn't that some hamburger joint will bring its gaudy, plastic building materials to the neighborhood as much as it is a fear that new residents will dream up million-dollar homes, sending property taxes sky-high for everybody else.

"People here see Taos and Santa Fe," says Dan Cassidy, forty-year-old great-grandson of the Cassidys who built and ran the Cleveland Roller Mill. "They remember their ancestors' adobe home selling for $700,000 and how the kids were forced out when prices skyrocketed. Mora, I believe, would like to back away from that sort of growth."

Already, however, Cassidy has seen an increasing number of realty signs. In bright lettering, they adorn some of Mora's older downtown buildings, ranch fences on the outskirts of town, and even a few landmarks such as the Almanzar Motel, which its owners have put on the market because of illness. Realty agent Leyba is pitching a combination general store, hotel, and warehouse that belongs to a relative and sits dead square in the middle of the small downtown skyline in Mora.

Indeed, the very fact that property owners in close-knit Mora are even willing to sell, much less advertise the idea with bright realty signs, is telling in itself.

"You know what's striking?" Cassidy asks. "Ten years ago, you'd never see a real estate sign around here. Now they're all over the place. You get the impression the whole county is for sale."

He feels someone is buying—though he, like some of his neighbors, gauges the activity by the tourist traffic. In his particular case, Cassidy sees good arguments for both sides of the tourism issue. As operator of the Cleveland Roller Mill Museum, he knows increased traffic would mean more visitors paying the admission fee to see his "roller mill in action." Yet Cassidy likes the quiet life of today's Mora and, in fact, speaks badly of time spent in Colorado and Santa Fe.

At the county tax assessor's office, Angela Romero is keeping track of newcomers who walk into her office to ask questions about various properties up for sale. Most of them, she says, ask for maps before leaving.

"I think Mora will grow," says Tony Martinez as he sits with a cup of coffee at a table near his bar's small bandstand. "I get people in my place from everywhere. And I am seeing the tourists come in more and more. But these guys don't spend that much money in Mora. Most of them come in their tourist wagons, and they carry everything on it: food, beds, and television."

Rancher Salman, who served as the area's state representative for five terms until retiring in 1979, sees Mora at the proverbial crossroads. The risk being run, he argues, is that in trying to preserve the community's seventeenth-century roots, anti-growth proponents in Mora eventually will see it become just another Western ghost town.

"Mora is already an anachronism," says Salman. "It hasn't died because people here are, by and large, elderly, unskilled, and have no place to go. A lot of it has to do with some people patronizing their own people. I think they enjoy seeing them in poverty. These same people think they can go back to the seventeenth century."

Allen A. Nysse is a former Wisconsin resident who's lived in many places and last hung his cowboy hat in Santa Fe. Last month he packed his belongings and the tools of his woodworking business and trucked it all up to Mora. With big plans in mind, he got himself an abandoned building right downtown in exchange for a little handiwork. He's a newcomer, and to hear him talk, he feels it.

"You know, I was real anxious to leave Santa Fe after four years of rising rents," says the forty-seven-year-old Nysse, who, in his pony-tailed hair, stands out in Mora. "Everything isn't perfect here, but I think I'll stay."

He has a woman friend in town. His building is owned by an acquaintance. A large portion of the false ceiling has caved in, and the only signs of any improvement on this day are two posters of Cuban revolutionary Ernesto "Che" Guevara that Nysse has nailed on an overhang directly above his lathe.

"This is like returning to life in the 1950s," Nysse adds. "The whole world is racing, losing its values. Here it's a lot simpler."

Never mind that, try as he might, he's been unable to get the phone company to install his service. Even for that, Nysse has a ready answer: "You could say I grew tired of the fast lane and found Mañana Land. I don't need my phone by morning. I can wait."

If the myth that has long dogged the Mora Valley—that it is cold to strangers and especially cold to Anglo strangers—is accurate, Nysse has no chance. He, however, is unconvinced.

He is going places in town to speed up his assimilation. On this Saturday afternoon he is drinking beer at the Cleveland Bar. Around him, stocky Hispanic men in working clothes drink together, jousting noisily like good friends as they shoot billiards. Nysse sits by himself, conversing only with owner and bartender Tony Martinez, who tells him he should've stopped in the night before.

"Big crowd, huh?" he says to Martinez. "I walked over to The Lounge [another local bar] last night, but they were having a wedding dance there. The third place was full of old men. Sorta dead, so I went home."

Nysse is too much of a newcomer to have come to conclusions about the town. But he is nonetheless convincing when he says he has never believed the myth about coldness toward Anglos and thus feels no danger. "Most of my girlfriends have been Hispanic," he volunteers. "Maybe that'll help."

Bar owner Martinez believes the myth was created and is perpetuated by outsiders. "This county is about Mejicanos in charge, and it bothers a lot of people who do not live here," he says. "But Anglos can't say that they're mistreated. It's not that way at all. I have all sorts of customers, and aside from a few fights, which every bar has now and then, everybody gets along."

"It's a lie," adds school board member John Romero. "A damned, damned lie. That's just something that was published years ago and easy for people to repeat. The other myth is that we prefer outdoor privies out here. It's bullshit, of course."

Tuesday night at the Cleveland Bar: Tony Martinez and his wife, Connie, behind the bar. Eight Hispanics playing billiards, another three seated at the bar, one playing an out-of-tune guitar. Loud norteño music screaming from the jukebox, followed by a pair of tunes by the Texas Tornados in English. Rough-looking hombres; no fights this night.

Saturday afternoon at the Cleveland Bar: Young Anglo men and women on break from repair work at the Catholic church in nearby La Cueva play billiards, Hispanic cowboys play on a nearby table. Loud music. Boisterous chatter. No fights or arguments.

Father Walter Cassidy, seventy-six, has lived all his life in Mora.

"I know there are people who are absolutely isolationists," he says of some of his neighbors. "They won't talk to strangers. I call them xenophobes."

He remembers when trains rolled into Mora, when the now-gone Butler Hotel hosted gala Saturday night dances featuring the beloved Mora Jazz Babies of the 1920s, when the valley's agriculture helped feed people elsewhere in the state, and he scoffs at the myth of unsociability.

"My father came here and practically forgot he was Irish," the retired priest adds. "He grew up with Spanish kids and herded goats with them. He got along famously with Hispanics."

Mora County is a Hispanic stronghold. Hispanics hold every seat on the three-member county commission. A Hispanic serves as county manager, sheriff, treasurer, magistrate, and county clerk. This pleases the population, which, depending on whom you talk to, is anywhere from the federal Census Bureau's estimate of 85 percent Hispanic to, if you accept the local figure, 95 percent Hispanic.

Sit inside Theresa Marie's and hear a language that is a mixture of English and Spanish. ("Ese earthquake in California," one man is telling others at his table. "Es muy amazing tan pocos died, no?") Also obvious to a visitor is the bond, the community. With each patron entering the cafe comes a round of greetings, handshakes, and abrazos. The only ones left out of the circle are the tourists, who invariably stop what they're doing and look up and smile.

Still, as school board member Romero put it, there is little the community can do to replace its less-than-complimentary reputation. Romero believes bad publicity has hurt the region for years.

Just what are they saying about Mora, anyway? A call to the New Mexico Tourism Department yields this information:

"Mora is not a big community, but we're really not that familiar with it, sir. We do not have a tourist brochure on it, for example."

"Is it safe for travel?" we ask.

"You should visit Los Alamos," replies the woman pleasantly over the telephone.

"No," we say next. "Not Los Alamos. We're thinking of visiting Mora."

"Mora?" she chips in. "You're still stuck on that one? No one has ever called us to ask for tourist information on Mora, sir."

In June 1989, on the occasion of a visit to Mora by then-governor Garrey Carruthers for Government Day in Mora County, Antonio Medina rose to give a speech he wanted the governor to hear. It concerned the area's economic future, and it came soon after the governor's special force had identified socioeconomic problems facing Mora.

Medina read from a prepared text outlining his ideas of how to usher Mora into the twenty-first century. Surprisingly, he conceded that the idea's time had come, but he told the governor and the others in attendance at the high school gymnasium that economic development would have to be a process "of the people, by the people, for the people."

"That is, economic development from the bottom up, so that those who have the greatest need benefit the most," he said at the time. "Our long-term goal is to live gracefully and die proudly," he concluded.

When he recalled the speech, Medina explained that the conclusion was a jab at the governor, who, he says, had answered a question about the future of New Mexico's poor rural towns by saying he hoped they'd all simply die gracefully.

Medina won't let Mora die, but just how hard would he fight the arrival of tourism?

"It would be the Mora Bean Dip War," he says without hesitation.

A Passive Town in Utah Awaits Its Fate

Florence Williams

reprinted from *High Country News*, November 18, 1991

On a breezy October Saturday in Moab, Utah, a sea of mountain bikers clad in brightly colored Lycra flows down Main Street to commemorate this year's Fat Tire Festival. Over two thousand bikers from across the country have converged on this town of four thousand to ride spectacular canyon trails rated "gonzo/abusive" and to play games like bicycle polo and bicycle rodeo. Some are even wearing Nike's bright new $115 cross-training desert sneaker, the Air Mowabb.

In 1989 this busted uranium town was dubbed by *Outside* magazine its "favorite mountain bike spot." The town has not been the same since.

Just over a century ago Mormon leader Brigham Young sent disciples to colonize the ruddy, barren valley along the Colorado River in eastern Utah. Today Moab is a different sort of mecca: tourists come from all over the world to visit nearby national parks, and recreationists hike, bike, and four-wheel the canyon country with a near-religious zeal. In the last three years the area's popularity has exploded.

The pedaling Fat Tire flotilla looks strangely out of place in downtown Moab, until recently dominated by eighteen-wheelers and drilling rigs. For all its surrounding scenic beauty, Moab may be one of the ugliest towns in the West. Writer Edward Abbey called it "the metal building capital of the world." When uranium hit eastern Utah in the 1960s, the town's population exploded from two thousand farmers to ten thousand miners. Uranium left a sprawling legacy of trailer parks, industrial service shops, and giant utility poles.

The town's reluctant embrace of tourism has also followed an industrial approach. Visitors are greeted by a main street festooned with giant neon signs advertising rooms with cable TV and fast-food specials. But as more and more upscale urban refugees seek sport and solace in the surrounding canyons, Moab's days of atomic cafes and uranium drive-ins are numbered.

Taking advantage of cheap real estate—a result of the collapsed mining industry—and Moab's own planning vacuum, developers are tumbling into town. Moab's earlier settlers, the Mormons and the miners, are struggling to hold on.

From both environmental and demographic perspectives, the tourism boom is not without its ill effects. As one planning consultant put it, "Everything is up for grabs."

Although tourists have been coming to the area since the mid-1960s, when nearby

Arches and Canyonlands national parks were born, the recent spate of recreation seekers is unprecedented. Since 1986 the number of visitors to Arches National Park has risen 75 percent, to nearly 700,000. Canyonlands National Park, an hour away, has seen a similar increase.

But more and more visitors are bypassing the national parks in favor of the equally spectacular federal lands administered by the Bureau of Land Management. On the millions of acres of canyon country surrounding town, public use is free and virtually unregulated; anyone can pitch a tent or ride a bike anywhere, and only a few areas are closed to vehicles.

Overwhelmed by the current wave of tourism, federal administrators of the surrounding public land say they are unprepared to handle the environmental impacts of off-trail biking, four-wheeling, and unregulated camping.

What the Fat Tire Festival is to Halloween, the Jeep Safari is to Easter. Last year some ten thousand people took part. The town, however, has only four hundred hotel rooms. Most of the Jeepers and other springtime revelers drive into the slickrock around town to camp out.

Such use takes its toll: Most of the damage occurs along the Colorado River, where the dense tamarisk along the water can't cover the stench of human waste and the sight of garbage accumulated over seasons of weekends.

"It's disgusting," observes Scott Groene, an attorney in the Moab office of the Southern Utah Wilderness Alliance.

Until last spring there were no latrines near the river; now there are several, but the county can't find funds to maintain them. Says Ground County Commissioner David Knutson, "We've run out of money [to maintain] Port-o-potties along the river, and we have three more months left in the year. That's how out of money we are."

Environmentalists, who initially welcomed the town's switch from an extractive economy to a service-based one, worry about the impacts of recreation. "At first people thought, yeah, great, tourism, it's great, it's clean," says Groene. "But now people are running around out of control, looking for a place to camp, pushing into sensitive areas. The desert bighorn sheep barely survived the uranium boom; now the mountain bikers may finish them off."

BLM biologist Linda Seibert says the bikers and Jeepers destroy sensitive microbiotic soils. In the arid desert, mountain bike tracks make ruts that can turn into gullies and cause erosion, she says. Disturbing wildlife is also a concern; along one popular biking trail, a pair of endangered peregrine falcons recently deserted a long-used nest.

Now, says Seibert, the BLM will have to reassess its policy toward recreationists and write a new management plan. "A few years ago we were promoting the area," she recalls. "Now we have to say, 'oops, there's too much.' "

Gene Nodine, the BLM's recently retired district manager in Moab, says the agency lacks funds and personnel to handle the impacts of recreation. "We have a staff of seven people for all of southeastern Utah," explains Nodine. "That's 885,000 acres per person." He says the last management plan for the area was written in the early 1980s, before the mountain biking craze. "It was not a forward-looking document," adds Russ Von Koch, the BLM's recreation planner.

Nodine says the BLM is writing a new management plan and, in addition to asking the national office for more money and staff, the Moab office may implement a fee system for bikers and campers. More latrines are also in the works, as well as an educational campaign to teach visitors how to tread lightly on BLM land.

While the BLM is attempting to regulate the influx of people to the area, the same cannot be said for Moab or surrounding Grand County. Town officials have failed to keep up with the pace of growth. With weak zoning, Moab is virtually indefensible against the assault of subdivision developers, chain store giants, and megahotels. The county's sewage system, jails, fire department, and hospitals are already at full capacity, open space is dissolving into pricey subdivisions, and few are happy about the rapid changes to their town.

Moab is just beginning to suffer the classic resort-town symptoms of nearby Park City and Telluride. As second-home development increases, few affordable rentals are available for seasonal service workers. Much of the existing housing has been bought by out-of-towners, and apartments have been converted into overnight accommodations.

To handle the influx of tourists, the town's lodgings have more than doubled in just three years. Bed-and-breakfast establishments have quadrupled in that time. Local real estate prices have also more than doubled. Recently, an orchard owned by the Mormon Church was sold to a Las Vegas developer who plans to build a three hundred–room deluxe resort. Land speculators from Aspen and Telluride have bought up numerous properties. From a demographic point of view, Moab is changing fast.

"We're a playground now for the rest of the world," says local Realtor Ray Tibbetts, who grew up in Moab. "You can't buy a pair of Levi's here anymore, only T-shirts. It's not a real world for working people."

Tibbetts doesn't hide his anger at mountain bikers. "A lot of them have no respect for the traffic. They ride three or four abreast. Why one hasn't been killed, I don't know. You get the seed planted in your head you'd like to be the one to do it."

Says Commissioner Knutson, "It's like having company at your house all the time. You begin to feel like it's not your home anymore. You wish they'd leave."

The town's beef with bikers goes beyond traffic or crowds. In a town still predominantly run by members of the Mormon Church, the inevitable culture clash between visitors and natives runs even deeper than in most resort spots.

"Tourism promotes self-indulgence," explains Commissioner Knutson, a fifth-generation Moab resident. In his early thirties, wearing a T-shirt and a neat, clipped beard, Knutson hardly seems a reactionary. He leans across his desk in the Grand County Courthouse to tell me his wife is also a fifth-generation settler and that they may even be related.

"The Mormon work ethic is definitely at odds with tourism," continues Knutson, who runs a Jeep-rental company for tourists. "These people bathe in City Market. They pick food out of the salad bar. We are going to have difficulties when we base our economy on play. There's no productivity." Knutson's idea of productivity is mining. With a nostalgia typical of Moab's old guard, he says he made more money supplying oil rigs in four months than he's made in four years of renting Jeeps. He also says that tourism does not provide the solid tax base that mining did.

It's no surprise that many from Moab's working class resent tourists, who more often than not represent values antithetical to the town's history of Mormon settlement and mining. This is, after all, the place where local commissioners drove a bulldozer into Negro Bill Canyon to protest its designation as a Wilderness Study Area. The town also drove out one BLM district manager in the early 1980s for attempting to assert federal control over the area's public lands. Since then the Moab BLM office has applied a relatively hands-off approach when it comes to oil and gas oversight, grazing, and now recreation.

But federal presence has also been a blessing for Moab in that it provides visitors with a playground free of local investment. Other recreation-based economies such as skiing demand large amounts of capital. In Moab the federal government provides the jungle gym, and the tourists swing.

Ever since Arches and Canyonlands national parks were designated, Moab's destiny has been to serve visitors to the spectacular lands surrounding town. But it is a destiny filled only with the greatest reluctance.

"Every day I see a backlash of sorts against tourism," says Robin Groff, co-owner of Rim Cyclery, Moab's original bike shop. Groff, a mining engineer who turned to biking when the energy bust hit, says he is alternately praised and vilified for bringing biking to Moab. "There's a lot of local resentment against the bikers, who are for the most part really good people."

"Tourism is a different kind of culture than they are comfortable with," explains Myles Rademan, a planning consultant to numerous former mining towns in the West, including Moab. "At least Moab is lucky enough to have a culture clash. It's stressful, but it's better than blowing away."

Despite the concerns of both the newcomers, who are mostly environmentalists, and the old-timers, who would prefer a mine to a mountain bike any day, Moab appears disinclined to help plan its own future. Even the mayor, Tom Stocks, seems uninterested. "It's not my place to do anything about it. I'm not worried about controlling growth. The concentration of people in this town is lower than in Europe."

Stocks's laissez-faire approach to development echoes through the old-guard community. In rural Utah, where wilderness is a dirty word and where sagebrush rebels still await the day they can gain ownership of federal land, the concept of any governance meets with wary suspicion.

"If I had my druthers, I'd stop it all right now," comments Realtor Tibbetts. "I don't want it overcrowded. But you either go ahead or you go back. You don't control it and you shouldn't control it; that's wrong. Our constitution says everyone has a right to a good life and making a living."

In short, in Moab anything goes: giant plastic signs on Main Street, big hotels, little hotels, ugly hotels. One developer wants to build a giant water slide, and others have plans for chain stores and restaurants. As one land speculator from Telluride puts it, "It's like Jay Leno on the Doritos commercial: Eat all you want; we'll make more. Moab is saying: Build all you want."

Recently local business owners signed a petition protesting a proposed ordinance to limit the size and height of signs on Main Street. Bowing to the opposition, the town council voted the proposal down. According to the town's draft master plan, new buildings of any kind are not subject to design reviews. Residential and commercial neighborhoods are mixed; open spaces and hillsides are unprotected.

Grand County's rules for developers are even more diluted. The most prohibitive zoning for agricultural land allows for one-acre subdivisions. In Colorado counties, by comparison, land can't be broken up into tracts smaller than thirty-five acres without a county review. Grand County does not even employ a planner. In fact, its total planning budget is $300, says David Olsen, the planner employed by the town of Moab. "The county's philosophy is free agency, free market, Adam Smith."

Although Olsen is Moab's planner, the title is an oxymoron. "It's frustrating," says Olsen, a recent college graduate. "People don't want rules."

Despite the power of the old guard, a growing segment of town is lobbying for better planning, controlled growth, and a preserved environment. Not surprisingly, the two factions routinely clash. Debates polarize the community on everything from wilderness designation to the proposed construction of the several-thousand-seat Kokopelli Theater in what is now scenic open space outside of town.

Craig Bigler, who moved to Moab from Washington, D.C., says that without a collective vision, the future looks bleak. "We have two worst-case scenarios. We'll either become a rich people's paradise, or we'll become a tacky tourist trap with big billboards and windshield tourism."

Bigler, who ran for county commissioner last year and lost, says no consensus exists on anything. "No community ever had a better opportunity to control its destiny and turn it to its benefit, but we're so damn contrary we'll blow it."

There are small signs of reconciliation. Robbie Swasey, president of the town's chamber of commerce, says she supports modest regulations on development. "We need to direct growth in a positive manner. Telluride, Aspen, Vail—they're dirty words around here. We don't want to become one of them, but Moab is twenty-five years behind in planning."

One of Moab's newest restaurants is Eddie McStiff's Brewery. Under a striped umbrella on the patio, owner Steve Patterson recommends Cajun french fries. He recently moved his business from the upscale resort of Telluride, which had become "prohibitively expensive." Patterson promptly bought several houses and vacant lots in town. "Is Moab going to be like Telluride?" he asks. "It's done. It's finished. By allowing bikes on the slickrock, by allowing second homes and not closing the door . . . Moab now reminds me of Telluride in the early days."

If Patterson is right, Moab's fifth-generation families are opening the door to a future that excludes them. "By boosting this kind of economic development, the old guard will destroy the very way of life they love," observes Jim Stiles, editor of the *Canyon Country Zephyr*, a local monthly.

With its seven-lane-wide downtown street, its utility parking lots, and giant store signs, Moab still seems a far cry from Telluride. Says planning consultant Rademan, "There's a certain charm to Moab being tacky. I wouldn't want it to be cute." Stiles agrees: "Keeping Moab ugly may be the only thing that saves us."

Mountain Passages

Richard Manning

reprinted from *Wilderness*, Fall 1992

W hen the first winter storms off the Continental Divide leave the storefronts of Cooke City, Montana, buried to the eaves, only about thirty stout souls remain in residence. The strip of businesses that feeds off the summer's flow of tourists into Yellowstone National Park has shut up shop. Plows have abandoned two of the three highways into and out of town to the high-country snows. Most of Cooke City's approximately two hundred residents have left on the remaining road and escaped through the park's Lamar Valley to Gardiner, then to the interstate, then on to warmer points south. Jammed into a narrow slit of canyon between the Beartooth and Absaroka mountain ranges, the nearly empty town seems forgotten and closed down.

It isn't though, not entirely, and in this slack time between the high-summer season and the midwinter boomlet of snowmobilers, news travels fast among those souls who stick it through the winter. Joan Humiston was in town to oversee the school board election and attend afternoon Bible study at Flo Zundel's motel. When she heard the news about the television broadcast, she postponed the three-mile snowmobile ride back to her ranch over the unplowed Beartooth Highway so she could watch the show at the Zundel's motel, which has a big satellite dish.

The program had to do with a gold mine that a Canadian company proposes to establish three miles outside town, a project conservation groups of the mine-riddled Northern Rockies region have called "the mine from hell." From a narrow strip of patented mining land on a tender alpine ridge overlooking Yellowstone, the Noranda Corporation of Canada wants to spend the next twenty years pulling ten thousand tons of crushed rock every day from two strip mines and a brace of tunnels blasted into Henderson Mountain. During construction, the mine would put as many as three hundred workers into the narrow furrow of the canyon that holds Cooke City and two attached hamlets: Colter Pass and Silver Gate. Both Joan Humiston and Flo Zundel vehemently oppose the mine—which is something new for them, and for Cooke City too.

Times are changing, this much we know. But what comes as something of a surprise is that electronic gadgetry like the Zundels' satellite dish is helping to subtly and fundamentally alter the economic realities of the Northern Rockies. A recent study of the twenty counties surrounding Yellowstone National Park, for example, showed that the region has an unusually healthy economy. More importantly, in terms of the way the region sees itself, the same study demonstrated that economic vigor and conservation are not mutually exclusive. In fact, the economy of the Greater Yellowstone Area was virtually unaffected by the recession—and it depends directly on the preservation of the natural amenities of the region.

This has never been understood as well as it might have been—or even admitted. At virtually any chamber of commerce, university business school, or Forest Service ranger district in the Rockies, you would still be told that the butter for the region's bread comes almost entirely from the extractive industries—ranching, logging, and mining. Lately, though, more tourists have been pulled to the area for the wild beauty of the mountains and to hunt, fish, refresh their spirits, or just plain spend money. The question is beginning to be asked: If we mine and log all the mountains, will the tourists still come?

The tussle between tourism and resource development is not entirely new in Cooke City. In 1869 four trappers stumbled onto gold "float" near the headwaters of the Clark Fork of the Yellowstone River, and Cooke City was born. By 1876 there was a smelter and 1,450 gold, silver, and copper claims on the sharp-faced hills around town. The whole complex became known as the New World District. Its mines continued producing until 1954, when the McLaren, the last operating mine, finally shut down in the last of the boom-and-bust cycles to which Cooke City, like so many other towns in the Rockies, has been vulnerable. The district's name lives on in the present controversy as the New World Project of Crown Butte Mines, Inc., the controlling interest in which is held by Noranda.

Cooke City's tradition of tourism is not quite as old as that of mining, but it has a pretty respectable vintage nonetheless. Local merchants set up the first tourist campground in 1921, and by 1956 at least one writer appeared somewhat disappointed in Cooke City's complete conversion to tourism. "Shiny, peeled-log facades," she said, "support neon signs to lure tourists and fishermen off the road for a coffee break, souvenirs, or a night's lodging. Cooke, as it is now called, is a wide-awake resort town with gas pumps and juke boxes."

Still, tourism was how most people in Cooke City earned their living even then. It still is, especially in summer, when the highway over Beartooth Pass to the interstate is freed of snow and open to car-borne tourists, who stop for meals and motels before going into Yellowstone through the northeast entrance. And some tourists come even in winter now, driving in through the Lamar Valley at the opposite end of the park. Cooke City has taken advantage of the closed highway and a network of unplowed roads surrounding town to produce 120 miles of groomed trails for snowmobiles, the vehicle of choice for the winter trade.

Cooke City and nearby Silver Gate are mainly a rustic row of motels, log cabin cafes, and convenience stores, with names like High Country Motel and Grizzly Lodge. Still, there are other signs that promise (or threaten) a return to the old days of boom and bust. A mobile home office bearing the logo of Crown Butte stands just at the edge of town, and at the opposite end, in place of the old All Seasons Motel sign, there is now a billboard-sized shingle dubbing the building the All Seasons Mine Co.—Hotel & Casino and Prospector Restaurant. The town bar, once simply called the Elkhorn, has been newly christened the Miners' Saloon, Casino & Emporium.

Noranda has been in town for several years now conducting what is technically called "exploration," since the relevant state and federal agencies have not yet granted the necessary permits for the company to start mining. The permit process will take several years and require a full-blown environmental impact statement (a requirement the company is fighting every step of the way).

Inside the All Seasons there is a plexiglass model of Noranda's proposed operation prominently displayed. Owner Patricia Crabb takes a break to argue her support for the mine and for the business it would generate in the community. She says she understands that her tourist trade is directly dependent on the natural values evident all around the town, but she has faith in the company's ability to preserve these and still get the ore out. "You build a house and you tear up the ground," she says. "You clean it up afterwards. Whatever impact they have I believe they would deal with in a positive manner. God put us in a stewardship position."

Roberta Williams, another winter resident, comes into the restaurant, listens to Patricia Crabb quietly for a while, then says she agrees. Mrs. Williams has lived in Cooke City since 1949. In some of those years her table was set with wages from the old McLaren Mine. "I think the new mine will help," she says. "My husband was a miner. People need jobs."

Flo and Eddie Zundel certainly don't disagree about the need for income. They fought hard for theirs. They bought their motel in 1985 and have watched a steady increase in the tourist trade produce for them what is now a secure living. "God, it's tremendous," says Eddie. "I thought I was going to lose my ass the first year. I borrowed $8,000 just to get by, but now I'm putting $8,000 a year in the bank."

"We have a lot at stake here," says Flo. "We own this business. It's our livelihood and I don't want to see it ruined."

In the beginning of the controversy over the Noranda project, Flo was concerned but neutral, listening and thinking things out. "I have been to more meetings and learned more things in the past two years than if I'd been to college," she says. Flo is now unalterably opposed to the project, a transition that has placed her in unfamiliar territory as a member of the Beartooth Alliance, an ad hoc group of 160 people, most of them local, that is fighting the mine. She has become an activist: a card-carrying, testifying, petition-signing, letter-writing environmental activist.

Her friend Joan Humiston underwent the same sort of transformation. Joan has lived in Cooke City since 1949 and remembers clearly the roar and rumble of the old McLaren Mine. At first, she says, the new mine seemed like a good idea. She was in business too. She and her husband Bill ran a cafe which, according to one source, furnished "the best pies in the ecosystem."

She and Bill are retired now (though they still stop in to say hello to the customers and help out their daughter, who now runs the place). She has time to appreciate the peace of her town—the peace and the clean water. But she has begun to worry that these will not survive the mine. "I guess I've had to evaluate what's important to me," she says. "Now I've realized there are certain things so important in my life I'm willing to speak out."

Not that either of these Beartooth Alliance activists could be called a wilderness advocate. People like Flo and Joan, while opposing the mine, are still against the designation of any more wilderness areas. They've had enough, they say. They can't ride their snowmobiles in wilderness. In Cooke City and in similar towns in the Northern Rockies, wilderness is still a fighting word.

But if pressed, Joan says, "I'd be willing to have that [mining area] all put into wilderness to protect it." The mine site would not qualify for wilderness designation, of course; the claims of which it is made predate the Wilderness Act of 1964 and the area is pretty torn up with "exploration" work already. Still, her statement indicates how far Joan Humiston already has gone in her thinking—and how much farther she might be willing to go.

As viewed through the concerns of these opposing pairs of women—Patricia Crabb and Roberta Williams, Flo Zundel and Joan Humiston—the conflict over the Noranda project can be interpreted as one more battle between sectors of the economy, tourism versus mineral development. But obscured by all the standard rhetoric are hints of a broader, more interesting, and potentially more significant development—a subtle shift in the local economy that may be a more powerful argument against extractive resource developments like the Noranda project than all the best arguments of tourism.

One can see the possibilities in the form of a young couple named Bill Blackford and Tami Johnson, English majors and would-be writers who have been here only a year. They were hired by Noranda up at the mine site to work on reclaiming exploration disturbances. Their jobs paid well, but they got tired of watching the company seed pristine alpine terrain with exotic species, despite sound advice that only native plants had the slightest chance of surviving. They quit Noranda and opened a bike shop. Blackford and Johnson believe they are successful transplants and will root in Cooke City simply because it's a good place to live. "I'll spend two or three hours just walking up the street," Bill says, "because I stop and talk to people the whole way."

You get a hint of the possibilities from Dave Majors too. Dave makes a living by maintaining seasonal homes in the area. He also oversees the town's volunteer fire department and serves as chairman of the town's quasi-governmental planning committee. Wearing the latter hat, he is statesmanlike, speaking of the need for an impartial assessment of the mine. Wearing his own hat, a baseball cap with a bill that overlooks an omnipresent but seldom lit pipe, Majors talks about his old town in the mountains of New Mexico, a place of 225 inhabitants that became overrun with economic development. He moved to Cooke City to get away from that.

"I wasn't forced to come here," he says. "I chose to be here. I chose to come here because of the way it was, not because we're going to have a big economic boom. There's a hell of a lot of people up here for the same reason." His feelings about Noranda are blunt: "I wish they would go to hell and burn."

The new possibility expressed in and by people like Tami Johnson, Bill Blackford, and Dave Majors—and Joan Humiston, too, when she describes the evening quiet out at her ranch—can be called "quality of life," for want of a better term. It is based on a kind of economy of amenity—and it is not only in Cooke City that the outlines of the future it promises can be seen. Economic changes are taking place throughout the entire Greater Yellowstone Ecosystem—indeed, throughout much of the Rocky Mountain West. Down in Dubois, Wyoming, for instance.

Geographically, it's not far from Cooke City to Dubois, but mountain roads make the distance seem greater, even in summer when the most direct roads are open. At first you might mistake Dubois for a dusty cow town. It is not. Or because of a big tepee burner at the edge of town designed to dispose of wastes from lumber mills, you might think it is a logging town. This time you would be half right. It used to be a logging town—and that is an important part of the story.

Today, Dubois (pronounced "*Doo*-boys" and the French be damned) is a town offering an intriguing view of the future—though as recently as 1987 Dubois didn't look like a town *with* a future. It was as tied to the past as the horses that are still tied to hitchrails in front of log-faced buildings on the main street. But the tie was slipping. That year officials in surrounding Shoshone National Forest adopted a new forest plan that included a severe reduction in the amount of timber they would allow to be cut from the hills around town. Louisiana Pacific, operator of the mill once served by the tepee burner, went into action immediately: it closed the mill. Two hundred jobs left the town of two thousand, nearly 30 percent of the total employment of Dubois, 35 percent of its payroll. The town's economy, it was feared, was crippled beyond recovery.

Nearly five years later the economy of Dubois not only isn't crippled, it doesn't even limp, and regrets over the passing of the mill are hard to find. "We were delighted to get rid of that mill," says Mary Allison, a forty-three-year resident of Dubois who, with her husband, runs a real estate office in town. During the first four months of 1992 her office sold $1 million worth of property, a figure that was unheard of five years ago. Pat Neary, the county's director of economic development, agrees. "It was time to close the mill," he says. "I don't think the forests could tolerate that level of cutting."

It is not the arrival of large new employers that has changed attitudes. In fact, when Conoco wanted to drill for oil on surrounding public lands, the town's chamber of commerce filed a formal appeal of the Forest Service decision to lease the land. So did the town council. Their objections stated that allowing oil exploration could damage the town's blooming economy, a fact they alleged the Forest Service had not sufficiently taken into consideration when it decided to allow the leasing. Equally remarkable was the fact that the Forest Service acceded to the town's appeal and reopened the case. "We basically felt like we didn't take a good look at the economics of the Dubois area," explains Brent Larson, the Forest Service's district ranger. "We agreed to go back to look at further analysis."

Among Western towns, Dubois is not unique in beginning to understand that its fortunes are no longer entirely dependent on the once-holy trinity of mining, logging, and ranching—but it may be unique in that it knows why. And how it knows why is largely the work of John Murdock. Lunching at the Wild West Deli, Murdock can't cross the room without greeting diners at every table. He divides his time between small-town hospitality and drawing bell curves of statistical profiles and probabilities on the backs of napkins. He is seventy, retired, and has been a full-time resident of Dubois since 1978. He comes by his bell curves honestly. He holds a PhD in economics and was chairman of that department at the University of Missouri-Columbia, as well as the institution's director of research administration.

Retirement notwithstanding, Murdock's research continues. But now his lab is Dubois, and what he has discovered over five years of detailed surveys and investigations has caused this town to rethink its life. First, just three years after the Louisiana-Pacific mill closed, the gross personal income of Dubois exceeded that of 1986, when the mill was running normally. During the same period, real income grew by 8.5 percent a year, a rate the national economy would enjoy. Such growth has not come from traditional extractive industries nor, for the most part, from tourism. "Timbering," Murdock writes in a summary of his research, "is a minor fraction of its 1986 level. Agriculture and the tourist-oriented sectors, if they have expanded at all in this period, have done so only marginally." The explanation for the town's prosperity reverses conventional thinking that the way to economic growth is to create jobs, after which the people will follow. In Dubois and other communities in the region, it seems that people do not follow jobs—they bring the jobs with them.

The economic success of this little town is predicated almost entirely on the fact that it is a nice place to live. Traditional sources of income, especially ranching and tourism, have not disappeared; they continue to contibute something to the community's health. But the key to the future is a phenomenon known as "footloose business." Many jobs in the modern American economy, especially information-age jobs, are portable. One's work can be as close as the nearest post office, Federal Express drop, computer modem, or fax machine, and it is beginning to occur to a lot of people that such jobs can be performed anywhere—so why not perform them where the quality of life is high, the country is beautiful, the air is clean, and the streets are generally safe? Why not in Dubois?

Murdock's research is clear: it is just such "footloose" newcomers who are fueling the new economic boom of Dubois. They have moved to town in numbers approaching the mill's old payroll. They bring paychecks from outside or from sources such as Social Security, pensions, or investments, and they spend their money. The community's mountain-town ambience provides the equivalent of a factory payroll.

The core of Murdock's work is a survey of thirty-one newcomers. He found that their after-tax household income was $40,300—35 to 40 percent higher than the rest of the households in Dubois. Sixty-one percent of this income came from outside the area. These households spent an average of $120,000 on new houses, more than the average for the area. This alone spurred construction in town and absorbed some of the workers idled by the mill closing. Contrary to some assumptions, the newcomers were not all retirees. The average age of a householder in the survey was forty-eight, with three times as many people in the sample younger than forty than were older than sixty. Nearly half the households had children.

Most important, though, the vast majority of the newcomers brought their lives and incomes to town for reasons that had nothing to do with its economic opportunities. They were not looking for new jobs, nor were all of them seeking a market for new businesses. The survey indicated that 71 percent of the sample moved to town for "noneconomic" reasons. Their most important considerations in doing so were the "physical setting and community tone plus residents' lifestyle and attitude," Murdock says, citing the town's "newly emerging function: as a long-distance bedroom community. We sell quality of life, just as the suburbs do with central city populations. But the new feature is that technology and economics are progressively relaxing the distance constraint which requires that suburbs *be* suburbs."

William Gustafson is one of the newcomers. He runs a construction company that does no business in Dubois itself. Recently he was headed for Washington, D.C., to bid a job in Nicaragua. Gustafson used to run his operation in Pennsylvania, but when it occurred to him his mobile job could be done anywhere, he decided anywhere might as well be Dubois. Bill and Gwen Bruner moved to town in 1988 to buy a main street motel, but that is mostly a nest egg for later years. For now, Bill works on oil rigs as an electrician—but not on Conoco's rigs in Wyoming. He works offshore rigs. Offshore *African* rigs. He works for a French oil corporation, a month off and a month on the job. His commute to the office covers seven thousand miles. "He could live anywhere," Gwen Bruner says. "We just decided this was the way we wanted to do it because we like living here. There aren't any shopping malls, but that isn't what makes people happy. We just like the lifestyle here, the small-town atmosphere. There's no stress, no traffic. The town is very friendly."

It is the concept of "the good life" that ties together the stories of Cooke City and Dubois—and it ties them not just to each other. The vision of the good life, of life in a *community* and not just another urban agglomeration, of air and water and natural beauty, is spreading up and down the Rockies. Like most such visions, it is part hope, part reality; but there is no denying its power or its ability to effect change. It may indeed be the future.

That certainly was the implication of the Wilderness Society's 1991 study, *Yellowstone: The Wealth of Nature*, an economic analysis of the twenty counties in Idaho, Montana, and Wyoming that cluster around Yellowstone National Park. Traditionally, the communities in this 18-million-acre region—which also include the Greater Yellowstone Ecosystem—are regarded as sleepy timber and cow towns, places fed by industries in trouble. The traditional wisdom is wrong.

In fact, if those twenty counties were combined into one to become the nation's fifty-first state, it would be among the fastest growing states in the nation, says Ray Rasker, the economist who conducted the two-year study. What is more, the counties in the area have a consistent economic profile, and the profile is healthy. During the two decades from 1969 to 1989, the total number of jobs in the region increased by 68 percent. Population rose 32 percent, while personal income doubled during the same period. Meanwhile, direct employment in extractive industries shrank in importance, from one in every three workers in 1969 to one in every six in 1989. Ninety-six percent of the new jobs and 89 percent of the growth in labor income occurred outside the extractive industries. The number of non-farm, self-employed jobs in the total region grew by 39 percent in the 1980s alone, while the number of salaried workers grew by a little more than six percent. More than twenty-one hundred new businesses popped up in the study counties in the decade. More than 90 percent of these employed fewer than twenty workers.

The trend was toward diversity, a large variety of individuals successfully working the niches that emerge. And as with natural systems, one measure of an economic system's health is its ability to survive external shocks. The impact of the national recession was not unfelt in the Rockies. The decline in manufacturing and housing starts nationwide greatly suppressed demand for lumber and minerals. Likewise, unemployment and consumer pessimism tended to keep travelers at home. But in spite of this, the economy of the Yellowstone region grew. Unemployment in Bozeman, Montana, for instance, hovered at about 5 percent throughout the period, several percentage points below the national average.

This durability is largely a measure of the degree to which the region's economy has freed itself of dependence on the traditional extractive industries. The public lands managers in the area are finally beginning to realize that recreation and tourism dollars flow from the forests, and the importance of those dollars has to be balanced against extractive income to foster intelligent long-term economic development. Yet *The Wealth of Nature* shows that the battle is not between tourism and extraction—not in the most significant sense. Throughout the counties, employment flowing from the forests is only a very small part of the picture. The national forests, through both extraction and recreation, account for only about 9 percent of the total number of jobs. Yet the forests play a major role in providing much of the very definition of "quality of life." They are nature, a big part of what most people—including loggers, miners, and cowboys—cite as their reason for living in the Rockies.

And if clearcuts, streamside erosion, mining pollution, overgrazing, and other bad land-management practices damage the character of the land and the quality of life it provides, so, too, can tourism. Replacing logging with tourism can be a bit like replacing a coal-fired electrical plant with a nuclear reactor. On the surface it looks a lot cleaner, but occasionally you get a meltdown. Around Dubois, for example, people think not of the China Syndrome, but of the Jackson Syndrome.

Jackson, Wyoming, they point out, was once a sleepy little resort town near the Tetons. But about a decade ago it began to overheat on money, and suddenly growth was out of control. Between 1980 and 1990 there was a 40 percent increase in the number of dwellings in town. Cabins became condos and prices went stratospheric. Sixty percent of the houses sold in 1990 cost more than $150,000. Outlets for J. Crew and Ralph Lauren claimed downtown hitching rack space once held by the Cowboy Bar. Suddenly, many people who had always lived there didn't want to live there anymore.

The residents of Dubois did decide that tourism would have a part to play; a main street lined with rustic storefronts and giant plaster grizzly bears testifies to that. But they were determined not to let tourism become the tail that wags the dog. The challenge is to prevent tourism from looming so large it scares the newcomers and residents. That is not an impossible goal, as long as an important facet of tourism remains defined as "recreation." Biking, hiking, fishing, camping, skiing, hunting, horseback riding, and wildlife viewing are, after all, part of what comprises the quality of life that draws people to the region in the first place and keeps them there. Properly restrained, tourism and recreation, like "footloose industries," could become cogs in a new kind of "development." New age. Information age. No smoke.

But, say some, where there is no smoke there is no production, and that can't be good. "That's what people are saying," remarks Pat Neary, the economic development director in Dubois. "In most ways I think they are right. All of those things [in Murdock's survey] may be true, but looking at it from a larger picture we are no longer producing wealth. The issue is, America is no longer a producing nation, and Dubois is no longer a producing community."

The argument comes out of the old school of thought that insists that wealth comes from the ground and that all other forms of economic endeavor prey upon the original form of production. The argument does not easily go away. Recreation *is* play, and neither a nation nor a region can afford to base its economy on play. And as for portability, how does a personal computer and modem produce a chicken—not to mention the steel for the pot to cook it in?

Critics say that the new economy is simply an escape from reality to a playground, but proponents argue just the opposite point. Writing in *The Atlantic*, Harvard economist Robert Reich maintains that the nation needs a new idea of just what we mean by "production." That is, as more sophisticated designs to meet specific needs arise, the value of a product—for example, a bicycle—is not merely the steel that is in it. If it were, we would price bicycles by the pound. What makes one bicycle better than another is design: *information*. Traditionally, we have regarded this design, this information, as if it were somehow inferior to the physical product. Yet with the value of the bicycle so dependent upon design, does this division make sense? As goods become more specialized and technologically sophisticated, Reich says, it makes less sense all the time.

"The idea of goods as something distinct from services," he writes, "has become meaningless. Steelmaking, for example, has become a service business." So it is in other industries. In 1915 the wages of production workers accounted for 45 percent of the cost of a product. By 1975 that had fallen to 25 percent. Today 80 percent of the cost of a computer goes into the wages of the people who design it. Further, modern communications technology has fragmented what once was an integrated workplace. Design, administrative functions, and production no longer take place all in the same factory—or even in the same city, region, or nation. And it is just that separation of functions that allows people looking for quality of life in places like Dubois to play a key role not merely in the national economy but even the world economy. Reich argues that problem-solving competence will be the driving force of this emerging economy and that a region's ability to attract capital and wages will depend on its ability to attract educated people. The jobs will follow. "Increasingly, educated brainpower—along with roads, airports, computers, and fiber optic cables connecting it up," he writes, "determines a nation's standard of living."

It is a new and only partly understood world that Dubois and Cooke City and other Rocky Mountain communities are entering. Understandably, there is some trepidation, even among those who perceive these changes as opportunity. They worry, some of them, that the newcomers will love the West to death. Environmentalists might like to assume that newcomers will have an abiding interest in formal protection. Not necessarily. Murdock's survey indicated that his sampling of people generally was against the designation of any more wilderness areas, although they did hedge a bit when it came down to a couple of *local* roadless areas—a sort of ironic twist on the Not in My Back Yard principle. And just as often as they cited environmental values as the chief attraction of the town, they cited human considerations—the slow pace of small-town life, the friendliness, the absence of traffic, crime, and noise. The sense of community.

Still, nothing is simple, as Bob Baker suggests. Baker is a former mayor and town councilman and was the manager at the LP mill when it closed. After that, he bought the town's only lumberyard and now makes a living selling materials for the new houses built by the newcomers. He made his money in the old world, and he is making it in the new one. And he doesn't argue with Murdock's general thesis. He says his business at the lumberyard is clear evidence that the town is better off today economically than it was when the mill he managed was running. But he does worry about the cultural changes brought on by the new economy. Baker says that while the newcomers are generally opposed to logging and ranching, they like the community. The irony, he says, is that logging and ranching shaped the existing community. "Dubois is what it is because of its past," he notes. He says the mill drew blue-collar folks who took part in the community's affairs, but now that is gone. "I guess I liked it better back then."

Nevertheless, everyone, including Baker, agrees that the town gets along better now than it did when it was a one-industry community. Meetings are less rancorous. No clear lines divide the town, as they tended to do when Louisiana—Pacific ruled as the economic elephant dancing among the chickens. There's extractive business in Dubois still, even logging business, but it is small, diverse, and independent—the sort of development that typifies the emerging economy of the region. There are no more elephants.

But over the mountains in Cooke City, as the little town wakes from winter for another rush of Yellowstone tourists, one elephant named Noranda is still having an impact. The mine already has brought about a dozen workers to town, and the implications of what an influx of three hundred could do is lost on no one in this town of a couple of hundred. Already the strain shows. Bill Blackford thinks about this as he and his partner, Tami, talk about Cooke City. He is the fellow who takes two hours for his morning greetings around town. That pattern already is changing as bare-knuckled corporate politics emerge.

"It's hard to go to the bar and have a beer without talking about the mine," says Tami.

"It's just uncomfortable," adds Bill.

Careless Love
An Unfinished Report on the De-development of Yosemite National Park

Richard Reinhardt

*M*y mother and father spent their honeymoon many years ago in Yosemite National Park. I used to hear them reminiscing now and then about "the Valley"—the balky little mules that carried you up the trail to Vernal Falls, the perfect image of Half Dome that you saw in Mirror Lake, the pancakes with maple syrup at Camp Curry, the firefall that tumbled down each night from Glacier Point. I have some pictures that my father took with a box Kodak. One of them shows my mother sitting on a boulder at the edge of Mirror Lake. She is wearing knee-length pants and long woolen stockings, and her hair is bobbed in the fashion of the Twenties, with bangs across the forehead. Her wistful smile is reflected in the water.

Although I have no reason to believe that I was either conceived or contemplated in those sublime surroundings, I grew up sensing a deep, proprietary bond to Yosemite National Park. Like millions of other Californians, I looked upon the Valley as my allotted share of paradise. Yosemite was a unique, almost sacred place, a destination to be longed for, saved for, stayed in and talked of, not only for its wind-blown wisps of falling water, its translucent leaves, its lustrous granite cliffs, but also for its comforts and diversions: the Christmas revels in the great candle-lit dining room at the Ahwahnee Hotel; the summer bonfires at Camp Curry; the ranger talks; the trout streams; the feeding of the bears. As one grew older, Yosemite became the place to get a summer job making beds or washing dishes. It was the place to meet adventurous, warm-hearted girls, the place to go fishing for a week, just after college, before starting to look for work. Someday Yosemite might even be the place for one's own honeymoon. Yosemite was familiar, friendly, fixed in time, as changeless as its rocks.

We were wrong, of course. Yosemite was far from changeless. It was temporal and precarious, and its comforts, its accessible delights—the very aspects we had learned to love—were putting the Valley in terrible jeopardy. With regret and shame, I began to understand what our careless love had done.

It was in the early 1960s, when my family and I came back to California after several years in other parts of the world, that I first heard and read reports about the appalling deterioration of Yosemite. A friend of ours had gone up to the Valley on a midsummer weekend with some visitors from the East Coast. When I asked how it was, he shook his head.

"It was unbelievable. I'm never going back."

Never going back to *Yosemite?* Wasn't that laying it on pretty thick?

"Hot. Dusty. Noisy. Cars everywhere. Never again."

If you could manage to avoid the Valley, he said, it might be possible to enjoy other parts of the park. Even the Valley might be tolerable if you went there out of season. . . .

Tolerable? Yosemite?

A magazine in San Francisco published a furious, denunciatory article by a professor of English who had spent three summers working as a ranger in the high country and around the campgrounds. Recognizing heresy, the magazine took the precaution of stating that the author did not speak for the National Park Service or the park administration. His article was called "Down with Yosemite City!" and it was illustrated with photographs of an enormous parking lot at the foot of Half Dome, television antennae silhouetted against Yosemite Falls, kids in swimming trunks drinking out of cans, motorcycles racing across a meadow, trailer camps seething under a veil of smoke.

What the article said was that this precious valley, which we presumed had been protected for nearly a century as an irreplaceable national treasure, was being destroyed by its current owners: us.

"You may never have heard of Yosemite City," wrote Starr Jenkins, the summer park ranger, "but it is a fair-sized city—40,000 to 60,000 people—complete with smog, crime, juvenile delinquency, parking problems, traffic snarls, rush hours, gang warfare, slums, and urban sprawl. It sprouts every summer in the congested upper end of the spectacularly beautiful Yosemite Valley. . . ."

At the heart of this disaster was the open, uncontrolled campground—long a tradition in the park—which regularly accommodated six thousand visitors and sometimes provided habitation of a sort to thousands more. Jenkins was astounded to discover that nearly 30 percent of all the camping in all the national parks in the United States took place in Yosemite—and that most of the camping in Yosemite was concentrated in the most scenic portion of the Valley. He wrote:

> Soggy cartons float downstream among the air mattress riders. Tent cities choke the peaceful scene with cars, dust and smoke. Bears are seen only on nightly raids on garbage cans, where they compete with the raccoons for the privilege of dumping out the rubbish in search of food. Drunken or rowdy groups of teenagers, few of whose parents are within fifty miles, regularly terrorize their camping neighbors, keep hundreds awake all night, push cars into rivers and stop traffic on Stoneman Bridge. Bicycles, motorcycles, cars, stores, gas stations, people, more cars and more people have taken over Yosemite Valley. . . .

On one holiday weekend, Jenkins reported, seventy-six thousand people had poured into the national park. An uncounted, uncountable number had set up housekeeping in the "mob camps." Civilization, in its most unattractive form, had captured Yosemite and turned it into a rough equivalent of an urban slum.

Shortly after reading this, we too went up to the Valley in midsummer with some visitors, American friends who lived in Germany. We found that what Jenkins had written was exactly true. The campgrounds sweltered in a smoglike haze of smoke and dust, locally known as "smust." The bridges on the Merced River were impenetrably thronged with bodies in T-shirts, cut-off jeans and sandals. Happy Isles, the lovely woodland where Vernal Creek runs down in half a dozen rivulets to its confluence with the Merced, resembled a schoolyard at recess: children rioted through the woods with Frisbees, whiffle balls and dripping ice cream bars. Music from a hundred portable radios stabbed the air. There were so many hikers (and runners) on the trail to Vernal Falls that we continually had to step aside to let somebody pass. I kept saying to myself: "They have a perfect right to be here. Same right as we have. It's a public park." What I felt was misanthropic rage.

Soon after that, in the anarchic decade of the 1960s, the assault on the Valley came to a dreadful, highly publicized climax on an Independence Day weekend when rangers ordered several thousand young people out of a meadow where they were smoking joints, undressing, dancing and pounding on bongo drums. Three dozen rangers, wearing plastic riot helmets, wielding clubs and spraying Mace, charged into the crowd on foot and on horseback. They made 186 arrests. For some time afterward, young campers called rangers "tree pigs." No longer could anyone doubt the ugly reality of Yosemite City nor pretend that the Valley was being protected from the destructive effects of commercial development and overpopulation.

The trouble was, too many people like me had assumed that Yosemite was indestructible. We had taken for granted the privilege not only to go to the Valley, but also to do whatever we wanted when we got there: to eat and drink and spend the night; to play golf, swim, ride horseback, gas up our cars, kennel our pets, convene conventions, stage pageants, put on wine tastings, weddings, beer busts, weeny roasts, rock concerts—anything. Wasn't that what a national park was for? Wasn't it supposed to be a beautiful place, run by the government and open without limits to the public, where people could go and play and look at pretty scenery? Let's go Yosemite!

In any case, we figured that Yosemite National Park was so vast and high and empty it could swallow up our annual lilliputian invasion (which by the 1990s was approaching four million visitors a year) like a swarm of mosquitoes: 760,000 acres in the central Sierra Nevada, surrounded on all sides by national forests, and 95 percent of it without a road. The seventy-five-mile boundaries of the park embraced tawny gold Sonoran foothills and naked, wind-scoured alpine peaks, lakes and meadows, oak woods and pine forests, river canyons, glacial cirques and groves of giant sequoia trees. Tucked into this immense playground were some relatively puny works of humankind: 750 miles of trail, four or five hotels, a score of shops and restaurants, a museum, a lot of offices, dozens of campgrounds, two golf courses, a major trans-Sierra highway, a ski resort and the watershed of San Francisco's municipal water system, including a couple of storage dams. These intrusions were numerous, but they had accumulated gradually. We occasional visitors regarded most of them as *improvements*. Everybody had his favorite project for the adornment and enhancement of Yosemite: a photographic studio here, an ice rink there, a parking lot, a storage shed, a doughnut shop, a jail. For decades only the most alert and intransigent conservationists realized that such innocent accretions were threatening the very existence of the park.

In other words, the "degradation" of Yosemite, as ecologists would now call it, had gone on for so many years that it seemed like the natural and proper way to treat a great public resource—to make it accessible, comfortable and entertaining for a larger and larger public every year. In fact, the development of the Valley into a useful and profitable site for human enterprise had begun way back in 1851, with the first foray of American cavalry volunteers into the Valley in pursuit of some uncooperative Indians who were making life difficult for gold miners in the foothills. The Indians chose to avoid the rendezvous. They and their ancestors had been using this land of the Uzemati— the Grizzly Bear clan—as a hunting ground for food and a route across the Sierra for perhaps four thousand years, and they knew how to melt into the mountains when an enemy came around. The cavalrymen, however, liked the look of the deserted meadows along the Merced River, at the foot of the astonishing granite cliffs. They carried away impressions of lush grass, big timber and clear streams from which one might pan chips of gold.

The ensuing military conquest of the Yosemite took a couple of years and cost the lives of several settlers and a larger number of Indians. Immediately afterward a bloodless, pastoral conquest began. In fewer than a dozen years settlers and visitors managed to commit an inordinate amount of lasting, sometimes irreparable damage. They brought in cattle, sheep and horses that ate the native vegetation down to the gravelly red earth. They brought in grains and grasses and other exotic plants and animals. They felled and milled virgin forests of conifers, turned meadows into pastures, toppled and virtually obliterated the hardwood oaks of the valley floor, built roads and houses, saloons and stables. They mined for gold and quarried granite. In short, they carried on the various exploitative, extractive, pastoral, and commercial enterprises which are everywhere accounted "progress" and which were calculated to make Yosemite, as quickly as possible, a place like any other, but with waterfalls.

Just four years after the suppression of the Indians, the first party of tourists came up from San Francisco in the company of James M. Hutchings, the owner of a magazine extolling the wonders of California. They took notes and drew pictures, which Hutchings published in his magazine. In the next nine years (according to Hutchings, who was keeping count) no fewer than 655 souls braved the sixty-mile trail into the valley he called "Yo-Semite." The most luxurious indoor sleeping arrangements were in a barnlike hut called Lower Hotel, which offered dirt-floored chambers that resembled stalls in a stable, beds of ticking stuffed with hay, and toilet facilities down the path behind a tree. Among the visitors was Horace Greeley, the New York newspaper publisher, who arrived on muleback so chaffed and raw that he had to be lifted from the saddle, anointed like a baby with oil and alcohol, and carried to bed. Although he hated the ordeal, Greeley spread word back east that Yosemite was worth a look.

From that time on—and it was before the outbreak of the Civil War—the valley of Yosemite never faded from the mental landscape of the American people. While the Union was still fighting the Confederacy, President Abraham Lincoln signed an act of Congress granting the state of California fifty-six square miles of federal land in and around Yosemite Valley "upon the express conditions that the premises be held for public use, resort, and recreation [and] shall be inalienable for all time. . . ." Thus, Yosemite became, in effect, our first national park, although the distinction of that title actually fell to Yellowstone eight years later, in 1872.

The federal government, in setting aside an otherwise "worthless" scenic area as a park, intended that it should become a public playground. Public service, not ecology, set the standards for appropriate development. Although areas of inaccessible wilderness were included within the boundaries of the park, the government's chief purpose was to preserve and display natural wonders: the falls, the views, the giant trees, the soft-eyed deer and playful ground squirrels. Wild fires would be suppressed; roads and trails would be constructed to points of "natural beauty"; benevolent, attractive animals would be protected, while predators, raptors and poisonous snakes might be exterminated, as they would be on a well-run farm. As far as I know, it did not occur to many of the well-intentioned preservationists of the nineteenth century that visitors themselves might become the principal enemies of preservation.

After Yosemite became a national park in 1890, the rate of development accelerated. Lodges, campgrounds, hotels, roads, museums, amphitheaters and cafeterias made the Valley more enticing, more comfortable, more *civilized*. The first automobile came over the Big Oak Flat road into the Valley in 1900. Its noise and appearance so terrified the cattle grazing in the shadow of El Capitan that the park administration banned cars for the next thirteen years. The policy did not, and could not, endure. Fifty years later, cars had almost banned the park: there were more than twenty-five hundred day-use parking spaces in the Valley.

Shaken by the horrendous summer invasions of the early 1960s, the Park Service began some tardy experiments in crowd and car control. All private vehicles were to be prohibited from entering the east end of the Valley. The most rowdy and overcrowded of the campgrounds were closed, and the Park Service got busy marking and labeling all campsites to hold down the total number of parties in each campground. Roads through the Valley were converted into a series of one-way loops feeding into scattered parking lots, from which free shuttle buses carried visitors around the park. In response to the federal Wilderness Act of 1964, the Park Service proposed that some 624,000 acres of the roadless areas of the park be designated wilderness. Rangers began issuing permits to limit the number of persons entering the back country.

At the same time the Park Service declared that it would soon establish broad new policies to restrict the number of visitors to the carrying capacity of the park, to phase out the use of cars for access or circulation in the Valley, and to remove from the park all facilities that were not directly necessary for the use and management of the park.

Several years passed, however, before the Park Service had ironed out the details of a scheme to reach these goals. Part of the problem was that Yosemite Valley did not lend itself comfortably to the sort of zoning policies that the Park Service had developed over the years to control land use in undeveloped areas. In its national policy toward Class IV lands, for example, the Park Service had decreed that "nothing in the way of human use should be permitted . . . that intrudes upon or may in any way damage or alter the scene." In Yosemite Valley, however, the Class IV lands—that is, the areas of outstanding natural beauty and unique interest—were the very places with the most concentrated development. The entire Valley was comparable, in a sense, to Bright Angel Point on the south rim of the Grand Canyon or the Great White Throne in Zion National Park, to Acadia's Cadillac Mountain or the shore of Crater Lake above the Phantom Ship—it was the unique and irreplaceable scenic attraction. To many casual visitors, the Valley *was* the national park. Having drunk in the famous vistas, they would climb back into their cars and happily take off for Lake Tahoe, Bryce Canyon, Mount Rainier, or whatever attraction was next on the itinerary.

In Yosemite Valley, the area of concentrated wonder was, by no coincidence, also the area of concentrated commerce—of snack bars, parking lots, souvenir shops, and campgrounds. To eliminate the human use that intruded upon, damaged and altered the scene would require not only controlling current and future activities but actually moving or destroying many familiar (and profitable) pastimes, services and habitations. Who would dare propose such drastic measures? Who said they were necessary? While the Park Service was pondering the alternatives, a writer for *National Geographic* who professed to "know Yosemite well" declared he actually had gotten lonely in the national park. All you had to do, he said (completely missing the point of the controversy) was to "step off the beaten path."

The first draft of the general plan, published in 1978, purported to be a radical proposal to halt and systematically reverse the effects of a century of development. It called for an end to management practices that had damaged the ecological system of the central Sierra and to commercial ventures that existed simply to attract people to the park. Most importantly, the plan envisioned a purposeful *de-development* of Yosemite Valley.

"Fifty years ago we were busy building roads and parking areas to 'open up' Yosemite Valley and make it accessible to the new generation of mobile Americans," the draft plan said. "Today, we look with irony on the acres of pavement, the traffic congestion, the noise we have created."

Over the next ten to fifteen years (i.e., up to about 1993, when the contract of the private corporation operating the commercial concessions would come up for replacement or renewal) park managment would deliberately reduce the maximum level of both day-use and overnight visits to the Valley. This would be done in part by cutting the number of overnight accommodations in the Valley by 17 percent. At the same time there would be a "substantial reduction" in the number of structures in the Valley. Both the National Park Service and the concessionaire (at that time, the Yosemite Park and Curry Company) would move their headquarters offices out of the Valley to the village of El Portal, on the western edge of the park. The Park Service would relocate its central maintenance facilities (a tawdry corp yard locally known as "Fort Yosemite") to El Portal, along with the dwellings of all employees except those whose jobs required that they be housed in distant areas of the park. In the process, El Portal would become a full-scale town, with a seasonal population of about two thousand residents. Its principal industry, aside from the Park Service payroll, would be a huge two thousand–space visitor parking facility, linked by shuttle to the Valley. The number of day-use parking spaces in the Valley would be cut in half.

Recreational facilities with no relevance to the "resources of the park" (such as swimming pools, tennis courts, golf courses and skating rinks) would be removed. Programs of education or entertainment with no relevance (such as square dancing and the study of non-indigenous Indian cultures) would be terminated. The wilderness areas of the park would be enlarged by twenty-four thousand acres.

In managing its back country, Yosemite would follow the principles enunciated in the Wilderness Act: natural systems and processes would be permitted to follow their courses with minimum intrusion by man; the number of visitors would be limited to a level that would not significantly affect the natural environment; and in three wilderness and primitive areas that adjoin Yosemite Park—Minarets, Hoover and Emigrant Basin, totaling 251,000 acres—the Forest Service would maintain similar controls. In practice this would mean that the Park Service would continue its permit system to limit the number of users to about ten to fifteen thousand persons a year, and that the park concessionaire would be permitted to continue the immensely popular summer pack trips around the High Sierra Loop Circuit of tent-cabin campsites.

Devising rules to protect the wilderness areas of the park, where the intrusions of humanity were impermanent and few, would be relatively simple. It would be far more difficult, however, to reconcile the traditional qualities of Yosemite Valley—its accessibility, its comforts, its variety of entertainments—with the stern necessity to halt and reverse the deterioration of a priceless resource. The authors of the plan figured the task would take decades and cost around $80 million.

To no one's surprise, the publication of the draft plan provoked several thousand letters, petitions and demurrers, ranging from appeals to save the Tuolumne Meadows coffee shop to speeches opposing rock climbing. Critics pointed out that many visitor services (such as swimming pools, which would be banned or relocated under the new administrative standards) had developed a large and appreciative patronage. Did the benefits of de-development justify the loss of wholesome and popular recreational facilities? Granting that it was impossible to return the Valley to its primitive state, wouldn't it be prudent to enhance and beautify the existing visitor accommodations rather than to limit or remove them?

In general, however, the public appeared to support the plan—or at any rate, to accept it in silence. Even backpackers and fishermen gave "sullen agreement," in the words of the writer Ezra Bowen, "to keep us all from loving our wilderness to death."

The most unfavorable comments, surprisingly, came from conservationists. The Wilderness Society, for example, found the specific recommendations of the draft plan "inadequate" to reverse the long-standing pattern of overdevelopment in the Valley.

"The draft management plan . . . does not go nearly far enough in reducing the amount of development, commercial services, employee housing, and auto traffic," said William A. Turnage, who was at that time the executive director of the Society.

To put it bluntly, the plan promises much but delivers little. . . . The Park Service acknowledges that the level of overnight accommodations in the park has been a key issue, [but] if the plan as now written is implemented, a total of 190 units of overnight facilities would be eliminated [and] more than 200 new camp sites would be built, most of them designed for use by people in vehicles. This does not represent a significant change in the status quo. . . .

Yosemite, the Society said, was the most overdeveloped, overcommercialized area in the national park system. Under the proposed general plan, it was likely to stay that way.

Two years later, in 1980, the Park Service officially adopted a general plan, amended in detail but similar in principle to the draft document. Its goals were to remove administrative and managerial functions from the Valley, scale back overnight accommodations, eliminate irrelevant services and limit access by private vehicles to significant scenic portions of the park. Reading the plan, one might have concluded that only time and money were now needed to achieve the permanent de-development of the park.

During the decade of the Eighties, however, it became obvious that the high-minded objectives of the Park Service were not being achieved. A few dramatic, inexpensive and highly visible reforms (one-way roads, numbered campsites, permit control of wilderness areas) came quickly, but painful, costly and controversial changes (getting rid of superfluous buildings, moving employee housing, closing commercial concessions) were repeatedly postponed. The excuses were numerous and predictable: lack of money, resistance from the concessionaire, unforeseen complexities and hardships for park personnel, detrimental side-effects on the environment.

The site of a substitute hotel outside the Valley was found to be the breeding place of an endangered bird species. Another alternative site was short of water and lacked soil drainage for the disposal of wastes. The location of the proposed administrative center, parking facility and employee housing at El Portal was too small, too steep, too far away.

"Some of these ideas [in the general plan] sounded good, but they didn't hold up," a park official said not long ago. "If you work in the Valley, there's a lot of time lost coming and going, additional traffic on the road, gasoline used, exhaust fumes. How're you going to get all those shuttle buses full of people up and down that narrow road between El Portal and the Valley?"

Closely examined, virtually the only significant accomplishment of the general plan appeared to be the permit system to control seasonal population in the wilderness areas of the park. Gone, to everyone's relief, were the days when "cowboys" and "hippies" staked claims on their personal territories by defacing the rocks with rivalrous painted graffiti. The only remaining controversy in the high country was between those managers who would and those who would not replenish the supply of fish in the alpine lakes and streams; on this issue, the natural ecology advocates in the Park Service grudgingly yielded to the sports people.

As to closing or removing urban conveniences from the Valley, however, neither the Park Service nor the concessionaire made much progress. The Park Service transferred a few of its contemplative activities (such as research and record keeping) down the road to El Portal, while the concessionaire moved its reservations office, its laundry and its warehouses outside the park. In both cases, the buildings that had housed those functions remained in use. Worse, the sprawling village known to its detractors as "Yosemite's armpit" continued to flaunt its corp yards, offices, garages and housing clusters among the cliffs and meadows of the Valley, while the grand illusion of forcing all visitors to park their vehicles in satellite garages outside the Valley died quietly of official neglect.

When Allan Temko, the distinguished architecture critic of the San Francisco *Chronicle*, paid a visit in 1990 to Yosemite on the hundredth anniversary of its designation as a national park, he found the experience "inexpressably sad." At the heart of the fragile, incomparable Valley was a "meretricious theme park and shopping mall operated by a monopolistic concessioner." Even if the Park Service were to find the courage and intelligence to apply its "timid and partly outmoded" general plan of 1980, that inadequate document would do little to save Yosemite from the depredations of another hundred years as destructive as the last.

Like other critics, Temko laid much of the blame for the degradation of the Valley upon the concessionaire, but he pointed out that this inevitably resulted from the government's long-standing policy of allowing and encouraging private contractors to run the national parks as profitable resorts. At Yosemite the franchise policy goes back to the founding of the National Park Service in 1916, when farmers were still planting orchards in the meadows along the Merced River, foresters were chopping down the virgin timber and no less than twenty-four hotels of varying quality were luring visitors to dubious accommodations in the Valley.

One of the primary tasks of the Park Service, in the view of its first director, Stephen Mather, was to put an end to every sort of hit-or-miss exploitation and to create high standards of service to visitors throughout the national park system. Mather's strategy in Yosemite was to select the strongest and most reliable hotelier (in this case, the family-owned Curry Camping Company), force it to merge with its chief competitor (the Yosemite National Park Company), give the resulting firm a long-term monopoly franchise, and require construction of a luxury hotel (the Ahwahnee) to attract wealthy and influential travelers from all parts of the world.

Mather's policy worked so well that Yosemite Valley became the most popular tourist destination in western America. The Yosemite Park and Curry Company fattened into a vast concession that recently grossed more than $90 million a year and came to see itself as a full partner with the federal government in running the park. Most of Yosemite's millions of visitors lost track of who owned the park—the American people or the Curry Company. Curry-owned facilities—the Ahwahnee, Yosemite Lodge, Wawona Hotel, the high mountain camps—were everywhere, and the company offered every form of accommodation from tents to luxury suites, every type of recreation from skiing to wine tasting. It is fair to say that the Curry family and their staff were widely and gratefully admired for providing exactly what most visitors wanted to find in their favorite national park.

When the Park Service proposed its general plan in the late 1970s, however, it was the Curry Company that sounded the most audible complaints. Edward C. Hardy, the president of the company, questioned whether there was any "imminent danger threatening the park" that would justify the expense and pain of reversing the urbanization of the Valley.

Moving all the administrative functions to El Portal, for example, would be not only costly but useless. El Portal was fourteen miles from the Valley by a narrow, winding road.

"The additional traffic generated by employees going to their jobs on differing and often irregular schedules would more than offest any advantages of the move," Hardy said. More space and money could be saved just by consolidating managerial operations of the company and the Park Service right in Yosemite Village, where they had always been.

As for certain other proposals, Hardy argued that they would cause more problems than they would solve. Getting rid of the barber shop would cause employees to go unshorn. Getting rid of the branch bank would cause more driving into and out of the Valley. Getting rid of the post office would inconvenience visitors. Getting rid of the gift shops would cut into the justified profits of the concessionaire. Getting rid of the skating rink and swimming pools would serve no useful purpose. And eliminating 278 overnight accommodations within the Valley would simply frustrate thousands of visitors and do nothing to reduce peak-time traffic.

In 1963 Curry had signed what was to be its last contract with the Park Service—a thirty-year license to run its hotels, camps, expeditions, stores and restaurants for a fee of three-quarters of one percent of its gross yearly revenues, one of the lowest franchise fees in any national park. It was the kind of sweetheart agreement the government had traditionally offered the Curry Company in return for giving excellent service in well-maintained, company-owned facilities. But the company, which dated back to David Curry's simple camp established at the base of Glacier Point in 1899, was undergoing swift and startling changes. From a closely held family business, it passed through a series of corporate buyouts to become one of many operations of MCA, the Los Angeles–based entertainment conglomerate. In turn, MCA was absorbed by the Japanese-owned Matushita Electric Industries in 1990.

As the time approached for the Park Service to strike a new contract, dozens of would-be concessionaires appeared, most of whom professed their eagerness to pay the government more than Curry did, to run the facilities better, and to cheerfully acquiesce in the provisions of the general plan. Many found they could not raise the capital to better the existing concession; in October 1993, the government chose the Delaware North Companies of Buffalo, New York, out of six final bidders. The new fifteen-year operating contract, which was said to be the largest park concession in the world, provided that the government would buy all the facilities owned by the Curry Company and that the concessionaire would pay 20.2 percent of its gross profits for the privilege of running the show.

A spokesperson for the Park Service called the new contract "a tremendous advance." But the Sierra Club, which has faulted both the Park Service and the concessionaire for failing to carry out the modest dictates of the general plan, said: "We hope they will be good for the park. We are going to keep an eye on them. . . ."

While keeping an eye on Yosemite, it is appropriate to recall that the fundamental purpose of our national parks, as stated by Congress in establishing the Park Service in 1916, is to conserve the scenery, natural and historic objects, and wildlife within the parks and to provide that these be used only in ways that will preserve them unimpaired for the enjoyment of future generations. Broad and unspecific as this language is, it clearly does not say anything about establishing a large administrative facility in every park, providing hotel rooms, hosting conventions, selling souvenirs, and offering restaurants, sports and hangouts for every taste.

Frederick Law Olmsted, the distinguished landscape designer who headed the commission appointed by the state of California in 1864 to govern the Yosemite grant, wrote a wise and prescient report expressing his moral conviction that the government had a duty to preserve scenic places for the mental and spiritual recreation of all people. I have never seen a more persuasive statement of policy for the management of a natural park. Olmsted wrote:

> The first point to be kept in mind is the preservation and maintenance as exactly as is possible of the natural scenery; the restriction, that is to say, within the narrowest limits consistent with the necessary accommodation of visitors, of all artificial construction and the prevention of all construction markedly inharmonious with the scenery. . . . In permitting the sacrifice of anything that would be of the slightest value to future visitors to the convenience, bad taste, playfulness, carelessness, or wanton destructiveness of present visitors, we probably yield in each case the interest of uncounted millions to the selfishness of a few individuals. . . .

Olmsted was a strict constructionist of the ethics of preservation. Confronted as we currently are in Yosemite Valley with a conflict between the desire to maintain a large, popular, and profitable resort and the necessity to heal the damages of overdevelopment, Olmsted undoubtedly would have said, ''The resort must yield.''

The issue really is not whether there should be a hairdresser, an ice skating rink, or a boarding kennel in Yosemite Valley. Every facility can be deplored or defended according to one's taste. I, for one, enjoy swimming pools, ice cream parlors, small theaters and cosy pubs and dislike rifle ranges, Chinese take outs, fitness gyms and video game arcades. The question is, does *any* sort of commercial enterprise belong in the scenic heart of a national park? And the answer is that all commercial developments, with the exception of a few essential services for health and safety, basic nourishment, and temporary shelter, are equally out of place.

Applying that stern but simple criterion to Yosemite Valley, it should be relatively easy to decide which of the existing structures and activities are appropriate to this treasured land, this valley like no other place on earth, and which are there because of thoughtlessness or greed or whims of fashion. Given another hundred years of grace to undo the evidences of our careless love, we might even be able to reverse the process of ruin, although no one will ever again see the valley we so devotedly destroyed.

Camping Ranches and Gear Junkies:
New Scourge of the West

Linda M. Hasselstrom

When the modern family counts the kids and leaves on vacation, many trinkets associated with a comfortable lifestyle are jammed into the family jalopy. Even if they call it a camping trip, Dad takes an electric razor, Mom packs makeup, Sis can't leave without mousse. Junior wears his portable cassette player, headphones firmly clamped to shut out natural as well as parental noises. The overloaded car probably drags a miniature house containing a TV set to monitor current disasters.

Many folks head west to enjoy the beauty, fresh air, and spaces of the last wilderness. They want to camp safely, protected from the West's hazards: the wild animals they came to see, rabid environmentalists, gun-toting cowboys. Naturally, they don't imagine Western residents might consider a shiny camper scenery pollution or a subject for controversy.

Some will stay in a "camping ranch," a gaggle of concrete slabs lined up in straight rows close enough to hear neighbors argue above the air conditioners' roar. In this vacation paradise, "street corners" are lighted, strangers clean toilets serving every twenty or thirty families, and vacationers circle the wagons and amuse themselves with a heated swimming pool, golf course, stables, go-cart track, and video game room to make them feel at home in the wild West.

Such a facility now occupies a superb chain of alfalfa fields along a creek near my home. When the ranch was real and the road was gravel, driving down that valley guaranteed I'd see raccoons, deer, antelope, turkeys, skunks, owls, hawks, wild roses, plum bushes, cows, and joggers. In fall, yellow cottonwood leaves drifted like candles across the way. The seed of many a poem or essay sprouted as my car drifted through the curves, headlights off, on dark nights.

The road was paved when the ranch went public; friends who stayed there recently were thrilled to see three deer on the golf course. In two years I haven't seen a wild animal or rose, and the joggers lurch along like wounded rabbits, nervously loking over their shoulders at speeding recreational vehicles.

I accepted my friends' invitation to visit because I'd never been to such a commercial campground, and I finally found their trailer among the dazzling metal domes. Families huddled at picnic tables bolted down to prevent theft, discussing the cost of camping in style. "Thirty-five thousand dollars," murmured my hostess as a nervous husband backed into a site, while his wife, clutching a poodle, shrilled incorrect directions. Open-mouthed, I watched as an extra "room" pushed hydraulically out the side of the trailer.

Mentally, I was dividing $35,000 by $400, the price we got for a good yearling steer recently. That cramped dwelling would cost me eighty-eight steers, three times what I own, and the labor of raising them for a year. My old four-wheel drive couldn't pull the load, so let's see: $20,000 for a new pickup, making $55,000 for two vehicles designed for comfortable travel during two weeks out of the year if you have enough money to buy gasoline for them.

The American Heritage Dictionary defines *vacation* as "a period of time devoted to pleasure, rest, or relaxation; especially, such a period during which a working person is exempt from work but collects his pay." (The segment after the semicolon has never applied to me, since I've rarely collected a salary long enough to qualify for vacation time.) A rival dictionary mentions "freedom, release, or rest from some occupation, business, or activity."

My personal definition includes freedom from noise, from inane advertising, from crowds of people frantically trying to buy joy. Each of us selects our pleasures and pains to suit our own taste. My vacation could not happen in a camping ranch. Most folks wouldn't regard using a flush toilet, cooking over a modern stove, watching TV, and putting on makeup as work, but I prefer to escape any venture that's a reminder of the hustle dance we do in order to get money.

In theory, I don't object to anyone's choice of recreation. Practically and immediately, however, facilities installed to provide travelers with the conveniences of home have degraded a specific environment, turning a peaceful valley full of wildlife into a miniature city. The land used was not mine. I never owned, hunted, walked, or used it in any way except to admire it in passing. According to modern standards, because paving these fields did not take money from my pocket, I have no grounds for objection. But the camping ranch, part of a modern trend toward consumerism in recreation, is devastating what its customers hauled their accessories out here to see. That is my business. I live here.

When the governors of western states meet to discuss tourism—how to lure more visitors west to spend more money—I cringe. Of course, businessmen love tourism. Camping and wilderness stores profit from the sale, rental, and repair of expensive gear. Gas station and marina owners hope everyone brings a Winnebago, an off-road vehicle, and a boat or two. Clothing store owners want folks on holiday to buy new, exciting wardrobes. Each of these people has a legitimate desire, a right to make a living.

Yet each participates in destruction of the place I call home. We who live in the West mutter uneasily that tourism is less catastrophic than clearcutting, open-pit mining, growing wheat, and other enterprises which have damned our landscape. Can we persuade modern pilgrims that some methods of enjoying the outdoors may spoil it?

When most folks speak of outdoor recreation, including camping, they are apparently not speaking my language. To me, experiencing the outdoors means making time to live simply in the wild, to observe what nature is doing, without a telephone, television, radio, or other electronic noise-making machines. Camping means no mail delivery, little housecleaning. I eliminate garbage before I leave, since I haul it home instead of leaving it in vacation paradise. In my fantasy someone else cooks, but I'm not willing to stay in a commercial lodging for that privilege, so menus are simple to fix, with few utensils to wash. I cook home-canned meat with fresh vegetables over a wood fire, wash dishes after heating water from a creek, sleep in a canvas tent that lets in cold night air, soft grunts from unidentified critters, and indigenous insects. I understand that exposing myself to nature as it is may be harmful to my health.

Modern travelers who seek "wilderness experiences" often seem intent on hauling as much of their lifestyle along as they can. Magazines are filled with articles on new ways to enjoy the wilderness, most involving significant amounts of money. Each new sport requires new equipment to "enhance" the experience. One effect of this delirium is the implication that the wilderness is just a large gymnasium: it's acceptable to exercise there without thought for human or animal activities you may interrupt, because exercise is healthy, and health is good.

Many of us justify purchases by imagining they have real value or can improve our lives in several ways. An automatic potato chip maker is called a "health aid" and "labor-saving device." We're counseled to buy relaxation in candles loaded with crushed quartz and promised enlightenment with our "Personal Native American Experience" consisting of sage and cedar sticks, herb tea, and Indian music. When we're ready for a wilderness escape from consumerism, we'll buy powerful four-wheel-drive vehicles to take us deeper into the woods, carrying larger roof sacks loaded with lighter stoves, portable chairs, and smaller televisions sets so we can watch the bad news in comfort.

Most of us are eventually convinced that with better apparatus we will love the wilderness more, or understand it better. Subconsciously perhaps, we are beginning to believe that the raw, smelly, prickly outdoors is not safe or entertaining without particular clothing, sophisticated equipment—a protective coating of manufactured items. After all, we console ourselves, unlike historic pioneers, we're concerned about the ecosystem; they may have been tougher than we are, but they were meaner. They didn't enjoy the woods, just exploited them.

Those pioneers might have come west on a few tough ponies, carrying a few basic necessities; instead, they bought Conestoga wagons (not unlike Airstream trailers), hitched up the slowest and dumbest of domestic animals, and traveled in groups so large they devastated native grasses, polluted waterholes, and left tracks we can follow a hundred years later. They took with them everything they owned, including oak furniture and sets of china, and cluttered the prairie even more by dumping ninety-nine percent of these possessions along the trail. Some of them survived only by eating their oxen or each other; if they got to Oregon alive, they didn't have much left but their socks. Their descendants are the folks in the concrete campground, right beside the pool.

Lately, though, we've become more sophisticated, marketing not just equipment but entire experience packages, total consumer products. The language of articles about unique entertainment is almost indistinguishable from that of advertisements: a river-rafting company boasts the most talented guitarists and thickest steaks; mountain bikes can conquer steep trails, leap over rocks, and ford streams, thereby, the writer notes smugly, bringing "an entirely new sport to the masses."

The current concept of wilderness seems to mean taking everywhere both equipment and attitudes developed in concrete cities. Advertisements acclaim better restaurants at ski lodges, all built with no hint of regional architecture to look like luxury hotels. Hikers drink bottled water so they don't have to consider what might be in natural water as a result of mobs infesting the wilderness.

The back pages of many outdoor magazines are jammed with small-type ads attempting to lure me to places so remote, so politically unstable, so inaccessible they were once only a dream: Nepal, Tibet, the Yukon, Hindu Kush, the Amazon, Pakistan, Borneo, Patagonia, Copper Canyon—places once considered exotic, mysterious, safe from exploitation. Now, if you have the money, you can get there, tantalize the natives with artifacts they desire without thought for the consequences, and enrich them with the debris you leave behind. Apparently, money can buy not only gear but a politically correct attitude as well.

But even a spacious wilderness does not have room for thousands of equipment addicts careening up mountains and down rivers, clanking with carabiners and pitons, grunts of exertion mingling with the beep of digital watches. We're being trained to believe we can't survive the wild without special gear, and we're starting to believe we need professional help as well to understand and appreciate wilderness happenings. When we arrive in a remote spot with high-tech food, gear, and ideas, much of the trip is already so carefully engineered there may be no room for originality—or error.

Recent news has reported climbers or skiers lost on mountains in blizzards with no food, water, shelter, or safety lines. People take whitewater raft trips without knowing how to swim or row a boat; hunters kill companions by shooting at anything that moves. The narrators of such tales may not realize how close some parties came to disaster, yet their style and tone may persuade other innocents to attempt the same feats. Every wanderer who finds an enchanting secret spot writes about it, helpfully supplying routes. Writers always need money, editors always need stories. Only a writer's sense of responsibility could temper such impressions.

But the lesson an unwary reader might learn is that skill and sensible precautions no longer matter. Buy enough gear and you can do anything, go anywhere briefly, and return home to speak of your adventure at chic cocktail parties. Risk is exciting, runs the implied refrain. Don't worry about equipment failure, injury, or the specific perils of the latest sport. Anyone can do anything affordable in wilderness—the meaningful point is enjoyment.

Lean wraiths festooned with plastic water jugs, running in purple-and-green tights past the rock I sit on don't pollute my experience as much as nine drunken hunters in jeeps, or a logging operation—but they aren't wilderness.

Moreover, as the public discovers repeatedly, wilderness can kill. Expensive gear might raise an untrained fool's survival quotient but is no substitute for brains or competence. Everyone who goes into the woods and creates a disaster imperils rescuers and destroys a part of that wilderness. The headphone-wearing jogger killed by a mountain lion may have been enjoying the wilderness benignly. But he didn't heed the wilderness maxim: what you don't know can kill you. Or, as Rick Bass remarks more aptly, "The closer you get to Canada, the more things will eat your horse."

But my objections are broader: if we all take all the gear and attitudes we can afford into the woods, wilderness will become just another mall. We may forget how to live without sophisticated equipment and become unable to appreciate naked nature without explanations from experts. Wilderness is not nature swarming with people. Wilderness is not concerned with human exercise programs, or entertainments, or recreation, or production. Wilderness is. Without us.

Not everyone who goes to wilderness areas looks for high-tech solutions to old problems of living comfortably away from home. An underground force does just the opposite. Some of its members began with curiosity about the fur trade era and found a new avocation. We call ourselves "muzzle-loading" or "black powder–weapon enthusiasts" when we're in society, and "buckskinners" when we're among friends. Some are "mountain men"; others re-create an earlier era, such as the Civil War, complete with a character and role played in camp. Most of us enjoy the challenge of going into the woods with as little as possible, but even in our small company, divisions exist. Some serious fanatics require clothing to be hand sewn and insist on wire-rim glasses for the visually impaired. In "primitive" camps no object is allowed that did not exist in a fur trade camp in the 1830s: no zippers, no jeans, no cold beer or ice, no plastic spoons or paper plates, no disposable diapers. Less rigid camps allow modern items if they are hidden in a tepee or under a blanket.

The experience isn't for everyone. Late at night talk often turns to the number of marriages broken by an addiction to this way of camping. Trying to live simply in the woods can be like jumping out of an airplane without a parachute. Injuries are common, and ignorance or carelessness in a camp with wood fires, black powder, and sharp and explosive weapons can harm both the environment and humans. Nearly all of us, however, could learn something from the old ways.

A fellow named Ed Maurer, who re-creates the period of the Ohio River valley of the 1850s, once spent twelve days in the high Uintas of Utah on a horse trek by himself with equipment Jim Bridger might have used. Ed carries his personal provisions in a belt pouch and a small haversack, referred to as a "possibles bag" since it holds everything a mountain man could possibly need, even if separated from his horse and camp. In the belt pouch are a flint and steel kit, fishing supplies, and a burning glass: when sun rays are focused on tinder—light fuel such as dry inner tree bark or moss—a little patience can create a solar campfire. (Broken beer bottles can work, if you're cold that close to town.)

The haversack, full, weighs about five pounds. The average backpacker hauls thirty to fifty pounds—several hundred dollars' worth—of lightweight miracle fibers, tents that fold to the size of a postage stamp, and food so processed it might better serve as shelter. In a haversack pocket, Ed tucks two knife-sharpening stones and a small mirror to check himself for "tiny livestock," a pioneering problem we modern folk don't like to think about, though we know ticks can transmit serious disease.

Ed also packs a fly-fishing line, two strips of cotton fabric, and a sewing kit for wounds in himself or his gear. His haversack contains lengths of elkhide, a tin of beeswax and oil for waterproofing mocassins, and another tin of char cloth, a candle stub, and slivers of pitch pine to guarantee fire in wet weather. Maurer's food is jerky (dried meat), dried corn, beans, and peas, cooked in a tin cup or corn boiler. A weekend requires a half pound of dehydrated food. For "really bad weather," he carries a pouch of coarse fiber for cleaning his gun or starting a fire. (Don't you wonder what this guy considers really bad weather?) With that outfit, which you'll note does not include toilet paper, plus the rifle, knife, and tomahawk always carried on his belt, Maurer spends comfortable vacations in the woods.

Let's put aside contention over meat eating and weapons use and simply look at what George Carlin calls "stuff!" Ed Maurer has less to carry when he goes into the woods than the contemporary yuppie backpacker. His digital watch won't screech while he's watching a wild turkey—he can tell time well enough from the sun. If he gets hurt, sewing his own wounds will take his mind off stock quotations.

Put Ed, leather clad and smelling like smoke and sweat, in one aspen thicket and an urban gear junkie in another, and watch what happens. We can't know what's in their minds, but I can comfortably assume the woodsman is calm because he knows the dangers and knows his own ability to survive. He has time, space, and energy for spiritual perceptions. I'm likewise willing to assume, without ample evidence, that the backpacker, instructed by modern society, may be trying to understand her trip in terms of how much money and time it's "costing" her.

Twenty years ago I backpacked. I spent winter searching catalogs for lighter, more cleverly designed tools that folded or collapsed into ever smaller packages so I could pack even more paraphernalia into a pack designed more efficiently. I haunted camping supply stores, and my conversations with other campers were all about objects. I wasn't entirely sure what was missing, but I knew something was. I found that trying to write about wilderness was hopeless.

Then I met a man like Ed who persuaded me to try the older route. I was dubious, kept my backpacking stuff in the basement for years. But gradually the independence, the lack of agenda, enticed me. I began to understand what Thoreau meant when he spoke of allowing time for wild harmony to invade the mind.

For the past fifteen years I've hauled less to the woods. When I settle down, I'm not distracted by searching a dozen zippered pockets for the compass, the collapsible cup. My hearing isn't distracted by the metallic jingle and dissonant whisper of my clothing. Sitting is utter immersion in a wild place: listening with every filament of my body, seeing with every cell. I can't speak for all the buckskinners, of course—for many, their chief interest is more bang for their black powder. But I believe that, as a general rule, fewer possessions require less time and attention, allowing concentration on what is already in the wilderness before we get there.

But maybe I've been approaching the problem in the wrong way. Perhaps instead of trying to convince the average family to change its lifestyle before entering the woods, we should keep it out of the woods altogether by providing suitable vacation sites elsewhere.

By creating camping ranches and by providing modern conveniences in national parks, we've trained generations to expect camping to be like a shopping mall with real trees. We may have destroyed the truth of wilderness in American minds by devaluing it.

Some rock climbers, who used to carp that they hadn't time to find real mountains after work, are now building or buying artificial climbing walls—after being chased off highway overpasses. I admire the courage and bodies of these modern spider people, but they're too busy climbing to look at the scenery. By scaling fake walls inside gyms or in parking lots, they save their precious time and my landscape. They examined the problem and solved it in a unique way, suggesting a solution to overcrowding in national parks and wilderness areas.

Let's imitate the climbers' ingenuity and categorize recreation. Some folks just want exercise—they might be just as happy with fake mountains and self-contained rivers designed specifically for the frenetic activity of their choice. Designing arenas for their sport would keep them all together so they could communicate, protect them from wild animals (and vice versa), and provide a challenge for a new generation of landscape designers.

Some families want to simulate togetherness by sleeping together in a camper but would slaughter one another if they couldn't escape to video games, golf, or shopping during the day. Camping ranches are the answer.

First, we'll ban all modern camp sites in wilderness, retroactively. Construction workers idled by recession will tear down toilets, turn paved walkways back into grass, and haul soft drink machines, plastic tomahawks, and stuffed buffalo back to the malls where they belong. Rip out the cooking grates, burn the picnic tables, recycle the trail markers into license plates.

People who like flush toilets will camp on concrete pads where they belong: right by the West's big towns, close to drive-ins and electric outlets, fast food, and highways. We can erect billboards with scenic views on all four sides of each camping reservation, next to the chain link fence erected to keep campers from wandering into the woods.

If the camp site happens to be near a real forest, armed guards will ensure a biker doesn't accidentally pedal into the real thing while absorbed in the music from ear plugs. Brochures will explain that guards are to keep the grizzlies and scorpions out.

By eliminating modern conveniences in wilderness, and the ninety percent of the population who won't move without wheels or batteries, we'll solve half the problems of wilderness overcrowding. We'll trim the numbers still more by requiring a competency test for wilderness admission. Keep wilderness for those who cherish it. On its own terms.

Rabble-rousers who insist on the right of everyone to go everywhere will object that keeping some folks out of wilderness is "undemocratic." But the process of selection I propose would give everyone an equal opportunity. My plan would not necessarily eliminate wheelchair ramps in national parks. Instead, we'd strictly define wilderness, reserve entry to those capable of appreciating it, those equipped for wild living.

The aptitude test will be given by folks proven able to survive rough conditions— providing them with jobs will be a nice economic and psychological bonus, since some haven't worked since the Vietnam War. Outfitters who pass the test will earn their fees and risk fewer lawsuits, because no customer will fail to understand the dangers and skills involved in wilderness travel.

The test will be devised by a council, with consultants who are climbers, backpackers, runners, mountain bikers, outfitters, buckskinners, ranchers, environmentalists, foresters, fishing fanatics, and other groups who use the wilderness. Getting them together will be a nightmare, but each has something to gain: protection of a primary resource common to us all. The council will define its own membership on the basis of ability and then write a test for the general public. Here are some standards I'd suggest.

Start a fire with one match, or with flint and steel, and without using lighter fluid or paper: 150 points. Lose ten points for freeze-dried food. Lose twenty points if your tent or outer clothing is bright orange of blue; gain ten for a canvas shelter grimy with age. Let's see you defecate, camper; subtract 150 points for use of toilet paper or failure to bury the waste. Lose ten for footwear that can be inflated or any item made by a major corporate polluter. Visitors in wilderness would be on their own. Survivors get a decorative shoulder patch ensuring admission to other such areas.

The problems have less to do with shrinking wilderness than with our fecundity, and our belief in technology. If we continue to use wild areas as we are doing today, we will destroy them. The current definition of *use* seems to be that of the Forest Service, as in "Multiple-Use Area"—a hillside where grizzlies once nibbled strawberries on warm afternoons, now crowded with skinny people in eye-blistering clothing pedalling mountain bikes around stumps left after a clearcut.

Edward Abbey correctly insisted that wilderness is where the grizzly governs; bless his furry reincarnation, he's probably eating a motorcyclist in a roadless area right now. Among Thoreau's wise sayings is: "A man sits as many risks as he runs. The amount of it is, if a man is alive, there is always danger that he may die." I'd rather risk death in the woods, really living, than fade away in my living room surrounded by possessions.

Another Thoreau suggestion applies equally for an authentic wilderness expedition or our feverish daily lives: "Simplify, simplify."

What Price Tourism?

Glen Hunter

reprinted from *Santa Fe Reporter*, May 13–19, 1992

New Mexico's first director of Indian tourism, Calvin Tafoya, likened the scene to a church service in Disneyland. The scene was a hotel banquet room in Santa Fe, where a group of Pueblo Indians had gathered to perform a ceremonial dance for a meeting of government dignitaries and visiting business people. After the guests had quaffed a few cocktails, however, some in their party began to whoop loudly and to mimic the dancers' movements, turning a revered tradition into an occasion for mindless merrymaking.

While some blame for the disrespect must lie with the "uneducated" tourists, Tafoya says, part must also be borne by the American Indians themselves. "By putting on a show for tourists away from the pueblo setting, I'm afraid some [Native Americans] have started to turn a culture and a tradition into a commodity that can be bought and sold," Tafoya says.

"I personally don't think that auditoriums or hotels are proper settings for these types of activities, which on the reservations most often are geared toward the Native American religion," he says. "Unless we put in place some kind of controls or policies to govern these events, such distortion and devaluation eventually could lead to the destruction of our way of life."

The scene at the hotel illustrates the fine line between sensitivity and exploitation faced increasingly by Native Americans in New Mexico, where tourism—and Indian tourism in particular—has become big business. Faced with fewer dollars from the federal government and unemployment rates of over 50 percent on some reservations, more and more tribes are turning these days to the visitor industry as an economic development tool.

As they do so, they must deal with the question of just how much it's worth to open up their tribal and personal lives to the inspections—and possibly intrusions—of strangers. Though tourists usually find their experience enhanced by visits to dances, churches, homes, and sacred areas, in permitting this, tribal members must share sites and activities that to them have a much deeper and more important meaning.

Nevertheless, many Indians find that such sharing is one of the few available ways of moving beyond the poverty and bare subsistence forced upon them by an age-old lack of economic opportunity. Contrasted with this history, they see the burgeoning expansion of the state's overall tourism business, which is expected to employ forty-eight thousand people by the end of this year and to generate $2.4 billion in gross receipts annually.

Though no figures on tourism revenue are available for the individual Indian communities, it is estimated that many of New Mexico's twenty-two reservations have doubled their number of visitors in the last two to three years through their lure of history and traditions, arts and crafts, and natural beauty. In fact, a 1989 survey by the state Tourism Department and the Bureau of Business and Economic Research at the University of New Mexico attributed 55 percent of all the state's tourist visits to "Indian cultural opportunities." That reason for visiting New Mexico was the survey's third most frequently mentioned, trailing only "scenic beauty" (75 percent) and "historic sites" (62 percent).

Responding to the economic implications of such figures, Governor Bruce King's administration established a separate division of tourism last year within the state Tourism Department—the first division of its kind in the nation. Overseen by Calvin Tafoya, with an annual budget of about $100,000, the new venture will attempt to help New Mexico Indians manage and profit from tourism without sacrificing their homes, villages, and traditional ways of life. Clearly, however, it won't be an easy task.

"Tourism is a desirable, clean industry. Tourists take their pictures and leave, and they don't pollute the water and the skies," says Alfonso Ortiz, a native of San Juan Pueblo and a professor of anthropology at the University of New Mexico in Albuquerque. "Especially in a day of declining to non-existent federal dollars, it's much better [for tribes] to depend on their own resources, and tourism can be a major part of that.

"The problem, though, is in controlling the numbers of tourists so that they don't inundate the facilities—both the human resources and natural facilities—and take away the privacy completely," Ortiz goes on. "If the pueblos can [establish rules] to do that and then make their decisions stick, they can have the best of both possible worlds."

So far tribal approaches to the dilemma described by Ortiz seem to be as varied as the tribes themselves. (New Mexico's twenty-two reservations include its nineteen pueblos plus settlements of the Navajos and the Jicarilla and Mescalero Apaches.) At one end of the spectrum, for example, Zia Pueblo, some thirty-five miles north of Albuquerque, zealously guards its privacy by welcoming visitors only on certain days. At Acoma Pueblo, which sits atop a 360-foot mesa some twelve miles off Interstate 40, just southeast of Grants, visitors are allowed to enter the pueblo only by guided tour.

Adopting a more aggressive approach to tourism, the Mescalero Apaches successfully operate a major hotel, as well as a full-blown golf course and ski resort, on their reservation land near Ruidoso. At Santa Clara Pueblo, just east of Española, a growing number of visitors may knock on the doors of village painters, sculptors, and potters, whose prized polished redware and black-on-blackware have become nationally known. Santa Clara also is beginning to grapple with increasing numbers of visitors to its ancestral Puye cliff dwellings, which Tafoya refers to as a "hidden jewel."

Nine miles north of Santa Fe, Tesuque Pueblo caters to tourists with activities as diverse as a horse-riding stable, an RV campground, and a bingo parlor. However, tribal officials ask that visitors refrain from hiking or climbing in the surrounding hillside, which the pueblo considers sacred and wants to keep undisturbed.

Meanwhile, just outside of Albuquerque, Sandia Pueblo's Sandia Bingo operation plays host to a whopping half-million bingo-playing visitors a year. But, like the tribe's Bien Mur Indian Market, its Los Amigos banquet facility, and its Sandia Lakes Recreational Area, the Sandia gaming operation is located on the fringes of pueblo property, well away from the pueblo residences themselves.

A similar "separatist" approach to visitors has been adopted by Pojoaque Pueblo, some fifteen miles northeast of Santa Fe, where tribal members are using tourism not only for economic development but also to help them rediscover their cultural roots.

"How do we view tourists? With open arms, as long as they have money!" laughs Pojoaque governor Jacob Viarrial, slicing jalapeño peppers for his breakfast one recent morning at the pueblo's tourist-oriented P'o suwae geh Restaurant. (The eatery's name is a Tewa phrase for "water drinking place," a reference to the nearby Tesuque River.)

The Pojoaque restaurant, with items on the menu like the Taos Turkey Sandwich, the San Juan Egg Salad Sandwich, and the San Ildefonso Ham and Swiss, is located in the Pueblo Plaza shopping center, a bustling, tribally owned complex of buildings just off busy U.S. 285.

Most of the businesses in the recently expanded center are also owned by the tribe, which hires its own managers and employees, many of them non-Indian, to operate the enterprises. Among the center's tenants are a well-stocked grocery, a video store, a True Value hardware outlet, and a laundromat, the latter owned by Viarrial himself. Just up the road, the pueblo has opened a tourist information center as well.

But these enterprises, which generate some 90 percent of the pueblo's operating revenues, are buffered by the Pojoaque hills from the tribal residences and the pueblo headquarters office. "Each pueblo has its own way of dealing with tourists, and we have decided we don't want tourists in our residential area," says George Rivera, a Pojoaque Pueblo artist and Viarrial's nephew. "We treat the visitors [to the enterprises along the main highway] with respect, though, and hopefully that is their attitude toward us in return."

Now the smallest pueblo in northern New Mexico, with about 215 residents, Pojoaque is said by legend to have been the "mother village" at one time to all the historic Tewa people. Abandoned in the late 1600s after the Pueblo revolt against the Spanish, the settlement was reestablished in 1710, only to be decimated by a smallpox epidemic and eventually deserted again around 1900. Some thirty years later, however, four families returned to revive Pojoaque Pueblo once again, including Feliciana and Fermin Viarrial, Governor Viarrial's parents.

Some sixty-thousand visitors stopped at the Pojoaque Pueblo center last year. With authentic, Indian-made pottery, drums, and jewelry offered for sale in a room next to a Route 66–style curio shop ("This is where we sell the rubber tomahawks," Viarrial chuckles), the center's motto might well be "Something for Everyone." According to shop manager Gerri Lujan, many of the visitors stay to watch the tribe's traditional butterfly, eagle, and buffalo dances as they are rediscovered and reinterpreted by the pueblo's young people. The dances are increasingly popular, Viarrial says, both as an educational tool for the children and as an economic generator for the tribe.

"The kids that dance have a different perspective [on the dances] than the viewer might have," he says. "While a tourist might see it as entertainment, the dancers do it for a reason, such as for the religious aspect.

"Our kids are so happy to learn and to respect these dances," he adds, "that I doubt they would ever see them as an exhibition only to please someone else."

Some seventy-five miles northwest of Pojoaque, meantime, an estimated 200,000 to 300,000 visitors each year pour into Taos Pueblo, a traditional, multi-storied adobe settlement beneath the slopes of Wheeler Peak. Sometimes referred to as "Winnebago Village" because of all its traffic, Taos Pueblo attempts to manage the onslaught with entry fees and clearly posted rules (prohibiting photos at certain times, for example), and by opening and closing its doors at specific hours.

Even so, says tribal secretary Renaldo Lujan, some tourists still get out of hand, climbing onto rooftops, ignoring the posted hours, or just being plain nosy. "We want the same respect that the tourist would want if we went into their places," Lujan says. "If I were to go to California, for instance, I'd abide by all the rules and regulations. I'd say to the people there, 'Good morning. How are you?' "

Despite its appeal as the area's major tourist attraction, Lujan says, the pueblo earns only about 10 percent of the typical Taos visitor dollar, with the remainder going to shops, restaurants, and lodging facilities in the town of Taos proper. That dilemma is not unusual among New Mexico pueblos, says Ortiz, although the situation has improved since the "neo-colonialist" 1940s and '50s, when Ortiz was growing up at San Juan Pueblo.

"Back in those days, the tribes weren't organized to charge the various fees that they do now," Ortiz says. "So the Grayline tour bus would come in and let the tourists off under a tree, and then they would proceed to wander around and to peer into people's homes, as if it was a movie set constructed just for them. They'd ask us street urchins for a photograph, and then we'd get a nickel or a dime if we were lucky. We were expected to be mute and colorful, like props or scenery."

Today, Ortiz goes on, tour operators increasingly are employing Pueblo tour guides, setting up traditional meals on the reservations and encouraging the purchase of native arts and crafts. "The journey from the old days to now has been a long and painful one," he says. "Indians want to be dealt with not as stereotypes but as responsible, fully sentient human beings who deserve respect—not as people to be ripped off. They're people who need to make a car payment, for example, who need to send their children to college."

Toward that end, Tafoya hopes to have his Indian tourism division prepare a detailed "handbook of protocols" to distribute to visitors to New Mexico's Indian reservations. More importantly, he says, the office is aiming to shape a new way of thinking about tourism among American Indians themselves.

"We have to stop and ask, What are we doing to ourselves? Is the tourist industry going to peak in five or ten years and destroy our way of life? Or should we try to level this thing out and enjoy it for the next hundred years?" Tafoya says. "We are natives with roots here, after all, and we are going to stay. So we have to think about protecting ourselves and about taking control of our own destiny."

Aspen:
A Colonial Power with Angst

Harlan C. Clifford

reprinted from *High Country News*, April 5, 1993

*A*spenites sometimes quip that they live in "the center of the known universe." Hyperbole aside, there is a bittersweet truth to the phrase, at least for residents of west-central Colorado who live within commuting distance of Aspen.

In the past decade, Aspen has completed its transformation from funky ski town to full-blown power resort, from hip to rich. The residents half joke that billionaires have pushed the millionaires downvalley. The ski bums have been replaced by "yurpies" (Young Resort Professionals): lawyers, caterers, architects. Wealth from around the world flows into Aspen by the hundreds of millions of dollars annually, and the backsplash from that flood affects small communities many miles away.

At high season the town of forty-six hundred is festooned with fur coats, Range Rovers, and private jets. Yet Aspen, sitting at seventy-nine hundred feet in the Roaring Fork Valley, is swathed in angst. Many long-time residents believe the opening in December [1992] of the 257-room Ritz-Carlton Hotel marked the end of Aspen's small-town pretensions. Others hailed it as a great achievement. Old-timers say the town they know is gone, but newcomers are upbeat. There is a lot of discussion in Aspen about preserving "the community" but little agreement on what—or whose—community.

Even as Aspen is busy pondering what and who it is, its effect on the surrounding region has been profound. Aspen leaves a fat financial footprint on the West Slope of the Colorado Rockies. The resort's insatiable demand for employees, goods, and services primed the pump for an influx of Hispanics into the Roaring Fork Valley during the 1980s and has changed the lives of residents as far away as Rifle, sixty-six miles distant, and Paonia, a two-hour drive away.

Many people who cannot afford to live in the resort town now live in towns downstream of Aspen and even over McClure Pass, in the next major drainage to the south, creating a commuter culture. Money flows to those towns, too, in search of fresh fruit, baby vegetables, organic cider, art, automobiles, handmade furnishings, beer, natural gas, and a cornucopia of other things which can no longer be produced or warehoused affordably in Aspen but are still demanded by the town's privileged residents and visitors.

One of those privileged residents is industrial billionaire David Koch, who last summer [1992] offered to build an ice skating rink for Aspen on a downtown park. Most towns would have jumped for joy, but the Aspen City Council told Koch thanks, but no thanks. Some residents saw Koch's attempted largesse as the latest illustration of a disturbing phenomenon: new, monied Aspenites, often vacation-home owners like Koch, trying to purchase goodwill. "There are a lot of people who think they can buy their way into the community by writing a check. That's very new to me," says Pitkin County Sheriff Bob Braudis, a veteran social and political observer.

The money of the 1980s has largely overwhelmed Aspen's skiing culture, which in its own heyday overran traditional mining and ranching cultures. Today Aspen lives off tourists, and outlying communities increasingly live off Aspen.

In the '50s, '60s, and '70s it was skiing first and foremost which brought new arrivals to the valley. After World War II Aspen broke out of its Victorian time capsule and began to grow as a resort. But for many years it still had a small-town feel about it.

"I liked the old Aspen. It was about the right size," recalls rancher Connie Harvey, who runs cattle twenty miles away in Old Snowmass and maintains seventy acres on the edge of Aspen. "It seemed kind of a friendly thing, on the whole. . . . Now you get people who are a world unto themselves."

Skiing provided a common bond through the '70s. But the small ski town of Aspen is gone. Many veteran residents regret that passing and feel the new Aspen, whatever its merits, has been forged by different, richer people and doesn't include them. Most people like Aspen as it was at the time they arrived. More recent residents, consequently, are comfortable with the changes which upset old-timers. "If you've been here a year," says one local attorney, "you remember the good old days."

Aspenites from earlier decades point repeatedly to the influx of new money during the 1980s as the root of many problems. Aspen's "old money," they say, didn't show off. But the *nouveaux riches*, largely created by the economic boom of the Reagan years, felt—and feel—a need to demonstrate their financial muscle by building big houses, driving fancy cars, shopping in expensive boutiques.

"When I came here [in 1955], this was a classless society," says *Aspen Times* publisher Loren Jenkins. But that changed in the 1980s with the arrival of "huge classes of people that suddenly had buckets of money. The creation of a rigid caste system here is what threatens our community. A caste system is what has been imposed by people from outside who just want servants; they don't want neighbors."

That attitude was illustrated for some people when Florida developers Tom and Bonnie McCloskey bought seventy acres at the mouth of Hunter Creek Valley, a popular White River National Forest recreation area, and attempted to close an access route to the public land behind their property. Six years later the access battle between the family and the county continues in the courts.

Bonnie McCloskey, now volunteer president of the Aspen Valley Hospital Foundation, downplays the Hunter Creek fight and says she feels a part of the community—even as many old-time locals disdain the McCloskeys and what they have come to represent. At the same time, however, an increasing number of wealthy residents share the McCloskeys' desire for a mountain retreat. It is these people who are forging the new Aspen; those who disdain them are thinning in numbers.

Social events in the ski town Aspen were built around the Aspen Ski Club, the volunteer fire department, and the local churches. Modern Aspen swarms with groups like Les Dames d'Aspen, a gathering of wealthy women, and the Friday Men's Club, a weekly lunch meeting of the rich and powerful in town, encompassing people like Lee Iacocca.

"What defines you as a local, in my mind, is whether you give more than you take," says Michael Kinsley, a former county commissioner and now a consultant on small-town development who measures commitment in currencies other than money. "That's the essence of community." Kinsley believes that the new money in Aspen, for all its financial benefits, doesn't pass that test. Bonnie McCloskey disagrees and thinks the changes Aspen has seen are for the better.

"People who contribute to this community love this community. If people are bitter [about the town's changes], maybe they have withdrawn," she says. "I feel sorry for those people who are bitter. I think they need to get a handle on their attitudes and reinvolve themselves."

That prescription may be difficult to fill. The displacement of many less wealthy locals to towns down the Roaring Fork Valley has sapped Aspen of its vitality, Braudis believes. "Aspen merely imports a lot of mercenary labor every day that pulls a shift and doesn't have the energy for Aspen per se," he says.

An aggressive mesh of zoning, open space, and growth-control restrictions, while broadly supported by county residents as a way to preserve Aspen's small-town feel, has combined with an overheated real estate market to force many employees beyond county lines in search of affordable housing. Inside Aspen city limits a single-family home sold for an average of $1.2 million last year. The result is near gridlock on Highway 82, the two-lane road which winds northwest down the Roaring Fork Valley to Glenwood Springs, forty-five miles distant. Towns like the former ranching and coal mining town of Carbondale, thirty-two miles away, have become bedrooms for commuters. And commute they do: thirty-one thousand vehicle trips were counted into and out of Aspen from downvalley on a weekday last August, up from a daily average of fifteen thousand in 1972.

Growth pressures on Aspen have been unremitting. Pitkin County, which includes Aspen and the nearby ski resort of Snowmass Village, added a million square feet of commercial space between 1975 and 1989. Commercial passenger counts at the Pitkin County airport jumped from about 100,000 in 1977 to 218,000 in 1991. Second, or perhaps fourth, homes are so prevalent that the 1990 census found 40 percent of the county's residences unoccupied.

This growth is the basic cause of Aspen's delaminating community, as many long-time residents cash in and clear out. "So many people complain about the people who bought Aspen," says Jim Kent, an Aspen-based sociologist. "What about the people who sold Aspen?"

In the past decade the percentage of workers living in the Aspen neighborhood dropped from 63 percent to 30 percent. Beginning in the early 1980s city and county governments began building employee housing to try to stem the downvalley flight. About thirteen hundred rental and ownership units have been constructed, and a new "community plan" calls for another 620 units within nine miles of Aspen by 2015. The goal: preserve and even reintroduce the middle class to the town by providing price- and rent-controlled housing for a broad range of workers. It is a stated objective of local governments to re-create "messy diversity" in the community.

"What I see happening," says Aspen city manager Amy Margerum, "which I think is a microcosm of the rest of the nation, is the gap between the rich and the poor. There's a lot of animosity because the gap is so wide here.

"Our biggest problem is there's no middle class," continues Margerum, who lives nine miles away in Snowmass Village. "If we were known more as a community and less as a resort, maybe we'd be better. Maybe the lesson is not to put all your chips on one thing, because you'll become that thing."

The '80s and '90s saw a profound shift in the attitude of Aspen's visitors as well as part-time or year-round residents. Visitors demanded more resort amenities, and the town, in the interests of competing with Vail and Sun Valley and Park City, broadly acceded to those demands. These days business people are less likely to close up shop and take advantage of a morning of fresh powder skiing; there's money to be made.

Aspen today is a locus of what Edward Abbey termed "industrial tourism." There is such demand to see the namesake peaks of Maroon Bells–Snowmass Wilderness that the road to their base is closed to passenger vehicles during summer days and visitors are hauled in by bus. (The peaks have been promoted as the most photographed in the world.) The area around Maroon Lake—the bus drop-off point—attracts tens of thousands of tourists a summer and has become a sacrifice zone in the eyes of some local people who avoid it altogether.

Summer tourism has grown steadily, aided largely by the success and acclaim of several performing arts organizations. In recent years the arts have grown to become an economic force in their own right: one study claims they contribute $24 million annually to the Roaring Fork Valley's economy. And it is a booming economy. Since 1987 retail sales in Aspen have increased by one-third, to a 1992 annual total of $254 million. That doesn't include real estate, which is sold by 649 agents in the Aspen, Snowmass, and Basalt areas. In the 1980s real estate courses at the community college were packed. Aspen even has some things most U.S. cities don't have, including two daily newspapers, one of them edited by a Pulitzer Prize winner. There is also a weekly paper and a pair of commercial radio stations.

As a result, Aspen has become a conduit for money from around the globe, the dominant financial force in the region. "I think [Aspen's economic influence] is growing," says Rifle city manager Mike Bestor. Rifle is the home base for Aspen Limousine's vehicle fleet, a linen supply firm, and a glass company, all of which do a lot of business in Aspen. The Garfield County airport at Rifle is often the destination for aircraft which can't make Aspen's landing strip before its evening curfew. "I think there are probably quite a few people [in Rifle] that are extremely dependent on [Aspen]," says Bestor.

"The reality is that everybody here knows that [Aspen] is a source of sales," says Bernie Heideman, who runs Big B's Fabulous Juices in Hotchkiss and sells about 10 percent of his product in Aspen, two hours away over 8,755-foot McClure Pass. Other Paonia and Hotchkiss residents work in Aspen in construction, an industry which many Pitkin County residents believe is as significant as skiing, thanks to the second-home boom and constant demand for retail store remodels. A Paonia foundry casts large bronze sculptures, some of which dot Aspen—including a piece installed at the entrance of the new Ritz-Carlton. In Redstone, halfway between Paonia and Aspen, deer antlers are assembled into chandeliers and other exotic furniture to be retailed to designers and architects in an old Aspen building which once served as the hardware store.

Red Hat Produce, located in Austin, gets as much as 45 percent of its business from the Roaring Fork Valley during peak winter and summer seasons, and 80 percent of that is attributable to Aspen, according to general manager Gary Goad. During the summer Goad buys apples, cherries, peaches, corn, broccoli, cabbage, and other produce from farmers around Colorado's West Slope, and much of it ends up in the restaurants and catering dishes of Aspen. "People in Aspen love to have Colorado produce," says Goad, who sends as many as twenty trucks a week to the town, up from only three trucks five years ago.

In January [1993], Pitkin County's bus service was extended forty-five miles down the Roaring Fork to Glenwood Springs, in Garfield County. Some politicians and business people in Glenwood, including Ramada Inn owner Klaus Schattleitner, opposed the extension, fearing that easing access to the high-paying hourly jobs in Aspen would drive up wages at the bottom of the valley.

Glenwood, which hosts a half-dozen car dealerships, natural gas facility, liquor distributors, and bottling plant, has long been a service town for the region. In the early 1980s Glenwood helped service the oil shale boom in Parachute and Rifle. When Exxon, Unocal, et al. pulled out, it turned its attention to Aspen and Vail. Its Wal-Mart, only a few years old, recently doubled in size; on weekends many of the license plates in the parking lot sport Aspen prefixes.

"Aspen has always driven the economy of the valley to one degree or another," says Dean Moffatt, a Glenwood Springs architect and member of that city's chamber of commerce. "I think that the general economy of the area owes a lot of stability to the influx of money into Aspen." He points to the broad selection at Glenwood's City Market grocery store, a frequent stopping point for tourists headed to Aspen, as an example of the improved quality of life for the region.

"If they think the bus is the problem, the four-lane is going to be a hundred times the problem," fumes economic development specialist Kinsley. The range of Aspen's economic effect is largely a function of how easy it is for commuters, second-home owners, and suppliers to reach the town. Highway 82 is slowly being expanded to a four-lane road, despite heavy political opposition from Aspen residents. When that project is completed, people will be able to live farther away than they do now yet reach the resort in the same time.

"Basalt and El Jebel will become second-home communities," Kinsley says. "Rifle will become a bedroom community for Aspen. The most important sub-issue is transportation. The easier it is to get from a highly inflated economy to a cooler economy, the faster that cool economy is going to heat up. [And] the second-home phenomenon is the most dangerous thing for those small towns."

The fax machine, the computer modem, and the airplane may be the most powerful technologies faced by the West since the moldboard plow, for they free people to move their offices and their work out of urban centers and into the small towns where they would rather live. While most people cannot break completely from cities, greater numbers are able spend more time in places such as Aspen, Telluride, Jackson Hole, Vail, and Crested Butte than they could have previously.

"Every little town that is livable, if it is comfortable, safe and clean, and if there is an airport, even a funky airport, within an hour, is going to be inundated by the same phenomenon," says Kinsley. "This is the harbinger."

Residents of many small Western towns, Kinsley says, tell him they will avoid becoming "Aspenized" by not zoning their land or controlling growth. They believe such restrictions can make land more expensive, thus limiting a local person's ability to buy a piece and build a home on it. That is true, Kinsley says, only as long as a town remains undiscovered by outsiders.

Lack of growth controls doesn't change the demand for small-town life, he argues. It simply clears the way for developers to cater to the demands of rich "equity refugees" from cities without taking local needs into account. Given that developers will try to maximize profits by catering to the wealthiest potential customers, the result can be the same development problems but with less consideration for preserving the existing community. Once outsiders in significant numbers begin to move into a town, local people begin to be forced out of the places they grew up in.

The market for second homes in small towns has become international and is spilling across the mountain West: by all indications, this is the economy of the future for many small communities. "There's insatiable demand," says Aspen city manager Margerum. Consequently, many small Western towns look to Aspen with trepidation and occasional admiration, for their future may be a variation on Aspen's theme.

"It's certainly something that's happening already," says John Thrasher, assistant to the city manager in the northern Colorado resort of Steamboat Springs. "We have people that work in Washington but live here three days out of five, or work in Denver." Steamboat officials are trying to improve air and telecommunications links to draw such residents, whom some dramatize as "lone eagles" because they do not depend on the local economy.

Aspen has been the vanguard of this movement, and its effects have spilled down the Roaring Fork. "I know of individuals here who do their business out of their home with a modem, a fax, and a computer," says Davis Farrar, town manager of Carbondale.

Glenwood Springs, for example, is headquarters of Commodity Quote Graphics, a company with offices in Denver, Boulder, Chicago, New York, London, and Paris. The firm sells information via satellite about the world's commodity exchanges—exactly the sort of service that allows people to live anywhere they can erect a satellite dish.

"Already, in the Glenwood Springs area, people are looking for the ideal second-home site, and they don't mind the drive [to Aspen]," says Moffatt, who worries about the domino effect of vacation homes spreading down the valley. Community balance, Moffatt says, is "threatened by what we're talking about. Paonia is a good example: on the one hand you have artists who can sell their things; on the other hand the prices to live there are changing." Recently a tenant of Moffatt's, born in Glenwood Springs, moved out after he raised her rent.

What is a small town to do? "If [small towns] don't stand up to defend themselves, they will be taken over and exploited by others," says *Aspen Times* publisher Jenkins. "There's a tradition of exploitation. We've lived on exploitation. We're still living on it now. You leave it to the guys with the money, yeah, they'll ruin it."

"Somehow, we have to get a regional grip on it," says architect Moffatt, noting that Pitkin County tends to take aggressive positions limiting growth while Garfield and Eagle county officials don't. "I think we need regional land-use policies, and I think we need political coordination between the three counties, at least."

The growth of Aspen in so many directions has resulted in an influx of people to the valley who come for more varied reasons than those who were drawn in past decades by the skiing. Their common ground is not a love of sport but a debt to predecessors who made Aspen a highly desirable place to live by building ski lifts, forming cultural institutions, and limiting growth. Former Eagles drummer Don Henley, who has lived in nearby Woody Creek for many years, may have been thinking of Aspen when he wrote, "Call a place paradise, kiss it good-bye."

Many old-time residents have done just that. More recent arrivals, those who can afford the housing and the clubs, are thrilled to find a place which, developer Harley Baldwin once said, "has the heart of a small town and the soul of a big city."

"I'm very optimistic about Aspen," says Bonnie McCloskey. "I think it's better than it used to be, and it's going to continue to be better. I think there are more working people with family values, traditional values coming in. It's become more of a permanent community." She and her family, she says, "are becoming part of the future."

But Sheriff Braudis sounds bitter—the future McCloskey sees does not include him. It is a future where you must pay to play. It is not the future so many people like Braudis thought they were getting when they left America's mainstream to retreat to a small town in the mountains. The mainstream has followed them. "We have too many people trying to suck on the hummingbird feeder we call Aspen," says Braudis. He says he has watched dozens of friends leave town.

The rich are "fickle," Braudis believes, and he hopes they will turn their attention to the next discovery, some other small town which will be their Shangri-La. It's a wish others like him share, a wish that a new Aspen will make room for the old Aspen to resurrect itself. It's a wish that, by all indications, won't be fulfilled.

Tourism Trap
The Californication of the American West

Jim Robbins

reprinted from *Northern Lights*, Winter 1991

O ne year in a mythical kingdom the entire stock of grain became poisoned. Anyone who ate it would become insane. Grain had been stored from years past, but only a small amount. The king fell into a quandary. Should people eat and become crazy? Or starve to death? Finally the king decided to feed the people the contaminated grain. But he reserved a little of the unpoisoned grain for a handful of people so, the king said, someone will know the rest of us are crazy.

With its dramatic and surreal open spaces, its parks and wildlife, its dearth of people and crime, and the reasonable cost of living, much of the Rocky Mountain region is analogous to that unpoisoned grain. People on the West Coast and in the Eastern cities are discovering this in ever-increasing numbers. Tourism—the marketing of these virtues—is booming and now is trumpeted as the industry of the '90s and beyond for much of the West. It's being sold to the people who live here as clean and stable, the perfect remedy to the region's traditional boom-and-bust economies.

However, there are people who live, or used to live, in Jackson, Wyoming, just south of Grand Teton National Park, who argue that tourism is indeed an extractive industry. Frannie Huff is one. Huff, like hundreds of others, came to Jackson for the skiing, waitressing in the evening and spending her days on the slopes that loom over town. That was in 1969. Now she owns a successful outdoor clothing company called Wyoming Woolens, which makes ski clothes.

In the twenty-one years she's been here, Huff has watched Jackson change from a place where families came for a few weeks in the summer to browse knickknack shops, raft rivers, and eat around the chuckwagon into a resort town where members of a global elite come in their private jets to spend a month each year in $2 million houses ensconced in gated communities.

She doesn't like it. "They are a different kind of people," she says. "These people are cosmopolitan. I prefer the common folk. I don't go in for the fancy houses, the jets and the flash. In 1969 people on the street would say hello. But people are so transient, that doesn't happen here anymore."

Huff is a member of a diminishing population of "common folk" in Jackson. Though she owns a business, she started it from scratch, sewing wraparound can coolers to keep beer and soda pop cold, after her regular job as a waitress. Her income has allowed her to stay in Jackson. She knows dozens of people, however, who have lost their struggle to stay in Jackson. Forced out by an astronomical cost of living, they have fled to other places seeking work. Or they have settled in small Idaho towns on the "backside" of the Tetons and commute over Teton Pass every day to work in the upscale galleries, restaurants, and hotels of Jackson.

The convulsive change tourism has wrought on the northwest corner of Wyoming is different from the kind mining or logging brings to a town. The glacier-etched Teton Mountains, so dramatic they look like an illusion, remain the same. The sagebrush flats still roll along outside of town, their topography original and uninterrupted. The Snake River is still clean here, near its source on the Yellowstone Plateau. What has been extracted from one of the most beautiful places on earth, however, is people. Diversity. Some would say soul. Entire classes of people have largely disappeared, or are disappearing. Ranchers and cowhands drift on to other things or places. Many folks who have to work for a living must clear out. The people who once owned the stores and cafes have sold out to those with money from an outside economy. Ranches are leased at high prices to the few hunters who can afford to pay for them; access to trout streams is sealed off. The view and the landscape and the lifestyle at the base of the Tetons now belong mostly to the elite. Jackson feels as if it had been airdropped from some faraway place—but only after it was carefully designed by Ralph Lauren.

Of course, the phenomenon is nothing new. Aspen. Telluride. Sun Valley. Santa Fe. Park City. In all of these towns there has been a tremendous dislocation that in many cases rivals the kind of social upheaval that comes from a boom in coal or oil or gas. What is new is the intensity of the population shift. In Jackson, for instance, county officials have predicted that the town's population could soon surge from twelve thousand to twenty-five or forty thousand.

One of the most frequent complaints heard in booming resort towns is that people from other places, especially cities, bring their way of life with them and change the openness and friendly character of a town. Huff was particularly bothered by the advent of gated communities, an anathema to the spirit of a place like Jackson, she says. "There's a locked gate and a security guard. You have to know who you want to see to get in. It's a paranoid culture."

While the ranchers and loggers and others may be gone from Jackson, there is no shortage of real estate agents. In an area with some twelve thousand souls, there are between fifteen and twenty real estate companies and about 150 agents. And their eyes are turned westward, toward Californians who are bailing out of the smog and gridlock and heading to Wyoming. Californians can sell a home for $500,000 or $5 million and buy a nicer home for a third that much in Jackson. "It's really escalated in the past few years," says Bruce Simon of Prime Properties of Jackson Hole, a twelve-year veteran of the real estate business. "There's really a demand from urban areas. They're tired of crime, pollution, and crowds. With faxes and UPS they don't need to live in an urban area anymore."

So the past three years have seen a "tremendous boom" in real estate. In 1988 and '89, the price of land was doubling in a year's time. An average piece of ground might sell for $20,000 an acre in March and then jump to $40,000 by September. Starter homes that cost $70,000 went to $100,000. And there's plenty of new construction. It's quite common for a new home going up in Jackson to be from six thousand to twelve thousand square feet, starting at $2 million. There is no way people living in the local economy can begin to compete with those from outside.

Fed up and frustrated, John Wiesel, a partner in a small resort-designing firm who settled in Jackson back in 1980, moved his business to Bozeman, Montana. "The cost of living skyrocketed," Wiesel says. "After nine years of renting I wanted to buy and I couldn't. The pace of life changed. Tourism became the dominant element of life. Aggressively, assertively so. Traffic jams were terrible, and it was even hard to find a place to have lunch." Montana has become a refuge for other Jackson expatriates as well. Wiesel's United Parcel Service man moved to Missoula and bought twenty acres. Several friends have relocated in Bozeman. This, he said, really is the last best place.

The Last Best Place. That's a phrase that makes some long-time Montanans nervous. They said similar things about California a half century ago. Colorado's Front Range in the 1960s and 1970s. Seattle and Portland. And Arizona. Jackson and Sun Valley may be full, or close to it. But there are plenty of other towns waiting to be Aspenized. Big Timber, Montana, for one.

In March 1990 I wrote a story for *The New York Times* on the Great Montana Ranch Rush. Celebrities like Michael Keaton, Mel Gibson, Dennis Quaid, Meg Ryan, Emilio Estevez, Ted Turner, and Jane Fonda all bought ranches in Montana. I was uncomfortable writing the story. Montana doesn't need that kind of promotion. One of the main reasons I wrote the story is that people should know what kind of massive change is taking place here. It's not just film stars but also the rich and mighty from all over the world who are coming here to buy up Montana, Wyoming, Idaho, and other Rocky Mountain ranches.

The response to the piece was far beyond what anyone imagined. I mentioned Sonny Todd, a real estate agent in Big Timber who has sold to some of the stars. Within a few weeks after the piece ran, he told me he received more than five hundred phone calls from people who wanted to look at ranches and almost immediately sold $2 million in real estate. Other realtors in Montana reported a burst of business, though none so dramatic.

So what's wrong with allowing a town its tourist industry? Aren't people who complain about the outlanders coming in just whining because their own little corner of the world is changing? Isn't this just environmental bumper sticker jingoism?— "Don't Californicate Montana" and "Gut Shoot 'em at the Border."

Like every other change the West has faced, it is a matter of degree, a matter of preparedness. K. Ross Toole spoke to this change when he wrote, "There is little or nothing moderate about the state of Montana. It has ricocheted violently down the corridor of possibility. What is good in reasonable measure is often bad in full measure, and Montana has been a place of full measure." He could apply that as well to the entire West.

The problem, a lot of people feel, is that there is absolutely no planning for the impact of tourism or for the shift in population as computers and telecommunications free people from the constraints of place. Change is being allowed in full measure. State commerce departments still promote the hell out of Yellowstone, even though the smart money knows Yellowstone exceeded human carrying capacity a long time ago. A new business promotion center in Denver called Center for the New West, bankrolled by US West, is part of the free-for-all, promoting the West as a place for the world to come and tour and tap into. Planning for the lower elevation winter range lands and river corridors is largely nonexistent, even though these are the very places the New Westerners want to locate.

Tourism has turned Jackson upside down, along with people's lives. It has affected the environment. Yet there is no environmental or social impact planning process for this full-blown charge into a tourism-based economy.

Many proponents of environmental protection see a tourist and summer-home economy as a good thing. In the old Western scenario the corporations and captains of industry are colonial powers, who rule from afar and do as they please with our copper and coal and timber.

There's no doubt that tourism is an alternative to a boom-and-bust natural resource economy. It creates a native constituency for protection. It is clean and creates a more stable economy. It creates an economic argument for natural and historical preservation. What people haven't looked at is whether we're trading in one kind of colonial status for another. Is the Rocky Mountain West becoming a great theme park for people from the East and the Pacific Coast? For much of the world? Real cowboys and Indians become marketing tools. Tourists don't always go home. They stay and buy a house. A ranchette. A ranch. A trout stream. Or a whole mountain.

What is at risk? There's a laundry list of things. Much of the West's distinctiveness could be lost in the so-called New West. Many of the small towns are places where people have not yet totally overpowered the landscape. The freedom to escape the crush of humanity is still available. The mountains—which so beautifully suggest possibility—are visible from town.

There is the cultural landscape as well. Jobs in the bed-and-breakfast economy are by and large low-paying jobs. "I don't want my daughter making beds for tourists for $3.50 an hour," said one rancher. There is something to be said for the size and makeup of most small to middle-sized western communities. They are diverse and intimate. The last few remnants of real democracy linger. People know their representatives, state and federal. In some Western states the population is small enough, far-flung enough, that politicians must make personal contact.

The West has been overly romanticized. It has problems. Real problems. But above all else, there is human scale here. There is more to the corridor of possibilities than the extremes. The West, unfortunately, has never been able to find the middle ground between wilderness and the wasteland of overcivilization.

The Meadow at the
Corner of Your Eye

C. L. Rawlins

I could tell you about a place, though it might be better for it to stay secret. If you wakened there, you would hear a light wind, brushing downslope like a hand on a bare shoulder. The wind moans through rocky fingers along the ridge, combs the grass, lifts the skirts of a grove, silvers the dark water of the lake.

Then it stops. In the calm, a bird calls, is answered, calls again. The stream treads a staircase of boulders. At the corner of your eye, a doe and fawn step into the meadow and lower their heads. Where?

There's a yearning that can be expressed as a place more simply than as a feeling: for beauty, rest, purity, transfiguration. It is easier to think of it as unknown. A knowing love is difficult, like a marriage that persists despite boredom, bitterness, and grief. It can be easier to see love's essence in the face of a stranger, passion in a body you've never touched.

It can be like this with the land. There is a strange resemblance between national parks and brothels: one pays to gain entry, to witness something set apart from daily life. There is likewise a correspondence between a love affair and a wilderness hike: the urge to move beyond accustomed bounds.

Most of us live in cities. Nature, as we define it, is where we go on vacation. Wilderness is what our lives are not: noble, quiet, unhurried. At home our immediate worlds are defined by exclusion. We are irritable beasts, and we wish to keep out the sales representatives, the nosy relatives, the stray dogs, the tomato hornworms, the dandelions, the starlings. We go backpacking to get away from the content of our lives, to forget what we've become. For most of us, wilderness excludes more than it contains. We love the wilderness and hate the neighbors.

Generalized loves can be deceptions. One might claim to teach out of a regard for the young while treating one's students with cruelty. The students become, with their awkwardness and failings, an impediment to the higher purpose of education.

A man with a grand, vague love for women might be unsatisfied by individuals. He might discard them almost without regret—one for her impatience when tired, one for the appendectomy scar on her otherwise perfect belly—as imperfect versions of his dream.

One might also claim to love the land—aaah Wilderness!—but treat most of it as a doormat, a factory, or just a boring drive.

Out on my fieldwork, measuring air pollution in a designated wilderness, I read trail registers. There are one-word reviews: Awesome, Unreal, Radical, Perfect, usually with exclamation points lined up to shove. There are also complaints. Those who commute complain about the lines of packhorses. Those who flew out bemoan contrails and sonic booms. Those who hug the main trails are angry because the main trails are crowded.

"We did not feel," read one note, "that we had a high-quality wilderness experience as we were led to expect from the information we received. The weather was bad and there were too many mosquitoes."

The irony is awesome, unreal, radical, perfect.

In June a year ago I went up with my partner, Jim, to scout the snowpack for a sampling trip. Our truck stalled at the trailhead. The campground was still snowed in. We postholed up the trail, looked around, and decided to chance it in a few days, with snowshoes. We left the truck and walked back, high above the valley on a road between melting drifts. After an hour we were passed by a silver van. The driver stopped and we asked for a ride to town. "I'm going to the campground," he said.

We told him that it was under a yard of snow. He turned around and we got in. His poodle snarled at Jim. "You could camp by the overlook," I said, thinking he could watch the sunset over a nine-mile, glacial lake and sleep in his van. He stopped, surveyed it from the pavement and pulled back onto the road. "Too open," he said.

He told us he was on vacation from his executive job in Connecticut, seeing the West for the first time. Jim, a native Coloradan, asked him where he'd been. He gave a litany of places: the Grand Canyon, Mesa Verde, Canyonlands, Flaming Gorge. Each was followed by a dismissal: too cold, got a speeding ticket, smelly toilets, too desolate. In the pauses, the poodle snarled.

"Where are you headed?"

"Jackson Hole, the Tetons, Yellowstone, Glacier: all the places worth seeing." At our backs, pines hid the Continental Divide, a rank of granite peaks above 13,000 feet. I suggested camping on the big lake, where a campground held spacious restrooms. He glanced down. "Probably too windy," he said.

He let us off in town two hours before dark, then drove away. He would end up, I thought, in Jackson Hole in a motel, watching the news. The best I could hope for was this: that he would return home feeling lucky not to live in any of the spots he had visited. He would never find a place to fit his vision, which narrowed the further it was pursued.

Contempt for what is close corrodes the heart; it can't be escaped. The vision of a perfect love is a remedy for lovelessness. The vision of a perfect landscape is a drug. Only having abandoned the physical world can we love "wilderness" more than any real place.

So, wilderness is about as far from life as we can make it. We'd rather it was over the horizon, so we can fight for it without kicking our bankers and our brokers and our bosses in the shins. So we won't have to alter our ways. So that we can lie to ourselves that, in spite of what we do, someplace, somewhere, is safe.

When I show slides of my back-country work to conservation groups in cities, their eagerness to embrace my life as an ideal makes me sad. It's work, not a crusade. I measure air pollution, year-round, in a remote range of mountains: a sad fact in itself. It's a place I've begun to know, an obligation that I owe. I don't like being made a fantasy.

I started thinking about this years ago, rereading one of my favorite books, *The*

Monkey Wrench Gang. Abbey made the villain a greedy, rural, Mormon bishop, based on Calvin Black, a man I had met in Blanding, Utah. The excitement took place in the remotest boondocks. What began to amaze me was that the conflict was so completely projected onto a rural landscape, onto a sparse population of Mormons and rednecks, when the problem of environmental rape had mostly, as far as I could see, to do with cities and their staggering wants.

In 1985 I talked to Abbey at Arches, where he was the guest of honor at a party for a tenth-anniversary edition of the book. It was dark. There was a fire. Ken and Jane Sleight were frying steaks in a huge, black pan. Stiles, the ranger, was flipping out over the jam of cars locked in the group-camp loop, snarling at Spurs, who had sent out the invitations. Spurs growled back, gesturing with a right hand that clutched a foaming beer, then with a left that gripped a plastic dinosaur.

I'm tall and lanky. I had a can of beer. In the dark, four or five persons stopped to ask if I was Ed Abbey. "No," I said. "I'm looking for him too." I found him in the shadow of a Triple-A Springbar tent, looking mournfully toward the fire.

I echoed his posture, talking about nothing for a while, then asked: "How come you didn't set the book in New York City? You hate New York. Why didn't they blow up the Chase Manhattan Bank? Or Washington. What about Congress? Go for the heart. Limping Jesus Christ!" There was a lot of free beer at the party. Ed had kidney stones, so he wasn't drinking. I didn't have kidney stones.

"Because the cities are dead."

I didn't know how to reply. I was a range rider then, in Wyoming. I'd been offered a Stegner Fellowship at Stanford. Abbey had been a Stegner Fellow years before.

"I'm going to Stanford next fall," I said. "Bright people, good conversation. No cows."

"May God have mercy on your soul," he said. "Don't forget to cut the deck."

Five years later I came to Arches to read his elegy. Wilderness is a strange word, like truth. I think too of Emily Dickinson. Hiking down a canyon in southern Utah with her collected poems, I read such gems as this:

Had I not seen the sun
I could have borne the shade;
But light a newer wilderness
My wilderness has made.

And this:

But when all space has been beheld
And all dominion shown,
The smallest human heart's extent
Reduces it to none.

What we've been fighting for isn't places, but our souls. Wilderness is a fragment, a green ghost at the edge of sight. The land itself is large and various, full of complications, hard to encompass with mere mind. When we set aside a wilderness, we draw a boundary in our thought, divorce it from the scrape of daily life. Only the most acculturated Indians can talk of "wilderness" with conviction. Mostly, they talk about their home places, the fields and nearby hills, the windy grass, the sacred lake from which real water can be dipped. Love is a tangle of sense and memory, hard to sort out, harder still to condense into a neat declarative sentence.

Wallace Stegner said it well: "The marriage of people to a place may be close and considerate, and it may be hardly more than sanctioned rape."

How is such a marriage made? It takes time, generations, and more than time. No one is married to a place who has not gotten a mouthful of food from it, picked or grown or hunted down. It is easy to buy and sell ground when you've never known its taste, singular and certain, never taken the hard brown nipple between your lips, rolled your tiny fists against the mountain breast, warmed to the flow of the earth's own milk, rough and rich. Nothing could be farther from the ideal. you eat from it. In the end, it eats you.

We've driven out our hearth-gods, chased the elementals from hedge and gate, purged our lives of modest spirits: a voice in the fire under the kettle, a shadow in the arch of the door, a breath in the grass. Like wilderness, our heaven is remote. Only the dead can travel so far. It is strange to us that the living realm touches the sacred one, that the fit is so close.

But wilderness is out of reach, a place we can't inhabit. Footsteps alone make it less than sacred, less than wild. So we strain to hold it separate, to border it with laws, to keep it clean and out of reach.

What to worship, now? Under the altars of old churches lie the bones of saints, locked in reliquaries, jeweled and dead. Held apart, they yearn for the soil's kiss, for saturation, for the soft release. They long for dissolution, for the dark return. And the stones of the cathedrals long to fall, to travel in a streambed, to wash up, sandy, on a shore.

I could tell you about a place, but you know it well. The telling will not penetrate its peace. You see the blue, blue mountains, or the sea of windy grass, or the breaking waves that curl along the black rock point. The earth turns, one, regardless, mixing its waters in the sea. There is no wilderness but in our minds. The undiscovered country is not wilderness, but a change of heart. Above, below, around, air circulates and water runs, the clouds rise up and shed their rain and snow. And, somewhere, lawless animals cross boundaries without a blink.

Suicide and the
Way of Eccentric Tourism

William Corcoran

O n a long, hot walk without enough water, when your head aches, your legs shake, and your mouth is as dry as the desert you're stumbling over, the Grand Canyon greets you with indifference.

This may panic and even anger you as much as it did me. Later, contemplated over a beer, such an experience reminds us of the limited biological importance of our personal dramas. It is exactly this kind of experience that tourism short-circuits. Because the tourist travels without risk, he remains within the usual dialectic of idealizing and demonizing the land: he sees the spectacular wonderland and the forbidding desert. As travelers in the West, we need instead the clairty to see how we, in our current cultural matrix, do not belong on the land as much as how we do. Tourism, because it is a desire industry, thwarts a liberation from self and labors (at minimum wage) to make us feel welcome, that we deserve a welcome, that our presence is important. The arid spaciousness of the Southwest should engender humility. Instead, the tourist ecology cages travelers in a round of self-representation, making it difficult for the visitor to move beyond tastes and desires derived from spending money. We carry our baggage out into the world covered with labels bearing our names. Refusing self-displacement, the tourist imagines acts of possession, of having "done," say, the Grand Canyon.

Sitting at Cape Royal, I lean into the coolness of the rock and watch the swallows slide across the canyon's depths. The depths are a presence, one that frees me, for a moment, of my self-presence. I am a part rather than apart. Having entered a ritual state of amnesiac communion, I am interrupted by fellow tourists, almost all of whom practice rituals of distancing and containment. I watch them block their view with cameras as they try to shrink the Grand Canyon into something that fits in one hand. Instead of opening themselves to the canyon's scale, the groups of visitors with whom I share this point accept a point of view that fits within the boundaries of light-sealed boxes. Fathers puzzle over f-stops, focus rings, and lens flare, or wonder how best to videotape the silent, unmoving canyon. Tourism delivers us to the tyrany of the view and the viewing self, all of a piece with our culture's disembodied visual bias. These amateur photographers, like many professional photographers and painters of the West, participate in a pornography of access. Although we tourists want access and are willing to pay money for it, how many of us are willing to invest the effort to earn it? Most of us are busy enough earning our access into America's managed society of industrial hierarchy and bureaucratic certification. We accept the desired image rather than the place itself so that we may imagine a tableau of innocence larger than the social order that consumes and discards us. Spectacle and vicarious self-importance creep into our relation to the land. A cult of ease washes out its beauty.

In the round of tourism, destination and occasion replace a more humane flux of experience. Each step down tourism's signed path leads us back to a culture of domination and submission. Tourism follows a path but never a way. I tell myself that a trip to the Grand Canyon requires a walk without a "scenic" destination. I want to forget that it is *I* walking, so that I can quit leading the moment around. How else can whatever the Southwest offers be gathered? I purposely remove myself and try to forget how I got here, what I am going back to, and the accumulated destruction being wrought by me and all the other visitors to this park. I shuttle between amnesia and complicity. I cannot find an uncluttered way.

Tourism takes us toward the land only to turn back upon itself. Etymologically, *tourism* implies a circle, a return. This is not, however, a mythic circle or return, but a series of destinations. The tourist isn't at any one spot; he is on his way to having been there. The promise of a fun trip and a safe return blunts the power of a journey to transform. Within the borders of the tourist circle there is no time for time, but only for schedules. The canyon glimpsed over a day or two does not reveal its chronology or its own comparable youth in the history of the earth. To earn a return we should spend time and not save it. Ideally, we would spend time on Nature's scale and not our own. We would be profligate, drunken tenants of time.

How do we open the circle of tourism to the land instead of letting it crush us all within the interstate-motel-restaurant chain, the corporate chains that bind the country more tightly each year? How do we uncenter the circle and the self to make tourism *eccentric*? How do we shift from an infatuation with ephemeral beauty—national parks as fireworks displays—to an absorption of place, the fitting together of humanity and land?

Our tourist rituals do not tell stories of place and relation but instead reshape and rewrite the land to fit our desires. They fail to confront us with our ambiguous relation to nature and cannot guide us to the strangeness that is the first step toward a familiarity tempered by respect. The ease of access at the heart of tourism fosters a disrespect for the land. We need rituals of travel that bring us into true intercourse with the land. Ritual should involve us in and guide us through life's endless interplay of connection and separation, comfort and threat. At Grand Canyon National Park, the visitor confronts not his personal presence at the canyon but a strange combination of Enlightenment science and Romantic ideality—uplift and erosion jockey with the romance of Bright Angel, Point Sublime, and the Divine Abyss. The names of the Grand Canyon viewpoints preserve nineteenth-century notions of transcendence, as though the great absence at the heart of the canyon were a niche from which mankind could evolve to the next sublime height. The words *royal, imperial, sublime* feed our anticipations and guide our responses. Lacking significant rituals of connection, we accept labels in place of a nonverbal, nonrepresentational knowing which, despite postmodern skepticism, remains the unsigned way to the land.

True love, true knowing require an acceptance of complicity in the inescapable wrongs of human existence. At each national park visitor center there should be a history of tourism at the park. Panels that illustrate our intrusion on the land—showing, for example, how much carbon is emitted by the average RV that lumbers along our park roads, or how we might reduce our urban use of electricity to preserve the air of the Grand Canyon—should have equal prominence with pictures of rattlers and warnings of rock falls. On the way to the north rim, the visitor crosses the marvelous Kaibab Plateau. The national forest has no signs to explain that our government is turning the Kaibab into a ponderosa tree farm for construction lumber. Nowhere are we pointedly confronted with the cost of our desires or asked to question their appropriateness. Tourism (and its incestuous sibling voyeurism) aggravates the problem European culture has always had in the West: an inability to love the West as it is.

Growing up in an age that has habitually confused limits with pessimism, the West with Tomorrowland, I often wonder if I will ever make or find a legitimate place in the land. I am not even sure what "legitimate" means beyond something intuited. "With regard to Nature," Thoreau wrote in "Walking," "I live a sort of border life." For me, border life is my only life. Wherever I look in the West I see borders on the land created by different human values and uses, a history of construction and destruction. Contrails, interstates, uranium, off-road vehicles, nuclear testing, nuclear disposal, Glen Canyon Dam. All my life I have been a tourist, moving from state to state, suburb to suburb. I am a liminal tourist-citizen of the modern West, aware and wary of borders.

Because I am among borders, my strongest memory of the Grand Canyon is of a scene not found in any guide. My best tourist photo of the Grand Canyon is of a suicide.

Point Imperial juts like a thrust stage out over an amphitheater of the Colorado, north of the river's great turn west. My friend and I stand here as tourists, brought by the vagaries of a haphazard trip, agenda improvised, return date to be determined by mutual spontaneous decision (when we are hungry and dirty enough). Why the Grand Canyon? We want something bigger than both of us, another point of view. I want to face east, the house of birth, and feel possibility again. I want to bend back the arrow of time. Like any other benighted tourist, and despite my intellectual misgivings, I bring my unspoken desires to the canyon.

The closed circles of suicide and tourism converge in the desire for escape from the perceived drudgeries of life without the difficult work of learning to know a place, a lover, a people. That desire for escape abstracts the land, creates questionable representations, and produces fetish objects that carry the aggressive strength of blunted human connection. The American dream is of a destination, a stopping place, a utopia. Place is not destination, however, nor is it a stage. It is neither ephemeral nor final, but it is process and flux. It is life and not representation. Tourism is nothing but representations created to fulfill desires created by representations.

My memory of the view at Point Imperial is of a death. The visual impact does not fade away; the dead man has a permanence in my mind that the ephemeral stunning of my senses by Imperial, Royal, and Sublime cannot match. I feel the destination, the end of the round where the suicide must have opted out. Here again, though, I am still a voyeur, without real connection, without a sense of the shared risk which holds human beings together. Here I feel only that sensation most galling to the tourist and the one he or she is most carefully guarded from—indifference.

It is early. My friend and I have come to Imperial to watch the sun rise and fill the canyon with presence. We want the sun to take away the night and our contemplative doubts. Give us the theater of the canyon. Give us a show. I want to take away a piece of its presence, a sublime emptiness within me.

People have gotten here before us. A Park Service cruiser sits, its engine creaking as it cools. I do not see the ranger. Next to the cruiser is a red Mazda RX-7 with Florida plates. The car's hood holds the night chill. We walk to the point, cool air from the plateau sinking past us and into the dim canyon, which will, in a few hours, send back a hot wind. The sun rises and Navajo Mountain moves from silhouette to gray roundedness. The sky shows desert colors: rose, ochre, charcoal. Vultures have gathered in the morning air. They tame gravity in a way that makes me envious and humbled. Leaving the official viewpoint, we snake our way through some cliffrose and scrub oak to a ledge adjacent to the fenced-in point. The rails oppress us with their reminder that we are prisoners of gravity. Courtesy of the Park Service, we have been shown our cage.

Scrambling over rocks, I stop at a knee bent up into the air like someone lying on his back reading a book. The knee is awkward, swinging out toward John Burroughs's Divine Abyss, a posture anyone's intuitive desire for self-preservation prohibits. The ranger appears from around a rock that screens all but the raised knee from sight. He motions us to leave the ledge, waving his hands as though to brush away flies. We leave and swing around to another ledge to see what the ranger has shooed us from. We forget the sunrise and the canyon in our curiosity to see what he does not want us to. We climb onto a point and look over at the ranger looking back at us. He doesn't hide his contempt. We are tourists at a show not listed in the Park Service newspaper given out at the gate. The body sprawls backward; the head arcs back along the end of the point. A red stain clotted with black has splashed down the white Kaibab limestone.

I take several pictures but have only my 50mm lens: the scene easily fits within my viewfinder, one small outcropping against a silent depth. Above the body and the ranger, a group of people have arrived and are looking out into the canyon. They take pictures, of course, all the time oblivious to the death a few yards beneath their feet. The new attraction of a scenically placed body distracts me from shopping the landscape for revelation or relief, leaving me to stare at this small corpse which was never meant to be found but to fall backward unnoticed into the abyss.

Instead of imagining uplift and erosion, I imagine a man driving to the rim in the dry night air of the plateau, coming to the end of the road and parking. Conifers and scrub screen the canyon from sight. Out on the bare rock he looks up into the arc of the Milky Way, down into darkness. He walks out to the ledge, stops, and turns his back on the canyon. Sitting down on the rock, he holds the gun and puts the barrel into his mouth. The steel is cold from the night. His mouth is dry. A shot erupts into the gorge, not reaching, probably, the Navajo Reservation on the other side. He falls back, but not as far as he intended; he has instinctively stayed just shy of the edge and does not, like a rock, fall in.

Was this for show or not? He is my show this morning. Having accepted the pretense of the idealized canyon, he has used the canyon as a stage for his own spectacular self-destruction. By doing so, the dead man rejected the canyon as simply and miraculously a place. He taught me that as long as tourism is about shows then visiting the canyon will always be about me and you. The suicide's ultimate tourist sideshow took me even farther from the canyon than I already was until, reaching aphelion, I began my return journey. I forgot geological time in that early morning scale of time, the short span in which the report of a gun dies away and a body turns cold. I remember that scene at the canyon with more intensity than any other. I still feel that place because I felt there how displaced we have become. I felt the sublimity of tourism, the overwhelming collision of attention and indifference.

Tourism is a shell game in which life's direction, purpose, and immediacy shift from one destination to another while our only real capital, our life, dwindles away in a blur of deceptive motion. The suicide at Point Imperial stopped his own swindler's hand and found the empty shell he was looking for. An empty canyon. Like that suicide, tourism leaves marks on the land that inscribe the true emptiness of the self that craves distraction and escape. Both empty life to create meanings and significances that only mirror desire. The tourist is essentially meaningless. He is a person without place—an apt product of our age.

In "Carmel Point," Robinson Jeffers praises "the extraordinary patience of things" and warns:

> We must uncenter our minds from ourselves;
> We must unhumanize our views a little, and become confident
> As the rock and ocean that we were made from.

Is it possible for me to find an origin story for myself in the landscape of the West? The asphalt path of tourism leads us over the land. We drive past, air conditioning, stereo, and cruise control on, a cold drink in the beverage rack. The land outside blurs by as we hurry to a destination. But the destination—any destination—is another part of the possession hallucination brought on by driving too long. If we indulge our eccentric impulses, we will find that our destination is ourselves in the land. By being critically conscious of our presence in the land, we open the way to unthinking ourselves.

Once we become eccentric, we may be able to walk an opened circle as Thoreau hoped to do: "The outline which would bound my walks would be, not a circle, but a parabola, or rather like one of those cometary orbits which have been thought to be non-returning curves, in this case opening westward, in which my house occupies the place of the sun." I will not return to the Grand Canyon until I am not looking for anything, even a view. Without hope of return, I will walk until I cannot see.

Communiqué from
the Vortex of Gravity Sports

Ellen Meloy

The morning sun, already burning an 80° day, tops a cliff cut with fine strata of red rock and broken at its foot by emerald cottonwoods and the startling bronze of a river. I don khaki uniform shirt, shorts, 97-cent hot pink thongs and, clipboard in hand, walk from the trailer to a boat ramp plunked down in nearly a million acres of uninhabited desert. This is an act of courage. Courage to face the violation of isolation rather than the isolation itself, for I savour the remoteness and the rare times I am alone on this muscular river in southern Utah, a precious ribbon of wild water between reservoirs and the suck holes of industry and agriculture.

Officially, I am here to have my peace disturbed. Floaters must have a permit to run this stretch of river. During the peak season a ranger checks lottery-drawn launch dates and a short list of gear related to safety and environmental protection. The permit system allows the federal agency in charge to hold numbers of floaters to a maximum of about ten thousand a year, set in 1979, when use increased 250 percent in just three seasons. Each year since, the actual number of people down the river has hovered close to this ceiling, which the agency believes is the river's carrying capacity for a "quality wilderness experience." Socially, if not physically, however, "wilderness experience" seems to have become an illusion if not irrelevant. Right now I am the volunteer ranger managing both the illusion and the irrelevance.

Most people accept the permit system as a panacea to the explosion in numbers of river runners and the consequences for a fragile riparian corridor. Others find regulation about as painless as an IRS audit. They see the Southwest as a region of federally neutered rivers, where a person is no longer free to kill himself in a four-foot rubber duckie pulling an inner tube piled with beans, testosterone, and a small machete. Instead, some geek rangerette at the put-in asks to see his bilge pump.

The boat ramp is swarming with people and vehicles to be shuttled to the take-out. Someone's dog is throwing up what appear to be rabbit parts. I am approached by a pickup driven by a man waving a spray nozzle and hose hooked to a large barrel of allegedly lethal chemicals. He's from county weed control, he says. Have I seen the loathsome pepperweed? Not a leaf, I lie.

Cheerfully I sign the permit of the outfitter who specializes in theme river trips—stress-management seminars, outings for crystal fondlers or fingernail technicians from

East Jesus, New Jersey, overcoming, at last, their irrational fear of Nature. Today's load is priests troubled by lapsed faith—pale, anxious, overweight fellows in the early stages of heatstroke. I also check gear and answer questions about bugs, snakes, scorpions, camps, rapids, and Indians (one side of the river is reservation land). Do I live here full time, they ask. No, I respond, except for an occasional shift at the put-in, I am on the river eight days out of sixteen, seven months a year. Would I please call their mother in Provo to tell her they forgot to turn off the oven? Am I afraid of being all alone when an axe murderer shows up? Did Ed Abbey live in that trailer over there?

Some rafts look as if they barely survived World War II. Others are outfitted with turbodynamic chrome-plated throw lines, heat-welded vinyl dry bags, cargo nets spun from the fibers of dew-fed arachnids from Borneo, horseshoes, volleyball sets, sauna tents, coffin-sized coolers stuffed with sushi, a small fleet of squirt boats, whining packs of androgynous progeny who prefer to be at home fulfilling their needs electronically. All of this gear is color coordinated with SPF 14 sunscreen and owned by business majors in styrofoam pith helmets and Lycra body gloves, in which they were placed at birth. Once loaded these boats are pieces of personal architecture, stunning but nevertheless stuck on the sandbar six feet out from the boat ramp after a dramatic send-off.

Two commercial boatmen with platinum-blond buzz haircuts, Arnold Schwarzenegger bodies, neon green bicycle shorts, matching tank tops, and day-glo pink, insect-shaped sunglasses with lenses as luminescent as an Alaskan oil spill stand beside their rafts, arms folded across entirely hairless pectorals. Neither speaks; all communication consists of barely perceptible bicep movements. (This Mute Surfer look is new. The boatmen of a previous generation looked like anorexic ferrets—beards, missing teeth, a dagger on the life vest, ear-shattering, maniacal laughs as they slipped down the tongues of the wildest rapids.) "Trade you this clipboard for your sunglasses," I sweetly offer one of the Arnolds. His right bicep pops in boredom.

When check-ins are completed, I trudge wearily to the trailer, passing a group still in sleeping bags inside a crumbling log cabin, the remains of a ranch built nearly a hundred years ago. The doorway is strewn with beer cans; empty vodka bottles are perched on the end of each hand-hewn log. Unless it's raining and rangers take pity, people are not supposed to camp in the cabin, so I reprimand them gently. "Good morning!" I say in my sunshiny ranger voice. "Sleep well? Did you check your scrotums for black widow spiders?"

At the trailer a radio dispatch alerts me to ten thousand gallons of diesel fuel, spilled yesterday in a tributary upriver and now headed my way. Also awaiting me is an extremely animated man whose shorts are unzipped. So absorbed is he in his mission, he neither notices nor cares that he is exposing his underwear (turquoise bikinis) to a federal agent.

He is from Germany and seeks the cactus, he says, a claret cup cactus. He pronounces it "cactoose" but speaks English well, with a charming mix of words. "I am engineer but botanical by hobby," he explains. His colleagues in Germany told him he would find claret cups in this area, but "These botany friends are so secret and convenient, so much pride, they do not tell me exactly where are the cactus." Right. Let's begin with the 400,000 acres on my left.

I explain that claret cup grow downriver and take him for a walk atop the mesas to admire the prickly pear cactoose. He worries about traveling on the reservation side of the river. "It is wonderful to talk to Indians?" he asks apprehensively. Yes indeed, I say. His fine blond hair stands on end, his eyes are as blue as the sky. How lovely to be lost in the American desert in search of a claret cup.

Day's end. I have sent today's recreational flotsam down the river. I have "applied the minimal bureaucratic constraints associated with rationing a scarce resource," as the manuals say, and I have melted into the greasewood, leaving everyone to float ranger free into his or her wilderness illusion. I have advanced German-American friendship, I have communicated with a bicep, and I have fended off a deadly assault by herbicides. Yet I am much too weenie to be a ranger. Soon it will require a different breed: rangers trained in negative campsite-encounter negotiation, field liposuction, and the delicate art of chaperoning tasteful social events in exotic outdoor backdrops. After a day like this, I long to buy the Uranium Motel two counties south of here. No one will come there, I shriek desperately to myself; its name is like a leper.

Coyotes throw their songs from rim to rim across the river, and the breeze carries the heavy scent of heat on greasewood and salt cedar. Lizards chew quietly on my melon plants. I stroll down to the boat ramp, hoping to watch the nighthawks that feed there at dusk. Instead I find a small party of floaters—tomorrow's permittees, an excellence-management seminar from Boulder, Colorado. These totally excellent people are standing in a circle, holding hands and wearing funny pointed hats. I won't ask to see their permit. I am sure they have one.

Some Thoughts on Humiliation

John Nichols

I have been a tourist in many places. I don't think that makes me a devil, or a careless person. I know one can travel with positive intentions, which don't necessarily lead to hell.

At the same time I know that tourism—proclaimed the largest industry in the world, and growing—is largely an indulgence of affluence. It rubs the noses of the poor majority in the reality of the unequal distribution of wealth on earth.

Let me explain.

For starters, I have the great good fortune to come from a family with tricultural roots: in America, France, and Spain. I was raised with an awareness of those roots going back for centuries, and with a respect for the languages, cultures, and histories involved. My mother, a French woman raised in Spain, died when I was only two, and I had no opportunity to discover my European roots until I was twenty. But in the summer of that year I visited my French grandmother in Barcelona. It was a fabulous learning time. I began to speak both Spanish and French, and I became a bullfighting aficionado. I attended the festival of San Fermín in Pamplona, became acquainted with the avant-garde architecture of Gaudi, and made a pilgrimage to the Goyas at the Prado Museum in Madrid.

A friend of my grandmother's gave me a copy of Garcia-Lorca's *Romancero Gitano*, and she whispered to me stories of the Spanish Civil War. I read several books about that conflict and moved through Spain very much aware that it was a dictatorship and the people had limited freedom. In Barcelona, the capital of Catalonia, it was forbidden to speak Catalan, and books and newspapers in that tongue were banned. The poverty in Spain dismayed me.

In her modest apartment, my grandmother had three servants: a cook, a chauffer, and a maid. I had never been waited on like that before, and was terribly uncomfortable. I hated riding in a chauffeur-driven car. I created flaps by making my own bed, shining my shoes, and fashioning my own sandwiches in the kitchen, much to the consternation of the maid and the cook. I loathed servant-master relationships. Though I was white and middle class, I did not enjoy exercising such obvious power over others. This was a gut reaction, as I had scant political sophistication at the time. But it helped lay the foundation for a class consciousness that eventually followed.

And as a tourist I became a very ambivalent human being.

After graduating from college, I returned to Europe and spent a year with my grandmother, working on a novel. I taught English to earn a living. On several occasions, I visited a girlfriend in Paris. And I *loved* Paris. It seemed like the most wonderful city on earth. Wherever I went, I always had a map and a dictionary in hand. Each morning I translated articles from the newspapers. I pressed myself to speak with strangers, ask questions, learn. I visited aunts and uncles and grew more familiar with my European roots. Out of a grand mishmash of language, history, personality, and impressions I was constructing another couple of souls to join with my American spirit.

I was not some kind of politically correct and sainted Yankee in a foreign land. But I felt that I operated far from the negative arrogance of an ugly American. I was eager to speak foreign languages and to immerse myself in a brand new culture and history. I was proud to honor the countries in which I lived. Increasingly, however, I clashed with my grandmother over servants, power, the privilege of class. Of course, I accepted her generosity and was grateful for it. But when we parted company I was tremendously grateful to escape from her world, where inequalities were so clearly defined and observed.

In the spring of 1964, about a year after I had returned from Spain to live in New York City, I took a bus to Guatemala. I visited a friend who was on a Fulbright Grant studying illiteracy. I approached Guatemala as an adventure and a lark, without ulterior motive or preconceived opinions. In effect, I was very much the tourist.

That experience *really* changed my life. Spain had been rich and free compared to this Central American country. I was unprepared for the poverty and brutality of Guatemalan society, though in the beginning, I'll admit, I was fascinated by the country's raw energy and colorful despair. Guatemala was a "quaint" and dangerous place, and very exotic.

Most especially it was a land of prostitutes—and I am speaking now of women, and of paid-for sex, the "real" thing. To a puritan of my limited sexual experience, the availability of these women had great allure. My power as a monied North American was pretty heady stuff. And for a moment, in my excitement, I ignored the type of embarrassment over class inequalities that had characterized my sojourn in Spain.

Near my friend's apartment was a street of whores. The women occupied narrow storefronts with Dutch doors. You could walk up and down the sidewalk assessing the goods. The price was fifty cents a pop. One night I cruised the street and found a woman I wanted. A six-word conversation struck our deal. I entered the cubicle and followed her around a thin partition. She was young and pretty, wearing a simple dress and no sandals. I took off my clothes and hung them on a peg, but the girl simply lay on her back on the cot, hiking up her dress. I felt foolish for shedding my outfit. I felt exposed and vulnerable and profoundly *naked*.

Failing to perform, I became excruciatingly embarrassed. And not just because I was impotent. Suddenly, I saw the situation for what it was—appalling. And humiliating beyond belief to both of us. So I gave up, and, making an attempt at reconciliation, I tried to kiss the girl. She turned her head away.

Thus ended my lust for whores in Guatemala. And so began a very conscious education that radically altered my future. Guatemala was a cesspool, and the United States, I soon realized, had made it so. The country was a whorehouse for the Anglo powers up north. The economy, the oligarchy, the dictators were controlled by Yankee corporations. I read Guatemala's Nobel laureate, Miguel Angel Asturias, whose epic work *El Señor Presidente* castigates United Fruit, which once controlled much of the country. I conversed with many indigenous people who hated my country. They told me about the CIA-led coup a decade earlier that had overthrown their democratically elected president. And the shame I had felt with that youthful prostitute was multiplied tenfold.

After Guatemala, I struggled to build a useful social conscience. And almost twenty years passed before I traveled south of the border again. In the meantime I had moved to Taos, New Mexico. It was common for my Taoseño friends and neighbors to vacation in Mexico, in towns like San Cristobal, San Blas, San Miguel. But after Spain and Guatemala, I could not see myself as a tourist in the Third World. I knew that the minute I crossed the border I would feel like a blond, blue-eyed agent of North American imperialism. To take leisure in countries where the human misery and class inequalities were so pronounced seemed to me like an act of depravity. Even without malicious motives, how could a person feel comfortable floating around in their affluent, protected bubble while the people attending their every whim were in dire need of food?

In 1983, however, I overcame my prejudices and traveled south again, this time to Nicaragua. I had political reasons. I wanted to learn first-hand about the Sandinista revolution, so that I could be a more credible voice against Reagan's policies in Nicaragua. Before leaving I read books about the country to give myself more background. Then I spent eight days touring with a group of twenty other North Americans. We spoke to finance ministers and liberation theologists, union organizers and nurses. I took notes, filling up two hundred notebook pages. I think we were ideal tourists because we had a purpose, and the conscious intent *not* to exploit Nicaragua.

When I returned to New Mexico I wrote a long article for the *Albuquerque Journal*'s Sunday magazine explaining my favorable take on the Sandinista revolution. In following years I gave dozens of interviews and speeches on behalf of Nicaragua. In the end this did not stop the United States from destroying the revolution. But the effort made to halt the injustice was important. And what I learned in Nicaragua still informs the politics of my existence and is useful in other struggles.

My final "tourist" adventure (to date) occurred in 1987. That year my wife and I spent two months in Europe. Juanita is half Dutch, so we began in Amsterdam. Given the wealth of Holland, my conscience did not feel totally remiss—though I still felt like something of a cultural imperialist because I could not speak the language. We got a sense of the country, demanded very little service, and spent every minute learning. In France we hit all the museums and I babbled and chatted to my Gaulic heart's content, relearning French. We traveled out to Giverney and bicycled to the home of Monet. We paid homage at the grave of my great grandfather, Anatole le Braz, ate oysters in Cancale, chewed carrots at Mont St. Michele, and scarfed sandwiches on a cliff overlooking the ocean at Chateaubriand's tomb on the Grand Be at St. Malo. Heading south to visit relatives in Spain, we stopped at Ouradour-sur-Glane and walked through the burned-out town that the Nazis destroyed in reprisal for underground activity during the war. It isn't a tourist attraction, advertised with billboards and refreshment stands. And there's almost no comment within the empty village; just a few plaques commemorate where most of the people were herded together and shot.

Europe is an education, and I guess that always saves the day. In the end, though, I was glad to return home. I was tired of trying to be a responsible tourist, which can often seem like an oxymoron. Somehow, the fact that I was rich enough to be travelling thousands of miles from home among people who could not travel at all always muted the fun.

Given my attitudes about tourism, it is probably odd that I have chosen to live in a village which survives by being a major Southwest tourist destination. I moved to Taos in 1969 and I like it here; I plan to stay for good. We have scenic mountains, pretty mesas, and the dramatic Rio Grande Gorge. People can hunt and fish and camp, visit museums, buy paintings in some seventy art galleries, stay in a like number of B&Bs, or in more upscale hotels and Swiss-style chalets. They can ski in winter at several topnotch areas and visit Taos Pueblo, whose main dwellings are advertised as the oldest continuously inhabited buildings in the United States. Taos brags that it is a tri-cultural community where the three main ethnic groups exist in harmony. Sixty-five percent of the population is Spanish speaking, 30 percent is Anglo, and the rest is Native American.

Sounds interesting, and it is. There's one problem however: after decades as a tourist mecca, Taos is still poor. Put bluntly, it is a picturesque rural ghetto. Despite ski areas, galleries, and national forests, our socioeconomic stats are alarming. Official unemployment often rises above 20 percent. Underemployment, much of it close to minimum wage, is a fact for most of the work force. Many workers are "unskilled" and non-unionized and are prone to layoffs depending on visitor volume and spending habits. The glamour of Taos is supported by an army of workers earning limited wages for scrubbing toilets, washing dishes, and changing bedsheets.

Tourism, a seasonal, service, and menial industry in this area, has always promoted a poverty culture. And we have all the attendant problems that go with that culture: alcoholism, burglary, battered wives and children, poor health care, broken families, instability within the community. Many of our resentments and tensions relate to race problems, since the class differences—and there are great discrepancies in wealth here—break down principally along ethnic lines. The middle-class, largely Anglo minority controls most of the wealth; the Chicano majority is poor; the Indian people suffer most.

Nevertheless, a community long existed here. If it was not always harmonious, that community *was* a vital, coherent, and self-sufficient organism existing more or less in balance with the surrounding landscape and with the resources—the biological capital—of the valley. That balance is going by the boards today. Like most everywhere else in the world, Taos is caught in an upheaval from which it is unlikely to recover. Growth and development, largely around the tourism and recreation industries, are disenfranchising long-time locals and forging instability in the educational, agricultural, economic, environmental, political, and civic arenas. All that was once solid is melting into air.

The community, increasingly fractured, is undergoing a radical transformation. The health of its land base and its cultures, which were once integral and consistent, is evaporating. Our beauty has a new look, one more akin to that of a hooker making herself attractive to transients and outsiders who could care less about our personality, our body and soul, our history and aspirations. And whatever their intentions, tourists visit this country much as I entered Spain or Guatemala years ago. From the start it is not going to be an egalitarian exchange.

Immediately, the relationship of tourist to local folk is skewed. At worst it can be racist; at best simply patronizing. The class gap is wide. The Taos working class is closer to the Third World than to the first. Tourists have "power"; that it, they have money to spend. Unfortunately, most of them do not have a social conscience; they are not interested in the reality of our situation. Nor are they in search of education or insight or enlightenment. They simply want to be amused.

My dictionary defines *tourist* as "a person who travels, especially for pleasure." I'd amplify the definition to include anyone, approaching or living in a place, who remains uncommitted to that area's history, culture, environment, and social ethos. Of course, there isn't much "pleasure" to be derived from such a commitment. In our culture pleasure is usually translated as the search for entertainment, and entertainment is most often achieved through consumption. So the tourist is encouraged not to participate but to consume. Most importantly, tourists expect to be pampered, waited on, and deceived all in the name of comfort and convenience. That's what the money they spend is all about.

To make it palatable to visitors, our living culture in Taos is embalmed, sanitized, and presented much like a diorama in a museum: picturesque and safe. Tourists would rather not know that in many respects life here approximates the way four-fifths of the globe survives. In our town, a small proportion of the population controls a large amount of the wealth. In fact, all of New Mexico, a self-appointed "tourist haven," is much like a colonial country where a limited coterie of powerful outsiders, hand in hand with local big shots, controls the economy.

Unfortunately, then, the relationship between the town of Taos and the tourists who support it has all the egregious class and cultural conflicts that disturbed me in Spain and Guatemala. It is as if both sides of the human interaction have been programmed to create a humiliation similar to the one suffered by me and the young prostitute in Guatemala City. Of course, nobody defines the relationship in those terms. An effort is made by Taos business people and the chamber of commerce to paint a rosy picture and assure that the visitor's boat is not rocked.

By and large, however, the working people of Taos understand their humiliation and resent it. But they keep a low profile because, even if the work is demeaning, it is needed. And tourists rarely experience overt humiliation, either because they are oblivious or because they have been trained to accept the inequalities engendered by the class nature of our economic system. Visitors are rarely ashamed of their passively racist attitudes; for the most part, they probably don't even know that they exist.

Taos is New Mexico. It is the West. It is the United States: a typical American town. This means that much of the business and development community accepts the principle that growth for the sake of growth is *good*. They know resources aren't infinite, but they pretend resources *are* infinite, because that's what made America great. It's what profit is based on. You can't get rich without exploiting biological capital—lots of biological capital.

So Taos developers are planning to build a huge golf course/shopping center/condominium project called Las Sierras. Three-quarters of the town dislikes the project. But laws are stacked on the side of developers. Citizens need incredible time, energy, money and dedication to even slow down the process.

The powers that be also wish to expand the Taos airport so it can accommodate big jets. To bring in more tourists. To make Taos easily accessible. To put more pressure on our overcrowded valley. The pueblo is against the airport. Almost every social, environmental, and cultural group in town is protesting the airport. Yet the small band of local carnivores who stand to make a killing in their hotels and ski brothels are proceeding, undaunted, with their plans.

Taos Ski Valley is always in an expansion mode. Residents of the Valdez valley eight miles below are always fighting that expansion. It fouls their water, threatens their land, drives real estate prices out of sight, and leads to more condominium and hotel development. This ultimately disenfranchises the indigenous community, causing alienation, class tensions, general misery . . . you name it.

Locals can rarely buy land in Taos these days. New Yorkers and Californians, who initially arrived as tourists, consider thirty thousand an acre chicken feed. They sell a three-room cottage in Santa Monica and with the proceeds land a fifteen-room adobe mansion in Taos. Local property taxes are rising disproportionately.

Taxation is a thorny problem because we don't have graduated tax laws. Many poor people in Taos still have land because it has been in their family for generations. But they don't have money; they have low-paying jobs or are unemployed. If their property is taxed according to tourism and development values, they wind up selling portions of the land to pay the taxes until, ultimately, the land is gone. Assessing land at its development value guarantees that the indigenous population will eventually be eradicated.

We lure countless people to Taos but do not have a tax base capable of providing the services to which they are accustomed. Nor do we have the means to protect our existing resources from the onslaught. The tax burden is too heavy on the poor, while the rich get away with murder. And Taos flounders in traffic jams, sewage problems, inadequate fire protection, water scarcity, and so forth.

Middle-class newcomers would like to zone out trailers, the only housing affordable to the poor. Land zoned into five-acre parcels might look nice, but again it would box out the poor. Ironically, in Taos it is the poor who have traditionally cared for the land and maintained a balance on it. The newly immigrant rich are often unskilled in how to effect this harmonious relationship, and most of them could care less. They relate to the land as commodity and not as part of their emotional or spiritual being.

Over the past twenty-three years I have watched the pattern of retail sales in Taos change enormously. When I arrived here in 1969, the plaza was for locals. It had a few bars, a restaurant, the courthouse and jail, the police department, a department store, a hotel, a theater, a drugstore and soda fountain, a gas station. It was the heart of the community's shopping and socializing.

Nowadays, most stores on the plaza sell trinkets, jewelry, pottery, T-shirts, Indian gee-gaws, and other downscale or upscale tourist-oriented foofraw. Long gone is the courthouse, jail, police headquarters. Taoseños shop south of town at Wal-Mart, Smith's and Furr's. The rest of the city seems to have been deeded over to B&Bs and art galleries. The sense of community, place, and social cohesion fostered by the old plaza departed long ago.

When a town's principal occupation is pandering to monied outsiders waddling through in their Winnebagos, it loses a sense of identity, a sense of pride. Residents become the caretakers of a remembered history instead of a living history. They forget their own origins except as a watered-down commodity salable to the highest bidder, who promptly removes it to an alien environment thousands of miles away.

Where commerce and social interaction take place solely with transients, culture and responsibility die. The town itself adopts a transient soul. Everybody is scrambling for dollars from strangers instead of from each other. That changes the social contract. It eliminates respect, accountability, mutual responsibility. Merchants who wouldn't gouge their next-door neighbor will gladly join with that neighbor to gouge a stranger. Climax tourist exploitation leads to profit as the sole motivation for work.

It will take a radical shift in our national priorities to change these attitudes and interactions. Our economic culture is predicated on bland and careless consumption of both natural and human resources. Culture, community, history, language, and national parks and forests are all defined as expendable resources. Average tourists consume our Taos attractions with the same lack of feeling they have when consuming Big Macs,

Toyotas, fossil fuels, and fascist architecture. This insensitivity, magnified a thousand-fold, lies at the heart of every threat to our planet today.

A change in attitude can only begin with education; so starts any revolution. I know that my travels seriously shaped my life and my politics and all the books that followed. My eyes were opened, and my sympathies with other people and communities and cultures were powerfully focused and reinforced by those trips around the United States, Europe, and Central America. I learned to exalt in our universal connections. The tourist experience can be rich with possibilities. It is up to travelers and to the host communities alike, however, to realize those dreams.

To this end I constantly urge Taos visitors to understand the real situation. I preach that Taos, though small, is infinity in a grain of sand, no different at heart from New York, Chicago, Los Angeles . . . or Timbuktu. I tell visitors it is a crime to dehumanize this place; I suggest to my neighbors that it is a crime to dehumanize ourselves.

In August each year I help teach a photography workshop in Taos. Ostensibly, the twenty or so participants wish only to photograph the northern New Mexico landscapes. But I always begin with an overall view of Taos. I speak of our community, the economic situation and disparities, our problems and our struggles. I detail our building environmental tragedies. I caution the shutterbugs not to eat fish caught in our lovely rivers because they are full of mercury. I describe racial tensions, poverty statistics, the high crime rate. I talk about local groups striving for economic, social, and environmental justice.

I describe the acequia system that waters the valley, and I elucidate specific land and water struggles around issues of development, water pollution, and resource mismanagement. Because the pueblo is a main attraction for photographers, I pull no punches as I describe the appalling conditions out there. I also talk about our history. I suggest books, pamphlets, and other studies people can read in order to be well informed. I suggest civic, environmental, and human rights organizations to which visitors can contribute money. I explain that these organizations are determined to defend the natural and human resources that draw visitors here in the first place.

All during the workshop I talk about the reality and the vitality of my home town. It is the only way I know that workshop participants can take a valid landscape picture.

Bottom line: Taos is no place to escape to; no tourist destination ever is. Taos is real, alive, tragic, confused, beautiful, and floundering, just like the rest of the world. I hope to send photographers home full of information, contradiction, inspiration. My goal is that for them Taos should be their Guatemalan adventure, a challenge, an education.

In my book, that is the ideal way modern tourism should work. Not as an act of prostitution, but rather as a preamble to understanding, compassion and commitment.

Which might even evolve into love.

Swiss Wilderness

Reg Saner

In the United States there are more places
where nobody is than where somebody is.
That is what makes America what it is.
　　　　　　　—Gertrude Stein

Could a humble couple from an erstwhile mining town in the American West find happiness as guests at Villa Serbelloni? Anne and I believed we could.

Not least of what we quickly relished there were the little all-but-invisible touches; the adroit half turn of wrist, for example, with which—as they refilled our wine glasses—uniformed waiters named Sergio, Natale, Giovanni, and Vittorio kept even one droplet from the table's immaculate linens. But within such an opulent villa's sixty-acre dream of formal and informal gardens, long dinners, witty talk, Renaissance decor, any Coloradan's self-image might begin to blur.

Ours certainly did. Anne and I had flown to Italy from a home in Boulder where midnight was often sounded by coyotes, and where letters to the editor debated how to deal with the occasional mountain lion. What were we doing eating *filetto di salmerno al vino bianco* from multi-fork place settings? What were we doing eating *cavolfiori Mournay* or *coppa Romanoff*?

For that matter, what was my neck doing inside a tie? Dressing for dinner began to come naturally. Down marble stairs to the villa's spacious dining rooms, we descended for evening meals whose gourmet dishes never repeated, making each its own souvenir: *faraona al forno, zuccotto alla fiorentina, pappardelle alla carmagnola, filetto di nasello in salsa bianca*—and on and on. "Toto," I said to myself, "I don't think this is Colorado."

I had come to Italy to finish a manuscript about the quality of a few special places on earth as it now is but soon will not be, and *forever*, and about my reasons for being anywhere. In particular, out tall windows high over Lake Como—as a guest of the Rockefeller Foundation—I had meant to look at the size of life in the American West from its antipodes. Later, in Switzerland, I would see if I dare face Colorado's future. As the populous pre-Alpine terrain around Como now is, as the Swiss Alps now are, so our Rockies must become. A tomorrow sure as copulation, certain as money.

American Westerners of a hundred years hence will *read* about American space and nature as it once was—in our day, now—but will have no way really to miss what they'll be missing. Instead, they will temper nostalgia for what their own numbers will have long since trampled out of existence by preferring its remnants. The only world they'll be able to know and love firsthand will be whatever half inch they inherit. Compared to them, we live in a blessed hour.

Up till the twentieth century, nature had two lives, tame and wild. Now that its wild possibility has already sidled off into those highly artificial enclaves called "wilderness areas," nature untamed is forever exiled—unless we humans receive some setback such as "the great dying," in which, sixty-five million years ago, "something" wiped out 95 percent of life on earth. Otherwise, tame nature is the only foreseeable future.

The result may well be a sort of housebroken Utopia: its creatures genetically engineered, its flora hybridized, its ocean floors farmed, its air and sea currents harnessed, its virulent bacteria rehabilitated—all of which may pour into posterity's lap every conceivable advantage. When science has laundered our eventual bloodstreams beyond recognition, those rearranged psyches will, however bizarre *we* may consider them, consider themselves improvements.

Vistas glimpsed through an Italian promontory's araucaria trees, olive groves, palms, and palmettos soon revealed exactly how much Colorado had changed me. The smooth, young Fulbright student of the Sixties who once imagined he would enjoy living in Europe indefinitely—especially Italy—was now himself a souvenir. To recall his culture-vulturing, his cathedral-bagging, his devoted poring over tomb sculptures and lapidary inscriptions beneath pigeon-bedabbled statues made my smile wince. A much-crinkled devotee of high-country forests, canyon sand, adobe roads, and invisible air had long since replaced him. As for Europe's antiquities, no one can live amid the West's daily, inescapable enactments of geological time and consider an Etruscan wall or a Gothic cathedral *old*. By stone time, ancients are modern. All human past is now. Not only that. The charms of high art had waned the more I looked into nature. It has been said that our wilderness areas are America's cathedrals. For me, yes—only more truthful. In them, the greatest story that can never be told—and barely imagined—is the ongoing story called nature.

So while life in the West's widest-open spaces ended my callow genuflections before "culture," I found that it also made me mindful of the powerful fragilities we so loosely call *life*, thus much easier to appall.

As when Alain Blayac laughed. We'd been talking about Chamonix—a French mountain town I cannot stand but he adores. Though a literary scholar, Blayac goes in for macho stuff. He hunts, he climbs. The casually unbuttoned upper half of his shirt offers glimpses of a tanned, hairy chest set off by gold chain and medallion. Apropos of Chamonix's namesake animal, I asked, "Are many chamois left in the mountains around there?"

For the benefit of my regret, he laughed maliciously. "Ah, no! None. We have shot them." I asked about bears. He laughed again. "We killed them too, long ago." Insofar as his laughter expressed a low tolerance for American sentimentality, it seemed understandable. I too cringe from people who wear save-the-whales pieties like halos. Yet his cynicism struck me as very French. When it came to the extermination of bears, Blayac's only chagrin was that France had none left for him to shoot.

In Switzerland, the last bear was shot on September 1, 1904. I went there. Not to some blood-tainted handsbreadth of alp; on leaving Italy, Anne and I went instead to visit the Parc Naziunal, within whose present confines—but before it became the wildlife sanctuary it is today—that last bear was colonized by bullets.

The Parc Naziunal, as it's called in Romansch, was inspired by, but explicitly *not* modeled on, our American example. Sixty-five square miles may seem dinky compared to Yellowstone's nearly thirty-five hundred, yet considering that our national parks add up to only a bit more than half of one percent of our land, those sixty-five square miles make the Parc Naziunal proportionately comparable: a half percent of all Switzerland. Not bad. What did it matter that the Swiss have only one, or that its terrain is not state owned but *leased*? By the time they got round to it—a mere decade after the ultimate bear was blown away—that's how it had to be: rented or nothing. Which is how it still is, every square meter leased, long range, through public and private funding.

So upwards I find myself hiking, along a trail called the Höhenweg, happy in a rain of late May, a fine, all-morning rain that sizzles on my parka hood as I head higher in the Val Trupchunn. Maybe to see a chamois, who can say? Maybe even a steinbock, also known as the ibex, whose long, curving horns make it unmistakable. But, of course, never a bear.

Villa Serbelloni's own imitation "forest" was a civilized joy to stroll within. Often I walked for two hours there, uphill and down, under a dithering canopy of May's greenest leaves and the mewing of gulls, not once retracing my steps along its quiet paths—wide, easy, cone strewn. The forest effect, so casually manicured, seemed almost natural. Great beech trunks rose ninety feet without effort, each bole a smooth yet muscular rectitude, bearing branches that floated forth their foliage as if weightlessly, like green levitations. The umbrella pines rose just as high, maybe higher; yet on the ground underneath, there was no scruff of dead twigs such as litter our woodlands of ponderosa pine back home. No windfallen trees. No rotting logs. No shattered branches. Each turn of the path set off a grove brushed onto canvas as if by the French painter Corot. Even the romantic grottos and caverns, man-made, welcomed me into plausible rusticities.

Where not one tree marred the graceful verticalities of that forest with birth defects or hints of mortality, and where every massive trunk, every beech sapling grew exemplarily, my admiration deferred facing the question, "Without death how can a forest live?" Which is as much as to ask, "When is a forest a garden?"

"So what if it isn't 'natural'?" I scolded myself. "Would you have one twig of it otherwise?"

That final Swiss bear has come to live in my head, emerging from his mind cave whenever I notice, in the Bernese Oberland for example, a hotel boasting a handsomely savage black bear on its scutcheon. In the lake town of Thun, ursine images sanction every other hotel. Praising what's lost makes the remembrance even dearer, so the Swiss now pay homage to shot wildlife with pelts, antlered heads, bear simulacrums hung above ski shops, inside or outside any tavern—just as within or without town halls I find sheet metal bears in brass glaring down at me, frescoed bears, bears sculpted of granite. Fronting the Bären Restaurant at Trubschachen, for instance. From dozens of windowsill boxes, red geraniums cascade right and left, while—over the door—a life-sized bear welcomes me with jaws carved into more than a hint of a smile.

"In the Upper or Lower Engadine," I ask myself, "is there a single Swiss village without its teddy?" I have not visited all of them; possibly there is one. Two is not possible.

Certainly Switzerland's capital, Berne—whose very name refers to the creatures—has not for a moment lost sight of them. Not only do its civic buildings fly heraldic bears on the canton's official flags. Not only do its various scutcheons repeat the animal ubiquitously. Berne's loftiest fountain rises from a base circled by marching bears. Armed with muskets, dressed in Renaissance garb of days when such animals shared the environment with that town's first inhabitants and defenders, they hint that ursine courage comes with the territory.

Naturally enough, Berne's souvenir shops offer bears in every manner of craft: whittled, cast, welded, embroidered, enameled, watercolored, incised, sculpted, or stuffed. As further reminder of its most gloriously bygone animal, the city maintains a *bärengraben* where young and old can enjoy live examples of their town's totemic creature. And for enticing antics from this large open-air bear pit—stocked with *Ursus arctos* as it happens—people can buy a small, bear-healthful cornucopia of *barfuten*. On days I tossed them down to a half-dozen comically posturing bears, *barfuten* was carrots.

The happy hunting grounds of the European few—it was indeed their elitism that our American parks democratized. So even if Villa Serbelloni's well-behaved forest were but a vestige of earlier, wilder, more disheveled demesnes reserved to the king's pleasure in boar spearing, those aristocratic holdings had nonetheless shown the way. During each week of my stay there on the villa's peninsula, I marveled that someone in the Rockefeller Foundation had had the rare imagination to insist the villa's extensive grounds be clipped and tended in the authentic style of such pleasure gardens. Their "wild civility" made visible for me their historical origins: forested deer parks of medieval kings, queens, barons, and dukes—where my paternal ancestors might have been man-trapped for trespassing.

"Up to now," nineteenth-century Americans said to themselves, "game preserves have always been a monopoly of blue bloods. Why not extend that privilege to everyone? Besides, game is getting scarcer." Hence Yellowstone. Only when nature and humans have fallen apart does "nature" as such become visible. But once nature is "other," we can no longer sense that in felling trees six centuries old we are chopping down our own grandfathers, and setting an ambush for ourselves.

Across a broad river valley from the curiously named Swiss town of S-Chanf, I leave my rental car at the mandatory spot and, through forest half tame, half wild, leg it uptrail toward the border of the Parc Naziunal. Amid all its conifers I do not at once notice tameness. Instead, I splash along, amused by day-glo avalanche warnings in four languages, thankful for good rain gear and boots recently siliconed. Pleased with the weather difference between moist Europe and the aridity of our American West, I am finding the omni-wetness fascinating.

The ecology here is so new to me that my glances through rainy mist seem half to create what they dwell on. Larch trees grow in North America, but not near my home, so to walk at last among thousands of them is an occasion. No other conifer is deciduous, nor would even larches be had they been native to mountain soils, where meager nutrients make growing a fresh set of needles every year expensive. Like remnants of a losing tribe, they were once trees of the plains, till competition from other species forced them higher and higher, and finally into mountains. Their green needles, markedly lighter in hue than the green-blue of other conifers, turn color in fall to an ambered gold, but my May ascent takes me past larches whose needles, looking like asterisks, have only begun to leaf out.

Up close, mosses of a lush and emerald wetness make the drenched mountainside feel buxom, upholstered. Yellow-green mosses billow near the roots of fir and foot the thick boles of larches in ways I have not walked among before; nor have I ever seen lichen completely cover living boughs. A ghostly silver, this species hangs like hoarfrost on larch limbs, setting off their rain-blackened bark with its pale encrustings. Only after an uphill half hour of ambling and pausing, however, do I notice what isn't anywhere.

Not a single dead tree on the ground. None, nor trees half toppled. No standing dead. My years in American wilderness forests, where each day is ancient, make this feel *very* strange.

Then the instant I step from private land into the Parc Naziunal, the trail loses its vehicular character. Its mud is now laced with larch needles the color of rust, and like friends from home, fallen trees immediately appear. For number and size they cannot equal the wind-fallen timber in, say, the Indian Peaks wilderness of Colorado, because—given its beginning in 1914—the Parc Naziunal is not yet a hundred years old. Prior to 1914 every dead tree here became "useful" the moment it hit the ground.

Back in Colorado's gold rush days, many a mine swallowed whole forests. Even today more than one stump-stubbled mountainside recalls a West when the big idea was to "get and get out." Though such greed now euphemizes itself by speaking of "an extractive economy," the West, like the world, still includes men eager to kill beautiful animals they are seeing alive for the first time and to fell Douglas fir older than Milan's cathedral.

As for Europe, my Mozartian associations may flow into and out of the name "Salzburg," but in my great-grandfather's time, much Swiss forestation had flowed with the Inn River clean out of Switzerland—for timbering salt mines of the Tyrol. Thus from its inception the Parc Naziunal lacked old growth because its trees of longest standing had already been literally sold down the river. Which helps explain why none of the fallen trees I come across is either very big or beautifully rotten.

Nonetheless, I bless every mouldering trunk for returning its nutrients to living trees. I now feel myself at home in almost a forest. At the same time I smile to think how uneasy these same decaying trunks must make Swiss visitors to the Parc Naziunal. In this nation of carpenters, carvers, cabinetmakers, woodworkers, and of woodburning stoves, any fallen tree allowed to rot, just rot, must look wasteful, sinfully so.

"What do I see here in five hundred years?" Alice Goldstein repeated, as if trying to *will* her eyebeams through Lake Como's agreeable evening haze and beyond, into the mists of futurity. Not only was Alice one of the most radiantly friendly persons we relished being among at the villa, she was also highly qualified to hazard an answer.

We two shared a teak bench overlooking the lake, where sun—the same sun, glinting off those same wind-warps on the waters—had once attracted ancient Greeks and Romans to this incomparable setting. Panoramas that long ago dictated the siting and layout of summer homes built by the wealthier subjects of such emperors as Nerva and Trajan had survived, even though the villas themselves had sunk back into the earth. Two thousand years have left Lake Como's mountain profiles unchanged, despite shorelines that have since filled with vacation hotels and palatial second homes for Italy's affluent few, who are many.

Alice and I felt our evening complicated by the realization that both Plinys, Elder and Younger, uncle and nephew, had once known by heart the lake's same twilight reflections, the same forested mountainsides rising steeply above us. Not only had those Roman celebrities been born in Como—little more than two hours south by lake boat—but Pliny the Younger had built and occupied a pleasure villa on precisely the site where Villa Serbelloni now stands. Our evening twilight there was both ancient and modern, which is to say contemporaneous, because its ancients and moderns were us.

In fact, earlier that afternoon I strolled for hours reimagining Lake Como exactly as those imperial Romans had seen it. The problem proved easy as subtraction. Take away almost all buildings crowding the shoreline. Erase the highest farmhouses, those light flecks of stonework set off by green mountainsides. Take the twelve-foot-tall but almost invisible cross off a subpeak of Monte Tremezzo, opposite. Let weeds overrun the auto routes. Fill in the train tunnels. Diminish both the speed of the lake boats and their numbers. Think sails. Behold! Lake Como again perfectly Roman—or so I imagined.

My next trick came up against the limits of possibility: How would these same shores, their villages, their forested mountainsides look two thousand years in the future?

That stumped me. Peering backward, we have some idea. After all, Roman history is massively documented. But the future two thousand years hence? Any guess would be sci-fi. So I scaled my wondering down to five hundred. Equally impossible, of course. Star Trek stuff. Nonetheless, because Alice and her husband Sidney are professional demographers, distinguished ones from Brown University, with international reputations in population studies, I thought, "Why not at least *ask* them?" Isn't one aim of demography to guess how many may be coming to dinner?

So I posed that question to Alice. "What do I see?" she repeated. "Either a lot more or a lot less."

Epigrammatically shrewd, that. Five centuries down the road, technology will either have permitted global growth, Lake Como included, or the whole thing will have crashed. I then asked Sidney, "What do you think? What's the prospect? Is Paul Ehrlich's 'population bomb' real?"

After all, however humble one might feel, the drinks in our hands, the villa, its gardens and sixty-acre grounds, and its palatial decor were made available by the Rockefeller Foundation for the posing of just such questions.

Given Sidney's background, I was thus turning to somebody who should know. Not only are the Goldsteins demographers, they have spent decades studying trends in Asia, especially in China, whose 250,000,000 *unemployed* equal the entire U.S. population. A friendly, quiet man who never dramatizes, Sidney said, "I looked at the updates of the evidence not long ago. I'm afraid I have to come down on the 'real' side. The numbers may be worse than we thought." He did not elaborate, nor did he need to—beyond adding, "You know, in China, 'one percent growth' means ten million more people."

That little throwaway fact haunted me for days. As if the fuse on the population bomb was already shorter than the skin of our teeth is thin. But we hear such warnings, then shrug. We let catastrophe happen. Only when it happens does catastrophe get our attention.

Unsurprisingly, after Europe's he-men pumped slugs into the last steinbock alive in Switzerand, that country took thought. "What's to be said," the national Swiss conscience began asking itself, "of a people who permit the *extermination* of their own national animals?" The steinbock, at least, was "reintroduced."

Indeed, it was. My binoculars pick out, in an alpine meadow opposite me on the rainy Höhenweg trail, and across a roaring stream milky with glacial silt, no fewer than thirty-one steinbocks! Some hundred meters up-slope from me, they nibble away at alpine turf, sharing their May meadow with several chamois. A closer view would be nice, except that in the Parc Naziunal to leave the trail *ist streng verboten*, and when it comes to insisting that a rule is a rule, the Swiss do not mess around. The park's "rangers"—and I was chatting with one just minutes ago in Italian—can fine you on the spot. Frequent reminders in German and Romansch say: Verlassen des weges ist verboten / Id es scumanda da bandunar la senda. "Leaving the trail is forbidden."

Forbidden? To an American that admonition at first seemed quaintly absurd—as if the Swiss, imitating Yellowstone, had bungled and lost an important part in translation. But of course I was overlooking Europe's people density. As far as the Swiss are concerned, we showed them how, and how not to. Explicitly *unlike* ours, the Parc Naziunal puts recreation a distant second to flora and fauna. Recreation has been massively provided for elsewhere.

After all, a nation with eighteen hundred ski lifts has already gone some way toward replacing its evergreens with steel pylons. Not only trees. Swiss ski runs often descend slopes "corrected" by bulldozer. At Davos, for instance, even the once-wild peaks. High over town they still loom, but have been taught better behavior through the disfiguring use of snow fences, dozens per summit.

Thus, even if the Naziunal's terrain has been set aside, nominally at least, "for scientific purposes," science in this case may be mere pretext. Deep in their collective psyche, the Swiss may actually have felt a primeval qualm. Had they feared some vague reprisal from their old mountain spirits and bear-gods, the ones their forefathers had invoked before Christianity, long ages before Romulus slew Remus? Had they feared those bear-gods would not forever be mocked?

Thus, if the opposite of forestation is a ski lift, and it is, Switzerland may really have said, "This last, least space must be held. Must be held for nature to do as she chooses. Not we but she will decide. For as long as forever is. Untouchably." Yes. If no space is kept sacred, where is a people to keep its lost soul? Where on earth can we go to honor those days when we had one?

After locking my car at the Parc Naziunal's trailhead Number Seven, I walk over to a large signboard and, under an early June sun, stand daubing Piz Buin glacier cream onto my nose while, squintingly, I translate its litany of stipulations.

"In the National Park it is prohibited:
  to leave the indicated paths
  to light fires
  to take dogs with you!
  to pick flowers, to collect mushrooms, to pluck or dig up plants of any kind
  to cut or collect wood
  to kill, trap, or disturb animals of any kind
  to allow cattle to graze
  to hunt or fish
  to take arms or traps with you
  to camp or spend the night in any way, also on parking lots
  to throw away, leave, or bury litter
  to make undue noise
  to alter nature in any way
  to make commercial films
  to collect and remove natural objects, such as stones, roots, cones, &c.
  to bicycle, motor, or ski.

"Further, persons under fifteen may not enter the park unless accompanied by an adult. Infringements of these regulations are liable to a fine of up to 500 Swiss francs. Park rangers can demand a deposit from transgressors. The orders of the park rangers are to be followed implicitly."

So many "shalt nots"! Like a forefinger poked repeatedly into my chest. Yet with few exceptions our American parks forbid the same things. It is those exceptions. Under pressure from population densities matching Europe's, will similar areas in the U.S. have to be put off limits? No leaving the trail? No camping? No cross-country skiing? No solo juveniles? No dogs? Otherwise, no wilderness?

Also, if biologists have it right, no further evolution. Not for large vertebrate mammals. Without space abounding, space untrampled by humans, space free of hunters with gun or camera, of people like me just wanting to see them, large vertebrate animals cannot evolve. We have long known that our human way of being, by quenching thousands of species, has reversed evolution's direction, which *had* been toward ever greater diversity. But evolution squelched, ended entirely? That does take a while to sink in. Meanwhile the planet loses forest at an acre per second.

Prior to our heading out of Italy for the Swiss Alps, week followed week on Lake Como with every conceivable amenity. The setting was from the first enthralling. Anne and I were given rooms whose views . . . but no. It is best not to dwell on bliss retrospectively. Suffice it to say that we were there a full six days before I could pass by our tall and generous windows. Any glance out over that lake surrounded by mountain abruptions transfixed me, as if a hypnotist said, "Freeze!" On stage, his puzzled victims want to move and cannot. I could not move and did not want to. Stood gaping. At the center of satisfaction, desire disappears. So do we. That is, if what I was seeing was real—and I could *see* it was—I could not really be there. So that first week had been weightless, free floating.

As time passed a different puzzlement crossed my mind ever so briefly, almost furtively. I would find myself daydreaming of Utah, New Mexico, or perhaps Arizona. Flashes only. But in their implication, traitorous, ungrateful. How could I have dreamed of being anywhere other than there, where—till our actual arrival—I had never dreamed I could be?

As for missing Colorado's mountains, the summits immediately around us made that absurd. The Rockies are, yes, higher above sea level, but those pre-Alpine mountains rise far higher overhead than all but a very few peaks in the West. "Maybe it's this sea level altitude," I told myself, "the lake haze." Or maybe the soft skies, their slow, all but motionless weather.

"Well, then, perhaps it's these hillsides spattered with buildings, the towns strung and clustered along the shorelines." In theory I *ought* to have preferred Lake Como untouched. Fact is, however, the houses and lake boats give scale, make the shores more agreeable, the mountainsides even grander. As do church bells floating across the water from Menaggio, Cadenabbia. Pale yellow houses, houses of rooster red. Pinks and hot umbers and burnt siennas in roof tiles. The occasional maverick facade in moon blue. Those met the eye as more than just tolerable. I like them well, so help me. Didn't they add rather than detract? Of course they did. To me, bumpkin, it was a waking dream. Only a color-blind grump could have felt otherwise. Or Italians who knew Lake Como before the postwar building boom.

Which I had not. Instead that postwar scene was my *only* Lake Como—just as, a half century from now, a grossly overpopulated Durango and a high-rise Estes Park are the only ones posterity will ever know. *Adios*, Colorado.

So when I, *as somebody else's posterity*, stood enjoying views from the villa's promontory, I gazed across the lake at the town of Varenna and felt, "How Italian! A painting." As it all was. Each village "poetic." The whole place like that, all either "magnificently scenic" or "picturesque" or "romantic."

But despite the densely forested slopes, the towering cliffs, the summits higher above their towns than any in the U.S., and by far; despite my hiking all day on nearby Monte Tremezzo and meeting only two other hikers; despite the broken limestone of its mule trails being rugged as any trail up, say, Gray's Peak in the Rockies; despite the lovely buttercups, crocuses, Bavarian gentians I saw along my climb; despite dozens of ways you can get killed on any mountain around there . . . Euronature is not nature anymore.

Odd to think that our "conquests" have exiled us from our own planet. Odder yet when we realize that, in our evolving, it was what was not human that humanized us. Now, helpless against our locust-plague populations and power, Earth's very weakness threatens our strength. Nor does the paradox of reversal end there. Our separation from nature has become our connection to it. After that last Swiss bear was shot, the mountains he was killed among became a national park. There his kind would now be safe, if there were any. Old-growth trees, safe too. Except, does all Europe have even *one* left?

Atop a sub-peak of Monte Tremezzo, nicknamed "Crocione" for its tall but eroding cross of reinforced concrete, I stood looking forty six hundred feet down on the baked-clay house tops of Cadenabbia, surprised by how clearly I could hear its delivery trucks and whizzing Fiats honk or suddenly brake. The peevish whine of motorbikes. Scything arrivals of the hydrofoil, riding its underwater wings. The affable "too-ot" puffing up from the steam whistles of ferryboats—all of it was clearly audible. I had never been on a mountain you could hear traffic from.

Westward I looked down on clustered "development" strung along the busy road to Lugano, an hour's drive from Menaggio, across the Italian-Swiss border. There the northeasterly horizon was snow peaked, rugged as any Coloradan could wish. So what was my problem?

It was, to use a grammatical analogy, that nature's speaking had long ago been shifted from active to passive voice. It still spoke, but as setting, backdrop. "Nature." Its very name, thus set off and apart, called for a condescension similar to quotation marks. Great destinal powers had either become "scenic" or dumb bulk that nothing as yet had been done with. The picturesque villages all those thousands of feet below charmed me—their pastel walls, straw yellow or rouge, their ruddy tiles. But the ant race of buses, manic cars, the motorbike blat, the vast lake's graceful flow of big boats and little ones weaving their mazework of wakes, the forty sails of vacationers whose regatta I surveyed with binoculars up near the lake's hazy, northerly end toward Colico and Gera Lario—all were presence, human presence. Bulk loomed mountainously; still, our presence dominated. Every manner of flood, fire, rock slide, and storm would go on taking lives; even so, the struggle with nature was over. We humans had won.

Idyllic in April and May, by high summer—we were told—the lake becomes impossible. Every boat owner within a day's drive wants to carve up its waters. The inboard and outboard blat of its August weekends motorize the air, creating decibel levels said to frazzle the nerves. Then too, young windsurfers alone can turn the lake's southern expanse into an extravaganza of nylon and fiberglass. Being young, they do not know any other Lake Como. But one mustn't exaggerate. Even with the postwar boom in people and tourism, the lake shores are remarkably free of ballyhoo, billboards, neon.

All the same, nature there does as it is told. The "densely forested" mountainsides lack conifers and old growth. Fires are set to kill conifer seedlings lest they crowd out the understory browse that goats, sheep, and cows now wander nibbling among. Well and good. Our species is not yet ready to turn vegetarian, nor must trees be of great antiquity to give a hiker welcome shade. My stride has many a day been lightened on a steep European trail by the music of goat bells, cow bells. A herd of Swiss browns, for instance—I love their out-of-sync tinkling, as if a marimba band that can't agree on the beat.

Though the teeming human outlay below me was—in terms of sheer mass—"outwhelmed" by Alpine rugosities and peaks, even so little as the pontoon plane flying tourists to and fro, day long, low over the water made unavoidable the fact of human dominance. Instead of nature tolerating *us*, our species now gives it permission. From my lookout atop that Italian summit, I could not help seeing Colorado's populous future. But in that future, what will be missing, however "indispensable," will, once dispensed with, never be missed.

We mustn't kid ourselves. When wilderness was all there was, there was none. Our glances that way are necessarily retrospective. Created by its own absence, wilderness could only have come into existence disappearing. In a technological century, there is no "away." The goddess *Natura*, the nature of ancient times—"great creating nature," the nature of fateful powers unopposable—is beaten, defeated. Technology has it jumping through hoops. We got what we wanted. Real wilderness can be seen only in the rearview mirror.

9:30 p.m. The May twilight is cloudless but chilly. For spending a couple of nights deep in the heart of Swiss wilds, Anne and I have chosen a spot called Il Fuorn, which sits exactly as high as our house back in Colorado, fifty-six hundred feet above sea level. Because "it is forbidden to camp or spend the night in any way, also on parking lots," we are "camping out" inside: Hotel Parc Naziunal Il Fuorn.

To our north, conifered ridgelines—with snow Alps beyond: Piz Zuort, Piz Minger, Piz Sampuoir, Piz Murters, as they are called in Romansch. Above and beyond them, and everything, the evening's earliest stars shine auspiciously clear. The darkening air is too crisp for mosquitoes, so we open both windows wide to enjoy the constellations from under our goose-down duvets. Such, in the heart of these sixty-five square miles, are the wilderness rigors.

Having climbed Munt la Schera that afternoon, I brought down from its flat summit an appetite equal to the hotel's evening meal: bean soup, pumpernickel, the delicious house wine, Swiss grown, the big portions of beef filet, the browned potatoes and carrots, and the chocolate sundae—with, suitably, its Matterhorn of whipped cream. Our Swiss high-country meal included, too, a Portuguese waiter teaching us Portugal's word for *fox* as, through the dining room's glass walls, we watched a lone fox crossing the meadow right outside. There, each evening of our stay, a herd of red deer has, by ones and twos, seeped down from the forest of lodgepole pine to browse on the twilight meadow's lush grasses. "Just like back home," Anne remarked.

The chamois is not. From forelegs that knelt for better nibbling, it glanced up toward the trotting fox, stared a moment, then went back to its feeding. By the highway along that meadow's edge, cars slowed to a stop and tourists got out—despite the oncoming dusk—to try a snapshot or two, while big sisters or brothers pointed out yearling deer to their littler siblings.

During all this the American Westerner in us tried not to feel smug that our own sons grew up where deer, black bear, and mountain lions were part of their hometown's mixed feelings: how to make safe from, yet have; how to discourage, not quell.

To drive from the Parc Naziunal through Zernez, then Zuoz and S-Chanf and St. Moritz, over pass after pass on roundabout, mountainously up-and-down roads to Grindelwald, is to drive from nature's last stand toward the wonderful worst that can happen. Where Swiss wilderness begins at a railway ticket window.

More than just nature tamed, Grindelwald's world of glacier-shagged peaks is marvelous, appalling. Anyone who cares about mountaineering must go there. For the full effect, however, he must pay $190 to ride eleven highly unusual miles! Such are the rigors.

So, wanting two seats (second class) on the cog-rail train that winds upward to the celebrated Jungfraujoch, Anne and I fork over two hundred Swiss francs and climb aboard. The U.S. dollar may someday go further, but that will be in our next lives at the soonest. Meanwhile, this morning's weather around Grindelwald is a sparkling contrast to our visit years earlier, in whiteout. Never before has Switzerland seen fit to give us sunny skies so pristine and cloudless.

From the Grindelwald station we ride thirty-four hundred feet higher to a pass called Kleine Scheidegg. It is early June, with muddy heaps of leftover snow still melting near the big, blocky, hyper-conspicuous hotel, ugly as its surroundings are magnificent, but nonetheless a haven for serious climbers who dare attempt the famed Eigernordwand.

Our Rockies offer nothing remotely like its vertical difference: the Eiger's thirteen-thousand-foot summit, like a shape risen from the darkest past of creation, looks ten thousand feet *down* on Grindelwald. In fact, the English for its name is "ogre." Thus the Eiger's north face feels so awesome, so savage, so holy that none but the Swiss would have blasted and drilled a railway through it. That upwardly curving route through the mountain's innards is proof that if a hotel or restaurant can be built on one or another Swiss height, it probably will be, unless—even more probably—it already has been. No matter how many words Eskimos use or do not use for *snow*, the Swiss must have plenty of ways to say *engineering*. And if they lack ways to say *sacrilege*, it is because they simply do not grasp the concept. Or long ago decided, "no such thing." An official tourist brochure, the *Jungfrau Magazin*, helps foreigners digest this by way of a food simile: "The Swiss treat their mountains like their famous cheese, the Emmental; they put holes in them."

Up from Kleine Scheidegg's tundra pass, our train climbs, out of its switchyard where three separate train lines keep the rails clacking, and where the newly opened Sports Bazaar sits beside the newly opened Restaurant Eigernordwand, just below the improved Sesselbahn. Then somebody turns off the sky and we are enstoned. Inches from my face, rough rock blurs past our windows. We are more than encrypted. Within those mega-million years of a planet's oceanic and calcareous past, we have become lively fossils immured by sedimentation called the Eiger. Because there is nothing to see, the intercom wafts elevator music into our carriage, interrupting it for tour facts in German, Japanese, French, Italian, and English.

Equally bizarre, at several stations *inside* that mountain, we creep past illuminated ads for Patek watches, Rolex and Omega—as if it were the London underground—then unboard, moblike, with everybody else to peer through glass walls set high in the face of the famous Eigernordwand's snow and rock. While I stare seven thousand feet down on Grindelwald's summer-green valley, dozens and dozens of climbers who have been killed or frozen by the Eiger's north face gaze down alongside me. The corpse of one young climber, years back, dangled unreachable within less than a rope's length of the gallery where Anne and I are standing. Then that rope was cut from above, allowing his now famous cadaver to fall. Comfy, entunneled, I snap a photograph of glacial snow just the other side of the glass.

At the Jungfraujoch proper, a multi-floor complex caters to every touristic whim, both within and without the mountain. Punctual trains disgorge and absorb great surging loads of sightseers all day long, so wilderness rigors there include my waiting briefly in line at the official "Jungfraujoch Post Office" to buy stamps for our cards.

Further rigors: automatic glass doors opening onto the crisp, high-altitude air of terraces—where we are instantly blinded. Without cloud to mute it, and at 11,334 feet, the morning's June sun fires into our irises off the Altech Glacier. We squint down at a stiff river in motionless flow, streaming south from just below our feet—more miles of ice than I have seen since Black Rapids Glacier. Sun glares left and right off baroque snow billows piled every which way atop the Jungfrau proper. Sun blazes off similar snows whelming a neighbor peak called the Monk.

From our terrace, after swapping photo opportunities with fellow tourists not invariably Japanese, we look down on a near plateau of glacier where the much-advertised dog sled rides may be had. There too is the layout of a minuscule ski area, with rental outfits allowing a person to say, back in Osaka or Nimes, "You're not the only one who has skied the Jungfraujoch in June!"

Tame nature is a great convenience.

And hugely enjoyable. For the price of a train ride, some of the most feared peaks in the Alps will pose close up for your photos. Such is the Jungfraujoch. With its "Ice Palace," a blue-green catacomb of rooms and corridors carved into the living glacier, with its "snow plateau" for sunning and snowballing, with its multi-level cafeterias, with its souvenir shops, with its video monitors, with its museums of engineering history and scientific exhibits, there are roadside attractions for every taste. Also, inevitably, the Berghaus Hotel.

Swiss mountains are not the only ones that Europeans have housebroken. Southwest of where we stand lies the Italian ski town of Cervinia on the southern slopes of the Matterhorn. Eight hundred people live there year round, but during ski season Cervinia is a polyester and nylon anthill: beds for sixteen thousand tourists, half a hundred restaurants to feed them, and twenty-seven lifts to pull them uphill. Which is nothing. Whereas a *major* ski resort in Colorado may have eight or ten lifts, or—as at Vail—a couple of dozen, skiers farther west of here at the French resort of L'Alpe d'Huez can choose from no fewer than eighty-five! There the high-rise condos violate their alpine setting so aggressively, with such stark-naked venality, that on first sight I could only laugh and shake my head in disbelief: "People actually *pay* to come here?"

Aesthetically, France's L'Alpe d'Huez does not even try. To an American it can only be a sick joke, a landscape in ruins—but for tens of thousands it is a *tres chic* aspiration. At the height of ski season, the town's sewage system cannot treat three-fourths of the waste. *Que faire?* The town's owners, being French, solve that problem by passing it on. They simply pour the untreated sewage downhill, for "nature" to deal with. Winters at L'Alpe d'Huez, the big import is money, the big export is *merde*.

Is nature thus tamed what our Rocky Mountains, in less than a century, must come to? The answer may be another question: Can anything stop copulation? No? Then yes. That indeed is what we must come to: mechanized mountains.

In this age of mass tourism, with the lure of mountain terrain now drawing a combined 100,000,000 visitors each year into alpine areas of France, Germany, Italy, Switzerland, Austria, and Yugoslavia, overdevelopment has already produced backlash. Increasingly, people of the deutschmark, the pound sterling, the franc, the kroner, and the yen, are finding the grand expanses of the American West freer and easier. We offer cheap car rentals, cheap rentals on campers. We offer good roads, good motels, good campgrounds. Food of all kinds is a bargain. Compared to Europe's, our gasoline sells at giveaway prices. During my last Bryce Canyon visit, three-fourths of the persons I spoke with on trails were European. Any cursory inspection of the guest register at Navajo National Monument near Tonalea, Arizona, shows that at least a third of its signees are European also.

Increasingly, they and the Japanese flee their own gridlocked mountains, where—

compared to the American West—communing with nature can feel like an industrial experience. More pylons than trees? Switzerland already has eighteen hundred ski lifts and expects to add another two or three hundred in the next couple of decades, whereas Colorado—though five times bigger—has nothing like three hundred in the whole state. So, drawn by a U.S. national park system that for decades has been the envy of visitors whose countries include nothing remotely like it, either for extent or, yes, for *intelligence*, it is not surprising that more and more Europeans and Japanese fly toward a land whose legendary space and nature are still briefly real, nor surprising that its unique wealth in those things is being loved to death less and less slowly.

It would be fatuous to blame foreign visitors for that overuse. The problem is nature itself: the nature in us. Living things are encoded to propagate their kind. In my own lifetime, males and females in the U.S. have doubled their numbers. But if begetting thrives as it has, can anyone? Will our progeny? Which of us now alive is prepared to deny offspring to others? Which of us would deny that the main learning device of our species—thus far, anyhow—is letting itself get hit on the skull by an apocalypse? "Any catastrophe that hasn't happened to *me* is not a catastrophe."

Unfortunately, the very adaptability that makes us human may be our most lethal gift. Our shifty species is supple enough to call anything "home sweet home," no matter how befouled. In this, the very adaptability that makes Homo sapiens boss of all vertebrates may undo us. What blight can we not adapt to, project ourselves into, and love? We'll call desolation "nature" if that's all we've known.

Soupy weather is predicted for Grindelwald tomorrow. By then, however, Anne and I will be well on the road toward Montreaux—so the prospect of driving off into gathering rain has not dampened our final evening. On the contrary, it has made those briefly untypical skies of clear blue the luckier. At our hotel, *Die Alte Post*, on a far warmer terrace than the snow plateau up at the Jungfraujoch, we dawdle over supper *al fresco*, the better to enjoy a superb view of the still unclouded Eiger. Just to the left of its summit—which sundown is not quite done with—hangs a half moon of early June. And thanks to the mother of invention, our budget, we have discovered how to make mustard sandwiches.

Off a mountain just east of town, the Mettenberg, paragliders keep us entertained, impressing us with their skill at catching thermals. Green chute, yellow chute, red chute—it seems they can dip and soar, then rise sky-high again whenever they want. Forty-five floating minutes are as nothing for the yellow chute, though the red chute seems more adept in lateral maneuvers. Once upon an olden time, that mountain surely must have been the throne of some primeval spirit; but now, with its Fingstegg cablelift, it's merely a handy launching device, a limestone accessory those paragliders haven't needed to buy.

Adios, Colorado. As those floating colors and blithe levitations sweeten the evening—and they do—I realize that, as usual, the future has already happened.

New West Blues

Jim Stiles

reprinted from *High Country News*, August 23, 1993

> *This ain't the same old range.*
> *Everything seems to change.*
> *Where are the pals I used to ride with?*
> *. . . Gone to a land so strange.*
> —The Sons of the Pioneers

*I*n my never-ending quest to make some sense out of what is happening here in the rural West, I haven't "been to the mountaintop," but I've been to the Sand Flat, and the view from there is discouraging. A few days ago, my attorney and I took a drive to survey the destruction. (I hadn't been back since the "Easter Weekend Riots.") Besides being surprised at the number of campers still enduring the 100° heat, I was shocked at my reaction to another sight that should have only caused more aggravation. After wading through a hundred or more mountain bikers, we came around a corner and saw local rancher Don Holyoak with a couple of dozen cows. Smelly, stupid, fly-ridden cows . . . "stinking bovines," Ed Abbey used to call them.

I was glad to see them.

Don't get me wrong. I still believe that the mismanaged use of our public lands for cattle has done immeasurable damage to the land, fouled countless streams and water sources, and been a burden on the U.S. taxpayer. In fact, efforts by the extractive industries to literally tear up the West for maximum profit continue at a devastating rate. But I have become painfully aware of a bewildering shift in my thinking. There are more than a few of us long-time environmentalists who are suffering from an identity crisis.

Edward Abbey once wrote, "The idea of wilderness needs no defense; it only needs more defenders." But what it means to be a defender of the West has changed in fifteen years.

Just who poses the greatest threat to the West? Where does the real danger lie? I'm afraid it's become more complicated than I ever thought it could. This is not just another complaint about our changing town—the New Moab. What's happening here is happening elsewhere. And what's coming may be bigger than even we doomsayers would dare predict.

Barring a miracle, we are about to enter a new phase, the *last* phase, in the taming of the West. When it's over it won't be "the West" anymore. We all know "how the West was won." What we are about to see is "how the West was *done*." Pretty soon you will be able to stick a fork in it. And all of us, no matter how much we love the country, bear responsibility.

When I first moved here in the late '70s, threats to the canyon country were obvious: the extractive industries of oil and gas, uranium, timber, and cattle. Operations that actually reduced the quality of the resource were the natural target of environmentalists. In those years the desert was turned upside down by seismic crews and oil rigs, chaining operations, and a never-ending series of harebrained ideas to exploit the fragile western landscape. For almost a year we could see the big mercury vapor lights on an Exxon oil rig in Gold Basin, a place too beautiful for such a monstrous intrusion.

Seismic crews worked right to the edge of Arches and Canyonlands national parks, collecting geologic information that they could sell to other energy companies. In their wake, they left hundreds of miles of ugly scars that will take centuries to heal. The Department of Energy wanted to build a high-level nuclear repository adjacent to the Needles in San Juan County. The Bureau of Land Management continued to chain thousands of acres of piñon-juniper forest as part of its "range improvement" policy (one of my favorite euphemisms, I might add, next to "nuclear exchange").

In short, there was plenty to complain about. And we complained loudly and often. We, who actually lived here in the heart of the country we were trying to defend, felt honored and proud to be on the front lines. It was, after all, not easy to live in the rural West; it required sacrifices. Just trying to find a way to eke out a living was a challenge, for most jobs were low paying and many were seasonal. In addition, poor infrastructure, lack of cultural opportunities, underfunded schools, and an extremely closed, conservative population made it difficult for an "outsider" to survive. That is why, despite warnings by some about the threat of "industrial tourism" for more than twenty-five years, the effect on the West of all those millions of gawkers seemed trivial compared to the damage bulldozers could do.

There were, of course, blatant exceptions. Some of the West's national parks began to show the effect of abuse and overuse decades ago. Several small towns, from Aspen and Telluride to Jackson and Taos, were transformed from sleepy, even dying, little mining and ranching villages to bustling communities full of trendy restaurants and boutiques. They became rustic playgrounds for the rich and famous.

But they were the exception. The rest of the West changed very little from a demographic standpoint. Generation after generation grew up in the same small western communities. The towns looked the same, decade after decade. A person could go away for years and come back to his home town and find the same grocer behind the cash register, the same postmaster behind the same stamp window. But it was more than just the way these little towns looked. It was the *pace* that set such communities apart. While some may call it stagnation, it was comforting to find continuity in a world that turns itself inside out on a daily basis.

All that is changing at breakneck speed. We are watching, in effect, the last land rush, and when it's over the West will bear little resemblance to what it still is today. The decay of America's cities and urban areas, the congestion, the pollution, the crime, and the stress of urban life are driving millions to the wide open spaces. And the explosive growth of tourism is creating, for the first time, the climate necessary for that kind of exodus.

For the first time, West Coast immigrants can dream of moving to a rural community. No sacrifice is needed to sell a $500,000 home in California, buy a $100,000 home in a small western town, invest $200,000 in a business, and put the rest in the bank. A few hope to be modern-day Charlie Steens, who hit it rich on uranium. But this time fortunes won't be made with a second-hand drill rig and a thousand-dollar grubstake. Instead, speculators buy up land for JB's and McDonald's franchises the way miners staked uranium claims in the '50s.

As long as people in the cities can sell their homes at a great profit and can take that money and reinvest here, where the prices are still substantially lower, we will continue to see this remarkable inflow of humanity.

Is it all that bad? In some ways, it's not. Critics of tourism as an economic base claim that such an industry is too unstable, that a town that builds its economy around tourism is asking for trouble, that sooner or later the bubble will burst and all the tourists will go somewhere else. But I just don't see that happening. While energy towns have gone boom and bust for decades, I cannot think of a single tourist town that went belly up. Maybe business in these communities has ebbed and flowed with the national or regional economy, but dry up and blow away? Never.

So . . . with an established tourist base, a changing community profile that demands better educational and cultural opportunities, and a larger tax base, positive changes are inevitable. And yet, in a perverse way, those same improvements represent the final nails in the West's coffin, changes that guarantee the demise of the West as we know it.

For me, "the West" is a lot more than the sum of its parts. The West is the desert, the canyons, the mountains, and the wildlife that roams among them. It's the wild flowers that bloom in the most unexpected places and the gnarled spruce that clings to life at twelve thousand feet. It's the polished skies and the exploding cotton clouds that loom over the high peaks each afternoon. It's the kangaroo rats and fence lizards that we see all the time and the cougar that we wait a lifetime to see just once for a fleeting moment.

The intangible aspect of the West is as vital to its survival as the resource itself. It's the solitude, the silence, an almost pleasant loneliness that this country evokes in the souls of those who love it. These are an integral part of the West as a state of mind. Abbey could not describe this land without references to the "strange and mysterious" country that he loved so much . . . "the voodoo rocks." Even the inhospitable aspect of the West itself became a quality to be admired and respected. You loved the West on its terms and made the sacrifices required to be a part of it.

Solitude was not something to avoid, it was something to love and respect, and even to depend on.

So today, as I reexamine what the West is, I find a strange contradiciton in the experiences I seek out. For instance, I can hike into the badlands country north of Arches National Park, into country that was torn apart forty years ago by the uranium industry and which still bears the scars, and there amidst the rubble I can feel like I'm in the West. I poke my head into a deserted miner's cabin and find a great horned owl in the rafters waiting for nightfall. I sit down on the rocks above the Big Ape mine and watch the sun set behind the Devils Garden. Magnificent silence, brilliant light, only the wind and the hooting of that owl to disturb the silence of the evening—the West.

But I can hike to Delicate Arch, where the resource has been preserved, but also promoted to the far corners of the planet, and I feel like I'm in Disneyland. Surrounded by dozens of camera-snapping, video-taping tourists, screaming kids, and well-armed rangers, I think to myself: this is not the West.

But it may be the future of the West. It seems to be what people want. Those wonderful intangibles do not appeal to many of the New Westerners. In fact, all that solitude appears to scare a lot of them to death. Look at the way recent visitors, and even our most recent residents, "explore" the country. They travel in groups. Some might say they travel in herds—that we are seeing one herd (livestock) being driven from the country, only to be replaced by another. Where visitors once came here for the peace and solitude and beauty of the land, now they come for "breathtaking thrills." Those who found a trip to the canyon country to be akin to a religious experience have been replaced to a large degree by "recreationists," who regard this country as a playground and who seem to have a diminished or nonexistent environmental ethic. So people come here looking for organized ways of having fun.

Before skiing became popular, the mountains were cold and hostile and forbidding. They were nice to look at from a safe distance. But the sport changed everything. Here in the desert it was the same story. Hot, desolate, a nice place to watch from the comfort of an air-conditioned car, but who the hell would want to live in this godforsaken place? When I was a Park Service ranger, tourists thought I'd been assigned to Arches as punishment. "What did you do wrong to get stuck in this hell hole, boy?"

Again the sport, in this case mountain biking, changed everything. It changed the very reason people come here. We went from mystical to macho, from watching a hawk to "riding the rock." From "desert mystics" to "adrenalin junkies."

The sport, of course, and the reputation and notoriety it creates, spawn the ever-growing stream of businesses that are created to provide equipment and services for those organized thrills. And once a newer, more hip tourist infrastructure is in place, with a plethora of restaurants, boutiques, Southwest art galleries and jewelry shops, the nouveaux riches suddenly find the area much more appealing and start looking for little "ranchettes" upon which to build their million-dollar summer homes.

Here is the most frustrating aspect of the change. While some speculators see the West as a product to be marketed and sold like soap or headache remedies, a great majority of the new businesses that cater to the tourists and recreationists are simply people who are longing to escape their miserable, polluted, crime-ridden existences for the simpler life. The overwhelming number of new residents in Moab didn't come here to get rich. They simply want to live here. Once they arrive they wring their hands and hope that the situation doesn't get any worse. I've done my share of hand wringing. My paper's circulation has doubled in one year and I should be thrilled, but it's also an indication of what's happening to the town—we're booming. Does my paper somehow encourge more people to move here? The fact is, sheer numbers of immigrants alone will almost certainly mean that what they're running from—congestion, pollution, crime, and stress—will follow them here. That, in turn, will diminish the quality of everyone's life. But who has the right to say "Go away"?

Californians, Coloradans from the Front Range, as well as entrepreneurs from across the country are buying commercial and private property in rural counties all over the West. In Wayne County, Utah, out-of-state property sales are at an all-time high and property values have increased dramatically. There is a housing shortage in Emery County because so many homes are owned by absentee landlords. In New Mexico and Arizona the story is the same.

Is there a solution to all this? Is there a way to preserve the West? Can we protect the resource and those precious intangibles? I think the answer is no. Fighting strip mines and oil wells was easy. They were such black-and-white targets. What's happening now is much more insidious. Where would someone even begin?

The truth is, all the ordinances and regulations in the world can't change our life-style. We can't begin to see that the Real Enemy is the face we see in the mirror every day of our lives. Humans and their toys: what a deadly combination.

Someone once asked the great humorist Dorothy Parker to use the word *horticulture* in a sentence. She replied, "You can lead a horticulture, but you can't make her think."

Parker would have understood the New West.

Section Two

Photographs by Courtney White

Our West

Courtney White

*T*ourism and tourists, it seems, have always been the business of others. A tourist is somebody else; not me, but the person over there in the funny hat, wearing the silly shirt, or holding the map upside down. Tourism is the business of strangers, of foreigners crawling over the landscape with boorish manners and unattractive intentions. It is the category we use to separate ourselves, and our home, from the rapacious and phenomenally shallow attentions of these outsiders. This attitude can easily evolve into a form of backyard elitism with a quaint double standard: go away we hate you, but don't forget to leave your money.

Yet the simple fact is, unless you are a house-bound shut-in, you have been, at one time or another, a tourist. We are all tourists. Everyone has been somewhere "else," either physically or vicariously. Tourism is not the business of others, it is *our* business—our success and our failure. As tourists we must all share the burden of responsibility for our actions. One should not, for example, drive a car into Yosemite Valley and then complain about congestion; or whine about gawkers in one's home town and then boast to friends how Mexico City "blew my mind." Tourism is a mirror, reflecting our collective attitudes toward the land and ourselves, warts and all. Thus the photographs in this essay were taken from the perspective of a fellow tourist, another gawker away from home. I tried to capture the modern American West by simply being myself—just another traveler with a camera.

The Ghost of Route 66

'57 Chevy heading east on Interstate 40,
near Laguna, New Mexico

The Foreigner

French tourist with camera between mittens,
Monument Valley, Arizona

The Castle

Two white hats before a natural depression,
Montezuma's Castle, Arizona

Talking Beaver

U.S. Forest Service Spin Center,
near Abiquiu, New Mexico

Cheese

The story of Yosemite from a parking lot,
Yosemite National Park, California

Racetrack or Wilderness?

Off-road vehicle tracks in a wilderness study unit with cop,
Mecca Hills, California

The Wild West Lives!

Cowboys waiting for guests at their theater,
near Durango, Colorado

A Room with a View

Visitors patiently waiting their turn,
Mesa Verde National Park, Colorado

Boot Hill

Children standing in a graveyard full only of lies,
Tombstone, Arizona

The Killing Field

Dead Indian markers,
Big Hole Battlefield National Monument, southern Montana

The Apache Trail

This way on the road to Lake Roosevelt,
central Arizona

The Abyss

On the esplanade just outside the gift shops,
Grand Canyon National Park, Arizona

Power Included

A sign of the times found only in America,
near Springerville, Arizona

The Moon

Volcanic craters where astronauts trained,
Craters of the Moon National Monument, Idaho

Section Three

Academic Perspectives:
Tourism, Cultural Production, and Ethnicity

Art, Tourism, and Race Relations in Taos:
Toward a Sociology of the Art Colony[1]

Sylvia Rodriguez

*I*t is a sociological truism that ideology and expressive culture often give positive interpretation to harsh objective conditions, including oppression and exploitation. Indeed, oppressive, exploitative political systems inevitably employ justificatory ideologies in ways that are purposive, yet not fully conscious. Hegemonic process is not merely a matter of military force, economic control, or state ideology. It operates and reproduces continuously at myriad cultural levels from the broadest to the most minute. For all its pervasiveness, it sometimes calls forth contradictory impulses as well. Under modern industrial capitalism the process or processes are so multiple and complex as to defy holistic description, and therefore one must focus on individual, historical-ethnographic manifestations. The case to be examined here represents one such example. It illustrates a process of mystification which is the product of modernity on the one hand and an ongoing postcolonial history on the other.[2] It involves stratification, not only by class but by race as well, and reflects the symbolic transformation of this particular arrangement into a marketable commodity. It springs, in a word, from the modern economy of tourism.

Dean MacCannell (1976:8) has analyzed tourism as the quintessential sociological expression of modernity or postindustrial society, in which preindustrial or nonmodern societies do not vanish but instead undergo "artificial preservation and reconstruction" into objects or settings for leisure entertainment. Graburn (1977, 1983) and others have examined how tourism can variously shape the production of ethnic arts and how, as experience, it resembles pilgrimage and ritual. Other approaches focus on the impact of tourism development upon host communities (Jafari 1974; N. Kent 1983; Kottke 1988; Dann, Nash, and Pearce 1988). Scholars have identified various kinds of tourism, including historical, recreational, environmental, cultural, and ethnic (Smith 1977; Cohen 1979). Ethnic tourism, "wherein the prime attraction is the cultural exoticism of the local population and its artifacts (clothing, architecture, theater, music, dance, plastic arts)," is probably the most interesting type from an anthropological point of view because it can be seen to constitute a "special case of ethnic relations and can therefore be profitably analyzed as such" (van den Berghe and Keyes 1984:344).

The U.S. Southwest, particularly New Mexico and Arizona, is an excellent region in which to study the interaction between tourism and ethnic or race relations because these two factors, along with environmental aridity, have helped to shape its modern social history. Tourism in New Mexico was sired by the Atchison, Topeka & Santa Fe Railway, which brought the first resident painters to northern New Mexico in 1898 and for years provided them with an income from painting Indians for travel posters (Bryant 1978; Weigle 1986). The development of the Taos–Santa Fe art colony was both the product of and a stimulant to the growth of tourism as an increasingly important component of the state economy. It also had a deep and lasting effect upon the course and character of Indian-Anglo-Mexican relations in the region.

The term *art colony* refers to the hundreds of "Anglo" artists who migrated to Taos and Santa Fe between 1900 and World War II, as well as to the artistic products and social milieu they generated. This art colony was the mechanism by which a harsh environment and inequitable social conditions became symbolically transformed into something mysterious, awesome, and transcendent. In sum, the art colony unconsciously mystified a three-tiered system of ethnic-racial stratification within an arid, isolated, underdeveloped frontier region.

This study analyzes the Taos art colony in terms of the social conditions which surrounded its development and shaped its character, and it calls attention to the oblique, or unconscious, quality of this expression, an obliqueness that is part of its theoretical interest. The following discussion presents an overview of the regional setting and the general conditions under which the art colony developed, followed by a short history and then an analysis of the character of the art colony society. This involves scrutiny of the face-to-face relations between the artists and Indians and Hispanos, or Mexicanos, during the art colony years.[3] Several examples of cultural "text" representing different viewpoints are examined for what they reveal about the nature and structure of contemporary ethnic relations in Taos, and central, interpenetrating aspects of mystification as it operates in Taos are identified. The discussion concludes by locating the case within a larger context.

Taos

Art colonies exist in both Taos and Santa Fe. Although these colonies exhibit similar characteristics and followed parallel courses of development, the two cases differ in several respects. Santa Fe, which lies roughly sixty-five miles south of Taos along the Rio Grande valley, is larger, richer, and the seat of state government. These features have influenced the greater size, diversity, and sophistication of its artistic milieu. Taos is considerably smaller and more remote and rustic than Santa Fe. Its tri-ethnic composition, while exhibiting the same hierarchical pattern as Santa Fe's, seems more pronounced or stark and more prone to violent eruption. Both cities were originally established near aboriginal pueblos in the late sixteenth century, and both became centers for interethnic contact and trade; however, Spanish headquarters was located at or near Santa Fe from the beginning of colonization, while Taos remained the rugged outpost of the northern frontier, a lively center of activity conveniently beyond direct control. Taos Pueblo was the starting point of the Pueblo Revolt in 1680; under Mexican rule during the nineteenth century, the nearby Mexican town became a port of entry and a flourishing contraband center for the burgeoning Saint Louis–Santa Fe trade; and Taos was the locus of a joint insurrection in 1847, shortly after American occupation. Anglos established a firm foothold there but remained a numerical minority.

During the Territorial period (1846–1912), Taos, like the region in general, underwent enormous political and economic changes whose full social repercussions were felt only gradually. Land speculation by Anglo capitalists was rampant: American conquest and incorporation eventually dispossessed Mexicanos of roughly 80 percent of their lands and reduced them to migrant proletarians with stubborn ties to small, marginal, village-based farms, or *ranchitos* (Ortiz 1980:93). Indians were confined to reservations and made wards of the state with special administrative or legal status. In the meantime, regional mining, timber, cattle, and agricultural booms extracted natural resources and required cheap Mexican labor. By the time of New Mexico's statehood in 1912, Taos had become a significant exporter of labor, even while it was enjoying the last phase of an agricultural boom that won it a reputation as the "granary of New Mexico." In 1906 the public domain in Taos County, more than half of its land mass including the mountain wilderness, was declared a national forest and the property of the federal government. This curtailed both Indian and Mexicano traditional uses of the area and inaugurated the long-standing pueblo battle for the upper Taos watershed and Blue Lake. During the first decade of this century, the upper Rio Grande Valley slipped into a condition of economic stagnation from which it has never fully recovered. This development was more a crystallization of existing conditions or a change of degree, rather than of kind, since the region had also been peripheral to metropolitan centers in central Mexico.

Refuge Region

The U.S.–Mexican Southwest as a whole can be characterized geopolitically as a "refuge region" (Aguirre-Beltran 1979): a rugged, isolated geographical zone where marginal ethnic enclaves persist in subordinated relation to members of the national society. Other examples are found in the southern highlands and northern deserts of Mexico or in the Andes Mountains and Amazon basin. All these areas are marked by high proportions of enclaved ethnic minority populations whose sociocultural patterns retain a colonial, sometimes pseudoaboriginal, character. Because of their remoteness and climax ecologies, such regions are inaccessible to the kind of intensive resource exploitation and population growth that flourishes in less extreme, more hospitable, or more favorably situated environments. They thus remain sparsely populated and isolated and become progressively underdeveloped and backward in relation to mainstream urban society. The concepts of "core" and "periphery" have been applied by dependency and world systems theorists to the kind of dynamic macroeconomic relationship that obtains between metropolitan and postcolonially linked underdeveloped regions (see, e.g., Gunder Frank 1967; Wallerstein 1979; Wolf 1982).

New Mexico was a refuge region in the making by the time Americans began to arrive in growing numbers after 1821. Taos had always been isolated from Mexico City or even Durango. During the colonial centuries, the castelike pattern of relations between Spanish and Indian populations gradually yielded, through *mestizaje*, or miscegenation, to the overriding class orientation of nationalizing Mexico. Indian and Spaniard nevertheless remained the two poles of the local order, even while the middle zone expanded and the strata within ethnic levels grew more defined. Americanization both preserved and transformed the ethnic hierarchy by adding a new top level and distinguishing the legal status of Indians and Mexicanos. Whereas a trend toward deracialization developed in Mexican society (Harris 1964; van den Berghe 1967), American incorporation reracialized the region north of the border: Indians remained a race and Mexicans became one.[4]

The Hidden Role of the Art Colony

The social inequality and harsh material conditions of northern New Mexico are emphasized in order to underscore how remarkable the process was by which all these liabilities would become transformed, in the popular Euro-American imagination, into exotic, mysterious assets. Tourism and the art colony together constituted the means by which this extraordinary transmutation was accomplished. The art colony functioned to convert the disparity between social reality and touristic fiction into a highly marketable set of images. Taos art both reflects and expresses the social reality within which it was created and sold, albeit neither directly nor consciously. This complex symbolic function was achieved by various techniques including denial, omission, transmutation, and objectification of local conditions. In other words, the local social order is but obliquely reflected in Taos art. This very obliqueness and its apparently unconscious motivation are what call for explanation.

Several local features are credited with having attracted waves of artists and writers to northern New Mexico. These include the "spectacular" natural scenery and the long-standing presence of American Indians and Hispanics (Gibson 1983; Reeve 1982). Another important feature was the region's isolation and rusticity, or in a twentieth-century word, its underdevelopment. When artists first began arriving in Taos around the turn of the century, it was a small adobe village, barely accessible by road, with no electricity or indoor plumbing. Electrification and a paved highway from Santa Fe arrived in the twenties, while indoor plumbing and stucco did not become pervasive in town until well after World War II. In effect the Taos area was part of the Third World, which it still resembles in many ways, and it exhibited the usual indices of underdevelopment.[5] This quality was a major source of its appeal to the artists and the tourists the art attracted. In comparison to the industrial East and Midwest whence the painters came, the place was arid, empty, rugged, and foreign. It promised the quintessential frontier experience—vast desert-mountain spaces, wild but noble savages, and unlimited personal freedom. Fed by a generation of dimestore frontier novels (Broder 1980:38, 98, 117, 145), the painters' imaginations in turn produced the visual component for what would become the Taos–Santa Fe mystique.

Most of the early Taos painters were academically trained illustrators (Coke 1963: 1–27; Reeve 1982:2–3) who, along with other artists of their generation, sought to break out of a traditional European mold into a new, distinctly American aesthetic. Yet unlike the avant-garde of their day, the early Taos painters fled urbanism to live "out West" like pioneers and to paint Indians as romantic visions from a bygone world. Even though their urban expatriation implied a certain social critique, their behavior and work proved profoundly conservative. The Taos artists sought and portrayed a world best understood in relation to the worlds it negated: the modern industrial city on the one hand and the stagnant rural ghetto on the other. The reason for their imaginative transformation of the setting seems simple enough—no one would like, much less buy, socially naturalistic paintings of the actual conditions which prevailed in the region: racism, poverty, alcoholism, and perpetual drought. But this was not a matter of conscious or cynical deception, because it is clear from their own testimony that the artists visually saw what they painted. In any case, most of their work sold like hotcakes "back East" and advertised effectively for tourism.

Ourselves and Our Neighbors: A Social Anatomy

The first painters to reside in Taos permanently were Bert Phillips and Ernest Blumenschein, who arrived in 1898 on the recommendation of Joseph Sharp, another painter who only summered there until 1912. The breakdown of Blumenschein's and Phillips's wagon wheel north of Taos would later inspire the town's touristic origin myth. During the next three decades, they were followed by W. Herbert Dunton, Oscar Berninghaus, E. Irving Couse, Walter Ufer, and Victor Higgins. Along with E. Martin Hennings and Kenneth Adams, these resident artists made up the membership of the Taos Society of Artists, a social group and business association maintained between 1912 and 1927 (White 1983). Scores of other painters and artists passed through or lived in Taos between World War I and World War II, during the town's first tourism boom period. With the onset of World War II, tourism dropped off precipitously, the population declined, and the economy stagnated for the next two decades. Historians identify three general periods in the art colony's development: the early phase of romantic Indianist portraiture between 1900 and New Mexico statehood in 1912, a period of "flowering" and diversification that lasted through the twenties, and a "modernist" phase between the Depression and World War II (Coke 1963: 103–10; Gibson 1983: 50–68; Reeve 1982:9–11). These periods reflect the stages of change which unfolded as New Mexico moved into federal dependency and slowly modernized while tourism grew. This "golden age" of the art colony represents the first of two phases of accelerated tourism development in Taos during this century. It established the town's touristic reputation and laid the foundation for the second boom, which would begin in the 1960s and be based not upon art but the ski industry (Rodriguez 1987a).

In comparison to the natives' position and theirs at home, the artists from the beginning enjoyed an economic advantage and a higher social status in Taos. New Mexico was a cheap place to live compared to eastern cities, and because cash was scarce, the artists' presence was an immediate boon to the local economy. The painters purchased food and supplies, paid rent, and hired local labor. They were more educated than the natives and many other Anglos and immediately stepped into a patronlike role. They rented or bought old adobes houses from the Mexicanos, painted endless pictures of the Indians, and hired members of both groups as domestic labor. They differed from most other Anglos in that they were not primarily speculators or bureaucrats but, instead, allegedly came to appreciate, publicize, and preserve native culture, rather than to undermine or exterminate it. They sponsored social and artistic activities and became benefactors of civic services in the town. The early painters were politely welcomed and accommodated in Taos and soon came to feel more accepted and valued for their creative talents there than in the outside world (Gibson 1983:22).

The Taos and Santa Fe colonies tended to be more cohesive and inward turned than most other American art colonies, such as Carmel, Woodstock, or Greenwich Village. Indeed, in their heyday both were described as clannish and ingrown. Gibson (1983:37–38) connects this in part to the artists' practical need to cooperate in marketing their works. He also attributes it to the artists' emulation of the communal models presented by the Indian pueblos and Hispanic villages. A more likely reason was their geographic and social isolation in a region well over 90 percent Spanish speaking. Taos then, as now, was an ethnically stratified and segregated society, in which the three major groups—Hispanics, Indians, and Anglos—interacted in the workplace but kept to themselves socially. These groups were circumscribed by cultural boundaries as well as by the socioeconomic hierarchy.

The Taos artists therefore associated primarily with each other and with other nonnative elites in the town, including the merchants they patronized and certain professionals and federal bureaucrats. Their face-to-face interaction with Indians involved hiring them to sit as models for paintings and to perform domestic labor—two jobs which often went hand in hand. The men who worked for Couse and Berninghaus, for example, modelled in the morning and did yardwork in the afternoon, a general pattern followed by others, whose relatives sometimes also worked for the artists' households (Broder 1980:153). A man might do carpentry, construction, or gardening, while his wife or sister cooked and cleaned; and both modelled. These arrangements sometimes grew into lifelong relationships reflected in portraits spanning a lifetime, such as those Hennings did of Frank Zamora (Nelson 1980:105). Some models became so closely associated with a particular artist that they colloquially took on their patron's surname: Ben Lujan, for example, became known in town as "Ben Couse," and Jim Mirabal as "Ufer's Jim" (Nelson 1980:44–48, 79).

These patron-client, master-servant, artist-model relationships were perceived as mutually beneficial and were described as such, although there is a limit to what we can document about how the people of Taos Pueblo truly saw them. The art industry shaped the lives of some pueblo individuals by enabling them to sell their visage, dressed aboriginally, by the hour. A few became career models. Joseph Sandoval, for example, sat for many artists over the course of his long life, having begun at age six because his father, whom he grew to resemble strikingly, had also been a well-known model. When young, Joseph posed for Sharp, Phillips, Blumenschein, Couse, Ufer, Berninghaus, Dunton, Higgins, Leon Gaspard, Joseph Imhoff, and then many others. Later in life he offered this memory to the *Taos News* art editor:

> When sitting as a young child for Couse, Joe remembers that he became frightened at the idea of the artists "catching" his image in paint and ran out of the studio down the street. However, he was soon overtaken by Mrs. Couse who brought him back, chained him around the waist to a chair within easy reach of a great bowl of luscious fruit and a tempting mound of cookies. A blanket was draped over the chain, says Joe, and Couse, without further complications, completed the painting. (Cooke 1970)

It is important to emphasize that the Indian paintings were not realistic portraits of individuals as they actually appeared in everyday life, but rather romantic compositions for which the subjects dressed in prototypical costume. Indians tended to be portrayed as ideal types in harmony with Nature, caught at some pristine, eternal moment.

A few of the artists painted Hispanos as well as Indians, although Hispanos were never as popular a subject and modelling did not become a significant source of income for them. Hispanos were depicted differently: they were cast as distinct individuals in their traditional workaday world, usually at moments of labor, ceremony, or leisure. This contrast between Indian and Hispano portrayals is striking in Phillips's work, for example, as Broder (1980:108–9) notes:

> Phillips idealized the Indian and all aspects of Indian life. His Indian genre paintings are not scenes of everyday life inhabited by real people; rather, they are rhapsodies composed of flowing lines and of rhythmic repetitions of mass, color, and light. His Indian subjects are poetic figures in imaginary, poetic landscapes. Frequently they stand frozen in time in spotless snow—snow crossed by only a few carefully placed animal tracks. In these paintings, the Indians are in complete harmony with their idealized setting. . . .
>
> It is Phillips's paintings of the people of the Spanish community of Taos that are truly successful realistic representations of life in New Mexico. His *Three Musicians of the Baile* (color pl. 38) are real people who live in the village. They sit beside the stove in a traditional Spanish house, one tilting his chair in a casual, individualized moment. These sharp, detailed portraits contrast markedly with the idealized Indians in paradisaical [*sic*] landscapes, such as *Indian Flute Player* (color pl. 36). *The Santero* (color pl. 39) works in a real room, surrounded by the religious images he has painted. He is an old man with a lined face—the antithesis of the wraithlike figures in *Indian Courtship* (b&w pl. 85). The four members of *Our Washerwoman's*

Family—New Mexico (color pl. 13) sit waiting on a bench. The icons, windows, whitewashed walls, and bench identify the setting as a New Mexican interior. Here are individuals who are members of different generations of the family, each with a personal outlook on life.

Here Broder overstates the authenticity of the Hispanic setting, for a closer examination of two of the paintings reveals it to have been a studio contrivance: both *Three Musicians* and *The Santero* feature the same large Indian pot atop the same hand-carved wood trunk as part of the background. In *The Santero*, several *retablos*, or religious paintings, are included in a secular arrangement that would not occur in a Catholic Hispanic home but which reflects, instead, their "museumization" (MacCannell 1976:8). Ethnographically bizarre ensembles contrived for their picturesque effect were commonplace in the Indian paintings, a trait for which Couse is particularly well known (Broder 1980:140–44). Even Sharp, so esteemed for his ethnological portraits of the vanishing Plains Indians, was known to have painted Plains scenarios using Taos models (Broder 1980:44–50).[6] In either case the Indian was an image of the past. Although Hispanos were far less idealized than Indians, both types of portraiture presented a rarified, artificial view of the local setting.

Indians and Hispanos seem to occur in different time dimensions in most early Taos paintings and rarely, if ever, appear together in the same composition. Ufer's work represents a partial exception in that he tended to paint Indians in a recognizably modern setting, albeit one that was suffused with golden light and brilliant color. He did one painting that is truly unusual: *Lunch at Lone Locust* depicts an Indian man waiting table for an Anglo family of outdoor diners, against the distant backdrop of Taos Mountain (Broder 1980: b&w pl. 197). Ufer is probably the only early Taos painter who portrayed an Indian at a menial, subordinate task in service to whites, although this remarkable work can hardly be considered an example of social realism in the usual sense. Indeed, for a self-avowed socialist and Trotskyite, unique as such among the early painters, Ufer's vision of Taos seems amazingly benign. He painted several portraits of himself with his models, the most striking of which is the fanciful *Me and Him*, in which he appears not as an artist but as an Indian laborer. Here he is a young man with long dark braids, standing in a field with a rake, dressed just like his model and companion, a blanket around his waist (Broder 1980:211–19, b&w pl. 169).

The artists described their relationships with natives in glowing, if paternalistic, terms, devoid of critical reference to the daily workings of pervasive inequality, their own privileged position within the local order, or their role in perpetuating it. In addition to the paintings, their individual memoirs, poetry, and fiction, as well as all other promotional literature on Taos, are characterized by a naive, awestruck enthusiasm about the spectacular natural scenery, the town's rustic adobe charm, and the exotic, mysterious Indian and Spanish cultures (see Weigle and Fiore 1982). Even later painters, whose liberal political sentiments and/or professional training might have disposed them toward some form of social realism, assiduously avoided that direction once they began to work in Taos. These artists included Emil Bisttram, who, like Adams, had studied mural techniques with Diego Rivera, and Louis Ribak, an abstractionist influenced by the Ash-Can School in New York. A similar trend occurred in Santa Fe, where Robert Henri, a founding figure of the art colony there and a member of the Ash-Can School, turned away from his earlier urban "dynamic realism" toward a formulaic portraiture through which he sought to capture fragmentary reflections of "whatever of the *great spirit* there is in the Southwest" (Coke 1963:42). Similar creeping conservatism and stylization seem to have overtaken John Sloan's work in Santa Fe, where in the early days he had produced some pungent satirical studies of tourist scenes, attesting to a sensibility which with time yielded to the picturesque. As Coke (1963:54) writes of Sloan, "Life in Santa Fe was less challenging and he was no longer the revolutionary underdog as was the case in New York. In New Mexico, he was regarded as a major social figure as well as a distinguished artist, mimic, and raconteur. His pictures became less impromptu and lacked the rugged, realistic quality of his early work." Coke (1963:108) further summarizes the overall trend in both colonies:

> The painters in New Mexico did not involve themselves with social conditions or aesthetic theory, but rather reacted in an unreserved and directly enthusiastic manner to the immediate stimulus of the exotic quality of the Indians and the drama presented by the landscape. They saw no need to enlarge or deepen their artistic direction and felt no compulsion to deal with puzzling or ugly forces.

But despite their dazzled, bland, and often increasingly formulaic characterizations of the natives, some of the paintings unwittingly reflect the de facto relations which existed between the artists and the Indians and Hispanos. The nature of these relations is evident in other sources as well.

In addition to their labor, Mexicanos rented or sold their houses to the new immigrants. The first artists bought and remodelled houses within easy walking distance of the Taos plaza, while later arrivals extended toward Cañon, Taos Pueblo, Ranchos, and Talpa. For example, on Ledoux Street near the heart of town, the Blumenscheins gradually put together a fifteen-room house, a few rooms at a time as the inhabitants died. Blumenschein painted several of these people, including his adobe plasterer (Blumenschein 1979:23–33). In Cañon, the John Younghunters (who arrived in 1916) employed an entire family of former owners as servants and handymen, whom they regarded with the typical mixture of kindly, but stern, paternalism. The ambivalence inherent in this kind of relationship was differentially perceived and expressed by the interacting parties. A counterperspective to the dominant, publicized Anglo version of these arrangements can sometimes be glimpsed in a Hispano account like the following:

> The M.'s owned property that the Younghunters bought and became their hired help. B. [now about 40] waited the table at their dinner parties, attended by Mabel Dodge Luhan and other artists, as well as "the Indian" [Mabel's husband, Tony Luhan]. B. had very long curled hair and wore a white dress with red hearts. She was about eight. After dinner, the party would go to the living room and pull the drapes, and "the Indian" would sit apart and play the drum and sing, and all the artists would sit around on the floor on big pillows, listening for hours. They thought it was wonderful. B. thinks it is interesting because here they [the Mexicanos] were forbidden to speak Spanish in school, yet the artists learned Spanish and could speak it. They spoke other languages [than English] much of the time.
>
> The M. children who worked for the Younghunters were instructed to address them as Señor and Señora. Among themselves they called her *la vieja* [the old lady]. One time B.'s brother came in the kitchen and didn't see Mrs. Y and asked where la vieja was, and she answered "La vieja is in back of you." She used to give the children a midmorning break with a peanut butter and jam sandwich. They *had* to eat peanut butter and jam, not just the peanut butter or bread. Mrs. Y. made the jam, which tasted horrible, and when she wasn't looking, they would throw it on the roof for the birds to eat. One time it rained and the roof leaked, and la vieja went up and discovered all the discarded sandwiches, and she reproached

them and cried.

The Younghunters made a few improvements on the place like adding plumbing, but they didn't radically remodel the house. They even left B.'s grandfather's old harnesses on the walls. Mrs. Y. had the habit of leaving quarters or half-dollars lying around the house, basically to test their honesty. B. says she didn't think about it at first, but then one of her siblings called her attention to it. (Rodriguez 1987b)[7]

Several elements in this account invite comment. The first concerns the very nature and structure of the mistress-servant relationship and the ways in which domestic servitude embodies each form of stratification which operates in a given society. The evolving pattern of domestic service in twentieth-century America incorporates and reflects racial, as well as class and gender, classification, and it does this with local variation (Rollins 1985:55). In Taos, the history and contemporary dynamics of class and intergroup relations are manifest in any given set of master-servant relations. In the example described above, domestic service is a form of employment confined to particular ethnic groups and passed on from one generation to the next. This paternalistic pattern typical of colonial situations is accentuated by the fact that domestic servants are recruited and trained as children. The mother tongue is both co-opted and suppressed. At the same time, in mildly disrespectful reference to the boss lady and the constant small subversions of her coercive maternalism, the account reveals an oppositional, if covertly expressed, sense of resistance. Another, perhaps more symmetrical, kind of oppositional stance is hinted at in the reference to "the Indian," whose full name was known to the speaker. The Indian is faceless to the Mexican domestic, yet at the very center of the artists' deluded fancy. This image reflects the tragic irony of the Mexicano dilemma within the artist-native relation, a dilemma Bodine (1968) so aptly named the "tri-ethnic trap."

The "tri-ethnic trap" constitutes the historical predicament in which Hispanos in Taos find themselves: conquered, dispossessed, dependent, ghettoized, and, above all, witness to the Indian's spiritual and moral elevation above themselves in Anglo eyes. The ethnic triangle involves three different, differentially accessible, perspectives on historical relations among the groups. The Anglo view, articulated by the full range of tourism promoters, is the most accessible and, indeed, the official one, while the Indian perspective remains the least known or publicly articulated. An inverse relation appears to exist between relative empowerment and objectified portrayal in popular culture, while a conjunction occurs between power and media control. Thus, as Virginia Woolf (1929) observed about women in European literature, the Indian appears everywhere in Taos as a mystified ideal, yet nowhere in dominant discourse do Indians speak with their own unmediated voices. Hispanos are less sublime, yet nearly as mute. The ambivalence of Anglo-Hispano relations is not far from the surface in Taos art, but it is never represented directly.

Apart from the vanishing cowboy and Ufer's and Sloan's notable exceptions, Anglos rarely appear in the Taos–Santa Fe paintings, although their presence saturates the art in every other respect. Another noteworthy exception to this rule is found in Blumenschein's group portrait, *Ourselves and Our Neighbors* (Broder 1980:b&w pls. 254, 255), which depicts principals of the art colony standing together in a narrow, high-ceilinged, adobe room, facing the viewer or audience. All but three of the twenty-two figures are identifiably individuated, including one Indian (Tony Luhan) and one Hispano holding a trumpet. Three faceless Indians, two men and one woman, sit to one side. The nameless Indian in the Hispanic maid's account is the very one with a face here. This is the art colony as a self-contained world. It comprises a society unto itself, but one located within a larger system of which it is an inseparable part. It is a world both divorced from and embedded in its immediate context.

Cultural Conservatism and the Promotion of Underdevelopment

Many of the early artists became involved in local community and civic affairs, at least those surrounding certain issues. These mostly concerned cultural preservation, public welfare, and natural resource conservation. The early commitment of artists to conservationism is epitomized in Bert Phillips, who was instrumental in having the mountain wilderness and public domain around Taos declared a national forest in 1906. He later became its first forest ranger when he needed to rest his eyesight, strained by years of painting Indians by firelight (Broder 1980:104). Wealthy patrons like Mabel Dodge Luhan and Lucy Case Harwood donated public buildings such as the town hospital and library. Artists and literati in both Taos and Santa Fe became ardent and effective proponents of Indian cultural-religious and land-rights claims. They successfully lobbied against the Bursum Bill (1922)[8] and in support of Taos Pueblo's sixty-four-year struggle for tribal jurisdiction over Blue Lake.[9] They promoted the revival of native arts, crafts, and ritual practices and at every step vehemently opposed visible manifestations of modernization and assimilation. In this latter crusade they often found themselves in disagreement with Hispano and other Anglo elites but, interestingly, in concert with Indian leaders. They passionately supported the latter in their struggles to keep running water and electricity out of Taos Pueblo. They opposed nonadobe construction and street paving in town, along with neon and billboard advertising. In short, they actively worked to preserve the quaint, rustic, scenic, and foreign character of the region, as well as the "traditional" appearance and practices of its native people. The height of their conservationist influence was reached in the 1920s and 1930s when in-migration peaked and the town officially incorporated (1934), partly in order to promote itself as a tourist attraction.

An important factor in the growth of the tourist-art colony complex in Taos was the arrival of New York heiress and *salonnier* Mabel Dodge Evans Stern in the winter of 1916–17. She promptly took up permanent residence and built a palatial adobe estate between the town and Taos Pueblo. For the next twenty years she maintained a salon there, and to inspire interpretation of Indian culture and Taos, she entertained many of the notable literati of her generation. Taos's fame as a bohemian art colony stems largely from her activities. Dodge crowned her own Indianist mysticism by marrying a Taos Pueblo man, and thereafter she sponsored and contributed to a plethora of artistic-literary celebrations of Indian culture and the region in general. Prior to her arrival, the local colony of artists had not been especially bohemian in character but, instead, had resembled, in Nelson's (1980:11) words, "a frontier outpost of middle class form and propriety that they established among themselves, similar to that of military officers of that era sent to some remote army post."

Dodge's cultural influence on the character of town development was enormous simply because she had more money than anybody else in Taos, and for roughly two decades she spent it lavishly on the whole cultural conservationist enterprise. It is ironic that she helped to spawn the very commercialism she and other preservationists so detested. Taos grew into a modern town on the basis of the tourism originally promoted by the art colony. At the heart of this economy lies a contradiction between preservation and growth, a contradiction sometimes known as the "golden goose syndrome." This has been a prominent theme in town politics since incorporation. The entire appeal of the place for artists and tourists rested on Indian ethnicity, natural splendor, and a rustic Latin adobe ambience. Its promoters and connoisseurs were thus inevitably drawn into the task of protecting this delicate, "unspoiled" combination. At the conservative extreme of the argument stood the bohemians, a number of whom were independently wealthy, and most artists, whose major income was not local. Their usual cause and sometime ally was Taos Pueblo; their adversaries were business-men and Hispano elites who wanted "progress" and economic development. Another major player in this scheme has always been the state itself, which during the art colony decades became the single largest landowner and employer in Taos County.

During the 1930s Taos and other northern New Mexican counties moved into primary economic dependency upon the federal government. Already the major land-owner, the government acquired and then auctioned even more property for back taxes during this decade, while the New Deal inaugurated new forms of government subsidy that underwrote a wholesale shift from Republican to Democratic party domi-nation. At the same time, stringent limitations on grazing and other small-scale extrac-tive uses of the wilderness were enacted. The "Indian New Deal," under the direction of John Collier, an anthropologist and member of Mabel Dodge Luhan's circle, helped, with the best of intentions, to entrench Indian separateness. The role of the New Deal in intensifying Hispano economic dependency has been noted by Sara Deutsch (1987:208):

> The New Deal's pluralism . . . propagated a view of Hispanic culture as static. . . . By channeling relief funds for Hispanic areas into such projects as Spanish co-lonial crafts training, government programs encouraged cultural isolation, whether or not they intended it. Anti-modernist Anglos . . . saw in colonial cultural re-vival the economic salvation of the Hispanic villages, and the spiritual survival of modern America. . . . Spanish-Americans could not, because of their citizenship, be forever denied a place in the United States polity, but the place tendered them could remain on the margins. They could provide the useful "other" that anti-modernists wanted to preserve for balance as part of the human heritage.

Taos's population grew by 28 percent during the 1930s, partly through an influx of newcomers; but native Mexicanos who had migrated out for employment also came home during the Depression to get by on a combination of farming and welfare. This was the decade in which the town of Taos incorporated and actively began to develop itself as a tourist attraction. The art community took an active role in advertising itself and the historical, cultural, and spiritual wonders of Taos. Artists helped to create the "traditional" annual summer fiestas, which eventually replaced in commercial impor-tance the carnival that attended the pueblo's feast day in the fall. Like their counter-parts in Santa Fe, a group of artists and writers invented the fiesta "historical-hysterical" parade, which featured an opening procession that began with the Indians, followed by the Conquistadors, the Mountain Men, American Cavalry, and finally the Artists, broken wagon wheel and all (Taos Review 1940). The number of art galleries and other tourist businesses expanded, as did all promotional literature and activity (Gibson 1983:61–64). Thus, despite the Depression, tourism seems to have flourished in Taos during the 1930s.[10]

It was this combination of federal policy and tourism that helped to further en-trench and perpetuate the conditions of segregation and underdevelopment which had characterized the region even prior to New Mexico statehood. Federal policy deter-mined the political status of Indian and Hispanic ethnic groups and affected their economic status through the appropriation and allocation of land and other resources. The art colony converted inequality and backwardness into marketable assets and promoted the perpetuation of those conditions by which these "assets" were sustained. This is not to say that the artists performed the task of mystification consciously or with cynical intent; on the contrary, they mostly believed their own fiction. Thus while their paintings and writings certainly do not represent the situation as it actually existed in Taos, they do express what the artists saw, or what they wanted and needed to see. This kind of selective, softened vision is, however, hardly unusual. Indeed, one may argue, it is more the rule than the exception. Its very ubiquity may conceal its signficance.

Mystification Demystified

Several interpenetrating features or aspects of the artistic mystification process as it occurred in Taos can now be identified. These include: differential awareness, denial, and Indianism, intertwined with symbolic objectification, omission, co-optation, and transmutation.

Edward Spicer (1972) considers differential awareness of ethnic boundaries among dominant and subdominant groups to be characteristic of the Southwest as a regional system of ethnic relations. It is one way of referring to the fact that members of a racially or ethnopolitically dominant group do not typically think of themselves as part of an ethnic group at all. They tend to be less directly aware than are subordinates of the complex rules and markers which govern face-to-face interethnic relations. Thus members of different ethnic groups or strata actually tend to perceive and interpret interethnic interaction differently. Moreover, in mixed and in-group company, they are differentially candid about what they do see and feel. Power increases the dominant group's direct access to those subordinated as well as to universal attention, whereas relative powerlessness forces underdogs to learn their master's ways. Differential power accounts not only for the vastly unequal volumes of generally available material expressing different ethnic viewpoints in Taos, but also for the remarkable public consensus about what a marvel of interethnic harmony the place is. Privately and intraethnically, the story is often quite different, and occasionally these counterperspectives and the bitterness they involve erupt through the placid surface. Yet what is significant here is the success of the Taos mystique: it converts what is most brutal in society into something fantastic and wonderful—the land of enchantment. The mystique gained local currency simply because it sold well where little else seemed available. But there is something more than differential awareness operating in Taos: there is also outright denial.

Denial is a beautiful handwoven blanket draped over the chain in Couse's studio. Denial as it occurs in the Taos mystique is probably not universal to stratified systems but is confined to those, like the United States, in which an overt, central contradiction exists between ideal and real culture. The notion of such a contradiction was part of Gunnar Myrdal's (1944) thesis about American race relations: historical reality flagrantly belies the national ideals of freedom and equality for all, and this crack runs deep in the American character. In a stratified system where no contradiction of this type exists, the fact of domination may be frankly admitted but be legitimated, for example, by divine will. In a situation where a moral injunction for social equality prevails, the fiction may be perpetrated through denial. An imperfect analogy here is the concept of denial applied by clinical theorists to the communicational dynamics within the alcoholic or otherwise dysfunctional family. Here, denial is a mechanism whereby family members unconsciously accommodate and help to perpetuate the pathological behavior by claiming and pretending that everything is normal and going well—in effect, that what is happening is not really happening (see, e.g., Greenleaf 1981; Black 1982; Seixas and Youcha 1985). Denial also occurs at the extrafamilial or public level, where it may or may not turn out to be pathological, dysfunctional, or maladaptive. The phenomenon of denial characterizes contemporary race relations in this country in general, and, accordingly, it occurs in Taos, where part of its net effect has been adaptation to long-standing depressed economic conditions.

Indianism is the advocacy and emulation of Indian culture by non-Indians. As discussed here, the phenomenon is distinguished from nativist Indianism or ethno-political mobilization by Indians themselves. These latter have also occurred in Taos, perhaps first during the Pueblo Revolt and more recently in the legal struggle for Blue Lake, which was assisted by Anglo Indianism. The ideological roots of Indianism in America are almost as old as the colonial enterprise, having their diverse origins, for example, in the reformism of the Spanish missionary Las Casas or in Rousseau's ideal of the "noble savage." It began to assume its modern forms as nationalization took place and nations emerged. Indianism is found in both Mexico and the U.S. South-west, where during the twentieth century it has taken comparable, yet also signif-icantly different, forms. In the U.S. Southwest, its epicenters were the Taos and Santa Fe art colonies, both virtual breeding grounds for Indianism, where hundreds of "yearners" came to paint Indians; to write about them; to study, understand, or emu-late them; and to defend Indian difference against assimilation (Simmons 1979:218–20). Some even dressed like them or, as we have seen, painted (and photographed) them-selves as Indians, while virtually all adopted some items of Indian attire, such as moc-casins, certain garments, or jewelry. They collected Indian and Hispanic cultural arti-facts and sponsored the preservation or revival of various traditional native arts and crafts. In the latter case such arts became transformed, as Brody (1976) has shown for Indian pottery and painting (see also Deitch 1977), K. P. Kent (1976) for weaving, and Briggs (1980) for Hispanic woodcarving in Cordova. They promoted pluralism (and, unwittingly, the inequality it entails in the region) and pressed it into the service of their own class advantage and a tourism economy.

The other side of the coin of Indianism in the Southwest has been Hispanophobia, or anti-Mexicanism, which took shape during the period of Manifest Destiny and the Mexican War and probably reached its most virulent expression in Texas, and which forms part of the general Anglo-American heritage (Paredes 1977; Weber 1979). Hispanophobia and racism against Mexicans or mestizos is as prevalent in New Mexico as elsewhere in the Southwest, although it is complicated in the upper Rio Grande Valley by a demographic majority that gives Hispanics local electoral control. Although clearly subordinated, Mexicanos there enjoy a higher degree of practical parity vis-à-vis local Anglos than they do in south Texas or southern California, for example.

The "tri-ethnic trap" shaped Hispanophobia in Taos, where it represented a cul-tural means by which the Anglo minority could divide and rule the natives. It goes without saying that this division had a long-standing colonial precedent to build on. In New Mexico, the "fantasy heritage" of pure Castilian descent, a vestige of the Spanish preoccupation with *limpieza de sangre* (purity of blood) which served New World colonial elites, became entrenched and elaborated after American occupation, particularly among Hispanic upper and middle classes (Chavez 1984:85–106). It is noteworthy therefore that while Indianism occurs among elites in modern Mexico, it hardly appears among Hispanic New Mexicans, at least not until the post-Chicano movement period, and then only among certain urban middle-class youth.

Anglo Indianism in the U.S. Southwest invites comparison with the *indigenismo*, or Indianism, that developed among urban Mexican artists and intellectuals during roughly the same period. Unlike the Taos–Santa Fe painters, the Mexican muralists, for example, Rivera, Orozco, and Siqueiros, were stylistically innovative, often politically engaged social realists (or surrealists). Nevertheless, the two cases participate in a larger phenomenon identified by Graburn (1976:29): "In the Americas, too, each large nation has taken the arts of its crushed former peoples and erected them as symbols of 'national ethnicity' to distinguish each from the other, and all of them from their European homelands." In the U.S. and Mexico, Indian elements were incorporated into the "fine" art of the dominant society and ethnic group as part of an effort to define an essentially American national identity.

Symbolic objectification, omission, co-optation, and transmutation are intricately entwined with each other and with the aspects of mystification just discussed. For example, Indianism and especially the marketing, or "commodification," of Indian ethnicity cannot take place apart from the objectification of Indians and Indian culture. Conquest and colonization entail the objectification and dehumanization of subject populations, inevitably justified by some form of imperialist ideology. Indians in the North American imagination went from the subhuman to the sublime more or less as their numbers and military threat diminished. Nowhere more than in Taos were they seen and portrayed as the mystical Other instead of as regular human beings. Just as denial underlies omission, objectification underlies transmutation, in addition to co-optation. Omission is denial translated to the visual and poetic dimensions: the chain covered over, the trash and junk cars left out of the landscape.

Co-optation involves the insidious assimilative effect that mystification has upon both its objects and its purveyors. It seduced the painters away from risky aesthetic experimentation into decorative, formulaic, intellectually insipid renditions of "local color." But co-optation also seized natives, who learned to play out their scripted ethnic stereotypes, not merely as part of the inevitable choreography of denial that characterizes face-to-face interracial relations in contemporary America, but with increasing psychosocial investment in the fiction it perpetuated. Taking their cue from the artists, they learned to market, as well as to elaborate, their own ethnicity (Rodriguez 1986). Art in Taos became the grand commodity, itself based upon the objectification and marketing of ethnicity. Anglo artists co-opted native cultural and ethnic symbols, incorporating them into their own works and transforming their meanings forever. In addition to the ghettoization of natives as "folk," rather than mainstream (or "fine") artists, the Anglo appropriation of their "traditional" symbols has placed Indian and Hispano artists in an uncomfortable predicament in New Mexico, a situation which requires a separate analysis.

Finally we come to the matter of transmutation, the net accomplishment of all of these elements working in concert. It consists of imaginatively creating a prettier, more benign version of the world than the one actually prevailing. Transmutation is the most difficult aspect of mystification to define, partly because it involves an element of transformation that is universal to artistic creation. All art accomplishes the transformation of experience into plastic, verbal, or musical expression which somehow bears the cultural imprint of its historical setting. In Dupre's (1983:274) words:

> The genuine artist never merely depicts or describes: he symbolically transforms a given situation and thereby moves beyond the sphere of ordinary life. Even the "realistic" artist *chooses* the expressive details of his description and, in this process of selective symbolization, creates a distance between himself and the realities or ideologies in which his art originates. In doing so, he inevitably becomes a critic, however unwittingly, of the *given*. This may well constitute the major difference between genuine literature [for example] and ideologies: even if the writer accepts the ideologies of the ruling class, he inevitably transforms them in the process

of aesthetic symbolization.

The question thus arises whether all or only certain art amounts to mystification, a problem which is compounded if it is approached from an anthropological or cross-cultural perspective. Although the present discussion inevitably raises this question, it is not intended to resolve it nor to enter the domain of aesthetic theory. The purpose is smaller and more modest: to identify and describe one case of mystification. The products of the art colony comprise what some (e.g., Coke 1963:59) call "commercial" rather than "fine" art, or advertisement as distinct from "true art." Bateson (1972:136), scarcely concealing his disdain for this phenomenon, distinguishes allegory from art:

> Allegory, at best a distasteful sort of art, is an inversion of the normal creative process. Typically an abstract relation, e.g., between truth and justice, is first conceived in rational terms. The relationship is then metamorphized and dolled up to look like a product of primary process [the unconscious]. The abstractions are personified and made to participate in a pseudomyth, and so on. Much advertising art is allegorical in this sense, that the creative process is inverted.

It should be kept in mind that whereas Bateson considers allegory to be a falsified product of secondary process (conscious purpose), the claim here is that Taos art was largely an unconscious falsification. Perhaps it lies somewhere between what Bateson calls art and allegory. In any case, Taos art involves transmutation which, together with the other mechanisms already discussed, constitutes the process of mystification.

Conclusion

This paper has examined the Taos–Santa Fe art colony as a case study of the process of mystification. Mystification is defined broadly as a cultural process which perpetuates the social order by suffusing it with a shared sense of awesome, transcendent meaning. Mystification occurs in simple as well as complex societies and secular as well as sacred contexts. In modern society, where it serves both special and systemic interests, mystification assumes a multitude of sacred and secular forms. To illuminate how mystification works in one particular instance, the internal workings of art colony society have been examined here in relation to the art which portrayed the local setting.

We are left with several questions of a practical as well as theoretical nature. One of the most important is, Does all, or just certain, art involve mystification? In the first instance, one might wonder at the usefulness of so inclusive a concept; in the second, cross-cultural comparison requires considerable conceptual refinement of the diagnostic features. At least in vulgar Marxist guise, the concept might seem almost anathema to the anthropological interrogation of culture. Yet it contains a kernel of insight indispensable to social analysis. This study has tried to chart some of the uneven ground between these two positions. One the one hand, it represents an attempt to identify and analyze a specific historical phenomenon which occurred at a specific time and place. On the other, it represents an attempt to salvage the concept of mystification from a haze of assumptions about its vaguely hypnotic character. The concept is worth salvaging, it seems, not because it might lead to yet another sociological reification, but rather insofar as it helps us to analyze how particular historical instances of the process occur, perhaps especially those in which we ourselves may be entangled.

NOTES

1. This study is based upon research on interethnic relations in Taos, supported in part by grants from the Wenner-Gren Foundation for Anthropological Research, the American Philosophical Society, and the Academic Senate and ISOP-Mexico Program at UCLA. I also wish to thank the following individuals for commenting on earlier versions of this paper: Thomas Hall, Jacques Maquet, Louise Lamphere, Marta Weigle, and Philip Bock. Any inadequacies in the final product, however, are my own responsibility.

2. As defined here, mystification belongs under the general rubric of what Marxists call ideology, a concept neither confined to nor originating in Marxism, but which, according to Raymond Williams (1977:55), occurs among Marxist thinkers in three common versions: "(i) a system of beliefs characteristic of a particular class or group; (ii) a system of illusory beliefs—false ideas or false consciousness—which can be constrasted with true or scientific knowledge; (iii) the general process of the production of meanings and ideas." This study treats Taos art as a specific example of mystification or an expression of ideology in the first two senses. But it approaches the problem from a disciplinary perspective which encompasses and generally emphasizes the third sense.

3. The nomenclature for Mexican Americans is notoriously problematic. In this paper, "Mexicanos," an emic term (in Spanish) universally acceptable to people of Mexican descent in the U.S., including northern New Mexicans, is used interchangeably with "Hispanos," a term anthropologists now use to refer to these people, who also call themselves (in English) "Spanish Americans."

4. Race and ethnicity are often difficult to separate empirically, but they should be distinguished analytically: "race" refers to a group that is socially defined on the basis of physical or ostensibly biological criteria; "ethnic groups" are defined socially on the basis of cultural criteria (van den Berghe 1967:10–11). Race is a principle of stratification and an ideological instrument of subjugation, whereas ethnicity is a principle of cultural differentiation which, in state societies, is usually structural as well.

5. Relevant features of underdevelopment other than those already mentioned include: economic dependency; widespread use of nonindustrial technology; high rates of unemployment, underemployment, illiteracy, and infant mortality; and limited availability of modern public health and education services.

6. Many of Sharp's commissioned works portraying Plains Indians are owned by museums of anthropology, such as the Lowie at UC-Berkeley or the Smithsonian. Sharp delayed settling in Taos in order to document Indians in the Great Plains region, because he felt they would "disappear" sooner. In later years he used Taos models to execute Plains scenarios. That this was not always a happy process is indicated by the following anecdote: "One time he wished an Indian called 'White Weasel' to wear a hat, which he refused to do, saying it was 'bad medicine' for a Taos Indian to wear a hat, especially a Crow Indian hat. Mr. Sharp insisted, however, and got a picture of a real angry Indian in a big hat that looked decidedly uncomfortable on him" (quoted in Broder 1980:50). This account, like Joseph Sandoval's, describes the modelling situation as one of domination.

7. Rodriguez Taos field notes, August 5, 1987. This text represents a close paraphrase, not a direct quote, because the story was told during the course of casual conversation (and written down afterwards), rather than during a formal, tape-recorded interview. The speaker probably overstates the degree to which members of the art colony knew Spanish. Although Spanish was the lingua franca in Taos prior to World War II, few artists or other Anglos understood or spoke it, while both Indians and Mexicanos were required to learn English.

8. The Bursum Bill was introduced to Congress in 1922 by Senator Holm Bursum at the request of the Secretary of the Interior, Albert Fall, ostensibly to settle the problem of Pueblo land claims. It would have confirmed title to all non-Pueblo claims ten years older than statehood and placed land- and water-rights matters under state jurisdiction. This would have resulted in enormous land loss for the Pueblos. The bill was opposed and successfully defeated through the efforts of a devoted Anglo lobby which included artists, writers, and anthropologist John Collier (Simmons 1979:215).

9. Blue Lake, located between Taos and Wheeler peaks in the mountain wilderness above the Taos basin, is the source of the Taos Pueblo and town of Taos watershed. When the lake and many thousands of surrounding acres in the public domain were declared a national forest in 1906, they were placed under the administrative jurisdiction of the Department of Agriculture's Forest Service. This inaugurated the pueblo's legal battle to regain control and unrestricted access to the Blue Lake area, a case finally resolved in 1970 when President Nixon signed a bill giving the pueblo trust title to the lake and some forty-eight thousand surrounding acres. In effect this act transferred jurisdiction over the region from the Department of Agriculture to the Department of the Interior. The Blue Lake settlement represents a milestone in Indian land-claims cases because it is the only one in which the original tribal use-area was "returned" (rather than being compensated for in other lands or a cash settlement). The case was won on the basis of a religious-cultural argument that the lake was the pueblo's premier sacred-use area, its "church in the mountains"; without free and exclusive access to it, the Taos people and their culture would die out. The legal battle was assisted in important ways by a constant Anglo lobby more or less coextensive with the art colony (Bodine 1967, 1978).

10. The growth of tourism in Taos during the 1930s is further confirmed by the author's review of the local newspapers, which reflect an economy accelerated over the preceding and the subsequent decades.

REFERENCES CITED

Aguirre-Beltran, G. 1979. Regions of Refuge. Society for Applied Anthropology Series, Monograph 12. Washington, D.C.

Bateson, G. 1972. Style, Grace, and Information in Primitive Art. In *Steps to an Ecology of Mind* (by G. Bateson). New York: Ballantine Books. 128–52.

Black, C. 1982. *It Will Never Happen to Me!* Denver: M.A.C.

Blumenschein, H. 1979. *Recuerdos: Early Days of the Blumenschein Family.* Silver City, NM: Tecolote Press.

Bodine, J. J. 1967. Attitudes and Institutions of Taos, New Mexico: Variables for Value System Expression. PhD diss., Tulane University, New Orleans.

———. 1968. A Tri-Ethnic Trap: The Spanish Americans in Taos. In *Spanish-Speaking People in the United States* (ed. by J. Helm). Proceedings of the 1968 Annual Spring Meeting of the American Ethnological Society. Seattle: University of Washington Press.

———. 1978. Taos Blue Lake Controversy. Journal of Ethnic Studies 6(1):40–48.

Briggs, C. 1980. *The Woodcarvers of Cordova, New Mexico.* Knoxville: University of Tennessee Press.

Broder, P. J. 1980. *Taos: A Painter's Dream.* Boston: New York Graphic Society.

Brody, J. J. 1976. The Creative Consumer: Survival, Revival and Invention in Southwest Arts. In *Ethnic and Tourist Arts* (ed. by N. Graburn). Berkeley: University of California Press. 70–84.

Bryant, K. L., Jr. 1978. The Atchison, Topeka and Santa Fe Railway and the Development of the Taos and Santa Fe Art Colonies. New Mexico Historical Quarterly 9(4):437–53.

Chavez, J. 1984. *The Lost Land.* Albuquerque: University of New Mexico Press.

Cohen, E. 1979. A Phenomenology of Tourist Experiences. Sociology 13:179–201.

Coke, V. D. 1963. *Taos and Santa Fe: The Artist's Environment, 1882–1942.* Albuquerque: University of New Mexico Press.

Cooke, R. 1970. Taos Arts. Taos News, July 16, 1970.

Dann, G., D. Nash, and P. Pearce. 1988. Methodology in Tourism Research. Annals of Tourism Research 15(1):1–28.

Deitch, L. 1977. The Impact of Tourism upon the Arts and Crafts of the Indians of the Southwestern U.S. In *Hosts and Guests* (ed. by V. Smith). Philadelphia: University of Pennsylvania Press. 173–84.

Deutsch, S. 1987. *No Separate Refuge.* New York: Oxford University Press.

Dupre, L. 1983. *Marx's Social Critique of Culture.* New Haven, Conn.: Yale University Press.

Gibson, A. M. 1983. *The Santa Fe and Taos Colonies.* Norman: University of Oklahoma Press.

Graburn, N. 1976. Introduction: Arts of the Fourth World. In *Ethnic and Tourist Arts* (ed. by N. Graburn). Berkeley: University of California Press. 1–32.

――――. 1977. Tourism: The Sacred Journey. In *Hosts and Guests* (ed. by V. Smith). Philadelphia: University of Pennsylvania Press. 17–31.

――――. 1983. The Anthropology of Tourism. Annals of Tourism Research 10(1):9–33.

Greenleaf, J. 1981. *Co-Alcoholic, Para-Alcoholic*. Los Angeles: privately published by author.

Gunder Frank, A. 1967. *Capitalism and Underdevelopment in Latin America*. New York: Monthly Review Press.

Harris, M. 1964. *Patterns of Race in the Americas*. New York: Walker and Company.

Jafari, J. 1974. Role of Tourism in the Socioeconomic Transformation of Developing Countries. MA thesis, Cornell University, Ithaca, NY.

Kent, K. P. 1976. Pueblo and Navajo Weaving Traditions and the Western World. In *Ethnic and Tourist Arts* (ed. by N. Graburn). Berkeley: University of California Press. 85–101.

Kent, N. 1983. *Hawaii: Islands under the Influence*. New York: Monthly Review Press.

Kottke, M. 1988. Estimating Economic Impacts of Tourism. Annals of Tourism Research 15(1): 122–23.

MacCannell, D. 1976. *The Tourist: A New Theory of the Leisure Class*. New York: Schocken Books.

Myrdal, G. 1944. *An American Dilemma: The Negro Problem and Modern Democracy*. New York: Harper and Row.

Nelson, M. C. 1980. *The Legendary Artists of Taos*. New York: Watson-Guptill Publications.

Ortiz, R. D. 1980. *The Roots of Resistance*. Los Angeles: UCLA.

Paredes, R. 1977. The Origins of Anti-Mexican Sentiment in the United States. New Scholar 6: 139–65.

Reeve, K. A. 1982. *Santa Fe and Taos, 1898–1942: An American Cultural Center*. El Paso: Texas Western Press.

Rodriguez, S. 1986. Constructed and Reconstructed Ethnicity in Taos. Paper presented at the annual meeting of the American Anthropological Association, Philadelphia.

――――. 1987a. Land, Water, and Ethnic Identity in Taos. In *Land, Water, and Culture* (ed. by C. Briggs and J. Van Ness). Albuquerque: University of New Mexico Press.

――――. 1987b. Unpublished field notes on Taos; in author's possession.

Rollins, J. 1985. *Between Women: Domestics and Their Employers*. Philadelphia: Temple University Press.

Seixas, J., and G. Youcha. 1985. *Children of Alcoholism*. New York: Crown Publishers.

Simmons, M. 1979. History of the Pueblos since 1821. In *Handbook of North American Indians, vol. 9:Southwest* (ed. by A. Ortiz). Washington, D.C.: Smithsonian Institution.

Smith, V. 1977. Introduction. In *Hosts and Guests* (ed. by V. Smith). Philadelphia: University of Pennsylvania Press.

Spicer, E. 1972. Introduction and Plural Society in the Southwest. In *Plural Society in the Southwest* (ed. by E. Spicer and R. Thompson). Albuquerque: University of New Mexico Press. 1–20, 21–76.

Taos Review. July 18, 1940.

van den Berghe, P. 1967. *Race and Racism*. New York: John Wiley and Sons.

――――, and C. Keyes. 1984. Introduction: Tourism and Re-Created Ethnicity. Annals of Tourism Research 11(3):343–52.

Wallerstein, I. 1979. *The Capitalist World-Economy*. Cambridge, England: Cambridge University Press.

Weber, D. 1979. "Scarce More than Apes": Historical Roots of Anglo-American Stereotypes of Mexicans. In *New Spain's Far North Frontier* (ed. by D. Weber). Albuquerque: University of New Mexico Press. 293–307.

Weigle, M. 1986. Civilizers, Art Colonists, Couriers, and Civil Servants: The Role of Women in Popularizing the Native American Southwest. Paper presented at the Wenner-Gren International Symposium no. 102, Daughters of the Desert: Women Anthropologists and Students of the Native American Southwest, Tucson.

――――, and K. Fiore. 1982. *Santa Fe and Taos: The Writer's Era, 1916–1941*. Santa Fe: Ancient City Press.

White, R. R. 1983. *The Taos Society of Artists*. Albuquerque: University of New Mexico Press.

Williams, R. 1977. *Marxism and Literature*. Oxford: Oxford University Press.

Wolf, E. 1982. *Europe and the People without History*. Berkeley: University of California Press.

Woolf, V. 1929. *A Room of One's Own*. New York: Harcourt, Brace, and World, Inc.

Tradition's Next Step[1]

Dean MacCannell

Not long ago, around 1984, there occurred a convergence of opinion, a virtual consensus in the critical fields in the United States, that humanity was in a kind of stall. On the right, U.S. State Department official Frances Fukuyama celebrated the "victory of capitalism," calling it the "end of history." On the left, the distinguished critic Fredric Jameson, lamenting the same moment, wrote of "the death of the historical subject." We were told that we had entered *postmodernity*: from this point on we will recycle styles from the past and from different cultural horizons; we will live in a framework of greatly expanded possibility for gender and ethnic expression, but one in which difference no longer makes any difference; we will exist in a kind of emotionless state occasionally punctuated by manufactured and marketed euphoria. It should not go unremarked that this end of history, unlike the one Marx foresaw, did not happen under conditions of universal material equality and well-being.

Postmodern Replication of Colonial Arrangements

Since about 1975 I have been interested in another matter that is related. In my studies of tourism I noted a particular kind of cultural deformation that occurs in the production of "authentic native handicrafts" and "traditional artifacts" that are now for sale worldwide as souvenirs, decoration, and "tourist art."[2] My concerns about this material are not the usual ones: that tourist art, even that which faithfully reproduces traditional forms, is not really authentic or traditional; that it is fake and therefore tacky; that it has lost its original sacred significance and demeans those who make it. In this arena one finds the concepts of "modern" and "postmodern" applied to "ethnic art" which is valued but for something other than its "authentic," "traditional" qualities.[3] This approach to ethnic and tourist art strikes me as the transfer of a version of the "high versus low" distinction to expert aesthetic judgments of non-European art and music after it lost its utility for imposing value on Western art.[4] What intrigues me is that the valuing of *authenticity*, which usually goes without question in the appraisal of traditional arts, may eventually have a more profoundly negative impact on the cultures of native peoples than would a casual neglect of concern for this often embarrassing concept.[5]

Authenticity in discussions of tourist and ethnic arts usually means that the object is old, or pre-colonial, or in a pre-colonial style, that it was created for use by the people who made it, that it was actually used for practical or ritual purposes in a village context, that it is unique to a particular culture and not a product of external influences, and perhaps that it once had meaning for the peoples who made it that may not be fully understood today.[6] While the concept sounds innocent, it can be like a stake driven into the heart of local cultures. Once the standard of "authenticity" has been applied, one can only conclude that most art is not authentic and that most formerly traditional peoples live inauthentic lives. The concept of "authenticity" thus produces enormous leverage in the world art market, which is the true domain of its operation. The value of specific pieces is driven up because they are called "authentic," while others are driven down because they are not. Predictably, this leverage has been met with a myriad of clever dodges at the village level and among traders in native arts and handicrafts: copying an older piece, burying it in dung for several weeks to "age" it, encouraging chickens to peck at it to give it a patina of apparent use, creating fanciful narratives about its original function, etc.[7] The ongoing process of negotiating the status of art works and cultural artifacts in the interstices of cultures worldwide is potential ground for the production of new cultural forms. That it often resembles comic opera, I take to be a healthy sign.[8]

What is not healthy is the emergence on this same ground of subtle new forms of cultural hegemony which do not require military force or open declarations of Western religious or other cultural superiority. In fact, on the surface, quite the opposite kind of declaration occurs, where lip service is paid to the superiority of non-Western beliefs and traditions. I think it is possible in postmodernity, more specifically in postmodern admiration for the cultural other, most specifically in politically correct ("sustainable") tourism and ethnography, to discern a new kind of colonialism occupying the same ground as the old, operating as the old one did at the level of economic and other exchanges but also at the level of the unconscious.

I have not been able to prevent myself from asking how the world might look if everyone's dreams of authenticity came true. What if we actually realized the positive vision of a postmodern multicultural future? The cultural other that would occupy the site of "authentic tradition" would be condemned to a kind of historylessness, a flat existence in which past, present, and future are essentially similar, in which nothing happens other than a kind of masterful self-reproduction, in which everyone lives in the space between two deaths: the death of their culture, now beautifully preserved and presented, and their own physical death. Are these the conditions for the incorporation of "authentic, traditional otherness" into postmodernity?

In my studies of tourism and my travels, I have been naturally drawn toward things and activities which cannot be incorporated in the framework of oppositions: postmodern/modern/traditional or inauthentic/authentic. I confess to a deeply personal bias that drives me to search for cultural objects that do not yield to the new hegemonic incorporation, that refuse to participate in the reproduction of colonial hierarchies now under a positive sign. This has led me to sites of creative expression of new cultural forms and subjects and to a different view of the postmodern totalization, the death of the subject, and the end of history. The two artists whose work is discussed below clearly indicate a different path. Kafi Quaku and George Longfish are technically "post-tourist" artists in that both have reacted against an original positioning of their work as exemplary of ethnic artistic expression, but not by simply adopting a Western style. Quaku started out as a carver of African animals in "traditional" style for tourists but is now better known for his carvings of Western consumer goods. Longfish consciously rejected the "traditional" style of the Santa Fe Indian School—of "Bambi art"—taking an interesting route back to the grounds of Indian painting traditions. He comments:

> A reviewer of the first show I was in, because of my name, wrote about the "cultural information" in my work. He saw tepees and stuff that wasn't there. I was offended because I was trying to assimilate Anglo-European art values, color, and form. I was working with Barnett Newman, a hard-core New York Expressionist. I liked stripes and painted football uniforms. But I would be Indian no matter what, because of my name. [from notes taken in conversation between George Longfish and author at the Gorman Museum, Davis, California, October 1992]

Cultural Appropriation: How It Works

Willy Apollon has argued that art is the form of self-understanding that potentially has an opening for future subversion.[9] Closing this particular opening or gap—for example, by causing a people endlessly to reproduce themselves for others—effectively removes them from the stage of history.[10] In the great international cultural division of labor that is called "postmodernity," "authentic tradition" supplies humanity in general with the spectacle of a beautiful and frozen innocence lost. This is a brilliant design for the perpetuation of current hegemonic structures. Rather than killing the creative energy of formerly colonized peoples, this energy is channeled into endless repetition, which is praised and curated as the repository of "true human values." In postmodernity, anything and anyone that does not participate in "authentic" self-reproduction can be classed as a "victim" of development, abject and inauthentic, not suited for anything other than factory work.[11]

These issues have been authoritatively addressed more than once by the respected anthropologist James Clifford. In an important recent essay, "On Collecting Art and Culture," Clifford ironically inverts the usual formula of the "innocent savage" visited by the "scientific investigator," giving us a virutal ethnography of ethnographers now represented as innocent collectors, whom he compares to (white, Western, bourgeois) children:

> [A] boy's accumulation of miniature cars, a girl's dolls, a summer vacation "nature museum" (with labeled stones and shells, a hummingbird in a bottle), a treasured bowl filled with the bright shavings of crayons. In these small rituals we observe the channelings of obsession, an exercise in how to make the world one's own, to gather things around oneself tastefully, appropriately. The inclusions in all collections reflect wider cultural rules—of rational taxonomy, of gender, of aesthetics. An excessive, sometimes even rapacious need to *have* is transformed into rule-governed, meaningful desire. Thus the self that must possess but cannot have it all learns to select, order, classify in hierarchies—to make "good" collections. (Clifford 1990:143)

What Professor Clifford, for all his irony, may not see is that his formulation seemingly inadvertently places the anthropological collector over the rapacious and tasteless capitalist consumer *and* also over the people who created the objects that are assembled in the ethnological collection. Clifford radically asserts that "'cultures' are ethnographic collections. . . . [R]ather than grasping objects only as cultural signs and artistic icons, we can return to them, as James Fenton does, their lost status as fetishes—not specimens of a deviant or exotic 'fetishism' but *our own* fetishes" (151). According to Clifford, collectors and collections have absorbed culture at its source point. Even though something of the interaction between primitive other and Western ethnographer remains, the interlocutors have become hyperspecialized, with a culture *maker* on the one side and a culture *collector* on the other. The model of culture contact that is presented is dialectic but not dialogic. Ethnological collecting ingests the objects made on the primitive side. Issues of creativity, imagination, and innovation drain out, not just from the diminished "authentic," native, "traditional" creators of the things that are assembled in collections, but on the side of the collectors as well. All that remains of the original interaction of anthropologist and native cultures is a kind of maudlin appreciation for the ethnographic materials appropriated during earlier expeditions. In a displacement that is perfectly predictable under the circumstances, the *collectors* and *collections* of ethnological materials, not the people who made them in the first place, are now honored for having good taste, restraint, childlike innocent curiosity, and a desire for intellectual mastery. In Clifford's own words, noting Walter Benjamin as his authority on this matter, "The good collector (as opposed to the obsessive, the miser) is tasteful and reflective" (144). Thus, Clifford permits the original ethnographic subject gracefully and silently to slip away from the anthropological text.

Anthropology's postmodern theoretical project is really a kind of mourning and melancholia. Anthropologists would like to promote the idea that the melancholia they call postmodernity marks a death that they have not been able to accept, perhaps because they were accessories to it. It is not the death of the historical subject. Rather, it is the death of the ahistorical subject—savages or so-called primitive hunting and gathering peoples, the original form of humanity. It was our neolithic ancestors who gave us our history, who invented language, painting, music, sculpture, dance, weaving, ceramics, the spectacle of ritual, kinship structures, religion, community organization, writing, and agriculture—nothing less than the economic, moral, and aesthetic foundations of our common humanity. But they quietly disappeared sometime in the last decade, having kept from the "salvage anthropologists" their most precious secrets. Perhaps they were vengeful. Certainly the anthropologists did not deserve to be told their most precious secrets. What good did anthropology do them after all? It is as though their last words were, "We lived on earth for over a million years without destroying it or ourselves; now it's your turn." My take on all of this is that what is really being mourned is the passing of the anthropologist. A kind of cultural creativity that is worthy of being called savage is very much alive today. The only real question is whether anthropologists can develop observational and analytic skills sufficiently acute to recognize it even when they are holding it in their hands.

Hysterical Metaphoric Appropriation

Here I will argue that we (collectively—that is, tourists, anthropologists, collectors, curators, art traders, native artists, "informants") might get beyond the epistemological predicament which Clifford describes by attending to the fine-grained details in the various interactions that take place between tourists and natives, between natives and the officials of Indian schools and other administrators of government programs for native peoples, between the last anthropologists and their native informants. How *exactly* did it occur that tourists and anthropologists could come to think of themselves as politically correct, even believe sincerely that they admire the accomplishments of the native peoples they go to visit as much as or *more* than the accomplishments of their own civilization, while participating in the reconstruction of colonial hierarchies precisely opposed to the liberal values they think they hold and eventually aggressively participating in the destruction of the cultures they think they are admiring?

There is a scene in Dennis O'Rourke's film *Cannibal Tours* in which an American tourist admires a Papuan mask.[12] She uses a metaphor, "It is beautiful like a Modigliani." This particular type of metaphor is the most common trope in touristic discourse: It is "like the Greeks," etc. Here, as elsewhere, it is instructive to attend to the structure of metaphor at the scene of the crime. This expression of touristic innocence is incessantly repeated at the cutting edge of postmodernity; I think it *is* the cutting edge of postmodernity. Following Barthes and Lacan, a metaphor can be defined as a values statement with an alibi. To say, "My love is like a red, red rose" is a values statement about roses, but more important for the formation of the unconscious, it is also a values statement about petunias and everything else not metaphorically associated with love. To say "my love is like a red, red rose" is a negative evaluation of petunias, but it is a negative evaluation that need never confess, even to itself. Consciousness is entirely filled with the convergence of love and roses. It need never face the possibility that the love and roses metaphor is precisely equivalent to "my love is not like a petunia." The devaluation of petunias in the metaphoric equation of love and roses must reside in the unconscious, where it is unavailable for direct human exchange but still nicely positioned to shape the nuances of human discourse.

Now what of the tourist's remark, "It is like a Modigliani"? She obviously spoke honestly and with unsurpassable goodwill. But she also appropriated the mask for the West, even more powerfully than if she had purchased or stolen it and put it in a case in the American Museum of Natural History. Once "in metaphor" the mask was removed from itself. It is "like a Modigliani." It is *not* "like a Papuan mask" which, of course, is exactly what it is. This trope, in a single stroke, denied New Guinea as origin or took the idea for the mask away from New Guinea and gave it to Italy. I call this transfer *hysterical metaphoric appropriation*. It is based on utter terror in the face of the Papuan *as Papuan*. It contains and controls this imagined assault by inverting actual lines of creativity and influence. In this case it denies the influence of Papuan art on Modigliani, suggesting that Papuan art "is like" Modigliani, not vice versa as actually occurred historically. In short, the usage fully restores a Eurocentric perspective, aesthetic hierarchy, and control at the exact moment that it seems to embrace and appreciate non-European art.

Hysterical Metaphoric Appropriation in the Art Studio of the Santa Fe Indian School, 1932–37

Building upon the Santa Fe native art movement, then more than ten years old, Dorothy Dunn opened the first art studio in the Santa Fe Indian School. W. Jackson Rushing comments:

> Southwestern and Plains Indian styles of painting were synthesized and institutionalized at the studio, which was established in 1932 at the federal government's Santa Fe Indian School by Dorothy Dunn, a graduate of the Art Institute of Chicago. The resultant style—flat, highly stylized, decorative watercolors that usually depict dances, hunting, or genre activities—has since come to be known by Indians and non-Indians alike as "traditional Indian painting." (Rushing 1992:8)

By her own account, Dunn's first class was recruited from reservations across the entire United States but was mainly from the Southwest (Dunn 1968:251). Her stated goal was to give the Indians an opportunity to express their own aesthetic sense, drawing and painting "traditional" Indian scenes and symbols. She would help only with technique, color theory, and by providing quality supplies and an encouraging environment.

Dunn's art studio was the first institutional attempt to define and codify American Indian art. It was also a laboratory experiment in hysterical metaphoric appropriation.

The issues here go much deeper than the terms of the current debate over authenticity in recent African art: namely whether the incorporation of colonial themes renders the work "inauthentic."[13] At the Santa Fe school, colonial themes were specifically discouraged by Dunn. But that did not, I will argue, prevent the work produced there from having been appropriated even prior to its actual production.[14] This is evident in the lightning speed of the acceptance and positive reception of Santa Fe school work in Western art venues. Dunn's idea of "authentic Indian art" as taught at the school was apparently quite a bit influenced by the work of the young Pueblo, Awa Tsireh, who had been exhibited in galleries and museums in New York and Europe and had achieved some commercial success in the decade prior to her opening of the school. Tsireh pioneered the use of ultraprecise line rendition of geometric symbols drawn with india ink, ruler and compass, symmetrically framing figural representations of men, bears, etc. Dunn approvingly quotes an early collector of American Indian art, Alice Corbin Henderson: "Awa Tsireh's drawings are, in their own field, as precise and sophisticated as a Persian miniature. The technique which has produced pottery designs as perfect as those of an Etruscan vase has gone into his training" (230). And with evident pride, Dunn reproduces the *New York Times* review of the 1931 opening of the Exposition of Indian Tribal Arts at the Grand Central Galleries in New York: "The visitor may discern a yet comparatively untapped source of decorative inspiration. While we have had our eyes turned toward Europe with momentary vogues this authentic native American art has been overlooked. . . . [It contains] a Greek-like simplicity . . ." (235–36).

The language of these accounts is suspect and revealing. The expressions of admiration for the Indian art is clearly narcissistic: love of self is projected onto the other. The objects on display were obviously participating in the production of this narcissistic response in ways that the earlier Indian art (then still called "crude") never did. This is especially evident in the *New Republic* review which appropriated the displayed work not in the name of the Greeks, Etruscans, or Persians but for Christianity, or more precisely in the name of the Christian virtues of simplicity, purity, poverty, perfection, and cleanliness:

> The Indian artist may perhaps best be distinguished by his feelings for physical purity—the purity of abstract perfection and of extreme economy of means. This geometric quality is present alike in the simplicity of his forms, in the rhythmic reiteration of his dances and patterns, and the laconic neatness of his symbols. There is something fine in this severity, this directness and strict economy. . . . (239)

My point here is that metaphoric appropriation is not just a feature of the *reception* of this art.[15] It is a well-documented component of the actual conditions of its *production* at the art studio in the Indian school. In a fascinating three-page passage, Dunn reproduces excerpted and edited conversations between herself and her young Indian students in the art studio. The point which she desires to make in this extraordinary section (and which may have biased her memory of the conversations) is the degree to which she was nondirective in her teaching, urging students simply to express themselves. And this is the way it mainly comes across. But there are also moments such as these:

D.: Here are some pictures of Sioux paintings I thought you'd like to see. I think they are so fine in rhythm and clean-cut lines.

STUDENT: Who made them?

D.: These are only my sketches but the originals were made by an unknown Sioux artist many years ago. They have been preserved by the American Museum of Natural History in New York.

*   *   *

STUDENT: I don't know what to paint. I am tired of dancers.

D.: Why don't you try to think of some everyday happening which would make a nice picture—planting corn, or hoeing it or husking it and throwing it into big piles, all colors; or cleaning out the irrigation ditch in spring, or selling pottery. . . .

*   *   *

D.: Does this look to you as if it is falling down toward the bottom of the paper?

STUDENT: Too much white at the top? I can cut it off.

D.: You don't need to cut it off; why don't you try a design over the heads of the dancers—a design of clouds, or rainbow, or birds, or sun, or something else. (284–87)

The result, of course, was not "authentic traditional" art but a new genre in which Indian motifs were organized according to Western principles: a perfect expression of coloniality *tagged as* "authentic traditional" art.

While helpful, it is not strictly necessary to go to the material conditions of art production at the Santa Fe Indian School to discover the particular form of appropriation in operation there. It is also evident on the surface of the resulting paintings. The Santa Fe school paintings, in addition to using modern media, are balanced and formal appearing. Geometric symbols carefully rendered surround central human or animal figures. The frame of symbolic figures is arranged in a mirroring, bilateral symmetry on a central vertical axis. Also there is a conventional (Western renaissance) perspective at least implicit with the sky above and the earth below, the entire scene viewed as if from about six or eight feet off the ground.

The Longfish Critique

In his art Longfish states in effect, and works on, a problem that I have tried to make central to this paper: namely, How do native peoples get beyond the expectation or requirement that they turn themselves into a colorful version of themselves designed in the first place for hysterical metaphoric appropriation by the West?[16] This involves something more than resistance in the form of blatant political statement, and obviously something more than cleansing the work of "colonial references," which is now just another strategy of appropriation in postmodernity.[17] Since the status of Longfish's and Quaku's work in this paper is different from ordinary academic use of aesthetic "cases" and "examples," I should try to clarify my relation to it. I do not hold their work up as aesthetically exemplary, although it certainly qualifies as such, nor are the artists my "informants." Rather, they are colleagues and coworkers, intellectual guides and fellow travelers. I read their work for insight into a problem which we hold in common. They occupy a position here in my writing the same as that of Lacan or Willy Apollon and potentially anyone else who has addressed the ethical options in postmodernity with intensity and directness.

George Longfish specifically reacts against the Santa Fe school, saying of Dorothy Dunn:

She might be credited with creating the whole concept of Indian art as we now understand it in a high school setting. Her aim was to Europeanize technique, to make it world class. The work that came from the kids in her studio *did* have high production values and high decorative and illustrative value derived from sacred and secret traditional motifs. But in her effort to define Indian art, she limited it. The kids peaked out at about age eighteen. There was no sense of the next step beyond the traditional form now expertly rendered. Tradition does not take its own next step. Involvement with the Santa Fe school studio was a denial of the self and led to stagnation of cultural traditions. The students became victims of their art. (from notes—see previous Longfish quote)

To discover the specific elements in Longfish's critique of appropriation, which he mobilized in a remarkable series of paintings during the last twenty years, it is necessary to examine Indian art before and after Santa Fe and compare what happened before and after to the Santa Fe work.

The qualities of bilateral symmetry, balance, renaissance perspective, and formal relations between symbolic and figural elements are not strongly marked features of Indian art before Santa Fe or in much of the work after, including especially Longfish's.[18] Longfish often produces weird symmetries that turn out to be illusory; i.e., on close examination there is no resemblance between the "symmetrical" halves, or the axis of symmetry is not on the front plane of the painting so that the only way to experience the represented symmetry would be for the viewer to get inside the painting. In earlier buffalo hide paintings and other "sources of tradition" used in the Santa Fe school, the contrast, both compositionally and in terms of their rendering, between natural figures and geometric symbols is not clear-cut. Longfish often runs a "cloud symbol" across the top of his painting in an evident reference to the Santa Fe style of symbolic framing, but his clouds appear to be as natural, or present, as they are symbolic, full of water or casting a shadow, intentionally violating Santa Fe rendering standards for symbols. In their actual execution Longfish's "symbols" are more identifiable with the pre-Santa Fe work.

Nor do there appear to be obvious compositional rules governing the placement of symbols and realistic figures relative to each other in the earlier paintings and in Longfish's work. The symbols and figures exist in evident relationships, but their relations seem to be driven by the narrative function of the painting, historical marking, or ritual requirements, rather than by formal compositional rules as occurred at Santa Fe. Certainly there is no evidence in Longfish's work or the earlier paintings of simplified rules of spatial organization of the symbols relative to the figures, such as symmetrical framing.

In the older painting there is a strong tendency for each human, animal, or tepee represented to be clearly individually marked in such a way as to suggest the possibility of identification. In much of the older work infinitely close attention was paid to facial features and expression, bodily characteristics, markings of horses and other animals, designs on clothing and tepees. In the Santa Fe school paintings there is little tendency toward portraiture, with most humans and animals appering to be undifferentiated and interchangeable. Longfish's humanlike figures stand in an interesting relationship to both earlier approaches. At first glance they might seem to be allied with the Santa Fe painting. They appear as relatively shapeless, neckless silhouettes, just the suggestion of the form of the human. But closer examination reveals that no two are alike. Each humanlike figure has its own individual and very distinctive identity, but not one based on portraiture convention. Each has its own distinctive color, outlines, spots,

George Longfish, acrylic and collage on canvas.

and stripes. It is something that has never been achieved in the framework of white culture—an individuality of color.

There are other differences. In the Santa Fe school there is an explicit requirement of uniformly high technical execution across the entire surface of the painting, execution that leaves no trace of suggestion that this or that detail may have been more or less important to the artist. Earlier Indian and Longfish's paintings are often marked by very complex contours and microregions of involvement on the part of the artist. Some figures are sketched in, altered, and abandoned unfinished, while others in the same painting are lively and "complete,"and still others are overworked almost to the point of obliteration. Also, one finds differences in the apprehension of scale between the Santa Fe paintings on the one hand and Longfish and the earlier works on the other. At Santa Fe there was scrupulous attention given to uniformity of scale between and among all the figures in the painting. When they appear in the same painting, horses are larger than men and smaller than buffalo. The older work has not been policed by similar concerns for realistic scale. Sometimes men and horses are larger than buffalo. Sometimes a snake appears unrealistically out of proportion to the rest of the scene. One finds in Longfish's work, also, a tendency for scale to follow emotional contours more closely than spatial realism.

Finally, one finds in the pre–Santa Fe paintings and Longfish multiple perspectives in the same painting. In older buffalo hide paintings of war scenes and hunts, the figures and symbols are painted as if seen directly from above and from ground level (i.e., in profile) at the same time. Longfish uses this particular doubling of perspective and invents others. Narrative perspectives that admit of alternative points of view and interpretation are much more important in the earlier work and in Longfish than the singular viewpoint of a standing man for whom the scene is arranged after the fashion of a theatrical performance. In several paintings Longfish sets up a new perspective in front of the frame of Santa Fe perspective to include a viewing subject sitting spell-bound before a Santa Fe–style painting magnificently transformed.

What is interesting is that Longfish's painting bears no more surface resemblance to the earlier Indian painting that he admires than it does to the Santa Fe paintings, against which he rebelled. It resembles neither, but it is as distinctively and unmistakably Indian as the old paintings, certainly as the Santa Fe paintings. Longfish's sensibility reproduces the deep structure, not the surface structure, of the earlier work. The result is like what often occurs in the development of language when two dialects of the same language diverge, somehow becoming mutually unintelligible at the level of speech while remaining the same at the level of language. What binds Longfish's painting to the earlier work on a structural level is an indestructible sense of the deeply interactive nature of art. He honors and engages the viewer in a collaborative production of new unities which are also traditional unities operating beneath the surface. Unless, of course, the viewer is already blinded or incapacitated by the hegemonic drive. His paintings don't simply reassert the qualities of appropriated tradition—"wholeness," "balance," and "authenticity"—after the fashion of the Santa Fe paintings or anthropology. There is no manifest fear in Longfish or the earlier work of being seen as possibly not whole.

Kafi Quaku and His Mechanical Reproduction in the Work of Art

Kafi Quaku is the name by which the Ivory Coast artist Anoh Acou is known in the West.[19] The story of his art, like so many others, is entwined with the story of an ethnographic expedition. In the course of her studies of tourist art, Professor Bennetta Jules-Rosette visited several cooperatives in East and West Africa to observe the actual conditions of production and interview the wood carvers.[20] She quickly discovered that most of the profit in the tourist art trade was made by the middlemen who purchased from the carvers and other artists and sold to stores and galleries in Europe, America, and urban Africa. This, of course, was already well known to the carvers themselves, who felt powerless to do anything about it because they lacked the contacts and the means to maintain a sophisticated marketing operation. It happened that Professor Jules-Rosette carried a portable computer with her to use in her research. Several members of Acou's cooperative expressed a great deal of interest in the computer, which Jules-Rosette explained to them in great detail. They immediately understood the computer's potential for keeping lists of potential buyers, addresses, price agreements, orders, delivery dates, etc. In short, they saw that it could become the centerpiece of a direct-marketing operation and a greater share of the profits for their cooperative. Anoh Acou saw something more. On her departure, Professor Jules-Rosette left her computer behind.

When she returned for follow-up study the next year, and indeed to initiate new research on African uses of computers, not much progress had been made in the establishment of a direct-marketing system, but there was a second computer in the village. Anoh Acou proudly showed her his wood carving of her old computer with a folding screen, latching lid, keyboard, input and output terminals. Jules-Rosette asked him if he had other such carvings. Yes, he had always admired and desired formal Western men's clothing and he had carved himself several suits and pairs of shoes. He showed her his wardrobe neatly hanging on carved wooden hangers in his house. He had also carved himself a telephone, a stereo, and a small library.

Acou, or Kafi Quaku, is responding to his own need to control forces that are beyond himself and to a predicament of art after the industrial revolution. Walter Benjamin, in what is still the paradigmatic essay on the subject, comments:

> Even the most perfect reproduction of a work of art is lacking in one element: its presence in time and space, its unique existence at the place where it happens to be. . . . The presence of the original is the prerequisite to the concept of authenticity. . . . The whole sphere of authenticity is outside technical—and, of course, not only technical—reproducibility. Confronted with its manual reproduction, which was usually branded as a forgery, the original preserved all its authority: not so *vis* à vis technical reproduction. . . . [T]echnical reproduction can put the copy of the original into situations which would be out of reach for the original itself. Above all, it enables the original to meet the beholder halfway. . . . The situations into which the product of mechanical reproduction can be brought may not touch the actual work of art, yet the quality of its presence is always depreciated. . . . One might subsume the eliminated element in the term "aura" and go on to say: that which withers in the age of mechanical reproduction is the aura of the work of art. (Benjamin 1968:220–21)

Of course, all Benjamin means for us to understand by his term *mechanical reproduction* is the reproduction of art works—copies, prints, photographs, injection-molded plastic sculptures, etc. Acou restores the aura to the work of art, restores its ritual function in cult, by vastly expanding on Benjamin's notion of mechanical reproduction to include all the mass-produced consumer goods of industrial capitalism, Marx's "vast accumulation of commodities." He inverts Benjamin's formula by taking the mechanically reproduced object as his original and making a work of art from it. In Acou's hands, the aura lost by the original is transferred to the "reproduction," newly emergent as the work of art. This new aura comes from its uniqueness in time and place, just as Benjamin suggested. By using the techniques and materials of the African carver, Acou makes his statement with an intensity that eludes Andy Warhol's Brillo boxes, not in their conception, which is virtually the same as Acou's, but in their execution, which might have been accomplished in any Western artist's studio. Acou has established the grounds for his dialogue with consumer capitalism in his village in Africa. He freely confesses to the grip it has on his imagination and undertakes to contain and control its forces and make them his own.

His wardrobe and other carvings moved quickly to occupy a position in the international avant garde. But, again, they respond to the deep structure of tradition much more precisely than do the "traditional" carvings of giraffes and gazelles made by Acou

Western man's suit by Kafi Quaku.

and other members of his cooperative. They are magical incantations or prayers to bring some of the enormous power of industrial capitalism to him and to his village and to realize, even to take a certain responsibility for, the failed promise of the computer. Benjamin wrote: "We know that the earliest art works originated in the service of a ritual—first the magical, then the religious kind. It is significant that the existence of the work of art with reference to its aura is never entirely separated from its ritual function" (225–26). It should be noted that Acou's magical containment of consumer capitalism, like all true magic, is completely effective: with the price that one of his suits (or his computer, or stereo) can fetch in the world art market, he can buy ten "real" suits, or computers, or stereos, if he wishes.

At this exact point no doubt some will want to raise a hand and ask: Isn't Acou guilty of appropriating Western consumer goods, as surely as Western consumers have appropriated African art and artifacts? Isn't this just the hegemonic drive in reverse? No. While the two gestures are superficially similar, there is no comparison on either ethical or economic levels. In the hegemonic drive, the materials that are appropriated have all the blood and life sucked out of them. In the artistic response to hegemony, the life of the appropriated materials is restored. In the first case, value is taken away, in the second, value is given back. When an international food cartel includes Mexican fast food as a part of its product and franchise lineup, the process begins with a hysterical metaphoric appropriation: "Mexican food is *wonderful*, but no one would *really* want to eat it because it isn't safe." So what is created is a simulacrum of Mexican food that has been assembled by a food economist to "seem like" a Mexican meal at the smallest possible cost. Its "Mexicanness" now serves as a cover for the real basis for its existence, which is to squeeze value out of a product in a delicate balancing act with its marketability: the less value it contains, the more profits are made, as long as someone will buy it. The true test is whether Mexicans can be convinced to buy it. Hegemonic appropriation requires maintaining the idea of "tradition" as an outline or shell that is repetitiously filled in. Its global effect will be for everyone to be living a simulacrum of their former lives, paying for the food, art, clothing, and lifestyles that they themselves invented and that have subsequently been appropriated by capitalist firms— now only available at chain stores with all the value squeezed out.[21]

The opposite occurs in artistic appropriations. The pair of Western-style shoes carved by Acou took more time to make, had to be thought through to the essence of their value (not merely as consumer goods in general, but also for an African carver), and they are quite a bit more expensive. Acou has put value *into* the appropriated object, not taken it out. He may profit from it (one hopes), but this is a sustainable profitability. The shoes were in good hands when he was carving them and so was tradition. However much he may sell them for, he created more value than he destroyed.[22]

There is a similar move in a Longfish piece titled *Land O' Lakes*, which is part collage with the Indian maiden from the Land O' Lakes butter package in the center of a blaze of lightning bolts and spirit symbols. Land O' Lakes uses the symbol to sell their industrial butter as if it is "fresh" and "pure" and "natural" as an Indian maiden. It is straightforward hegemonic appropriation. Longfish consciously and carefully reappropiates the symbol. He does not hatefully deface and devalue the maiden because she "went over to the other side," so to speak, working for Western economic interests. Instead he respects and honors her and attempts to restore the value that was taken away from her in her colonial service. The image, encircled by powerful symbols, also makes clear that this Land O' Lakes maiden is ritually delicate, even dangerous.

The uniqueness of a work of art is inseparable from its being imbedded in the fabric of tradition. This tradition itself is thoroughly alive and extremely changeable.
—Walter Benjamin, "The Work of Art in the Age of Mechanical Reproduction" (Benjamin 1968:225)

Conclusion—Tradition's Next Step

The central ethical question of postmodernity concerns the appropriation of tradition. This is not an easy matter. Every appropriation becomes a kernel of history. We cannot just pronounce that any such appropriation is somehow wrong. Every cultural form is potentially subject to exchange, modification, new uses. Some forms which are justly admired—many types of music, for example—are already composite products, benefiting from hybridization. One could argue that Beethoven enriched Western classical music with his numerous borrowings from the folk music of his day and, at the same time, honored the figures he borrowed from. Structurally similar hybrids (e.g., Paul Simon's *Graceland* album or the movie *Dances With Wolves*) are more difficult to assess and clearly have entered ethically ambiguous territory. Other parallel examples seem ethically unambiguous—that is, wrong. When Taco Bell transforms ethnic cuisine into a fast-food product for the masses, it is perhaps mildly exploitative: insufficient return is given to the creators (who would probably not want credit anyway, given the nature of the product). But When Taco Bell recently opened its first franchise in Mexico City, it stepped into entirely new ethical territory. Clear exploitation occurs when aspects of everyday life of a formerly colonized people (their cuisine, music, or anything else that is important in the cultural life of the community) are taken from the people and turned into industrial products that *displace* the original—that is, when people are forced to buy back a devalued simulacrum of their former lives. This is unethical.

The first step in all hegemonic appropriation is a deformation of the idea of tradition as first undertaken by the field of anthropology. Much of the problem of addressing the appropriation of tradition will be one of reclaiming this difficult concept in its full sense. The deformation of which I speak is the idea that some groups and societies are *more* traditional than others, or that some groups *are* traditional while others are not. Technically, this is an impossible formulation which has substantial ideological implications. Wheresoever a group is found that lasts more than one generation, a tradition is sure to be. If a group successfully passes down certain values—for example, that its members should ignore what the ancestors did and solve problems by the most efficient technical means, or that money is as important as human relationships and so it is OK to exploit one's friends and family for economic gain, and to view every human contact as containing potential for gaining greater economic advantage—then this is technically a tradition. If this same ethos names itself as "nontraditional" or "anti-traditional" and successfully communicates this self-designation across generations, this too is a tradition. Only a group that pretends to have no traditions of its own can unconsciously appropriate the traditions of others. It only tells itself that it has no tradition in order to justify its appropriating the traditions of others. It has a tradition of appropriation.

It is almost too easy to discover the advantages which accrue to those groups which designate themselves as "nontraditional." They set themselves up as developmentally more advanced than those which are called "traditional" and justify a range of intervention in the lives of these peoples. Today this intervention includes delivery of technical expertise, religious conversion, scientific study including "salvage ethnography," the breakup of patriarchal structures and subsistence agriculture in the name of "liberation from tradition" so that young women can enter factory work, and most recently, the collection of "traditional" arts, artifacts, and ritual objects for use as decorative display in the universal drama of postmodernity.

What remains incomprehensible to me is the mechanism which allows experts on tradition in the fields of anthropology and art history to go against their own theories and the evidence of their senses, to repeat the arbitrary distinction—traditional/non-traditional—which can only have an ideological purpose in this not-so-postcolonial world. Against this tendency toward "weird science," I want to try to make explicit something that must remain unavowed in all the expert accounts of tradition which are on the side of arbitrary advantage while pretending, even to themselves, not to be: namely, that tradition is an *interactional* concept. Tradition, insofar as it covers the materials and values passed intergenerationally in every group on the face of the earth, is not and can never be a definable quality that resides in an account, artifact, practice, or belief. Tradition can only be an attitude that surrounds an *exchange*. We are again on the ground of Mauss's important question: "Who gives what and to whom and what is the obligation to repay?" Only this time we must deal with the emotional contours of the exchange—the feelings of good and ill will that build up depending on how the exchange has been handled.

For example, in the current debate about the repatriation of traditional cultural artifacts taken from Native American peoples during the period of their colonization, tradition is used in the first place as the justification for their removal as scientific evidence, as aesthetic objects worthy of plunder, as irreplaceable heirlooms from a dead past. And tradition is used in the second place as the basis for the demand for their repatriation, as in: "These are our sacred symbols; you stole them from us or cheated us out of them; you have no real understanding of their significance." I think it may be possible to resolve a series of problems anthropology faces as it tries to say farewell to the societies it liked to call "traditional" if we begin with a minimalist assumption: *Tradition* is the label we apply to the surplus value of anything that is potentially exchanged intergenerationally from the grave and may eventually be exchanged or appropriated across cultural and historical horizons.

The primary gifts that are marked by an attitude of tradition are the things given to the living by the dead: useful and other objects, formulas for conduct, music, dance, poetry, narrative. When these things are met with an attitude of respectful admiration and awe, the ground is established for a traditional exchange. This awe is not and should not be for the immediate symbolic impact on the living of the exchanged material. That is an attitude that leads to nostalgia, romanticism, sentimentality. In the traditional relation, the awe is for their probable signification for the elders. My colleague, the American Indian storyteller, professor of English, and specialist in biographical narrative Gregory Sarris, confesses, "I can retell some of the stories my Auntie Mabel McKay told me. I can describe the situation of the telling and some sense of their eventual impact on my life. But I do not think of myself as a storyteller in the same way my aunt was. Much of the time, I just didn't get it." Sarris has conveyed us to the ground of *tradition*: It is not something *in* the story (that might alternatively be missing from it) but rather an *attitude toward* the story and its hero on the parts of both the speaker and the hearer that renders its importance as probably beyond the grasp. It is this importance-beyond-the-grasp that is the surplus value of tradition, a surplus value that can only accrue to the community, which includes both the living and the dead and probably their plants and animals and spirits as well.[23]

What the anthropologists call "tradition" is a mask for intensity and pain, a pretense that everything is going along as it always has, uninterrupted, repetitious, "just fine," or "for the best," as we say when the worst has happened. What I am calling "tradition" here is more like an altar for intensity and pain. What is covered with the mantle of tradition always involves *the beautiful* and *death*. And it involves *metaphysical embarrassment* about the proximity of *beauty* and *death* in tradition. Even if Sarris produced a perfect simulacrum of his aunt's story after she died, a task much easier than the one he set himself, it, especially, could not convey the full significance of the original and the occasion of his hearing it.

Tradition is a challenge to the living by the dead to keep on living, to try to fill the real gap or void of death; a challenge that must be met with full awareness of the impossibility of telling the same story twice, fully honoring the dead and their accomplishments. Tradition is also a reminder that full speech and authentic meaning are constantly draining out of everything that is exchanged in human interaction. It is a challenge that can only be answered by art of a certain type, an art that in its first enunciation would probably not be seen as "traditional" but which moves quickly enough to fill the void opened by tradition, that is an art powerful enough eventually to open a new void of its own. The only thing that the living can give to the dead is the heart and passion the dead once gave but can no longer. It is the opposite of what passes for traditional in touristic exchanges or at the Santa Fe institute, where whites teach Indians how to paint in an Indian style—anything that involves copying the outlines of a dead form, standing in the place of one's father, trying to make present what is past, standing in for, marking an absence. None of this which is called "traditional" can be anything but grave markers for tradition.

NOTES

1. The author wishes to thank Jennifer Dowley and the staff and executive board of the Marin Headlands Center for the Arts for generous support while writing this paper. My fellow artists in residence extended the warmest welcome to the first scholar to live at the Headlands and helped me shape this paper by freely sharing their thoughts on creativity and tradition. Special thanks are due to Holly Blake, Fritzie Brown, Ann Chamberlain, Gabrielle Daniels, Sheila Ghidini, Robert Johnson, Mardith Louisell, Bernie Lubell, Juliet Flower MacCannell, Ce Scott, Stig Sjolund, Flo Wong, Elizabeth Young, and Victor Zabala.

2. Two pioneering studies of ethnic and tourist art to which I am much indebted are Nelson Graburn's *Ethnic and Tourist Art* (1976) and Bennetta Jules-Rosette's *The Messages of Tourist Art: An African Semiotic System in Comparative Perspective* (1984).

3. The two artists whose work is discussed in this paper are among those so called. George Longfish is called a "modernist" Indian painter, and Kafi Quaku is called a "postmodernist" sculptor. When I began this project I was excited to be surrounded again by terminology from my graduate school days in "economic development and modernization." I was not able to accept modernization theory as the whole story of what was happening in the Third World—the idea of the inevitability of technological progress, the eradication of human backwardness. This tells nothing of the struggle of the human spirit, or the "history of the human heart" as Rousseau liked to say.

4. W. Jackson Rushing, in his editorial statement introducing a very fine collection of essays on "Critical Issues in Recent Native American Art," comments on this in language that is adequate to the difficulty of the problem: "To insist on recognition, institutional and otherwise, for these artists—which they clearly deserve—by appealing to a hierarchical system (high/fine, popular, folk, primitive, tourist/kitsch) dependent on class and cultural otherness is to capitulate, conceptually at least. . . ." (Rushing 1992:6)

5. See also my earlier (1973) paper on "Staged Authenticity: Arrangements of Social Space in Tourist Settings."

6. The degree to which all of this is a Western romantic projection that is not especially rele-

vant to actual conditions in so-called primitive or exprimitive societies has been nicely documented by Sidney Littlefield Kasfir. See her 1992 article on "African Art and Authenticity."

7. All these practices are sympathetically and humorously documented in Ilisa Barbash and Lucien Taylor's excellent film *In and Out of Africa*.

8. Longfish in his painting and Quaku in his sculpture fully acknowledge the comedy that is never absent from emergent cultural forms. Anthropological writing is almost devoid of a corresponding sensitivity to what is funny about culture: that culture in all its manifestations, even funerals, always risks slipping over the edge of seriousness. The exception is the writings of James Boon, who can be trusted to attend to the comedic aspects of culture. See, for example, his 1984 paper, "Folly, Bali, and Anthropology."

9. In a paper on "Voodoo Art and Politics in Haiti" delivered to the Congress on African and Caribbean Art and Aesthetics at the University of California at San Diego, April 1993.

10. Art and artists are also targeted by the hegemonic drive in its violent phases, as occurred in Nazi Germany and more recently in Cambodia. Artists, along with "people who wear glasses," topped the list of "groups" targeted for genocide by the Khmer Rouge, who succeeded in killing every known Cambodian artist including puppet makers and actors. See Hélène Cixou's *Terrible But Unfinished Story of Norodom Sihanouk, King of Cambodia*.

11. Some native peoples have begun to speak out eloquently against what is for them the postmodern double-bind. Loretta Todd comments: "[A]rt critic Fredric Jameson has said . . . a change has occurred from the depth, historicity and affect of modernism to a place of depthlessness, surface and simulacrum that marks the postmodern. These terms—philosophies even—are forever linked, first to colonialism and now to decolonization. Yet increasingly, the two terms crop up with respect to First nations' cultural production. An artist's work is classified as modernist, and no doubt many Native artists incorporate modernism into their meaning. Our young people's negotiations between their traditional cultures and the late-twentieth-century consumer society are considered to be postmodern. . . . But it is the next step, where as artists we are encouraged to embrace these philosophies, that I worry about. . . . What does the use of these terms mean to our cultural production? And what relationship do they have to colonial history, and to our continued struggle with our own territorial and cultural sovereignty?" (Todd 1992:73). Kay WalkingStick (1992:15) comments succinctly, "Postmodern theory promised a more comprehensive critical viewpoint, but hasn't delivered it."

12. For reviews of *Cannibal Tours*, see Edward Bruner and Dean MacCannell.

13. For discussion of the African materials, see Kasfir 1992, p. 41.

14. This point is also made by Joy Gritton, who concluded her helpful article on the Santa Fe school as follows: "With 'outmoded tradition' relegated to the role of 'springboard for personal creative action,' the viability of intact native philosophies, religions, and political systems in insuring the continued survival and well-being of native peoples through time was obscured. Students were asked to be at once the 'Primitive' and the 'Primitivist' in a Western discourse wherein form took precedence over meaning, product over process, and 'universal' aesthetic (and market) value replaced cultural context. Within such a framework the recognition of the equality of divergent aesthetic systems, values and beliefs was precluded" (Gritton 1992:35).

15. The role of patron taste in shaping the work of art has been described with specific references to the Santa Fe school by J. J. Brody, 1971.

16. It is perhaps worth mentioning in this context that the current emphasis on performance and performativity in gender politics may be freighted with the same problem, insofar as there is no analysis of audience or the question of "performance for whom." To "perform oneself" for no one in particular and call it "liberation" certainly lays the groundwork for appropriation (of one's lifestyle, personal taste, etc.) by consumer capitalism, as much as it constitutes a personal statement and freedom of expression.

17. Longfish's work is interesting in this regard. It occasionally draws snarling commentary from the elite art press. See, for example, *Artweek* editor Bruce Nixon's snide remarks ("cheesy") on Longfish's contribution to the "500 Years Since Columbus" exhibition at the Triton Museum of Art (Nixon 1992:9). This suggests that Longfish's work is resistant to appropriation, perhaps even more so than that of Rick Rivett, Jimmie Durham, or Harry Fonseca, who make their anger toward whites the explicit theme of their work, often to considerable white approval.

18. The difference between the Indians of the Northwest Coast, Arctic, Plains, and Mesoamerica, and even within these areas, are such that one cannot speak of "Indian art" in general. For purposes of the remarks that follow, I have set before me several reproductions of nineteenth-century and earlier Sioux and other Plains buffalo hide paintings depicting hunts and battles. These are among the avowed sources of inspiration for the later work discussed below.

19. I am indebted here and elsewhere to my friend and colleague Bennetta Jules-Rosette for freely sharing with me her observations of the carver cooperative where Acou works and her photographs of his home and his collection of his own works.

20. Reported in Bennetta Jules-Rosette, 1990.

21. For an analysis of this and other "new sites of exploitation," see Dean MacCannell and Juliet Flower MacCannell, "Social Class in Postmodernity: Simulacrum or Return of the Real," forthcoming in Brian Turner and Chris Rojek, eds., *Forget Baudrillard* (Routledge 1994).

22. The idea that creating art for sale or exchange somehow reduces its authenticity and therefore its value especially serves hegemonic appropriation: "If this were of ultimate value you could never consider selling it." In his keynote address to the Eighth Biennial Conference of the Native American Art Studies Association, John C. Ewers remarks that "the 'Sioux-like' specimens Lowie referred to were not of Crow origin at all. They were Sioux-made pieces given or exchanged to Crow Indians by the Sioux after the intertribal wars ended and these former enemy tribes paid friendly visits back and forth" (Ewers 1992:38). In the same speech he helpfully reminds us that "during the 1830s Indians in Texas were painting robes sold to traders as were tribes on the upper Missouri. We may recall that Garrick Mallery informed us that Sioux were painting imaginary war records on buffalo robes for sale to whites during the 1970s" (43). To the extent that these "imaginary war records" cannot be distinguished from "real" ones, the art had not been subject to hegemonic appropriation even though it was made for sale.

23. See Juliet Flower MacCannell, *The Regime of the Brother: After the Patriarchy*, London and New York: Routledge, 1991.

REFERENCES

Barbash, Ilisa and Lucien Taylor. 1992. *In and Out of Africa* (film), Barbash Productions, 90 Poplar Ave., Berkeley, CA 94708.

Benjamin, Walter. 1968. The Work of Art in the Age of Mechanical Reproduction. In *Illuminations*. New York: Harcourt, Brace and World, Inc.

Boon, James. 1984. Folly, Bali, And Anthropology: Satire Across Cultures. In E. Bruner, ed., *Text, Play, and Story: Proceedings of the American Ethnological Society.* 156–77.

Brody, J. J. 1971. *Indian Painters and White Patrons.* Albuquerque: University of New Mexico Press.

Cixous, Hélène. 1994. *The Terrible But Unfinished Story of Norodom Sihanouk, King of Cambodia.* Translated by Juliet Flower MacCannell, Judith Pike and Lolli Groth. Lincoln: University of Nebraska Press.

Clifford, James. 1990. On Collecting Art and Culture. In Russell Ferguson et al., eds., *Out There: Marginalization and Contemporary Cultures.* Cambridge: the MIT Press.

Dunn, Dorothy. 1968. *American Indian Painting of the Southwest and Plains Areas.* Albuquerque: University of the New Mexico Press.

Ewers, John C. 1992. A Century of Plains Indian Art. *American Indian Art Magazine.* Vol. 17, no. 4. 36–47.

Graburn, Nelson H. H., ed. 1976. *Ethnic and Tourist Arts: Cultural Expressions from the Fourth World.* Berkeley: University of California Press.

Gritton, Joy. 1992. Cross-Cultural Education vs. Modernist Imperialism: The Insititute of American Indian Arts. *Art Journal.* Vol. 51, no. 3 (Fall). 28–35.

Jules-Rosette, Bennetta. 1984. *The Messages of Tourist Art: An African Semiotic System in Comparative Perspective.* New York: Plenum.

———. 1990. *Terminal Signs: Computers and Social Change in Africa.* Berlin and New York: Mouton de Gruyter.

Kasfir, Sidney Littlefield. 1992. African Art and Authenticity: A Text with a Shadow. *African Arts.* Vol. XXV, no. 2. 41–97.

MacCannell, Dean. 1973. Staged Authenticity: Arrangements of Social Space in Tourist Settings. *The American Journal of Sociology*. 79(3). 589–603.

———. 1990. Cannibal Tours. *Society for Visual Anthropology Review*. (Fall). 14–23.

——— and Juliet Flower MacCannell. 1994. Social Class in Postmodernity: Simulacrum or Return of the Real. In Brian Turner and Chris Rojek, eds., *Forget Baudrillard*. London: Routledge.

MacCannell, Juliet Flower. 1991. *The Regime of the Brother: After the Patriarchy*. London and New York: Routledge.

Nixon, Bruce. 1992. Across the Ocean Blue: ''500 Years Since Columbus'' at the Triton Museum of Art. *Artweek*. Vol. 23, no. 7 (February 20). 1, 9.

Rushing, W. Jackson. 1992. Critical Issues in Recent Native American Art. *Art Journal*. Vol. 51, no. 3 (Fall). 6–14.

Todd, Loretta. 1992. What More Do They Want? *Indigena: Contemporary Native Perspectives*. Hull, Quebec: Canadian Museum of Civilization. 71–79.

WalkingStick, Kay. 1992. Native American Art in the Postmodern Era. *Art Journal*. Vol. 51, no. 3 (Fall), 15–17.

Mudwomen and Whitemen:
A Meditation on Pueblo Potteries and the Politics of Representation[1]

Barbara A. Babcock

Out in this desert we are testing bombs.
                                        —Adrienne Rich[2]

The petit-bourgeois is a man unable to imagine the other. . . .
But there is a figure for emergencies—Exoticism.
                                        —Roland Barthes[3]

*A*s my title implies, I am concerned with the objects of others and the constitution of the colonial Other, the constructions of gender and ethnicity, and the
problematics of alterity and interpretation. This meditation on the representation of
the Pueblo subject within Anglo-American discourse is both a re-visionary and experimental text—a rereading through juxtapositions. "Re-vision," in Adrienne Rich's now
classic definition, entails "the act of looking back, of seeing with fresh eyes, of entering
an old text from a new critical direction." This particular re-vision was occasioned by
my leaving the Southwest and my work with Pueblo women and their potteries in
1987 and returning to it after a year in the Ivy League. My essay is experimental in
being a pastiche of images, quotations, and reflections—the sherds of over a decade of
studying ceramics and culture.[4]

I owe the first part of my title, "mudwomen and whitemen," to Nora Naranjo-
Morse, a Pueblo potter and poet. In 1989 we participated in a symposium on figurative ceramics at the Heard Museum, and Nora read a poem she had written about the
difficulty she had selling her first pieces because they were strange, not identifiable, not
"traditional" Santa Clara black pottery; about how devastating it is to put your heart
into a piece and then have it judged and dismissed. It was titled "Mudwoman's First
Encounter with the World of Money and Business." Her laughter, her parody of self
and other seems like the right place to situate this re-view of over a century of oppression, appropriation, and commodification. Better her poem than the scholar's statement that, "grasping for cultural legitimacy and survival in the industrialized West in
the past century, native peoples have accepted the economic option of converting
culture into commodity."[5]

As I struggle to put this critique together, I envy Nora her poetry, her pottery,
and especially Pearlene, her ceramic self-portrait and alter ego who "can say or do
anything she wants" (figure 1). "Pearlene," Nora says, "is a woman who doesn't
know where she is, and it doesn't matter. She is the antithesis of the characteristics
of Pueblo women that anthropologists love to point out." There is no question that
Pearlene destabilizes the authorized narrative of traditional Pueblo pottery—the story
of use and beauty told again and again by photographers, painters, collectors, and
scholars (figure 2).[6]

Figure 1.
Pearlene, ceramic self-portrait by Nora Naranjo-Morse, Santa Clara Pueblo, 1987. Courtesy of the Heard Museum, Phoenix, AZ.

Figure 2.
Water Carrier, (Mrs. Chaverria), Santa Clara Pueblo, ca. 1919. Photograph by Carter H. Harrison. Courtesy of the Museum of New Mexico, Santa Fe, NM; Negative No. 42726.

The "potteries" of my title is Pueblo English. Cultural critique in one word. The idea of a proper collective "pottery" is inconceivable from the Pueblo point of view. Every piece of pottery is a made being with a unique voice and spirit. But "politics"? Or "conflict *and* clay," as I once suggested in a lecture on Cochiti potteries? In response to presentations and proposals I have made in the last decade concerning the work of Cochiti potter Helen Cordero (figure 3), I've been told by Pueblo ceramic scholars and feminists alike that a little old Pueblo lady shaping dolls of mud is charming but trivial and unproblematic—affirming yet again that even, perhaps especially, among scholars, "the non-Western woman is the vehicle for misplaced Western nostalgia." I suppose we have progressed, for a century ago they said "eccentric" or "grotesque," and they called such figures *monos* (monkey, mimic, fool, or mere doll) (figure 4) and dismissed them as "tourist trash." [7]

And so I ask, what about these very "relations of power whereby one portion of humanity can select, value, and collect the pure products of others"? What about the way that Anglo America has been imagining, describing, and fetishizing the Pueblo Southwest for over a century? And why, indeed, has the study of pottery "generated more literature than any other aspect of Southwest culture"? Why was Nampeyo the symbol of Hopi culture in the minds of white Americans, and why did Maria Martinez become *the* single most famous Native American artist? What about "the pervasive metaphorical elision of colonized, non-European, and female" and the fact that woman is the "main *vehicle*" for "the representation of difference and otherness within mass culture"? And that raises the issue of the inverse relation "between relative empowerment and objectified portrayal in popular culture"—the fact that "the Indian appears everywhere . . . as a mystified ideal, yet nowhere in dominant discourse do Indians speak with their own unmediated voices." [8]

It is late July, 1988. Kit Hinsley and I are driving from Alamogordo to Las Cruces through White Sands Missile Range. It is shimmering hot. I have been away from the desert long enough to forget how you can see as well as feel the heat. I have missed the dryness, the emptiness, and the clarity of this landscape. I look at the map to see how many miles to Tucson. Along the road we're on I read, "U.S. 70 closed during short periods of firing." That prompts discussion of Trinity, Titan missiles, and the military omnipresence in the Southwest. No sooner said than we are halted by a military policewoman, who tells us that testing is about to begin and that we will have to wait at least an hour. She points us in the direction of the visitor center.

Inside it is cool and dark and soft as only fifty-year-old adobes are. The contents, however, are not so comforting. In the main hall are books for sale about desert flora and fauna, about southwestern Native Americans, and about the day the sun disappeared. An adjoining exhibit hall contains similar definitions, representations, and textualizations of natural, cultural, and technological objects and events. Displays juxtapose Mimbres pottery and other prehistoric Pueblo artifacts with the natural history of White Sands against a photographic background of missiles and mushroom clouds. This is a shrine naturalizing, domesticating, and celebrating nuclear power and militarism.

In the tourist shop, the same three classes of objects and images are for sale—vials of white sand and plastic missiles along with Indian souvenirs made in Taiwan. "Authentic" Indian-made pottery, jewelry, weaving, and painting are in a side room, dominated by a huge buckskin on which is painted a "traditional" Pueblo woman. Kit urges me to take a picture. I don't have to. It is, as the cover of the 1987 *Insight Guide— American Southwest* (figure 5) confirms, ubiquitous—a Pueblo woman with a pot on her head, encircled and frozen in time.

Figure 3.
Helen Cordero in her Cochiti
Pueblo home, 1979, shaping a
Storyteller with twenty-five
children for an exhibit at the
Denver Museum of Natural
History. Photograph by Dudley
Smith. Courtesy of the Denver
Museum of Natural History,
Denver, CO; Negative No.
4-79082-9A.

Figure 4.
Indian Pottery. Photograph of
Cochiti and Tesuque Pueblo
figurines for sale at Jake Gold's
Free Museum and Curiosity Shop
in Santa Fe, NM, taken between
1878 and 1881 by Ben Wittick.
Courtesy of the Museum of New
Mexico, Santa Fe, NM; Negative
No. 16293.

What preoccupies me and keeps returning to haunt our conversations for hours and weeks and months to come is the juxtaposition of Pueblo pottery, women, and nuclear power. They pasted a picture of Rita Hayworth on the bomb. They made it in Maria Martinez's backyard. Pueblo women cleaned Los Alamos labs and houses, and these "maids," Charlie Masters recalls, gave the Anglo lab workers "splendid pieces" of Indian pottery. A number of scientists and their wives "went native," for San Ildefonso Pueblo was one of the few places off the hill they were permitted to escape to. "It was this group," Masters tells us, "who changed, temporarily, the entire economy of northern New Mexico with their free-handed spending and their sudden demand of a handicraft people for something like mass production." They decorated their drab quarters with "strange and beautiful" Pueblo pots and carried these "pieces of New Mexico earth" back to Berkeley, Chicago, and Princeton as mementos of their wartime experience. Not surprisingly, in the recent opera *Los Alamos*, the voice and symbol of Mother Earth is Morning Star, ancient Indian maiden and contemporary waitress. Apart from the literal Los Alamos connection, the dialectic of nuclear destruction and Pueblo pottery is perhaps inevitable, overdetermined in a postmodern culture that "continually constitutes itself through its ideological constructs of the exotic," escaping from the power relations of modern society into, in this case, "the artistic otherworldliness" of the Pueblo.[9]

For this very reason, the *Insight Guide* olla maiden, posed to sell the Southwest, raises "ambiguous and disturbing questions about the aesthetic appropriation of non-Western others—issues of race, gender, and power." What does it mean not only that the Other is frequently presented as female—the feminization that Said discusses in *Orientalism*—but that women and the things they make are both symbols and sources of cultural identity, survival and social continuity, and also are mediators between cultures, vehicles of exchange and change? "It is," Gayatri Spivak has observed, "women's work that has continuously survived within not only the varieties of capitalism but other historical and geographical modes of production." For centuries pottery has been *the* primary Pueblo trade item, and pottery is women's work.[10]

In the past century pottery making has played a key role in the Pueblos' transition from an agrarian to a cash economy—a process that began with the Smithsonian Institution's first collecting expedition to the southwestern pueblos in 1879 and was accelerated by the coming of the railroads to New Mexico in the 1880s and Fred Harvey's marketing campaigns in the early decades of this century. Women sold potteries and demonstrated pottery making to railroad passengers, and images of women with pots were sold on Harvey/Santa Fe Railway postcards and playing cards as well as booklets and brochures and calendars (figure 6). As Marta Weigle has suggested, both the collecting of Pueblo potteries and the imaging of Pueblo women as "civilized" artisans using or selling their wares to tourists signify the transformation and domestication of the "savage," nearly naked, male warrior of the first Santa Fe Railway publications.[11]

This raises what I see as a key question and a paradoxical problematic, and politically charged situation: What happens when indigenous Pueblo "signifiers of stability"—women and potteries—become valued items of exchange, cultural brokers, and agents of change precisely because they embody a "synchronic essentialism" for postindustrial Anglo consumers? Why has a traditionally dressed woman shaping or carrying an olla (a water jar) become *the* metonymic misrepresentation of the Pueblo, and why has Anglo America invested so much in this image for well over a century? In *The Conquest of America* Todorov suggests part of the answer. If, he argues,

instead of regarding the other simply as an object, he [*sic*] were considered as a

Figure 5.
Olla maiden cover illustration,
Insight Guide: American Southwest
(Hong Kong: APA Publications,
1987). Courtesy of APA
Publications.

Figure 6.
*Comely Indian maidens and aged
squaws meet the train and sell their
wares.* This image of Pueblo
Indians selling pottery at Laguna,
NM, was reproduced both as a
"phostint" postcard, with the
preceding caption, and as the
five of clubs in "The Great
Southwest Souvenir Playing
Cards, made and published
exclusively for Fred Harvey" in
1911. Courtesy of Marta Weigle.

subject capable of producing objects which one might then possess, the chain would be extended by a link—the intermediary subject—and thereby multiply to infinity the number of objects ultimately possessed. This transformation, however, necessitates that the intermediary subject be maintained in precisely this role of subject-producer-of-objects and kept from becoming like ourselves.[12]

Examples of such image maintenance abound. As early as 1540 Castaneda, the chronicler of the Coronado expedition, reported that Pueblo women made "jars of extraordinary labor and workmanship, which were worth seeing." Under American occupation three centuries later, Lieutenant James W. Abert, with the advanced guard of the "Army of the West," made an "Examination of New Mexico" in 1846 and 1847 (with illustrations by C. R. Graham). Olla maidens are prominently featured in the foreground of the etchings of the Rio Grande pueblos of San Felipe, Santa Ana, and Santo Domingo. In his ethnographic reconnaissance for the Smithsonian Institution in 1879, Frank Hamilton Cushing painted similar images in words. He recalled his first evening at Zuni as follows:

> As I sat watching the women coming and going to and from the well, "How strangely parallel," I thought, "have been the lines of development in this curious civilization of an American desert with those of Eastern nations and deserts." Clad in blanket dresses, mantles thrown gracefully over their heads, each with a curiously decorated jar in her hand, they came one after another down the crooked path. A little passageway through the gardens between two adobe walls to our right led down rude steps into the well which, dug deeply in the sands, had been walled up with rocks, like the Pools of Palestine, and roofed over with reeds and dirt. Into this passageway and down to the dark, covered spring they turned, or lingered outside to gossip with newcomers while awaiting their chances, meanwhile slyly watching, from under their black hair, the strange visitors from "Wa-sin-to-na." These water-carriers were a picturesque sight as with stately step and fine carriage they followed one another up into the evening light, balancing their great shining water-jars on their heads.[13]

Within the same decade, in essays also written for popular periodicals and later collected in *The Land of the Pueblos*, Susan Wallace described Pueblo men as ploughing with a crooked stick, "the [O]riental implement in the days of Moses" and found much "to remind [her] of Bible pictures" in Hispanic villages along the Rio Grande:

> [T]he Mexican women, straight as a rule, carrying water-jars on head or shoulder, like maidens of Palestine. Now and then an old black shawl, melancholy remnant of the gay rebosa [*sic*], shrouding an olive forehead, suggested the veiled face of the gentle Rebecca.

And, in the summer of 1890, anthropologist John G. Owens described an evening at Zuni remarkably like the one Cushing had witnessed:

> Just before dark, the squaws all go to the spring to get an olla of water. I went over this evening to see them. It reminded me of the pictures of Palestine. . . . It certainly is a classic sight.

Again and again, this picturesque sight is figured in classical and biblical terms.[14]

It is probably neither insignificant nor coincidental that, at the same time that such inscriptions of Pueblo women and their potteries were proliferating, an anonymous article appeared in an 1880 *Harper's Weekly* on the revitalization of pottery among the women of Cincinnati, Ohio: "Handling dear old mother earth . . . does not leave much time for hysteria." The implied and valued proper role of woman—as well as relations between culture and nature, and production and reproduction—in this statement are made explicit almost a century later. In 1972 Marxist anthropologist Claude Meillassoux theorized "pre-capitalist formations" such as turn-of-the-century Zuni as follows:

[A]gricultural self-sustaining formations . . . rely less on the control of the means of material production than on the means of human reproduction: subsistence and women. Their end is reproduction of life as a precondition to production. Their primary concern is to "grow and multiply" in the biblical sense. They represent comprehensive integrated, economic, social and demographic systems ensuring the vital needs of all the members . . . of the community. A change towards a material productive end, the shift from production for self-sustenance and self-perpetuation to production for an external market, must necessarily bring a radical transformation, if not the social destruction of the communities, as indeed we witness the process nowadays.

Even more recently the following imagined conversation took place in the midst of an unstable African political situation between a CIA operative and a KGB agent in the best-selling spy thriller *Tass is Authorized to Announce*:

[The Russian:] "In this age of the rat race, only woman remains a symbol of stability, that is, beauty."
[The CIA agent:] "That's not bad. . . . Sell it to me, Ivan. *Beauty as a symbol of stability*. Ten dollars? Fifteen then. Imagine the report I could write for the swine back home."[15]

What these "classic" statements and images share is that he is speaking for and representing her and that she is valued because she is, if only in his imaginary projections, outside history, outside industrial capitalism. For many decades now Pueblo women have rarely worn *mantas* on an everyday basis or walked around with pots on their heads unless they were paid to do so. Such "picturesque" scenes exemplify "aesthetic primitivism," which is a form of colonial domination. Both Bhaba and Ong have pointed out that "colonial discourse produces the colonized as a fixed reality which is at once an 'other' and yet entirely knowable and visible"; that "by and large, non-Western women are taken as an unproblematic universal category." "The language of occupation" posits women as "receptacles and products of desire," for repeatedly "a female colored body serves as a site of attraction and symbolic appropriation."[16]

I have already implicated Edward Said's *Orientalism* in my argument, because I think that the Southwest *is* America's Orient. Like the Orient, the Southwest is an idea that has "a history and a tradition of thought, imagery, and vocabulary that have given it reality and presence in and for" the rest of America. And, as the preceding verbal and visual images amply attest, this Anglo-American tradition is explicitly figured in the trope of Orientalism. Repeatedly, "travellers passing the Pueblo villages of the Southwest in the [eighteen] eighties were invited to recall the villages of ancient Egypt and Nubia, Ninevah and Babylon, rather than to study the remains of American

aboriginal life; the people were 'like the descendants of Rebecca of Bible fame.' "
Contrary to what Pomeroy implies, however, such Orientalizing was not simply an
1880s phenomenon. In 1896 Philip Embury Harroun won a ten-dollar prize from
Eastman Kodak for a photo of a San Juan Pueblo woman titled *A New Mexican Rebecca*.
In 1920 Harriet Monroe compared Pueblo dances to Homeric rites and Egyptian
ceremonies. A few years later, in introducing the Santa Fe Railway's "Indian Detours,"
Erna Fergusson lured the traveller as follows: "Motorists crossing the southwestern
states are nearer to the primitive than anywhere else on the continent. They are crossing a land in which a foreign people, with foreign speech and foreign ways, offer them
spectacles which can be equaled in few Oriental lands." [17]

In this romantic dichotomizing and essentializing discourse that modern industrial
America began producing about the Southwest in the late nineteenth century, the
image of an olla maiden is a primary and privileged signifier and one in which considerable material investment has been and continues to be made. The 1987 *Insight
Guide* cover and countless other recent olla maiden images by contemporary artists and
photographers attest that the nostalgic aestheticism of the 1800s has persisted at great
profit for well over a century. Unsettled Indians were unsettling, and this authorized
image of the "civilized," domestic, and feminized Pueblo was popularized at the very
moment when "wild" nomadic Apaches were still killing whitemen and eluding
General Crook in these same southwestern spaces. Late nineteenth–century authors
such as Susan Wallace repeatedly juxtapose the "peace-loving," "pastoral" "maidens
of Palestine" with the savage, bloodthirsty "Bedouins" of the desert. The Indian wars
ended, but the Oriental tropology persisted, especially in the lyrical and escapist vision
of Fred Harvey and Santa Fe Railway advertising. Advertising that was intent on selling
the Southwest as "a last refuge of magic, mountains, and quaint ancestors"—"a gentle,
peaceful, and picturesque people." [18]

Calendars, playing cards, postcards. It was a sell whose time had come. Between
the Civil War and World War II, America had become, in Warren Sussman's words,
"a hieroglyphic civilization"—a culture that understands itself and others chiefly in
terms of visual symbols. At the same time, the arts and crafts movement had produced
countless statements such as the preceding about Cincinnati pottery making. For an
America which saw premodern craftsmanship as an antidote for modern ills, a technological America desirous of elegant articles of common use with, in Charles Eliot
Norton's words, "something of human life in them," what could be better than the
"timeless, authentic beauty" of a Pueblo pot? And who could better serve as an idealized alternative to modernity than a primitive "mudwoman" who, as Evans-Pritchard
has assured us, "does not desire things to be other than they are"? An Indian mother
shaping Mother Earth and gracefully carrying her burdens was/is indeed something
of a bourgeois dream of an alternative redemptive life as well as an imagistic transformation of an unmanageable native into a manageable one. Modern power, Foucault
argues, replaces violence and force with the "gentler" constraint of uninterrupted
visibility. The camera replaces the cannon, and "the gaze" becomes a technique of
power/knowledge, as the unruly other is managed through the creation and exploitation of a new kind of visibility. [19]

"The relegation of the tribal or primitive to either a vanishing past or an ahistorical,
conceptual present" influences not only the Western valuation but the production
and consumption of ethnic art, and that in turn profoundly affects gender relations
within tribal communities with regard to the reproduction of culture for sale. Scholars
and popularizers have been consistent in their refusal to see Pueblo women in their
"psychological, social, and colonial complexity." Natives, especially female artisan

natives, were co-opted into

> scripted ethnic stereotypes, not merely as part of the inevitable choreography of denial that characterized face-to-face interracial relations in contemporary America, but with increasing psychosocial investment in the fiction it perpetuated. . . . [T]hey learned to market, as well as elaborate, their own ethnicity,

and in the process they assumed powers and prerogatives that had once belonged to their husbands. Similarly, the repeated imaging of Pueblo pottery as useful beauty denies its complex embodiment of spiritual, commercial, and political, as well as aesthetic, factors. For both pots and potters, the olla maiden stereotype has not only influenced aesthetics—it has had profound economic and political consequences.[20]

Shortly after the turn of the century George Pepper went to New Mexico to collect for the American Museum of Natural History. A photo taken at Cochiti Pueblo in 1904 shows Mrs. Pepper and an Indian man packing potteries to be shipped to New York, and as the figures in the foreground attest, these barrels contained something more than utilitarian bowls and jars. Between 1875 and 1905, Cochiti and Tesuque potters produced an astonishing array of human and animal figures in addition to bowls and jars decorated with figurative designs. Many were satiric portraits of the whitemen, for one response of tribal peoples everywhere to Western invasion and domination has been to mock and caricature the light-skinned alien. Then and now, Pueblo men mimed the whiteman in clown performances on dusty plazas, and Pueblo women shaped his image in clay. Few whitemen who bought these figures, which were described as "eccentric" or "grotesque," realized that they were in fact portraits of themselves. These *monos* were not regarded highly, and because traders such as Jake Gold of Santa Fe encouraged the manufacture of these "primitive idols," they were (and still are) frequently dismissed as "tourist junk" and as wholly "commercial" in origin (see figure 1).[21]

In an 1889 note titled "The Debasement of Pueblo Art," William Holmes urged that the manufacture of such forms be discouraged and that museums not deign to collect or accept them. Collector and dealer Thomas Dozier was similarly disparaging. In his "Statement to the Trade for 1907," he attributed the manufacture of such "odd and attractive pieces" to "idle dallying in lazy moments" and predicted that, "in this utilitarian age, *she* cannot always go on making toys." From the perspective of these and countless other anthropologists and collectors, Pueblo potters playing and playing with the outsider's games did not make for a vision of authenticity, of timeless, useful, and subjugated beauty. The scholars were even more successful than the Spanish clergy in suppressing idolatry. As a consequence of this attitude, historic figurative ceramics have been more or less invisible, gathering dust in museum basements and attics for over a century. One can still view many exhibits and read countless books, catalogues, and essays on Pueblo pottery and not encounter a single figurative form. The pervasiveness of this use-and-beauty bias is also evident in souvenir postcards, photo albums, books, slides, and now even videotapes. Bowls and jars are featured as "authentic" items of everyday use. Figurines are basely commercial. To give but one example, an image of a Tesuque potter making "raingods," published in a 1930s souvenir folder of American Indian life, is captioned "Indian girl moulding lucky bucks."[22]

In contrast to these "tourist atrocities," the shapes that scholars call "utility ware" are, in fact, "receptacles of desire," for repeatedly authenticity is produced by removing such objects from their current historical situation or, even if photographed in the pueblo, by re-dressing the present in the past. In the established tradition of Charles Lummis and Edward Curtis, history is airbrushed out. Clearly, Ruth Benedict did not invent the stereotype of the peaceful, poetic, feminine Pueblo. She simply called it "Apollonian." To the extent that potteries are seen at all as containers of cultural value, as well as art objects to decorate Anglo lives, they are described as reiterating, affirming this world view. Nor is this view specific to the Pueblo, for it is widely assumed that primitive and folk art is tradition bound and conflict free. The idea that conflict, as well as clay, may be shaped in Pueblo ceramics is simply absent from the literature.[23]

When Helen Cordero shaped the first Storyteller doll in 1964, she engendered a revolution in Pueblo ceramics, caused a dislocation in the economy of cultural representations, and forced a taxonomic shift in Anglo classifications and valuations of Pueblo ceramics. When I first encountered a Storyteller figure (see figure 3), I read it as female and as a powerful image of generativity, of reproductive power. I soon learned that this was not simply another image of a Pueblo mother, of which Helen herself has made several, but a male figure: "It's my grandfather. He's giving me these. He had lots of stories and lots of grandchildrens, and we're all in there, in the clay." In studying these grandfather Storytellers, which are also images of cultural reproduction, I have discovered that synchronic essentialism and significations of stability in Pueblo art and culture are not entirely a matter of Anglo projection. Without pottery to store water and grain, settled Pueblo existence as it developed and was lived for centuries in the southwest deserts was literally inconceivable. Not surprisingly, therefore, the existence and well-being of the people was connected to the creation and maintenance of clay figures. Pueblo religion centers on reproduction or, in Haeberlin's terms, "the idea of fertilization." Connections between human fertility and agricultural subsistence were frequently made and have been the subject of both ritual and iconography, and a consistent theme in ceramic self-representation, for almost two thousand years.[24]

In the first half of this century, pottery production at Cochiti declined, as it did in many other pueblos. While scholars, collectors, traders, and writers were soon encouraging pottery revivals, they discouraged figurine manufacture and the production of "tourist atrocities." Santa Fe organizations such as the Indian Arts Fund and the Southwest Association for Indian Affairs combined aestheticism and activism, and in the 1920s supporters such as Mary Austin, Mabel Dodge Luhan, and Natalie Curtis promoted Indian art as a way to build popular sympathy for Indian political and religious freedoms and the preservation of Indian culture. The problem then and now was that they decided what counted as Indian art. Clearly, figurines did not.

Remembering her childhood, Helen Cordero has said, "For a long time pottery was silent in the pueblo." Among the few figurative forms that continued to be made at Cochiti, the figure of a woman holding a child, a water jar, or a bowl of bread was the most popular and was called "a singing mother," "a madonna," or "a singing lady." When Helen shaped the first Storyteller in response to Alexander Girard's request for a larger figure with more children, she revised the singing mother tradition in two significant respects: she made the primary figure male, rather than female; and she placed more than a realistic number of children on him. Helen's reinvention of this important mode of cultural production and tradition of representation controlled by women (pottery) transformed an image of natural reproduction into a figure of an important mode of cultural reproduction (storytelling) that is controlled by men and that both embodies and expresses generativity, the root metaphor of Pueblo culture.

By 1973 when the Museum of International Folk Art mounted its "What Is Folk Art?" exhibit, the success and popularity of Helen's Storyteller was such that at least six other potters had imitated her figure. A decade later over fifty other Cochiti potters and no fewer than 150 potters throughout the New Mexico pueblos were shaping Storytellers and related figurines. Many of these imitations are female figures, and as far as Helen is concerned, they are not "really" Storytellers: "They call them 'Storytellers,' but they don't know what it means. They don't know it's after my grandfather. At home, no womens are storytellers." When Helen Cordero insists upon the ancestral and masculine attributes of her Storyteller, she is both explicitly and implicitly "authorizing" her creation: explicitly, by invoking her biological connection to ancestral authority and power; implicitly, by identifying her pottery with a sacred masculine activity, a tradition that is both patriarchal and genealogical.

Women do tell stories at Cochiti, but they do not tell *the* stories—the sacred origin myths and legends. As Helen's uncle Joe Trujillo once remarked, "Our kivas are like men's clubs. Religion is a man's business with Indians." If women are practically peripheral, they are symbolically central to this "man's business," which involves a transcendental appropriation of the female principle. Moreover, in this world in which discourse is controlled by men, women's ideas or models of the world about them find expression in forms other than direct expository speech, and for generation upon generation of Pueblo women, pottery making has been a primary and privileged mode of expression. If Pueblo potteries were once a primary mode of production, a necessity of life, they were also and still are symbolic forms, containers of cultural values, models *of* and *for* reproduction and regeneration. But even here, men have traditionally controlled the marketing and distribution of pottery and other forms of communication with the outside world. Acculturation, automobiles, and an Anglo art market that names and wants to know its Indian artists have changed all that. Women have assumed control of activities and monies that were once their husbands' prerogatives.[25]

In the summer of 1982, when a Cochiti tribal officer tried to persuade the council to prohibit the women from having shows and demonstrating pottery making despite the obvious economic benefit to the pueblo, he was reasserting the traditional male role of mediating with the outside world and protecting what "he" deemed sacred discourse. He was also attempting to reinvoke his right to appropriate, control, and re-present female generativity and creativity. Perhaps he realized that in the remarkable revival of figurative pottery that Storytellers have engendered, women potters have done much more than reshape traditional roles in terms of economics, mobility, and communication. By creating Storytellers and other mythic and ceremonial figures, such as Turtles and Drummers, rather than bowls and jars, and in exhibiting and demonstrating their art, they are telling stories about storytelling and have assumed the right to re-present and interpret to the outside world at least some of the aspects of the very discourse in which they are displaced. Helen Cordero and her sisters are manipulating considerably more than clay. They are reproducing culture "with a difference."

As a consequence of Helen Cordero's creativity, Pueblo figurative pottery has also been rediscovered and redefined by Anglo consumers. There are now several categories for figurative pottery—other than "Pottery, Miscellaneous"—at Santa Fe's Indian Market, figurines win major prizes, and shapes once dismissed as "tourist junk" and relegated to museum attics and basements are now on display and commanding high prices. Nonetheless, it is doubtful if, from the white man's point of view, the shape of Pueblo pottery has *really* changed. In 1987 *American Indian Art* published a special issue on pottery that included two essays on historic and contemporary figurative ceramics—the latter shaped by Nora Naranjo-Morse. The cover, however, featured a very traditional, early nineteenth-century Acoma olla.

I don't think there's any question that Nora's Pearlene goes beyond such nostalgic Anglo categories of Pueblo women and Pueblo potteries. She got written about but did not appear on the cover of that glossy Indian art magazine, and I can guarantee that this Pueblo woman's representation of herself as postcolonial Pearlene will not be featured on any guidebooks to the Southwest. Nor is she likely to be the subject of Native American artists such as R. C. Gorman, Amado Peña, or Robert Redbird. Or Anglo Southwest artists such as Ross Stefan, Jacqueline Rochester, or Bill Schenck. They have very different ideas about these "mudwomen" than Nora Naranjo-Morse does. Fictions that sell. They don't want Pearlene, with all her ambiguity of dependency and rupture, for "man dreams of an Other not only to possess her but also to be ratified by her." They want those shiny black Santa Clara ollas (see figure 2) that look like "ancient" potteries are supposed to.[26]

To conclude this meditation on aesthetic appropriation and mystification: On October 15, 1989, *Money* magazine ran an ad in the *New York Times Magazine* titled "Adobe Sonata." Imaged as "the rewards of Money" was a casually elegant couple embracing at a grand piano in a Santa Fe adobe living room decorated with traditional ollas. The caption reiterated that, "to live in Santa Fe is to live amid the grandeur of nature and the beauty of the inspired artist's creation. The readers of *MONEY* magazine can easily afford to reflect this harmony in the paintings and crafts that illuminate their homes." In the late twentieth as in the late nineteenth century, such images not only are "invested with indescribable romance" but have become commonplace significations of incredible investment. Nine years ago Helen Cordero's potteries were photographed against a pastoral, Edenic background to advertise the 1980–81 Colorado Spring Symphony season and its sponsor, Otero Savings. The poster tells us that the art objects are from the Otero Savings Collections and that "the Otero Savings Blue Ribbon Collection reflects a corporate promise to offer excellence to all. The Indian art mirrors the Otero image of quality and lasting value."

In fin de siècle remarks that an "immense amount of romance is wasted on the old mud houses" and "tiresome pottery fragments," Susan Wallace might well be describing present-day Santa Fe. Adobes and ollas and olla maidens (see figure 2) and countless advertisements such as the preceding confirm that

> the need of our society both to engulf Others and to exploit "otherness" is not only a structural and ideological phenomenon; it has been at the root of the very development of capitalism, founded as it is on imperialist relations. . . . Economically, we need the Other, even as politically we seek to eliminate it. . . . Capitalism feeds on different value systems and takes control of them, while nourishing their symbolic difference from itself. . . . [D]ifferent systems of production . . . which are suppressed by capitalism are then incorporated into its imagery and ideological values: as "otherness," old-fashioned, charming, exotic, natural, primitive, universal—

the timeless beauty of a Santa Clara Pueblo pot shaped by, yet another ad tells us, "the warm hands of man." Confirmation yet again, as Luce Irigaray has pointed out, that "commodities, women, are a mirror of value of and for men." When "mudwoman encounters the world of money and business," she cannot but confront the nostalgic aestheticism, synchronic essentialism, feminization, and utilitarian biases that have shaped the Anglo valuation and imaging of Pueblo potteries. Among other things, Pearlene discovers that "tradition remains the sacred weapon oppressors repeatedly hold up whenever the need to maintain their privileges, hence to impose the form of the old·on the content of the new, arises."[27]

NOTES

1. This essay is dedicated to Helen Cordero, who has shared her life and work with me and by so doing has revised my own; to Marsie Cate, who has given me a home in New Mexico and never not challenged my own romantic vision of Pueblo life; to Marta Weigle, friend and fellow interpreter of the regional web of commodification in which our lives and work are entangled; and to Kit Hinsley, who has inspired, sustained, and contributed to this re-visioning. I would also like to thank Jay Cox for research and computer assistance; Linda Degh and Richard Bauman for inviting me to an Indiana University conference, "Folklore and Social Transformation" (Bloomington, November 1988); the editors of the *Arizona Quarterly* for inviting me to their first conference on American Literatures and Cultures (Tucson, March 1989); and John MacAloon for asking me to be Ford Foundation Lecturer in the social sciences at the University of Chicago (May 1989). These three presentations occasioned the rereading and rethinking that resulted in this essay, first presented at a Winterthur Conference in 1989—"The Material Culture of Gender/The Gender of Material Culture"—and forthcoming in a book of the same title.

2. Adrienne Rich, "Trying to Talk with a Man," in *Poems Selected and New, 1950–1974* (New York: W. W. Norton & Co., 1975), 185.

3. Roland Barthes, *Mythologies* (New York: Hill & Wang, 1986), 151–52.

4. Adrienne Rich, "When We Dead Awaken: Writing as Re-Vision," in *On Lies, Secrets, and Silence: Selected Prose, 1966–1978* (New York: W. W. Norton & Co., 1979), 35. For further discussion of the "question of how the third-world subject is represented within Western discourse," of "the mechanics of the constitution of the Other," see Gayatri Spivak, "Can the Subaltern Speak?" in *Marxism and the Interpretation of Culture*, ed. by Cary Nelson and Lawrence Grossberg (Urbana: University of Illinois Press, 1988), 271–313.

5. The Heard Museum, *Earth, Hands, Life: A Ceramics Figures Symposium* (January 21–22, 1989); Edwin Wade, "The Ethnic Art Market in the Southwest, 1880–1980," in *Objects and Others: Essays on Museums and Material Culture*, ed. by George W. Stocking, Jr. (Madison: University of Wisconsin Press, 1985), 167; for more on the commodification of ethnicity in New Mexico, the cooptation of the Pueblo and their marketing, and elaborating their own ethnicity, see Sylvia Rodriguez, "Art, Tourism, and Race Relations in Taos: Toward a Sociology of the Art Colony," *Journal of Anthropological Research* 45 (1989): 77–99. Nora Naranjo-Morse's poems have now been published in *Mud Woman: Poems from the Clay* (Tucson: University of Arizona Press, 1992).

6. The Heard Museum, *Earth, Hands, Life* (January 22, 1989). For examples of the official and predominantly utilitarian narrative of Pueblo ceramics, see especially Alfred E. Dittert, Jr., and Fred Plog, *Generations in Clay: Pueblo Pottery of the American Southwest* (Flagstaff: Northland Press, 1980); David L. Arnold, "Pueblo Artistry in Clay," *National Geographic* 162, no. 5 (November 1982): 593–605; Jonathan Batkin, "Pottery: The Ceramic Tradition," in *Harmony by Hand: Art of the Southwest Indians*, ed. by Patrick Houlihan (San Francisco: Chronicle Books, 1987), 74–106; and Jonathan Batkin, *Pottery of the Pueblos of New Mexico, 1700–1940* (Colorado Springs: Taylor Museum, 1987).

7. Aihwa Ong, "Colonialism and Modernity: Feminist Re-Presentations of Women in Non-Western Societies," in *Feminism and the Critique of Colonial Discourse*, ed. by Deborah Gordon, *Inscriptions* 3/4 (1988): 85; for discussion of nineteenth-century Cochiti ceramic "grotesques," which were in fact portraits of the whiteman, see Barbara A. Babcock, "Pueblo Clowning and Pueblo Clay: From Icon to Caricature in Cochiti Figurative Ceramics," *Visible Religion* 4/5 (1986): 280–300; and " 'Those, They Called Them Monos': Cochiti Figurative Ceramics, 1875–1905," *American Indian Art* 12, no. 4 (Autumn 1987): 50–57, 67. Only two essays have dealt at all with the relationship between politics and potteries, with the shaping of conflict as well as clay in Pueblo ceramics, and those quite recently: Edwin L. Wade, "Straddling the Cultural Fence: The Conflict of Ethnic Artists within Pueblo Societies," in *The Arts of the North American Indian: Native Traditions in Evolution*, ed. by Edwin L. Wade (New York: Hudson Hills Press, 1986) 243–54; and Barbara A. Babcock, " 'At Home No Womens are Storytellers': Potteries, Stories, and Politics in Cochiti Pueblo, *Journal of the Southwest* 30, no. 3 (Autumn 1988): 356–89.

8. James Clifford, "Histories of the Tribal and the Modern," in *The Predicament of Culture: Twentieth-Century Ethnography, Literature, and Art* (Cambridge: Harvard University Press, 1988),

213; Batkin, "Pottery: The Ceramic Tradition," 77; Helen Carr, "Woman/Indian: 'The American' and his Others," in *Europe and Its Others; Proceedings of the Essex Conference on the Sociology of Literature*, Vol. 2, ed. by Francis Barker et al. (Colchester: University of Essex, 1985), 46; Judith Williamson, "Woman is an Island: Femininity and Colonization," in *Studies in Entertainment: Critical Approaches to Mass Culture*, ed. by Tania Modleski (Bloomington: Indiana University Press, 1986), 101; Rodriguez, "Art, Tourism, and Race Relations in Taos," 87.

9. Charlie Masters, "Going Native," in *Standing By and Making Do: Women of Wartime Los Alamos*, ed. by Jane S. Wilson and Charlotte Serber (Los Alamos: The Los Alamos Historical Society, 1988), 117–30; Marc Neikrug, "Los Alamos" (unpublished manuscript, 1988); Clifford, *Predicament*, 272; Helen Carr, "In Other Words: Native American Women's Autobiography," ed. by Bella Brodzki and Celeste Schenck (Ithaca: Cornell University Press, 1988), 151.

10. Clifford, *Predicament*, 197; Edward W. Said, *Orientalism* (New York: Vintage Books, 1979); Gayatri Spivak, *In Other Worlds: Essays in Cultural Politics* (New York: Methuen, 1987), 83–84.

11. Frank Hamilton Cushing, "My Adventures in Zuni," *The Century Magazine* 25, no. 1 (November 1882): 191–207, 25, no. 4 (February 1883): 500–11, 26, no. 1 (May 1883): 28–47; David Snow, "Some Economic Considerations of Historic Rio Grande Pueblo Pottery," in *The Changing Ways of Southwestern Indians: A Historic Perspective*, ed. by A. Schroeder (Glorieta: Rio Grande Press, 1973), 55–72; Terry Reynolds, "Women, Pottery, and Economics at Acoma Pueblo," in *New Mexico Women: Intercultural Perspectives*, ed. by Joan M. Jensen and Darlis A. Miller (Albuquerque: University of New Mexico Press, 1986), 279–300; Wade, "Straddling the Cultural Fence," 243–54; Marta Weigle, "From Desert to Disney World: The Santa Fe Railway and the Fred Harvey Company Display the Indian Southwest," *Journal of Anthropological Research* 45 (1989): 115–137; T. C. McLuhan, *Dream Tracks: The Railroad and the American Indian, 1890–1930* (New York: Harry N. Abrams, Inc., Publishers), 34.

12. Homi K. Bhabha, "The Other Question," *Screen* 24, no. 6 (November–December 1983): 24; Tzvetan Todorov, *The Conquest of America: The Question of the Other* (New York: Harper & Row), 175–76.

13. Cheryl J. Foote and Sandra K. Schackel, "Indian Women of New Mexico, 1535–1680," in Jensen and Miller, *New Mexico Women*, 21; James W. Abert, "Report of Lieutenant J. W. Abert, of his Examination of New Mexico, in the Years 1846–47," in *Notes of a Military Reconnaissance, From Ft. Leavenworth, in Missouri, to San Diego in California, Including part of the Arkansas, Del Norte, and Gila Rivers* by Lt. Col. W. H. Emory (Washington: Wendell and Ven Bethuysen, Printers, 1848), 417–548; Cushing, "Adventures in Zuni," 197.

14. Susan Wallace, *The Land of the Pueblos* (New York: Columbian Publishing Co., 1891), 43, 51, 52; John G. Owens to Deborah Stratton, July 20, 1890, John G. Owens Papers, Peabody Museum Archives, Harvard University.

15. "Cincinnati Art Pottery," *Harper's Weekly*, no. 1202 (January 10, 1880): 342; Claude Meillassoux, "From reproduction to production: A Marxist approach to economic anthropology," *Economy and Society* 1, no. 1 (February 1972): 101–2; Julian Smyonov, *Tass is Authorized to Announce . . .* (New York: Riverrun Press, 1987), 73.

16. For discussion of "aesthetic primitivism" in the representation of Native American women, see Carr, "In Other Words," 146; Bhabha, "The Other Question," 23; Ong, "Colonialism and Modernity," 82; Trinh T. Minh-ha, "Introduction," in *She, The Inappropriate/d Other*, ed. by Trinh T. Minh-ha, *Discourse* 8 (Fall–Winter 1986–87): 8; Clifford, *Predicament*, 272.

17. Said, *Orientalism*, 5; E. Pomeroy, *In Search of the Golden West: The Tourist in Western America* (New York: Alfred A. Knopf, 1957), 39; quoted in Marta Weigle and Kyle Fiore, *Santa Fe and Taos: The Writer's Era, 1916–1941* (Santa Fe: Ancient City Press, 1982), 17; quoted in D. H. Thomas, *The Southwestern Indian Detours: The Story of the Fred Harvey/Santa Fe Railway Experiment in "Detourism"* (Phoenix: Hunter Publishing, 1978), 196. For more on Orientalizing in the imaging of Pueblo women, see Babcock, " 'A New Mexican Rebecca': Imaging Pueblo Women," *Journal of the Southwest* 32:4 (1990): 400–37.

18. Clifford *Predicament*, 268, points out that while Said is right to identify an essentializing and dichotomizing discourse as an element of colonial domination, such discourse is not specific only to the tradition of Orientalism; Santa Fe Railway ads, quoted in McLuhan, *Dream Tracks*, 19, 45.

19. Warren I. Sussman, *Culture as History: The Transformation of the United States in the Twentieth Century* (New York: Pantheon Books, 1984); T. J. Jackson Lears, *No Place of Grace: Antimodernism and the Transformation of American Culture, 1880–1920* (New York: Pantheon Books, 1981). See especially Chapter 2: "The Figure of the Artisan: Arts and Crafts Ideology," Charles Eliot Norton quoted, 66; E. E. Evans-Pritchard, *The Position of Women in Primitive Societies and Other Essays in Social Anthropology* (New York: The Free Press, 1965), 45; Michel Foucault, "The Eye of Power," in *Power/Knowledge: Selected Interviews and Other Writings, 1972–1977*, ed. by Colin Gordon (New York: Pantheon Books, 1980), 146–65 and *Discipline and Punish: The Birth of the Prison* (New York: Pantheon Books, 1977). See also Nancy Fraser's discussion of "Foucault on Power," in *Unruly Practices: Power, Discourse, and Gender in Contemporary Social Theory* (Minneapolis: University of Minnesota Press, 1989), 17–34.

20. Clifford, *Predicament*, 201; Carr, "In Other Words," 150; Rodriguez, "Art, Tourism, and Race Relations in Taos," 93; for further discussion of the effects of pottery revivals on Pueblo gender arrangements, see Wade, "Straddling the Cultural Fence" and Babcock, " 'At Home No Womens are Storytellers.' "

21. For further discussion of Pueblo portraits of the whiteman in both ceramic caricature and Pueblo ritual clowning, see Jill Sweet, "Burlesquing 'The Other' in Pueblo Performance," *Annals of Tourism Research* 16 (1989): 62–75 and Barbara A. Babcock, "Ritual Undress and the Comedy of Self and Other: Bandelier's *The Delight Makers*," in *A Crack in the Mirror*, ed. by Jay Ruby (Philadelphia: University of Pennsylvania Press, 1982), 187–203; " 'Arrange Me Into Disorder': Fragments and Reflections on Ritual Clowning," in *Rite, Drama, Festival, Spectacle*, ed. by John J. MacAloon (Philadelphia: ISHI Press), 102–28; "Pueblo Clowning and Pueblo Clay"; and " 'Those, They Called Them Monos.' "

22. William H. Holmes, "The Debasement of Pueblo Art," *American Anthropologist* 2 (1989): 320; Thomas S. Dozier, "About Indian Pottery," *Statement to the Trade for 1907* (Santa Fe, 1907); in "On Collecting Art and Culture," *Predicament*, 232, Clifford remarks that playing and playing with the outsiders' games "does not seem worth salvaging"; for representative texts on Pueblo pottery, see note 6.

23. Trinh T. Minh-ha, "Introduction," 8; for discussion of the production of authenticity by removing objects from their current historical situation, see Clifford, *Predicament*, 228; Trinh T. Minh-ha, *Woman, Native, Other: Writing Postcoloniality and Feminism* (Bloomington: Indiana University Press, 1989), 89 ff. similarly discusses "planned authenticity" as a "product of hegemony" which "constitutes an efficacious means of silencing the cry of racial oppression"; Sylvia Rodriguez, "Art, Tourism, and Race Relations in Taos," 83, makes this same point regarding the Indian paintings of the Taos painters; Ruth Benedict, *Patterns of Culture* (Boston: Houghton Mifflin, 1934); Babcock, " 'At Home No Womens are Storytellers.' "

24. For discussion and documentation of the revolution in Pueblo figurative ceramics engendered by the Storyteller, see Barbara A. Babcock and Guy and Doris Monthan, *The Pueblo Storyteller: Development of A Figurative Ceramic Tradition* (Tucson: University of Arizona Press, 1986); statements by Helen Cordero were made in conversations with me between 1988 and 1986; H. K. Haeberlin, "The Idea of Fertilization in the Culture of Pueblo Indians," *Memoirs of the American Anthropological Association* 3 (1916).

25. Quoted in Edith Hart Mason, "Enemy Bear, *The Masterkey* 22 (1948): 85. For further discussion of traditional gender roles and the disturbance thereof as a consequence of the manufacture of pottery for sale, and of the Storyteller revolution in particular, see Babcock, " 'At Home No Womens are Storytellers.' "

26. *American Indian Art Magazine* 12, no. 4 (Autumn 1987): "Pottery Issue"; in her "Introduction," p. 4, Trinh T. Minh-ha discusses "the ambiguous relation of dependency and rupture that the female writing/speaking/looking subject maintains towards both the West and men"; Simone de Beauvoir, *The Second Sex* (New York: Vintage Books, 1974), 170.

27. Susan Wallace, *The Land of the Pueblos*, 13; Judith Williamson, "Woman is an Island," 112; Luce Irigaray, "Women on the Market," in *This Sex Which is Not One* (Ithaca: Cornell University Press, 1985), 177; Trinh T. Minh-ha, *Woman, Native, Other*, 106.

The Commercial Canyon:
Culturally Constructing the "Other"
in the Theater of the West

Mark Neumann

*I*t's difficult not to become buried alive in the nostalgia and romanticism that is the American Southwest. Traveling its roads can be like wandering the pages of a dreamy story, a tale that finds its drama in the contours of the land and the characters encountered along the way. Signs and markers everywhere envision the region as a scenic wonderland, a Native American homeland, and a Wild West. All of these become guideposts for visitors, ordering and shaping the landscape through mythic stories of nature, culture, and history. "The world's landscapes are but the screen on which the past, present, and anticipated cosmic vanity of mankind is written," says geographer James Houston. "Land is the palimpsest of human need, desires, meaning, greed, and fears." [1]

National parks are also part of the Southwest's narrative landscape, telling a story that often conjures a sense of American nationalism, the majesty of nature, cultural identity, and the drama of westward expansion. Freeman Tilden, an early proponent of park interpretation programs, suggested that the purpose of national parks "is to preserve, in a condition as unaltered as humanly possible, the wilderness that greeted the eyes of the first white men who challenged and conquered it." [2] While Tilden valued highly the preservation of national antiquities and natural monuments, his remarks remind us how national parks are linked to an ideology of American progress and control over the natural world. For Tilden, the national parks were "national museums" that displayed the scenic wonders, scientific curiosities, and the cultural and historic evidence of how others had previously occupied the land. Like museums, national parks rescued and saved places and things from becoming lost to the transitory forces of the modern world. And, like museums, national parks are also modern institutions that construct images of nature, history, and culture. Although the parks may seem like enchanted islands frozen in time, they are places that mediate and interpret the "natural" world in the scientific, historic, and aesthetic terms of modernity.

In the landscapes of national parks, then, we find how land and people have been inscribed with the visions and values of their makers. What may seem at face value a preserved natural environment or indigenous cultural tradition is, instead, a reflection of selective *production* where, as Raymond Williams points out, "from a whole possible area of past and present, certain meanings and practices are chosen for emphasis [and] certain other meanings and practices are neglected or excluded." [3] National parks and their surrounding regions exemplify how the industries of tourism are often centered in the manufacturing of particular cultural images of regions and people that reveal political relationships among culture, state, and power as they produce visions of the past and present. "Why are certain practices singled out as cultural traditions while others are forgotten or ignored?" asks Wai-Teng Leong. "Who, in particular, links people and practices to the past and for what purposes? Who defines the cultural traditions for which groups? Which group is able to impose its version of the past on other groups and why?" [4]

In this essay, I examine how an image of the Grand Canyon and its surrounding region was produced by commercial forces of tourism at the turn of the century. Through the efforts of railroad and hospitality entrepreneurs, and due to a growing public interest in the anthropological reports of indigenous cultures, the Grand Canyon was one of many Southwestern destinations recast as a fascinating and mysterious landscape populated with "primitive" natives. For many Easterners experiencing a sense of alienation in the modern city, places like the Grand Canyon offered a promise of redeeming spiritual and traditional values through contact with nature and people who lived in the natural world. Through the growth of tourism, the Grand Canyon not only became an accessible destination for visitors but was also a theatrical stage symbolizing an ongoing drama of Native American cultural life in a romantic vision of the Southwest. As native life was transformed by warfare, government policy, and a politics of marginalization, it reappeared at places like the Grand Canyon in the form of images, performances, and architecture produced and anchored in place by the rise of a tourist industry that capitalized on Native American cultural tradition.

Visitors who wander through the Grand Canyon region today find that this image largely remains in place. While the tourist landscape of the Grand Canyon may seem at times to be a museum displaying native culture and history, it is also an exhibit that materializes the politics of a struggle and desire to hold on to a disappearing past. Since the turn of the century, the commercial tourist world of the Grand Canyon has in many ways been shaped by a dramatic allegory of loss and redemption. An "appreciation of the transience of things, and the concern to redeem them for eternity, is one of the strongest impulses of allegory," noted the German critic Walter Benjamin. [5] For Benjamin, the "ruin" was the physical symbol that paralleled the idea of allegory. The ruin is "an always disappearing structure that invites imaginative reconstruction." [6] And it is in the romantic and sentimental representations of Native American culture at the Grand Canyon, found along roadsides and in the scenes along the canyon's rim, that the present remains populated by the phantoms and ruins of an imagined past.

Driving on state road 64, approaching Grand Canyon National Park from the east, I come across a faded yellow sign at an abandoned roadside souvenir stand that reads: Welcome To Navajoland. These words, painted on a square of rotting plywood, lean against a fifty-five-gallon drum overflowing with garbage. This is the Navajo Reservation. Skeletons of abandoned cars rust in the desert, and small shack homes sit at the end of dirt roads falling from the shoulders of this route to the national park's east entrance. The decaying wood and peeling paint of the sign seem to reflect a larger poverty that afflicts the area and leaves me feeling anything but welcome on this land.

This well-traveled path through Navajoland is spotted with Navajo souvenir stands that fly flags from different countries in hopes of luring travelers from Germany, Japan, Switzerland, and Canada toward their tables of merchandise. And there are more signs: See A Live Wolf! Turquoise and Silver Jewelry, calls one. Another trader places signs in the serial style of Burma Shave advertising. Next Chief Yellow Horse, says the first; Indian Trade Center—No Tax! For You, says the second; Indian Silver—Pottery—Rugs, says the third; Dealers Welcome, followed by, Chief Yellow Horse Next Stop—Yellow Horse Loves You—Bankcards Accepted [with images of MasterCard and VISA] Pottery Sale. As I drive past the stand, Yellow Horse makes another pitch. We're Back There Folks, begins a new series of announcements; Nice Indians Behind You, says the next; the third sign, posted upside down, reads, Turn Around—Come On Back.

Traveling through Navajoland toward the park, I meet a man dressed as an Indian warrior standing on a rock in view of the passing tourists. I park on the worn dirt turn-out where two teenage Navajo boys lay necklaces on a table and set up for another day of souvenir sales. The costumed man is Jake, they tell me, and he works the road.

A Sioux originally from North Dakota, Jake started working the road in 1985. He had gone to Brigham Young University in Provo, Utah, for a few years but left because he had "a difficult time fitting into that society." He was planning to leave for Europe to dance and do expositions after he saved enough money. "Working the road" meant standing on a rock from the middle of June until the end of August dressed in a traditional Indian costume. Tourists would see Jake and stop to take his picture, and he would charge them for posing.

"I had the opportunity to travel to Europe on several occasions, and each time I went there I was fascinated by the costumes the people wore," he says, waving at a motor home heading east, away from the park. "I loved taking pictures over there of the people in the costumes, and when I got back over here I noticed that most of the Indians don't like to have their picture taken, so I got this idea." Behind the rock where we stand talking, I notice, Jake has parked his Honda CX500 motorcycle out of view from the road. "They use their film, their camera, they take the picture and I pose," he explains. "Three dollars if the picture is of me alone, and it's five dollars if they want to get in the picture."

"But you're in either picture," I ask. "Why do you charge more for them to stand next to you?"

"Well, it's an added thing. It gives it more of a personal identification," he says. "A single shot of me is just like a postcard. But for them to be in there, with this kind of setting, with this kind of costume, gives it a more personal value. And I guess it's what the market will bear, to speak in capitalist terms."

Jake tells me he earned nine dollars yesterday, but "June [is] usually a slow month." When business is good, he claims, he makes as much as 250 dollars a day. After the busy season is over at the Grand Canyon, he works as a stuntman in a Western theme park near Scottsdale, Arizona.

"It's called 'Rawhide,' " he says. "I get shot and fall off buildings for the tourist shows." The season at Rawhide typically lasts from October to May. Jake says the summers there are too hot and working this reservation road offers a much better climate. The traffic seems rather slow today, but it is not yet noon.

"What do your friends and family think about this kind of work?" I ask.

"Some of them laugh at it, and I guess it is out of the ordinary," he confesses. "I mean, how many people do you see standing all dressed up by the roadside like this? You don't see any." He pauses to put a blanket around his shoulders. The wind has picked up, and his costume exposes much of his skin. "But I'll tell you something, they've got the wrong idea about these stands here," he says pointing to the two teenage boys waiting for customers at their table of earrings and necklaces. "If you look, they've got these nice pickup trucks by the stand there. And they've got on green army fatigues and T-shirts with 'Ted Nugent' and 'Whitesnake' on them. It seems like they're trying to break out of the mold that society wants to put them in. Which isn't bad, I guess, but they don't know what they're passing up." He pulls the blanket off and waves at a station wagon cruising toward the park.

"If I were a tourist coming through here," he continues, "I'd want a little old lady sitting on a rug so I could get a picture of her. And a man with a silver belt, and some turquoise nuggets, and some moccasins and leggings, the whole bit, so he'd look the part rather than try to fit into mainstream society. I wouldn't care what they asked me for a price because that would be an experience you couldn't get anywhere else. I know that must sound like some Harvard Business School deal," he laughs.

A van pulls up next to my Volkswagen, and a family pours out to look at the jewelry at the Navajos' stand. A man with camera equipment walks toward the rock where we are talking. This could be a customer for Jake, so I say goodbye to him.

"Can I give you some money for taking up your time?" I offer awkwardly. "How much would be appropriate, do you have an interview price?"

"No," he laughs, "whatever you want is fine." I have a five and a twenty in my wallet. I give him the five, hoping it's enough.

"Good luck, man," Jake says, and I look at his hand shaking my own. We have done business. As I start down the rock toward my van, one more question comes to mind.

"What kind of costume is that you're wearing?" I ask.

"It's a Sioux warrior's costume," he grins. "It's what General Custer saw for about fifteen minutes." I nod, feeling privy to an inside joke, and continue down to my VW. On the way, I pass the man with the camera, who breathes heavily as he lugs a tripod and a bag of gear up the rock to where Jake stands waiting.

"To be an Indian in modern American society," argues Vine Deloria, "is in a very real sense to be unreal and ahistorical." [7] Deloria suggests that anthropology stands behind many modern Native Americans' ambivalence toward a firm cultural identification. "The massive volume of useless knowledge produced by anthropologists attempting to capture real Indians in a network of theories has contributed substantially to the invisibility of Indian people today," he argues.

> Over the years anthropologists have succeeded in burying Indian communities so completely beneath the mass of irrelevant information that the total impact of the scholarly community on Indian people has become one of simple authority. Many Indians have come to parrot the ideas of anthropologists because it appears that anthropologists know everything about Indian communities.[8]

Anthropology initiated public curiosity about native cultures and remains as an institutional authority on questions of United States government policy toward Native Americans. But anthropology was only part of the machinery that produced an ambiguous cultural space where many Native Americans today find themselves. "The Indian, by 1893," argues Alan Trachtenberg, "seemed a 'vanishing American.' "[9] But as native populations receded, killed by government soldiers or forced to reservations, they reappeared as imaginative constructions in American culture and commerce. As Jake waited on the rock for the man and the camera lens, he stood in the shadow of a mythic Indian cast for nearly a hundred years. The Sioux costume that linked Jake with the victory over Custer at Little Big Horn, now consciously worn by this tourist thoroughfare, connected him also with a sense of native culture made simultaneously real and imaginary by the commercial forces of tourism.

The tradition that constructed the Native American as a "noble savage" was strong at the turn of the century, stimulated by a larger urban dissatisfaction with the kind of world produced by technologically based industrial society. Many looked to the natural world, and to the native people who lived there, as a source of relief. The idea that experiencing nature could rejuvenate people entangled in the routines, pressures, and anxieties of city life has been popular in America since the mid-nineteenth century. "Thousands of nerve-shaken, overcivilized people are beginning to find out that going to the mountains is going home," observed John Muir in 1898, "and that mountain parks and reservations are useful not only as fountains of timber and irrigating rivers, but as fountains of life." [10] Near the end of the nineteenth century, many European and American elites recognized that "the triumph of modern culture had not produced greater autonomy (which was the official claim)," argues Jackson Lears, "but rather had promoted a spreading sense of moral impotence and spiritual sterility—a feeling that life had become not only overcivilized but also curiously unreal." [11] For Lears, this "antimodern impulse" reflected deeper uncertainties held by people whose days had been captured by the institutions of a progressive life. An increasingly secularized and industrialized society had failed to account for culturally internalized desires for individuality, morality, and spiritual fulfillment. Sensing that something was missing in their world, many nineteenth-century Americans went looking for an "authentic experience outside the bounds of Victorian respectability and the intense spiritual ecstasy of communion with God." Yet, even as Easterners left their urban homes for leisure excursions into the landscapes of the Southwest, they found that the forces of tourism had begun to recast the natural world into the shape of modernity's dreams.

Native American cultural life was one aspect of the natural world which promised, in part, to restore something of the traditional and spiritual character that seemed absent from city life. "A growing interest in patterns of life other than our own took root and came to have validity and significance," writes T. C. McLuhan. "The American Indian emerged from a position of banishment to a fanciful, factual, and appealing place in the American imagination." [12]

D. H. Lawrence observed this phenomenon nearly seventy years ago. "Just a show! The Southwest is the great playground of the white American," wrote a disgruntled Lawrence after attending a Hopi snake dance ritual with three thousand other tourists in Arizona in August 1924.

> And the Indian, with his long hair and his bits of pottery and blankets and clumsy home-made trinkets, he's a wonderful live toy to play with. More fun than keeping rabbits, and just as harmless. Wonderful, really, hopping round with a snake in his mouth. Lots of fun! Oh, the wild west is lots of fun: the Land of Enchantment. Like being right inside the circus-ring: lots of sand, and painted savages jabbering, and snakes and all that. [13]

Lawrence considered the American Southwest to be a strange and confusing theater. "All the wildness and woolliness and westernity and motor cars and art and sage and savage are so mixed up, so incongruous, that it is a farce and everybody knows it," he wrote. The Southwest was "like a comic opera played with solemn intensity." [14] Lawrence's reluctance toward the theatrics that surrounded him was, perhaps, consistent with his own feelings of dislocation. He described himself as "a lone lorn Englishman, tumbled out of the known world of the British empire onto this stage" of the West, a place "not like the proper world." [15]

Lawrence was right. Western regional identity has always been a problem. Instead of pinning the West down geographically as a specific and distinctive region, John Milton suggests that it may be more appropriate to think of the West as "an attitude, a state of mind, a way of looking at the world that is non-European, distinctly American." [16]

Such a view implies that we might consider the practices that constitute "Western experience," rather than think of the West in strictly geographic terms. In this sense, the West is, as William Goetzmann suggests, "a theater in which American patterns of culture could be endlessly mirrored."[17] At the turn of the century the American Southwest reflected an image that simultaneously dramatized progress and celebrated the wilderness and the "uncivilized" Indian. Today that image, still reflected in the structure and design of places like Grand Canyon National Park, recalls an early synchronization of tourism and anthropology. At the Grand Canyon, Native American culture became inscribed into the structures of tourism as a series of performances, art works, crafts, souvenirs, and architecture by entrepreneurs since the first decade of the twentieth century and have remained that way to this day.

Beginning in 1876, Fred Harvey, an entrepreneur of Southwest tourist facilities, and the Santa Fe Railway started a lucrative business collaboration that developed tourist facilities throughout the Southwest. But they brought more than railroads and hotels to the Grand Canyon area. They were also responsible for manufacturing a vision of Southwest culture and transforming the region into a popular tourist destination. "In commodifying the Indian Southwest as a tourist or secular pilgrimage center," says Marta Weigle, "Santa Fe/Harvey corporate image-makers transformed it into a mythological holy land of grand natural wonders, inspirational primitive arts, and domesticated, artistic 'natives.'"[18] The Southwest region became a kind of early "ethnic theme park," argues Weigle, that found commercial success in a corporate vision of the region that romanticized native culture as it dramatized the imposition of "civilized" life on the West.

The Santa Fe was also fundamental to the growth of tourism at the Grand Canyon. The railroad operated the stage lines that carried tourists to the rim in the 1890s from Flagstaff and by 1901 owned and operated the railroad spur that brought tourists to the canyon's rim from Williams, Arizona. Yet the railroad more than physically developed the means of transporting people to the canyon; it also helped create a vision of the Grand Canyon region as a destination. The Santa Fe Railway, climbing out of bankruptcy and under the leadership of a new company president, E. P. Ripley, began an ambitious and elaborate campaign designed to create an image of the Southwest that would draw tourists to its line. Ripley wanted to shake the Santa Fe Railway's reputation as a company that served greed-driven land speculators, gold prospectors, and buffalo skinners. The Santa Fe's new advertising campaign built on a new image of respectability, promoting the desert landscape as a region safe for travel and native life as a compelling display of cultural difference. "The landscape is wholly unlike the East," claimed an early advertisement for the Santa Fe's California Limited.

A land of wide horizons, of peaks miles high and titanic chasms. A world of color, too. These four are unique in all the earth: The Grand Canyon, the Petrified Forest, the Painted Desert and the Indian Pueblos. Reached only by the Santa Fe.

The campaign commenced by bringing artists to the Southwest. In 1892 Santa Fe executives commissioned artist Thomas Moran to paint the Grand Canyon. Moran was given transportation, lodging, and food in return. Ripley purchased Moran's *Grand Canyon* as well as rights for reproduction. The painting was lithographed in six colors, framed, and sent to thousands of schools, homes, stations, hotels, and universities throughout the world. By 1901 Santa Fe trains had arrived at the rim of the canyon. The railroad brought more artists to paint canvases of the canyon and other scenes in the Southwest and then purchased the best of their works.[19] In 1907 the Santa Fe began a general mailing of an annual calendar illustrated with images depicting romantic and primitive themes of native life. "In dire need of a powerful symbol to catch the public's imagination, the Santa Fe appropriated the Indian and his culture to establish for itself a meaningful emblem that would galvanize the American imagination," observes McLuhan.

> The railway's advertising images of the landscape and the Indian were glazed with beauty and picturesqueness, promoting a "last refuge of magic, mountains and quaint ancestors." But they also evoked a sense of mythological place—a distant West as a land filled with natural wonders, with the promise of a whole new set of different experiences implying a "rite of passage" from the familiar East to the wild, exotic, and slightly dangerous West, where "normal" rules don't apply.[20]

The Santa Fe circulated their romantic image of the Southwest and the Indian in a variety of media. Apart from the annual calendars, the railroad advertised its vision of the Southwest through brochures, posters, lithographs, postcards, and maps. In addition to these, travel lectures with lantern slides shown in businesses and schools also helped popularize the region.

McLuhan suggests that, "in assuming the cultural legacy of the American Indian, the [Santa Fe] ad men gave the impression that they were a knowledgeable 'ethnographic authority,' confidently imposing themselves on another culture by encapsulating it both in image and aphorism." [21] Anthropology had produced the initial accounts and gathered the artifacts that led to a larger public curiosity about southwestern Indian culture. The advertising department of the railroad also recognized that anthropological knowledge of the region carried a prestige which could work in the interests of the railroad. In 1903 the Santa Fe Passenger Department published an ethnographic account of southwestern Indian culture written by George Dorsey, who was a curator of anthropology at the Field Columbian Museum. Dorsey's work combined the voice of anthropological description with that of a travel guide. In one passage, for example, Dorsey authoritatively evaluates Navajo religious rites through the sensibilities of anthropological observer from the "civilized" world:

> That the power of the medicine-man should be curtailed there is no question. For while there can be no objection to the performance of purely religious ceremonies among any of the native tribes of America, there is an objection to the entrusting of the life of a person to the nine day performance of a shaman and his assistants, as is the case in this particular tribe. Remove this power of the shaman and give the Navaho work and see to it that his pasture lands are not encroached upon, and he will work out his own salvation without the assistance of higher education or donations of cast-off clothing.[22]

Here, Navajo culture was dually represented as a site of redemption and observation. Under the guidance of Dorsey's anthropological expertise, the Navajo could potentially be redeemed through the civilized management of their cultural order: Take away spiritual power, give them work, and they will be saved on their own terms. Yet, in nearly the same breath, Dorsey offers up the Navajo to the curious gaze of the potential visitor by recommending that those who "wish to know the Navaho intimately should visit the reservation in the winter and should be prepared to spend, not days but weeks or months, roaming from hogan to hogan, where they may always be sure of a welcome." [23]

The Santa Fe's advertising efforts succeeded in transforming Native Americans into something to be looked at, and their works were collected for private and public exhibit.

For instance, one 1900 guidebook advises travelers on their way to the Grand Canyon that "at the train itself you are likely to see members of the tribe, dignified and dirty and shrewd at a bargain, ready to sell baskets or blankets, perhaps crude but effectively decorated pottery by the aboriginal proprietors of this part of the world." [24] Another early guide complained that "the 'simple savage' with his 'untutored mind' does not propose to do anything for nothing; and he will do very little for anything. Why, he will even charge you 'two bits' if you take a snap shot at him with a kodak [sic]." [25] Even though the camera and the commercialization of crafts and souvenirs had obviously transformed Native American life, guidebooks maintained the idea that a "primitive" native culture was still available for a visitor's curiosity. "Indians of the Grand Country are one of its most fascinating lures," notes a 1929 guidebook. "The district is one of the very few areas in the United States where the 'red' man still lives in his native state, primitive but happy, contented, unchanged by the white man's civilization." [26]

Along with the Santa Fe, the Fred Harvey Company also perpetuated a romantic-mythic image of Native Americans. In 1902 Ford Harvey, who took leadership of the company after his father's death a year earlier, established the Fred Harvey Indian Department to merchandise southwest Indian crafts. Here, too, the synthesis of tourism and anthropology took the shape of architecture and tourist activities.

At the Grand Canyon, Mary Colter, an architect and schoolteacher from Minnesota, was responsible for designing many of the buildings that travelers today see and move through. Hopi House, styled after a pueblo, and the Watchtower, reminiscent of native ruins, are two of Colter's imaginative re-creations that fuse together a diverse combination of Native American cultural styles.

Colter designed Hopi House in the style of the Hopi dwellings found at Oraibi, Arizona. An early brochure described Hopi House as a native culture exhibit and craft exchange:

> Several rooms of Hopi House are devoted to an exhibit of rare and costly specimens of Indian and Mexican handwork. Here is displayed the priceless Harvey collection of old Navajo blankets, winner of a grand prize at the Louisiana Purchase Exposition. Here, too, is a Hopi entholographic [sic] collection . . . and a Pomo basket exhibit, the finest of its kind in the world. And a room filled with buffalo hide shields . . . and a salesroom. [27]

In addition to these exhibits, a Totem room displayed carved masks from tribes of the Northwest. A Spanish-Mexican room attempted to re-create a portion of a typical Southwest dwelling with a caballero's saddle, spurs, and sombrero placed near a corner fireplace. Native artisans could be watched making blankets, pottery, jewelry, and other salesroom articles. The distinctive differences between cultures, however, were subsumed by the larger cultural machinery geared toward merchandising "otherness."

These artifacts were only part of a larger design that allowed visitors themselves to become "anthropologists" and move around in the world of "the other." For example, one 1909 Harvey brochure described the world of the Hopi that lay waiting inside Hopi House:

> Go inside and you see how these gentle folk live. The rooms are little and low, like their small-statured occupants. The floors and walls are as cleanly [sic] as a Dutch kitchen. The Hopis are making "piki," twining raven black hair of the "manas" in big side whorls, smoking corn-cob pipes, building sacred altars, mending moccasins— doing a hundred un-American things. [28]

At the turn of the century, the commercial interests of the Harvey Company and the Santa Fe had assembled a world that juxtaposed the progress and comfort of modern life with a reproduction of the premodern past. Beside the elite El Tovar Hotel with its European styling, visitors could walk a few feet and find themselves in the primitive world of the Hopi. This brochure's description played upon a desire to escape the familiar world of home by telling visitors that they would witness a number of interesting, "un-American" activities and people. It also assured them that the inhabitants were clean, gentle, and safe. "The stylistic choice on the part of Miss Colter and the Fred Harvey Company was primarily commercial, designed to stimulate interest in Indian goods," notes a park service architectural report. "Hopi House symbolized the partnership between commercialism and romanticism that typified so much of Fred Harvey architecture." [29] The aesthetic of commercialism and romanticism easily blended architectural styles and combined tribal and ethnic cultural differences under the same roof.

Hopi House (built in 1905) and the Indian Watchtower (built in 1932) represent the beginning and end points of Colter's design career at the Grand Canyon (although the Bright Angel Lodge, the last building she designed within the park, opened in 1935). The stylistic variations between Hopi House and the Watchtower reflect Colter's movement from realism toward fantasy in her appropriation of native designs. Colter described the Indian Watchtower as a "re-creation" (rather than a "copy") of the prehistoric watchtower ruins she had seen throughout the Southwest. [30] The tower, standing seventy feet and measuring thirty feet in diameter at the base, was larger than any tower she had seen at Mesa Verde, Canyon de Chelly, Hovenweep, or Wupatki. The ground floor of the structure was designed in the style of a ceremonial kiva but functioned in the Watchtower as a circular observation room with large windows providing views of the Grand Canyon. Constructed from natural stone to blend with the surrounding environment, the Watchtower's outward appearance suggested that one had come upon the ruins of an ancient civilization. The inside of the tower was decorated with Indian cave and wall drawings, by Hopi artist Fred Kabotie, which told the Hopi story of the Grand Canyon as a place of legendary origins. Like Hopi House, the Watchtower also served as a salesroom for native cultural crafts.

Although more imaginative in design than Hopi House, the Watchtower is a bricolage of several native styles that evokes a dramatic energy from the cultural *differences* between Native American life and the white, urban world of the visitors who find themselves wandering through these scenes. Reporting on the May 1933 Watchtower dedication ceremonies, Sallie Saunders noted these differences in her description of the people who had gathered for a celebration that included native dancing, costumes, and a spiritual blessing of the structure:

> The white men in the audience suddenly appear almost pathetic, dressed in the world's common clothes—poor, drab male creatures divested of their heritage of glory. Even the cowboys, part of the intently watching audience, fail to be completely gorgeous in their wild-patterned shirts, neck bands and ornate boots. It is the Indians' day. [31]

While the Watchtower represented a monument to Native American history and cultural life, it also marked a larger modern quest for spiritual and cultural redemption and for the values of tradition that seemed absent to many who were bound to the progressive rhythms of the urban world. "These visitors will return to the troubled, throbbing tempo of their days," Saunders suggested, "with new thoughts, new visions granted them by this insight into an age-old culture." [32] The romantic image of native life offered by tourist productions like the Watchtower at least *suggested* a momentary retrieval of the kind of time-honored cultural tradition (and its promise of stability) which seemed absent from the forward-looking face of urban life.

The sweeping view of the Grand Canyon from the Watchtower was "like liberty itself," suggested Saunders, proposing that the "building stood so concretely for the recognition of an intangible thing—the relation between the white man and the Indian."[33] Yet, as visitors stood on the Watchtower's observation deck, they could also turn their attention away from the canyon, look toward the east, and find the Navajo Reservation on the distant plateau. And in this way the Watchtower (as its name so clearly captures) also stood as an ironic monument to vision, a reminder of the multiple ways that Native American life had become fixed for the visitor's gaze in a spectacle that combined anthropological observation with cultural imagination. In the simulated tourist landscape of native dwellings and ruins at the Grand Canyon, the history of difference and *division* between Native American culture and the modern world is, as Jean Baudrillard notes of such monuments, only able to "express the nostalgia of history,"[34] a yearning for a stable past and place that exists apart from the prefabrications of mass culture. As these monuments suggest a hope of recovering the traditional and spiritual dimensions of native culture, they also represent a tangible politics of vision and images which translate history through an aesthetic of sentimentality. These, perhaps, are the deeper relations between the modern world and Native American life that, indeed, found a *tangible* form in the developing tourist world at Grand Canyon in the early part of this century.

Today these relations of vision and commodity exchange are carved deeply into the tourist landscape at the Grand Canyon. Hopi House remains devoted to the same diverse collection of Southwestern souvenirs such as beaded belts (often produced overseas), silver and turquoise jewelry, pottery, baskets, serapes, and ponchos. Alongside these are more common items such as T-shirts, postcards, decals, and bumper stickers. As I wander the Hopi House sales floor through the displays of souvenirs, I notice a young African-American girl, wearing a feathered headdress and carrying a toy tom-tom, waiting as her mother scans a moccasin "conversion chart," which cross-references men's, women's, and children's shoe sizes for the U.S., Europe, Britain, and Japan. Such souvenirs not only invite a playful participation in the tourist tableau along the canyon's rim but also offer a means of mobilizing the region's drama in the distant context of home and everyday life.

Walking through the Watchtower at Desert View, I see a Navajo woman sitting at a loom weaving rugs while visitors watch. A sign above her reads: It is customary to donate money before taking picture. Dressed in traditional Navajo garb and adorned with turquoise and silver jewelry, she is another performer in this Theater of the West. The Watchtower room, designed in the style of a ceremonial kiva, is lined with souvenir pottery, wool blankets, polished stones, and baskets. Near the cash register, I watch video images of Hopi ceremonial dances on a small television screen.

Grand Canyon: A Journey into Discovery is one of several videotapes available for purchase. While the images of Hopi dancers move to the sounds of flute and drum, I hear the voice of Telly Savalas, the video's narrator, say: "Contact with the Spanish conquistadors and missionaries, and later the reservation system, has had little effect on the political and religious fears of their life. [The Hopi] are perhaps the most representative precontact cultural entity surviving in the United States today." Sealed in the flickering images of videotape, these Hopi dancers seem to have escaped the political and cultural transformations that have moved through their homeland. Yet, dancing on the TV screen behind the cashier, they somehow mock the visual and commercial relations of tourism that seek to keep this place at a distance from the passage of time.

At the Grand Canyon these spectacles point to a paradox where the tourist is asked to reconcile the past and the present. In the collective fantasy world along the rim, places like Hopi House and the Indian Watchtower reveal this paradox as a discovery of a naturalized image of native culture. Although such places suggest an imaginative look at history, they also mediate between the history of confrontation and the ongoing fascination with "the other" in the Southwest. They offer spectacular images of native life for visitors longing to experience a sense of tradition and heritage that seemed absent from their lives in the modern world.

In the time between the construction of Hopi House and the Watchtower, Colter designed three other structures that remain in Grand Canyon National Park today: the Lookout (1914), Hermit's Rest (1914), and Phantom Ranch (1922). These buildings differ from Hopi House and the Watchtower in that they gravitate toward a more general fantasy reproduction of a rustic West. These other buildings were part of a major expansion in Grand Canyon facilities initiated by the Fred Harvey Company in 1914. For instance, the Lookout Studio, designed by Colter, was constructed with native stone. Perched on the canyon's rim, the Lookout matches the stone of the surrounding cliffs in both form and color. In the case of the Lookout, Colter's sense of "historical romanticism and nostalgia evident at Hopi House [is] tempered by fantasy—a metamorphosis away from archeological authenticity and toward pure romanticism."[35] Colter's buildings expressed a desire to return to a simple life of nature and the frontier. According to the architectural historian David Gebhard, for Colter and other architects,

> the pristine purity of simplicity was to be found not in their European heritage but in the art and architecture of primitive man. . . . By the late nineteenth century the only American Indian groups which still possessed an active culture were those of the Southwest.[36]

Within that culture Colter sought the ideas for her architectural pastiche.

The new buildings that Colter designed at the Grand Canyon added to representations of Native American culture by appealing to visions of rustic Western life. Like Hopi House and the Watchtower, these buildings were also imaginative constructions of the West that represented a fanciful world of hermit miners and dude ranches. For instance, one early Santa Fe brochure described Hermit's Rest as "a new resting-place for wayfarers, built in solid rock of a little hill, like a hermit's cave of prehistoric times, yet furnishing modern refreshments and the warmth of an enormous fireplace when the day is chilly."[37] It is an architectural style that sought harmony with the landscape and evoked the efforts of pioneer labor but, at the same time, recalled a modern vision of progress. This spirit of design was not only found in Colter's works but was reflected in the general development of National Park Service buildings as well as the Bright Angel Lodge and El Tovar Hotel erected on the brink of the canyon. For example, an early Harvey brochure for the El Tovar calls attention to materials of the building that create a rustic Western ambience.

> Boulders and logs for the walls and shakes for the roof, stained a weather-beaten color, merge into the gray-green surroundings. The inside finish is mainly peeled slabs, wood in the rough, and tinted plaster, interspersed with huge wooden beams. Triple casement windows and generous fireplaces abound. Indian curios and trophies of the chase are liberally used in the decorations.[38]

El Tovar Hotel opened in 1905 on the south rim, only thirty-five years after John Wesley Powell made his first exploration through the Grand Canyon on the Colorado River. In that brief period not only was the American Southwest explored and mapped, but it also assumed a place in the American imagination as a theatrical stage playing an ongoing Western drama. A 1915 Santa Fe Railway brochure advertised the Grand Canyon as a place "for a genuine Out West outing." The canyon was a place where the visitor could get a good suntan, "the kind that goes with a Stetson and 'chaps' and khaki suit. In a week you will look like a native, and the tan on the native son's face is something worthwhile." [39] Such advertising was an invitation to a place absorbed with its own romance, a place where a visitor could experience a unique landscape and culture and perhaps indulge in a Western fantasy by becoming, albeit temporarily, a player on its stage.

The West that found form on the rim of the Grand Canyon at the beginning of the twentieth century exemplified a modern vision of American culture that juxtaposed an imagined frontier past with the comforts of middle-class luxury. "Everywhere you are reminded that though away from home this is another home," the Santa Fe Railway told prospective visitors. The Grand Canyon was a place where visitors were "furnished horses that would grace a city park" or could tour the park in "a big auto—the easy-riding $5,000 variety," a place where the "only modern note in the picture is the throbbing, high-powered auto. All else seems to have come from a different world and a different time." [40]

Taken together, the architectural styles Colter and others created at the Grand Canyon remind us of the floating regional identity that has long inhabited the West. The early engineering of the park was essentially a commercial production that played upon an urban imagination of the frontier, the West, and the Native American. It was a place that was at once different from the insulated world of the modern city yet safely civilized for the turn-of-the-century traveler. These designs remain in place as a contradictory image of Southwestern life expressed through the forces of tourism. The region today connects an American vision of progress with a nostalgic desire for an unchanged past. Dean MacCannell argues that, under modernity, the nonmodern world is artificially preserved and reconstructed. "The separation of nonmodern culture traits from their original contexts and their distribution as modern playthings are evident in the various social movements toward naturalism," argues MacCannell. "These displaced forms, embedded in modern society, are the spoils of the victory of the modern over the nonmodern world. They establish in consciousness the definition and boundary of modernity by rendering concrete and immediate that which modernity is not." [41] At Grand Canyon National Park and the surrounding area, modernity is reified by objectifying and romanticizing an unattainable past. To be sure, Navajoland is a theater and a theme park. It is an idealization and representation of Native American culture that extends beyond the world of the reservations and resides in the structure of the park as a commercial and aesthetic dream; one that provided, and still provides, the architecture of leisure experience.

NOTES

1. James M. Houston, "The Concepts of 'Place' and 'Land' in the Judaeo-Christian Tradition," in *Humanistic Geography: Prospects and Problems*, ed. by David Ley and Marwyn S. Samuels (Chicago: Maaroufa Press, 1978), 225.

2. Freeman Tilden, *The National Parks: What They Mean To You and Me* (New York: Alfred A. Knopf, 1951), 18–19.

3. Raymond Williams, *Problems in Materialism and Culture* (London: New Left Books, 1980), 39.

4. Wai-Teng Leong, "Culture and the State: Manufacturing Traditions for Tourism," *Critical Studies in Mass Communication*, 6, no. 4 (1989), 356.

5. Walter Benjamin as quoted in Richard Wolin, *Walter Benjamin* (New York: Columbia University Press, 1982), 71.

6. James Clifford, "On Ethnographic Allegory," in *Writing Culture: The Poetics and Politics of Ethnography*, ed. by James Clifford and George E. Marcus (Berkeley, University of California Press, 1986), 119.

7. Vine Deloria, Jr., *Custer Died for Your Sins: An Indian Manifesto* (New York: MacMillan, 1969), 2.

8. Ibid., 81–82.

9. Alan Trachtenberg, *The Incorporation of America: Culture and Society in the Gilded Age* (New York: Hill and Wang, 1982), 28.

10. John Muir as quoted in Tilden, *The National Parks*, 18.

11. T. J. Jackson Lears, *No Place of Grace: Antimodernism and the Transformation of American Culture 1880–1920*, (New York: Pantheon, 1981), 4–5.

12. T. C. McLuhan, *Dream Tracks: The Railroad and the American Indian 1890–1930* (New York: Harry N. Abrams, 1985), 8.

13. D. H. Lawrence as quoted in Keith Sagar, ed., *D. H. Lawrence and New Mexico* (Salt Lake City: G. M. Smith, 1982), 64.

14. Lawrence, "Indians and An Englishman," in Sagar, 2.

15. Ibid.

16. John Milton, "A Sense of Place in Western Writing," *The Bloomsbury Review*, 7, no. 4 (1987), 3.

17. William H. Goetzmann, *Exploration and Empire: The Explorer and the Scientist in the Winning of the American West* (New York: Alfred A. Knopf, 1967), xiii.

18. Marta Weigle, "From Desert to Disney World: The Santa Fe Railway and the Fred Harvey Company Display the Indian Southwest," *The Journal of Anthropological Research*, Vol 45, no. 1 (Spring 1989), 133. Weigle's study provides an excellent account of the commodification of Native American culture throughout the Southwest region between 1882 and World War II.

19. James Marshall, *Santa Fe: The Railroad that Built an Empire* (New York: Random House, 1945), 287–88; and Merle Armitage, *Operations Santa Fe: Atchison, Topeka and Santa Fe Railway System* (New York: Duell, Sloan and Pearce, 1948), 111–19.

20. McLuhan, 19–20.

21. Ibid., 20.

22. George A. Dorsey, *Indians of the Southwest* (Chicago: Passenger Department of the Atchison, Topeka and Santa Fe Railway, 1903), 176.

23. Ibid.

24. Frederick S. Dellenbaugh, *The Grand Canyon of Arizona: Through the Stereoscope* (New York and London: Underwood and Underwood, 1900), 31.

25. P. C. Bicknell, *Guidebook of the Grand Canyon of Arizona: With the Only Correct Maps in Print* (Kansas City: Fred Harvey, ca. 1900), 78.

26. Miner R. Tillotson and Frank J. Taylor, *Grand Canyon Country* (Palo Alto: Stanford University Press, 1929), 27.

27. As quoted in James David Henderson, *Meals by Fred Harvey: A Phenomenon of the American West* (Fort Worth: Texas Christian University Press), 30.

28. W. J. Black, *El Tovar: Grand Canyon of Arizona* (Chicago: Norman Pierce Company, 1909), 22.

29. William C. Tweed, Laura E. Soulliere, and Henry G. Law, *National Park Service Rustic Architecture: 1916–1942* (Washington, D.C.: GPO, 1977), 8.

30. For a history of Colter's architectural career, see Virginia L. Grattan, *Mary Colter: Builder upon Red Earth* (Flagstaff: Northland Press, 1980).

31. Sallie Saunders, "Indian Watchtower at Grand Canyon is Dedicated by Hopi Indians," *Santa Fe Magazine*, Vol. 27, no. 8 (July 1933), 28.

32. Ibid., 31.

33. Ibid.

34. Jean Baudrillard, "The Anorexic Ruins," in *Looking Back on the End of the World*, ed. by Dietmar Kamper and Christoph Wulf (New York: Semiotext[e], 1989), 38.

35. Tweed, et al., 11.

36. David Gebhard, "Architecture and the Fred Harvey Houses," *New Mexico Architect*, (January–February 1964), 18.

37. *Grand Canyon Outings*, (Chicago: Passenger Department of the Atchison, Topeka and Santa Fe Railway, 1915), 3.

38. Black, 4.

39. *Grand Canyon Outings*, 2.

40. Ibid., 2–3.

41. Dean MacCannell, *The Tourist: A New Theory of the Leisure Class* (New York: Schocken, 1976), 8–9.

Selling the Southwest:
Santa Fe InSites

Marta Weigle

> *I can hardly imagine how [Santa Fe] is supported. The country around it is barren. At the North stands a snow capped mountain while the valley in which the town is situated is drab and sandy. The streets are narrow. In the morning this place is crowded with men, women and children who come in from the country with articles for sale. A Mexican will walk about the town all day to sell a bundle of grass worth about a dime. They are the poorest looking people I ever saw. They subsist principally on mutton, onions and red pepper.*
> —Letter from a traveler with the Little Rock Company,
> *The Arkansas Banner*, 31 August 1849[1]

> *Although blue corn could easily be either the latest yuppie gastro-abomination or a New Age health-food miracle, it is, in fact, an ancient Native American staple and one that distinguishes New Mexican cuisine from its near relatives—Tex-Mex, Cal-Mex, and Mex-Mex food. Corn, whether blue or yellow, forms with chilies [sic] and beans the triumverate [sic], some would say trinity, that make up the basis of so-called gastronomy in northern New Mexico. This may sound like poor people's food, and it is. Despite all published reports of celebrities and other rich people moving in droves to Santa Fe, regardless of fancy stores selling big-ticket merchandise, this is not a wealthy state. Nevertheless, the food is as richly satisfying to visitors as soul food can be, and one has only to look at the lines outside The Shed, La Choza, and Rincon de Oso to have the point proved.*
> —Zanne Early Zakroff, "Gourmet Holidays: Santa Fe,"
> *Gourmet: The Magazine of Good Living*, December 1989, p. 214

New Mexico achieved statehood on January 6, 1912. On August 28 of that year its capital's chamber of commerce commissioned a new-old Santa Fe style exhibition (opened November 18, 1912) with a twofold purpose: "1st. To awaken local interest in the preservation of the Old Santa Fe and the development of the New along the lines most appropriate to this country. 2nd. To advertise the unique and unrivalled possibilities of the city as 'The Tourist Center of the Southwest.' "[2] The year before New Mexico observed the seventy-fifth anniversary of statehood, contemporary Santa Fe style was canonized and widely popularized by the 1986 publication of Christine Mather and Sharon Woods's 264-page *Santa Fe Style*.[3] The front flap of this full-color bricolage proclaims: "Here is not only the romance of Santa Fe, but the irresistable [sic] appeal of its life-style—a casual elegance enlivened by a dynamic, ever-changing mixture of the old and the new, the West and the East, the plain and the sophisticated."

Both exhibition and book are but two from myriad twentieth-century examples of what John D. Dorst terms auto-ethnographic self-inscription. In his analysis of the "distinct postmodern microclimate" of Chadds Ford, Pennsylvania, both a tourist site and a suburb in the Revolutionary War–Andrew Wyeth country of the middle Brandywine River valley between Philadelphia and Wilmington, he claims that "the culture of advanced consumer capitalism . . . consists largely in the processes of self-inscription, indigenous self-documentation and endlessly reflexive simulation . . . [and thus] 'spontaneously' does for itself, and massively so, the sort of thing ethnographers and other species of documentarist claim to do." In the case of the suburb of Chadds Ford, visual experience is privileged, particularly as that is framed by the automobile, which acts as "a kind of stylus," an inscription that Dorst terms "auto-writing."[4]

Post-statehood Santa Fe in large part derives its textuality from the commerce of the Santa Fe Trail and its successor, the Atchison, Topeka and Santa Fe Railway. The Santa Fe Railway and its close associate the Fred Harvey Company marketed the Southwest first as an Orient in Edward W. Said's sense and then as a world's fair midway of exotic goods and peoples.[5] Between the wars, this spectacle was further enabled by the Couriers and Harveycars of the Indian Detours from Santa Fe to various ruins, Indian pueblos, and Hispanic villages from Raton to the Grand Canyon.

By 1940 Santa Fe had established itself as a "Site" in Dorst's terms, "as an image, an ideological discourse, an assemblage of texts."[6] This textuality is evident on the Santa Fe Chamber of Commerce stationery of the period. The reverse bears a full-page, full-color design by Wilfred Stedman.[7] Titled "Old Santa Fe Year 'round Playground," the text is enclosed in a central medallion:

> The finest vacation of your life awaits you at the end of the Santa Fe Trail. Here, amid the color of Old Spain, preserved for over three hundred years by the descendants of the Conquistadores, is such a playground as you have never imagined. Cool summers, when the thermometer never rises above ninety degrees, bring added pleasure to active sports—the winter days are bright and mild, making our developed ski areas more enjoyable. If you like romance, Indians, Fiestas, Old World beauty, and true western hospitality you must spend your next vacation in Old Santa Fe.

Four small, circular images on the four sides of the page show a skier, a fisherman, a couple on horseback, and Indian dancers. The rectangular images that border the page depict two of Santa Fe's public buildings (Fred Harvey's La Fonda hotel and the Museum of New Mexico's Fine Arts Museum), two scenes from Santa Fe Fiestas (revived in 1919), an Indian pueblo, a kiva at Bandelier National Monument, and a street scene with a wood-laden burro driving by a serape-draped man past chile ristra–hung adobe houses. At the bottom right is El Santuario, the healing shrine at Chimayó, some thirty miles from Santa Fe. As Site, then, Santa Fe includes within its recreational, secular pilgrimage destination a traditional, sacred pilgrimage center.

Burro(wed) Alley

The first time I visited Santa Fe, the obvious things impressed me. The colorful vistas, striking personalities, sophisticated lavish hospitality and cosmopolitan conversations merged into a pictorial whole that exhilarated at every turn. The mind and all the senses seemed to be supplied delightfully.

"Where in America can such another spot be found?" I cried with a childish delight of discovery. Remembering the exquisite Diwan-i-Khas palace in Delhi, I transposed its ancient Persian inscription to the sun-baked walls of Santa Fe: "Be there a Paradise on earth; it is this, oh, it is this, oh, it is this!"

> —Carolyn Bancroft, "Calcutta Feels Like Santa Fe,"
> *New Mexico Sentinel*, 22 December 1937

To believe that the Orient was created—or, as I call it, "Orientalized"—and to believe that such things happen simply as a necessity of the imagination, is to be disingenuous. The relationship between Occident and Orient is a relationship of power, of domination, of varying degrees of a complex hegemony, and is quite accurately indicated in the title of K. M. Panikkar's classic *Asia and Western Dominance*. The Orient was Orientalized not only because it was discovered to be "Oriental" in all those ways considered commonplace by an average nineteenth-century European, but also because it *could be*—that is, submitted to being—*made* Oriental.

—Edward W. Said, *Orientalism*, 1979[8]

In the 1930s Marian Russell told her daughter-in-law about a trip over the Santa Fe Trail in 1852, when she was a child of seven. She vividly recalled Santa Fe, where "often the narrow streets became choked with a wiggling mass of humanity":

The market place in Santa Fe was a wonder. In open air booths lay piles of food stuffs. Heaps of red and green peppers vied with heaps of red and blue corn and heaps of golden melons. There were colorful rugs woven by the hands of the Mexicans and deep-fringed shawls, gay with embroidery. There were massive Indian jars filled to the brim with Mexican beans. There were strings of prayer beads from old Mexico . . . Mexican turquoise in heavy settings of silver. Silver was then cheaper than tin. Here was to be found exquisite Mexican drawn work and intricate bead work.

In deep, old hand-carved frames were pictures, mottoes, wreaths of flowers all cunningly fashioned of human hair, red, black, brown and yellow. There were beaded moccasins and chamois coats, leather trousers, silver trimmed saddles, spurs and knapsacks; great hand-carved chests and cupboards, Indian baskets and jars without number. So many things that were fine and splendid, so many things that were rude and clumsy, the Santa Fe market afforded.

Moving among the people were "long lines of burros all but hidden under enormous bundles of faggots, . . . taking good care not to step on [the children]."[9]

Early in 1990 Burro Alley achieved a new notoriety because landlord Richard (Dickie) Montoya evicted barber Joe Gonzales and bootmaker David Gallegos from their shops to make way for more tourist stores. Bob Quick declared in the Business Section of *The Santa Fe New Mexican* for February 2, 1990, that the departure of "Gonzales and Gallegos, who have been in business in Burro Alley for 38 and 54 years respectively," meant that "Santa Fe's downtown is now down to a precious few old businesses that aren't just for tourists—Woolworth's [5&10], Dunlap's [department store], Evangelo's [bar], Tía Sophia's [restaurant], the Lensic Theatre [movies]." Quick announced that some three hundred people had signed a petition to dissuade Montoya.

Carl T. Gilbert advocated political action in a letter to the *Albuquerque Journal North* (February 16, 1990). He deplored Montoya's facilitating more "fast-burn, high-rent, trendy shops targeted to the out-of-towners."

One of the very last places a local could go downtown for practical needs has been overrun by trinket peddlers. The "old timers" have truly been delegated second-class citizens to the tourists and [are now] condemned to shop in our segregated South Side.

About the only thing we have left over the tourists is our ability to vote in city elections. I hope everyone will turn out in March and impress upon our elected officials that Santa Fe's recent overemphasis on the tourist economy is unhealthy and permanently damaging to our city.

Gilbert's pleas were partially heeded. In a May 27, 1990, commentary piece for *The Santa Fe New Mexican*, "Santa Fe's Blessings Outweigh the Tourism Complaints," newspaper staff member Dan Vukelich reported:

> Objections about shameless pandering to tourism played a role in the mayoral race in March when City Councilor Debbie Jaramillo charged that Mayor Sam Peck had sold out this city's residents to hoteliers and resort developers. Jaramillo got about 30 percent of the vote to Peck's 39 percent, but the vote reminded us yet again we're not all of one mind about living in what many Americans describe as the nation's most desirable place.

Other letters to the editor were full of terms like *Disneyfication* and *Aspenification*. The latter was prompted by reports such as staff member Kelly Richmond's "City Limits: Growing Pains a Sign of the Times" in *The Santa Fe New Mexican* of March 19, 1990. Richmond cited growth questions faced by Taos, Aspen, Irvine, Petaluma, and Boulder. In Aspen "the median cost of a house has risen to $1 million, prompting city officials to require new business projects to build affordable housing for 60 percent of their employees." As it is, traffic is congested "because the average worker can no longer afford to live in town and must commute" to serve the "up-scale tourists and part-time residents" who double the town's population in winter.

"Aspenification" is the theme of Gene A. Valdes's letter about the Burro Alley situation, published in the *Santa Fe Reporter* of March 7–13, 1990:

> Santa Fe's most precious commodities are its people and culture—not the value of its real estate nor the tourist dollar.
>
> As to the remark attributed to Dickie Montoya that we need more tourist shops because "tourism keeps the local people working," the other side of the coin is that the majority of tourist jobs barely pay minimum wage. Local people do not need more jobs as busboys and waitresses in restaurants serving crab-meat enchiladas and black beans. Nor do they need employment as bellhops and maids in hotels where most Santa Fe residents could not afford to stay. Nor is there a future for our people as salesclerks in trendy boutiques whose only relation to our city are the words "de Santa Fe" after their names.

By mid-May 1990, the Santa Fe Convention and Visitors Bureau placed ads in the local papers admonishing against such thinking. According to the one in the *Albuquerque Journal North* of May 17, 1990:

> Is Santa Fe Style a whim? A fad? A farce? We don't think so, and neither do the readers of 450+ articles printed throughout the USA in the last year. Do you live in Santa Fe because it's a fad? No. We live here because it is "timeless" [Fort Worth, Texas], because we love the "[spicy] cultural mix" [New York City], because we are forever "falling for Santa Fe" [Austin, Texas].
>
> When tourists visit for these same reasons, they are spending resources that boost our economy. They increase our gross receipts tax, they pay lodger's tax and they buy our goods and services. They directly increase the number of jobs available in Santa Fe.

So when you see a tourist in need, flash a smile and point the way—they are bringing more than questions and confusion. They are bringing $'s too!

Efforts to stop the Burro Alley eviction were unsuccessful, and on Saturday, May 26, 1990, automobile traffic was stopped for a festival with "mariachi band, refreshments, mountain men, face painting" from 10 a.m. to 7 p.m. According to the ad in the *Santa Fe Reporter* of May 23–29, 1990, the stores opening were: Down & Outdoors in Santa Fe: The Quality Down Outlet Store; 31 Burro Alley: Art, Accessories, Furnishings; Pueblo Trading Co.: Jewelry, Pottery, Kachinas; and Jeff Lewis Trade Roots Collection: Fetishes, Rugs, Pillows, Folk Art. All these are well-established goods of the new Southwesternism.

Edward W. Said defines "Orientalism as a Western style for dominating, restructuring, and having authority over the Orient," which must be examined "as a discourse" whereby "European culture was able to manage—and even produce—the Orient politically, sociologically, militarily, ideologically, scientifically, and imaginatively during the post-Enlightenment period." [10] In late twentieth-century America the Orientalism guiding Western and Southwestern commerce in all senses (of goods and ideas) has to a large extent been supplanted by Southwesternism, a "discourse" whereby a functional capital city has been managed and produced as a regional, expressive cultural center.

Detoured to Yesterday

The many drives possible out from old Santa Fe penetrate a region as rich in archaeological and ethnological interest as it is in scene beauty and grandeur. American history, vivid and fascinating, was being written here long before the founding of Jamestown, the Voyage of Henrik Hudson or the Coming of the Pilgrims.

In threading these roads to Yesterday you may come to know well the mountains, canyons and valleys that girdle the old city—and still miss half the feast. On every side you will find visible records of the Forgotten People, the enduring impress of the Spanish padres and conquistadores, the life of the Indian, the Spanish-American and the frontier Southwest demanding interpretation. The country about you is saturated with history, legend and human interest—for those who know it.
—Foreword to late 1920s Harveycars Indian Detours brochure:
Roads to Yesterday: Motor Drives out from Old Santa Fe

Automobiles, middle-class tourists, and the new desire to experience the wilderness signaled a defeat for the railroads in their quest to control access to the far western landscape. They also confirmed the powerful new role the West played in American culture. The area represented all that seemed indigenous, vigorous, and characteristic to Americans. It offered a history that provided a kind of cultural grounding. Americans could look to the West and find splendid ancient history as well as evidence of more recent glories. It contained wilderness, the testing ground that many Americans believed was vital to their national development. Most importantly, it offered a landscape whose forms and colors had given Americans distinctive language, artistic styles, and architecture, which were crucial to the development of a national culture.
—Anne Farrar Hyde, *An American Vision:*
Far Western Landscape and National Culture, 1820–1920, 1990 [11]

A 1926 *National Geographic* ad heralded Indian Detours as "the newest way to see oldest America on your Santa Fe–Fred Harvey way to and from California." The first tours, begun on May 15, 1926, offered three days of a "personally conducted motor tour in luxurious Harveycars through a region rich in history and mystery—the Enchanted Empire." Detours founder, the Scottish major R. Hunter Clarkson, proclaimed the company's philosophy for success: "There is more of historic, prehistoric, human and scenic interest [here] than in any similar area of the world, not excepting India, Egypt, Europe or Asia. . . . The big idea is not only to let people know what is in Northern New Mexico but to tell them what it is when they see it."[12] Erna Fergusson undertook the job of training young women "Couriers" to serve as knowledgeable hostess-guides whose performances marked and interpreted the lands, sites, and particularly the native peoples with whom automobile tourists had to interact.

The Couriers' performed authenticity was designed to make them appear as knowledgeable, neonative, slightly bohemian art colonists. They were trained to emulate these predominantly Anglo cognoscenti. Sharing their company enabled "Detourists" to enjoy similar license and esoteric insight. A 1928 Santa Fe Railway Booklet titled *They Know New Mexico* features a list of former "strangers . . . [who] have learned the secret of New Mexico through years of association and study" Included on the list is poet Alice Corbin Henderson, who came to Santa Fe from Chicago in 1916:

> Mrs. Henderson . . . since coming to Santa Fe has actively participated in the interesting life of the Southwest. On horseback and by motor car trips have been made through New Mexico, southern Colorado and northern Arizona, thereby qualifying for membership in the circle of "those who know," as well as furnishing the background for intimate studies of Indian and Spanish-American life in out-of-the-way places.

In his foreword, Indian Detours publicist Roger W. Birdseye exhorts readers themselves to become temporary art colonists: "When the time comes to break over the narrow horizons of the railroad to follow the Southwest's Roads to Yesterday, may you indeed then find yourself an honorary member of that intimate circle who really know New Mexico."[13]

The early Indian Detours focused primarily on Indian ruins and contemporary pueblos, although some Hispanic villages were also included.[14] Detourists, also called "dudes," disembarked from the train at either Albuquerque or Las Vegas; spent the first day touring ruins, pueblos, or villages; and stayed overnight at La Fonda in Santa Fe. On the second day they toured the Puyé cliff ruins, had a basket lunch at Santa Clara Pueblo, and visited Tesuque Pueblo before returning to Santa Fe. There they enjoyed a "conducted tour of old Santa Fe, including old Museum and Art Gallery" and an evening lecture in La Fonda's Indian Lecture Lounge. The third day included more ruins, pueblos, and villages on the way to rejoining the train at either Las Vegas or Albuquerque, depending on where they had begun the Detour.

Much of the Couriers' success as mediators of these "roads to yesterday" can be attributed to Erna Fergusson, who pioneered guided car tours in New Mexico. From 1921 until 1926 she and Ethel Hickey, also a native New Mexican, operated Koshare Tours. Fergusson claims their tours "attracted the Harvey people, who set up their Indian Detours really in imitation of my Koshare Tours. Then I went with them for a couple of years."[15] Her first book, *Dancing Gods: Indian Ceremonials of New Mexico and Arizona* (Knopf, 1931), is the direct result of these 1920s experiences as a guide and trainer of guides.

In Koshare Tours Fergusson had "billed herself as the first woman dude wrangler," who would personally escort visitors through New Mexico, "a state still 'unspoiled by

civilization. In a few years, its primitiveness will be gone forever.' " Her brochure statement also reflects her approach to guided-tour mediation: "It is one thing to see a
place. It is another to see it knowingly." [16] For their role as guides, Couriers were
"periodically trained and examined by an advisory board of nationally known authorities on the archaeology, ethnology and history of the Southwest" and backed by an
active bureau of research to answer "new questions [that] are constantly arising." A
1929 brochure assures tourists that this "information is not intruded; it is simply a
store of remarkably interesting facts from which casually to develop the full interest
of a strange country." [17]

Detourists were treated "not as tourists to be bundled about, but as part of a little
group off on a private exploration where one of the party knows and loves the country
and is going to do her utmost to make you revel in every hour you spend in it." In
town they could participate in authentic art colonist life at La Fonda, which was not
only the center for Indian Detours, "a mecca for tourists to the Southwest, but a
haunt for Santa Feans as well." Its dining room was the only one in the Fred Harvey
system that did not require a coat, as Santa Fe's bohemian art colonists would not
allow the company to enforce its long-standing rule. Art colonists like novelist and
activist in Indian causes Oliver La Farge frequented the Harvey House, and "you
might meet [him] any day in the frescoed Fonda café eating a savory sixty-cent lunch
(wine included) [and] doffing his broad-brimmed hat to the zooming of the Mexican
orchestra in the patio." [18]

Indian Detours established authenticity for tourists motivated by what Dean
MacCannell calls "a desire to see life as it is really lived, even to get in with the natives."
In part this means "being permitted to share back regions with 'them,' " to find out
about and perhaps participate in their "real life" behind the scenes or "backstage."
This "variety of understanding held out before tourists as an ideal is an *authentic* and
demystified experience of an aspect of some society or other person." [19]

In effect, the Detours commodified what by then had been defined as "authentic,"
i.e., the relationships between 1920s Santa Fe art colonists and Indians. Erna Fergusson
later satirized this domestication:

> Witter Bynner bought and wore and hung on his friends a famous collection of
> Indian jewelry. Alice Corbin introduced the velvet Navajo blouse. Stetson hats,
> cowboy boots, flannel shirts, even blankets were the approved costume. Everybody
> had a pet pueblo, a pet Indian, a pet craft. Pet Indians with pottery, baskets, and
> weaving to sell were seated by the corner fireplace (copied from the pueblo), plied
> with tobacco and coffee, asked to sing and tell tales. . . . It was obligatory to go to
> every pueblo dance. Failure to appear on a sunny roof on every saint's day marked
> one as soulless and without taste.[20]

Indian Detourists sought just such authentic encounters, and the goal of their colorful
hostess-guides' performed authenticity was to make visitors feel as though they had
traveled with a real bohemian art colonist, and had gone backstage to meet the natives
in the exotic setting of Santa Fe and environs.

New Mexico Lourdes, Lurid

El Santuario has been called the "Lourdes of America." No one seems to know
exactly how this came about. . . . Fr. Sebastian Alvarez in his letter to the Epis-
copal See of Durango, dated November 16, 1813, expressed his feelings of the
people coming from afar to seek cures for their ailments and the spreading of the

fame of their cures, induced many more faithful to come in pilgrimage. . . . In time, the mass media paid attention to the little Shrine in the Sangre de Cristo mountains. Newspapers from Chicago, Denver, New York and Los Angeles; Time and Newsweek magazines have all taken it upon themselves to inform the public about the Shrine. This has resulted in a considerable flow of mail requesting information about the Shrine. People come to the Santuario in the thousands, close to 300,000 a year. They come to ask for peace in the world and in their hearts, to fulfill a promise, to feel the healing touch of God.
    —1990s brochure: *El Santuario de Chimayo: "Lourdes of America"/*
    A place to pray and meditate and to experience peace of mind as well as of body

Even if one regards tourism as voluntary, self-interested travel, the tourist journey must be morally justified by the home community. Because the touristic journey lies in the nonordinary sphere of existence, the goal is symbolically sacred and morally on a higher plane than the regards of the ordinary workaday world. Tourists spend substantial sums to achieve the altered state—money that could be invested for material gain or alternately used to buy a new car or redecorate their homes.
    "Human exploratory behavior," says Berlyne, . . . "is behavior whose principle function is to change the stimulus field and introduce stimulus elements that were not previously accessible." Thus, as art uplifts and makes meaningful the visual environment, so tourism provides an aesthetically appropriate counterpoint to ordinary life. Tourism has a stated, or unstated but culturally determined, goal that has changed through the ages. For traditional societies the rewards of pilgrimages were accumulated grace and moral leadership in the home community. The rewards of modern tourism are phrased in terms of values we now hold up for worship: mental and physical health, social status, and diverse, exotic experiences.
    —Nelson H. H. Graburn, "Tourism: The Sacred Journey," 1977[21]

Chimayó's first Hispanic settlement is now known as Plaza del Cerro, mentioned in 1714 documents and definitely established as Tzimayó by the late 1740s. Its already significant commerce in fruit, chile, corn, frijoles, blankets and other wool textiles benefited in the nineteenth century when

between 1813 and 1816 the Santuario de Nuestro Señor de Esquipulas was built just down the road from the plaza, bringing in many pilgrims and greatly augmenting the economic standing of the plaza. Another chapel near the Santuario, built in the 1860s, further stimulated business and other activity.[22]

The chapels' builders and their families controlled the profits of pilgrimage. The better known El Santuario was privately owned until October 15, 1929, when a group of Santa Feans, including writer Mary Austin, painter Frank Applegate, architect John Gaw Meem, and newspaper editor E. Dana Johnson, organized the Spanish Colonial Arts Society, bought the shrine from the Cháves family and deeded it to the Archdiocese of Santa Fe, "to be held in trust by the Church for worship and as a religious museum, intact, and no alterations to be made in it without our consent."[23]
    Writing in 1916 for the fledgling *El Palacio*, begun in 1913 as the "Journal of the Museum of New Mexico, Archaeological Society of New Mexico, and the Santa Fe Society of the Archaeological Institute of America," journalist and amateur historian Paul A. F. Walter called Chimayó a "New Mexico Lourdes." Among the etiological legends he recounts is one associated with the third of the holy images (Santiago, San

Rafael, and the Niño) carved for the miraculously sited chapel:

> Last of all, they carved out of wood the image of a Christ child. On its feet they
> put shoes. But lo and behold, the next morning, the shoes of the Chirst child were
> worn out. New sandals were fashioned, but each morning they had to be replaced.
> At the same time, sickness disappeared, the crops were abundant, the number of
> sheep multiplied, better markets were found for the Chimayó blankets woven in
> the homes, and the Chimayós prospered wonderfully. It was evident that the
> Christ child each night went up and down the valley to bless its people and its
> households. The story of the miracle spread abroad. The earth on which the chapel
> stood became holy ground, and the clay that formed the floor of the tiny side
> chapel of San Rafael healed the pilgrims who came from far and near. The place
> was called "Santuario," and to this day pilgrims from as far away as Colorado,
> Texas and Arizona come to the chapel to be cured of bodily ills and to receive a
> spiritual blessing.[24]

In March 1992 a dozen national magazines, including *Travel & Leisure*, *Holiday*,
and *National Geographic Traveler*, ran a full-page ad sponsored by the New Mexico
Department of Tourism. The caption under Mark Nohl's full-color photograph of
the entrance proclaimed, "An open gate awaits those who come for the healing earth
found in El Santuario de Chimayó." The text reads:

> Every Easter, the faithful make their pilgrimage to Chimayó.
> Before dawn, pilgrims will begin arriving by the thousands. They will come on
> foot from hundreds of miles around, some chanting, some praying, and others
> bearing crosses. For centuries the faithful have come to this, the "Lourdes of
> America," to partake of the *tierra bendita* or blessed earth, which is said to heal
> the sick.
> As you roam the town in search of its famed Ortega weavings or wonder at the
> crutches of the healed that line the walls of the shrine, you'll learn that Chimayó
> is more than a place to pray and give thanks. It is a place to heal the soul.
> El Santuario de Chimayó. It's just one of the many wonders of New Mexico,
> and it's waiting for you.

The *Albuquerque Journal* of March 21, 1992, ran a top-front-page headline reading,
"Chimayó Ad Outrages Pilgrims: Archdiocese Questions Exploitation of Event."
Reporters interviewed Nancy Everist, advertising and marketing manager for the Department of Tourism, who explained, "It's a culturally authentic thing, and that's
what people are interested in seeing." However, Nambé resident, writer and santero
Orlando Romero protested: "Is there nothing sacred anymore? . . . This is totally
tacky, outrageous. To a great many people, the pilgrimage is a very sacred ritual, and
for the tourism department to make it an attraction for people to come and gawk at
is very offensive to me." Romero and others planned to circulate a petition among
pilgrims during Holy Week for later transmission to the Department of Tourism. It
read in part, "The pilgrimage is not a tourist attraction and its advertisement as such
demeans and exploits a religious experience as a method of attracting tourists. Its
advertisement is inappropriate, insensitive and should never occur again."

Pilgrim Arlene Mestas, an Española resident employed by that school district,
shared these sentiments. In "The Unholy Walk to Chimayó," a public forum article
for the *Santa Fe Reporter* of April 15–21, 1992, she lamented:

Every year, a handsome young man shoulders a huge cross all the way from Santa Fe to the Santuario. The first year [that he did so], he arrived at the front of the chapel and put down his heavy burden. He sat wiping the sweat off his face, leaning against the wall. At that moment, amid much dust and noise, the Sky 7 helicopter arrived, and the reporters rushed up to him. They asked him to pick up his cross and step across the entrance once more.

The young man looked pained because his private act of faith had become so public. Even so, he took up his burden once again and crossed the entrance while the TV cameras recorded the scene as if it were just happening—live.

Once there was a time for silence, but not since the intrusion of the TV camera.

The Chimayó debacle is an extreme instance of the tourist gaze presaged by Erna Fergusson in *Our Southwest*, one of the first full-length interpretive studies of the region:

This highjacking of one people's practice by another has speeded up the interfusion which was going on anyway. Doubtless it will hasten the coming of something that may, in time, become a true Southwestern culture; except that by then it will be on the way to transforming itself into something else. Nothing is surer than change, nothing more futile than to mourn it; nothing more instructive, really, than to watch it. And, in this case, we may watch the lumps of various widely different types and stage of culture bobbing, still undigested, in a sort of sunny stew.[25]

In this case both tourism and church officials were implicated in the highjacking. Marsha Adams, deputy cabinet secretary for the Department of Tourism, was "shocked" by the outcry over the appropriation. According to the *Albuquerque Journal* of March 24, 1992,

Adams said neither she nor others in the department consulted the Archdiocese of Santa Fe for opinions about the advertisement. She also said officials didn't ask Hispanic Catholics who work in the Department of Tourism about the potentially sensitive advertisement.

"That was probably an oversight that we shouldn't have made," Adams said in a telephone interview. "It was an oversight not running it by church officials."

Rev. Richard Olona, chancellor for the Archdiocese of Santa Fe, was also quoted:

Olona said the potential for tourists to invade an essential part of Hispanic Catholic culture outweighs the potential benefit of tourism. . . .

"We don't need to have something very close to faith and culture exploited in any means," he continued. "I know the Department of Tourism wasn't trying to do that, but they should have contacted us. They shoot themselves in the foot when they do something like this."

Olona noted that many places and events connected to religion—including the Vatican—are tourist attractions. The difference is many who make the pilgrimage to Chimayó don't want the attention of tourists, he said.

A cartoon by Jon Richards on the Opinion page of *The Santa Fe New Mexican* of March 31, 1992, lampooned the Department of Tourism. A man in slacks, shirt, tie, and jacket with a "N.M. Tourism Dept." button tells a woman in a dress and sweater and carrying a camera, "Of course, you'll always have some die-hards who'll oppose progress. But I tell you, this is the wave of the future for pilgrimages." The two are looking at a crowd of people watching a brass band leading a parade of balloons, one in the shape of a person on crutches and another a priestlike figure holding a cross, along a route with a sign pointing toward Chimayó.

When he returned from state business to Mexico, Michael Cerletti, the secretary of tourism, addressed a letter to *The Santa Fe New Mexican* on April 2. The paper reported on April 7, 1992, that Cerletti

> expressed regret for "whatever pain or misunderstanding this ad may have caused anyone."
>
> But he said that if the department had meant to plug the tion [*sic*] it would have run the ad several weeks earlier to give tourists time to plan a trip to see the event.
>
> Cerletti also said that people who have contacted the state about visiting New Mexico because they had seen the ad did not interpret it as an invitation to experience the pilgrimage.
>
> So far, callers were "inquiring about Chimayo and New Mexico in general," Cerletti said. "Not one has asked about the pilgrimage."

Nevertheless, *Time Magazine* of April 13, 1992, included among its Business Notes on page fifty-three two paragraphs titled "Hey, Look at the Pilgrims!" noting that "worshipers are signing a petition condemning the ads . . . [and] in another manifestation of their protest, pilgrims say they will bar tourists from photographing their procession."

Fanta Se

It has been said that Santa Fe is a "vortex for transformation." Anyone you talk to can tell you their own story that even amazes themselves about the changes that have taken place in their life after being here awhile.

If you feel yourself suddenly feeling like Santa Fe is calling you—like a siren song—you may have been chosen to be one of the ones ready for their own transformation. The change that comes may be a change of clothes—to the relaxed Western style, or a change of lifestyle—become more easygoing in this gentle "land of Mana [*sic*]"—but the real change that is going on is in your heart.

—Judith Cameron, "The New Age: A Change of Heart,"
Travelhost: New Mexico North, Santa Fe/Taos,
31 December 1989–27 January 1990, p. 8

I have made much of Chadds Ford's self-referentiality and auto-ethnographic self-inscription. But this is not to say that these controlling processes of reproduction and self-citation are "aware" of themselves *as* processes. One might go so far as to suggest that the ideological efficacy of Chadds Ford depends upon a misrecognition of itself. . . . It simply would not do for Chadds Ford cultural production to theorize its own postmodernity, that is, become fully conscious of its pervasive textuality. Were it to do so, Chadds Ford would have to be categorized as a different kind of postmodern Site. . . . The closest approximation we have to this other kind of Site, one that is not only infinitely self-referential but also aware of its textuality and capable of textualizing (and commodifying) even this very awareness, is the theme park. Of course we might turn this around and say that Chadds Ford is a species of postmodern Site for which we have no good name but that might be described as like a theme park minus the self-consciousness. One symptom of this lack of detachment is the seeming absence of a self-directed sense of humor in Chadds Ford's cultural production. For the most part Chadds Ford takes itself quite seriously.

—John D. Dorst, *The Written Suburb: An American Site, An Ethnographic Dilemma*, 1989[26]

By 1989 Santa Fe jokes included this version of a familiar contemporary genre: Q. How many Santa Feans does it take to screw in a light bulb? A. One hundred; one to screw it in and ninety-nine to attend the opening. Residents and visitors sported T-shirts bearing the inscription "Fanta Se." Those who purchased newspapers regularly read alarming, amusing, and sometimes acerbic reports, cartoons, and commentary. The October 14, 1989, *Albuquerque Journal North* published a Teaford cartoon showing a checkpoint at "$anta Fe City Limits, Elevation 7000.00," in which an officer tells the male tourist driving a station wagon packed with luggage and children, "Sorry— You have one child too many—and one credit card too few. Have a nice day."

On March 16, 1990, Denise Kusel, editor of *The Santa Fe New Mexican*'s cultural section *Pasatiempo*, offered citizens an alternative census. Its initial questions read:

1. I first got to Santa Fe:
   A: On vacation.
   B: On the train and lived in Lamy for four years before I knew there was a Santa Fe.
   C: I have been here all my life and want the rest of you to go back to California, Texas and New York.
2. Living space:
   A. I live in a typically charming Santa Fe–style adobe with no closets. No windows. No hot water. No heat. But lots of vigas and the floor slopes a lot.
   B. I live in 750 square feet with four of my best friends and two guides who have channeled themselves into our lives and won't leave.
   C. I am from another planet and so are half the people I know who live here. The other half are just passing through on their way to Taos.

The jokes, cartoons, and commentary are part of Santa Fe style victimology. Impetus for this sarcastic theme park consciousness came from a 1989 postcard by Jerome Milord. Titled *Another Victim of Santa Fe Style*, the black-and-white design shows a woman in full-style regalia of boots, prairie skirt, velvet Navajo blouse, concha belt, squash blossom necklace, bracelets, and rings who lies with eyes closed, face up on the Navajo rug on the floor beneath the viga ceiling of her living room. An Indian pot sits on the ledge of the kiva fireplace, and to its left seven carved wooden snakes decorate the wall above the banco. An eighth is partly visible slithering out the door just beyond the woman's head.

When Milord made the postcard into a full-color poster, he portrayed the woman as a blonde, omitted one of the wall snakes, and added an O'Keeffe cow skull above the door and a nicho with a santo inside on the wall to the right of the fireplace. An Indian drum and a pink, wooden, howling coyote sit on the floor on either side of the kiva fireplace with its unlit piñon logs. Poster sales increased significantly after the *New York Times* of December 7, 1989, announced—under the title "The West Again? Enough!"—how copies could be ordered by mail at $16.95 each, postage included:

For those who have seen one Pendleton-cosseted, turquoise-draped Navajo too many, from Santa Fe, NM, there comes this poster, spawned by Lewis E. Thompson, an advertising man, and Jerome Milord, an artist.

"It's about time we started making fun of ourselves," said Mr. Milord, who has lived there since 1964 and has thereby earned the right to fight the hype. He admits to living in a piñon-scented adobe house filled with niches [*sic*], santos and trasteros. But he is eyeing his decorative pink coyote as kindling for his kiva fireplace.

Finally, perhaps, there have been two victims of Santa Fe style: the one made famous by artist Jerome Milord's 1989 postcard-turned-poster and the other "drawn and quartered" by cartoonist Jon Richards in the *Santa Fe Reporter* of December 11–17, 1991. Richards's cartoon, also titled "Another Victim of Santa Fe Style," simply shows a pickup truck loaded with cut logs and displaying a tailgate sign which reads "Piñon Firewood" leaving a hill of stumps.

Santa Fe style became its own victim on December 24, 1992, when Ann Japenga announced in the *Los Angeles Times* that the nation was "on a northwest course":

Forget adobes and coyotes and deserts. Southwest style has come and gone. Think cabins and salmon and forests, as the anti-style of Seattle takes over what we see, hear and wear.

However, someone forgot to tell movie actor Shirley MacLaine, interviewed by Bob Thomas for an Associated Press release printed in the *Albuquerque Journal* of January 26, 1993:

Q. Are you still living in the state of Washington?
A. Yes, but I'm going to sell the place and move to New Mexico. I'm interested in the high desert now. There are too many Californians now in Washington. . . .
Q. What do you do out there in New Mexico?
A. First of all, I have a satellite (dish), so I have all the shows I have to see. "Entertainment Tonight," "Nightline" and so forth. I write, I read, I've got friends there, I'm learning how to dowse for water, I'm learning what the crystal deposits are in the mountains and the high desert lands. I'm learning about the plants and the birds and Native American stuff.

In this inversion Shirley MacLaine brings to a close nearly a century of Southwesternism. Her New Age, New Southwest may not have been fully anticipated by Erna Fergusson's sunny stew and certainly not by Fred Harvey's girls and Couriers, but it remains true to the sitings set up by the world's fair midway Orientalism of Santa Fe's Trail and Railway.

NOTES

With a few minor changes, portions of this article have appeared elsewhere: "Burro(wed) Alley" and parts of "Fanta Se" were in Marta Weigle, "Southwest Lures: Innocents Detoured, Incensed Determined," *Journal of the Southwest* 32 (1990): 499–540; "Detoured to Yesterday" comes from Marta Weigle, "Exposition and Mediation: Mary Colter, Erna Fergusson, and the Santa Fe/Harvey Popularization of the Native Southwest, 1902–1940," *Frontiers: A Journal of Women Studies* 12, 3 (1992): 117–50. I would like to thank *Journal of the Southwest* editor Joseph Carleton Wilder and *Frontiers* editor Jane Slaughter for permission to include these sections.

1. Quoted in Marta Weigle and Kyle Fiore, *Santa Fe and Taos: The Writer's Era, 1916–1941* (Santa Fe: Ancient City Press, 1982), 3.

2. Carl D. Sheppard, *Creator of the Santa Fe Style: Isaac Hamilton Rapp, Architect* (Albuquerque: University of New Mexico Press with the Historical Society of New Mexico, 1988), 75.

3. Christine Mather and Sharon Woods, *Santa Fe Style* (New York: Rizzoli International Publications, 1986).

4. John D. Dorst, *The Written Suburb: An American Site, An Ethnographic Dilemma* (Philadelphia: University of Pennsylvania Press, 1989), 2, 4.

5. Edward W. Said, *Orientalism* (1978; New York: Vintage Books, 1979); Marta Weigle, "From Desert to Disney World: The Santa Fe Railway and the Fred Harvey Company Display the Indian Southwest," *Journal of Anthropological Research* 45 (1989): 115–37. See also Barbara A. Babcock, " 'A New Mexican Rebecca': Imaging Pueblo Women," *Journal of the Southwest* 32 (1990): 400–37.

6. Dorst, 3.

7. A photograph of this design appears in Marta Weigle and Peter White, *The Lore of New Mexico* (Albuquerque: University of New Mexico Press, 1988), 76.

8. Said, 5–6. Said cites K. M. Panikkar, *Asia and Western Dominance* (London: George Allen & Unwin, 1959).

9. Marian Sloan Russell, *Land of Enchantment: Memoirs of Marian Russell along the Santa Fe Trail*, as dictated to Mrs. Hal Russell, ed. by Garnet M. Brayer (1954; reprinted, Albuquerque: University of New Mexico Press, 1981), 53, 55–56.

10. Said, 3.

11. Anne Farrar Hyde, *An American Vision: Far Western Landscape and National Culture, 1820–1920* (New York and London: New York University Press, 1990), 301.

12. Ad reproduced in Albert D. Manchester, *Trails Begin Where Rails End: Early-Day Motoring Adventures in the West and Southwest* (Glendale, California: Trans-Anglo Books, 1987), 118; D. H. Thomas, *The Southwestern Indian Detours: The Story of the Fred Harvey/Santa Fe Railway Experiment in "Detourism"* (Phoenix: Hunter Publishing, 1978), 52–53.

13. *They Know New Mexico: Intimate Sketches by Western Writers* (Passenger Department, AT&SF Railway, 1928), 39, 3. The "strangers once" who "really know" are: Charles F. Lummis ("The Golden Key to Wonderland"), Alice Corbin Henderson ("Old Spain in New Mexico"), Mary Austin ("Modern Lore of the Pueblos"), Witter Bynner ("Pueblo Dances"), Eugene Manlove Rhodes ("Neglecting Fractions"), Elizabeth Willis De Huff, once a Courier ("Children of the Indian-Detour Country"), and fifteen poets whose works are in "And the Poets: A Little Collection of Verses About New Mexico, Edited by Alice Corbin."

14. Thomas, 122.

15. Barbara Young Simms, "Those Fabulous Fergussons," *El Palacio* 82, 2 (Summer 1976): 46.

16. Scott Sandlin, "Erna! Travel Guide Par Excellance [*sic*] Remembered for State Tours," *Albuquerque Tribune*, 30 April 1987, B12.

17. In the January 1, 1929, *Harveycar Motor Cruises* brochure, the national advisory board is listed as : "Dr. Edgar L. Hewett, Director, School of American Research; Dr. A. V. Kidder, Department of American Archaeology, Phillips Andover Academy, Andover, Mass.; Dr. S. G. Morley, Associate of Carnegie Institute, in charge of expeditions, Central American Archaeology; Dr. F. W. Hodge, Director, Museum of the American Indian, New York; Dr. Charles F. Lummis, author of 'Land of Poco Tiempo,' 'Mesa, Canyon and Pueblo,' etc.; Mr. Paul F. Walter, President, The Historical Society of New Mexico."

Couriers' abilities to inform were satirized in "The Great Southwest," a full-page feature by W. E. Hill in the *Chicago Tribune*, 24 November 1929 (in Thomas, *Southwestern Indian Detours*, 225): "The girl guide. Indian detours couriers are smart girls. A girl guide taking a party of inquisitive tourists on a sightseeing trip must have her geology, zoology and languages right at her tongue's door. She must know enough about geological formation to be able to point and say, 'Look! That's a mountain.' And she must have a smattering of Mexican and Spanish so that when visiting an Indian pueblo she will be able to say, 'Why, Manuelito, aren't you ashamed to charge two dollars for that!' "

18. *Indian-detours—Most Distinctive Motor Cruise Service in the World* (Chicago: Rand McNally,

1930), 5; Virginia L. Grattan, *Mary Colter: Builder Upon the Red Earth* (Flagstaff: Northland Press, 1980), 54; Elizabeth Shepley Sergeant, "The Santa Fe Group," *Saturday Review of Literature*, 8 December 1934, as reprinted in Weigle and Fiore, *Santa Fe and Taos*, 131.

19. Dean MacCannell, *The Tourist: A New Theory of the Leisure Class* (1976; New York: Schocken Books, 1989), 94.

20. Erna Fergusson, "Crusade from Santa Fé," *North American Review* 242 (Winter 1937): 377–78.

21. Nelson H. H. Graburn, "Tourism: The Sacred Journey," in Valene L. Smith, editor, *Hosts and Guests: The Anthropology of Tourism*, second edition (1977; Philadelphia: University of Pennsylvania Press, 1989), 28. Graburn cites D. E. Berlyne, "New Directions in Motivation Theory," in T. Gladwin and W. C. Sturtevant, editors, Anthropology and Human Behavior (Washington, D.C.: Anthropological Society of Washington, 1962), 152.

22. *Historic Preservation: A Plan for New Mexico* (Santa Fe: New Mexico State Planning Office, 1971), as cited in Samuel Larcombe, "Plaza del Cerro, Chimayó, New Mexico: An Old Place Not Quite on the Highway," in Marta Weigle with Claudia Larcombe and Samuel Larcombe, editors, *Hispanic Arts and Ethnohistory in the Southwest: New Papers Inspired by the Work of E. Boyd* (Santa Fe: Ancient City Press; Albuquerque: University of New Mexico Press, 1983), 173.

23. Mary Austin, "Frank Applegate," *New Mexico Quarterly* 2 (1932), as cited in Marta Weigle, "The First Twenty-Five Years of the Spanish Colonial Arts Society," in Weigle with Larcombe and Larcombe, 185. See also Elizabeth Kay, *Chimayo Valley Traditions* (Santa Fe: Ancient City Press, 1987); Marta Weigle and Peter White, *The Lore of New Mexico* (Albuquerque: University of New Mexico Press, 1988), 39–46.

24. Paul A. F. Walter, "A New Mexico Lourdes," *El Palacio* 3, 2 (January 1916): 3.

25. Erna Fergusson, *Our Southwest* (New York: Alfred A. Knopf, 1940), 340.

26. Dorst, 115.

Conclusion

A Wave of the Hand

Charles Bowden

The ceiling light paints the windows milk and we sit in the ranch house sealed off from the summer night. On the walls are huge oil paintings of Indians and of mountain passes. She is talking and there is this simple strand of things I notice—her quick bright words, the light painting the windows milk, the big paintings. The house is not her house; it is not my house. It is a kind of no man's land. The occupant is a friend of mine and he is on the run. That is why he has come to this place, Chorizo, because it is where so many are on the run from something and yet have come to ground. My friend's story is simple: he got caught, he agreed to a wire, his testimony put ten or fifteen Mafia guys in prison. Now for him it is no known address, no phone, a 9 mm. by the bed, an AK leaning against the wall in the corner, that sawed-off shotgun, and always a careful look over his shoulder.

The light is clean, the air cool, the two males, sixteen, hitch by the road hoping for a ride into Chorizo. They are ready, the afternoon is fine, a car slows and then stops.
It is time.
They get in—they know the guy, what the hell?—and talk to the man who has been hanging around the El Tonto the last week or two.
The car moves, runs through the gears, and it is nice, it is good, moving down that road with nothing facing one but the laze of the afternoon and the promise of the night.

For her it is not the same but similar. She . . . is very quick, with eyes that can only be called bright—blue, focused, alert, intelligent—eyes waiting like a hungry cat and ready to pounce. I'll tell you a simple story that will save time. The Border Patrol likes to descend on Chorizo like wolves and prowl about peoples' property looking for dope. These visitations violate various parts of the Bill of Rights and she cannot abide such behavior. So one night she hears the squad car prowling down her country lane, and she leaps out of bed around four in the morning and storms out. She is standing in the glare of the headlights giving the officers a piece of her mind when she notices she is buck naked.

She came here in 1976 she tells me as the night rolls on and on. She hitchhiked from New York state with her four-year-old daughter in a car with some drug dealers.

They paused in Missouri—*"Well, I was almost gang raped"*—and she landed in the Arroyo. Everyone lived in tepees and scrounged for food and did not much of anything. The mountains were beautiful, the hills pulsating with the seasons from withered brown to lush green and Mexico was just over the hill. On the line, on the border, on the edge and "I knew I had come home." The first day or so she made it the ten or twelve miles into Chorizo, bought some canned goods for herself and her daughter and then carefully stacked them in the tepee. She took a walk through the hills, and when she came back the cans were gone. She thought, "These people are hungry," and so she did not get upset. After all she had $200, plenty to start a new life with, especially when you have just finally found home.

But I keep noticing the way she talks, that quick, well-enunciated speech, the words almost crackling with this snap in her voice. And from time to time there is laughter but it is always choked off, a kind of self-mocking laughter, and when she laughs she does not expand the way many people do—their chests heaving, their bellies going slack and then contracting, their faces melting into new forms No, she does not do that, she does not release something from within herself but tends to suddenly look down at the table where we are sitting and pull back. And then after the laugh passes, her head comes up, the eyes flash, the black mane of hair shines, the skin is very smooth and clear, and she moves on as if the moment of laughter were an interruption, a delay, and now the time must be made up. Because she has something to say, a line running through her random talk like a hard wire. She wants to capture this place, Chorizo, to protect its past so that what has happened will be a conscious part of its future. She wants to be a historian yet escape the contamination and limits of both that word and that way of acting.

(She shows me a photograph. A tepee stands on a hillside and the landscape is white from a snow. She is standing there in blue jeans and a sweater, hair long, safe by her home. She says she built the tepee when the Forest Service tore down her shack. The mesquites look white and alarmed as they bend in the background with the unexpected weight.)

Out there, past the window, that glass eye blinded now by the ceiling light, there waits the land, oak-dotted mountains with the lion, the javelina, the deer, the cow. Flats with mesquite, cactus, brown soil. And then the heartbeat, water, the stream flowing lazily through Chorizo, and the ciénaga, the big bog where a slab of tilted slate drives the moisture to the surface and creates a broad, green tongue that laps at the valley, a tongue rimmed with cottonwoods. The water is part of what this place is: for at least a thousand years human beings have lived here in small numbers because of water. There is a history, though a fragmentary one. Everyone stops by this spot for a drink but few stay and fewer leave any record of their life in this place. Also, there are many, many holes in the hills, deep holes where people have dug into the earth seeking minerals. For centuries this place has been mined and for centuries the mines have failed—at the moment they are all pretty much dead—but this does not stop men from looking in the hills for the big rock candy mountain.

(Virgil, an old man I know in Chorizo, says that when a horse is gentle broke, the horse works with you, but when you simply break a horse, you work the horse. The old man sits in front of his trailer at dusk shooting coyotes that have foolishly forgotten their fear. He sips his beer from time to time.)

Chorizo is a prospect, always a prospect. But never a success. It is still unincorporated and no one knows exactly how many souls live in the area—one thousand, two thousand, five thousand? No one seems to care. This is a great place for pretending, which is what I am doing now. The name, Chorizo, that is not the real name. I will not use the real name out of caution. There are not enough places left where people can freely pretend. Somehow the United States has become a nation with a permanent air of unreality and yet—by law, custom, or magic—has managed to severely restrict the choice of fantastic roles available to players in this unreality. Halloween is the last night left. Everyone I know can rattle off numbers they have been taught as essential to their own identity.

Chorizo is a redoubt, struggling not to be a Masada. The fanatics here have a special twist. God did not seem to call them to this place. They are fugitives from our world, from Peace is Our Profession, from Law and Order, from the Great Society, from the Light at the End of the Tunnel, from Just Say No, from Star Wars. From stars for that matter, except for the billions that clutter up Chorizo's dark midnight sky.

> They have made it a desolation;
>   desolate, it mourns me.
> The whole land is made desolate,
>   but no man lays it to heart.
> Upon all the bare heights in the desert
>   destroyers have come. . . .
>   —Jeremiah 12. 11–12

This place is nowhere. These people look to be trash. Dopers. Welfare bums and bumesses, food stamp junkies, tax dodgers, traffic violators. Gun nuts. I've been coming here since I was a boy. Places like Chorizo have been dwindling for years, murdered in the lean hours of the night by golf courses, subdivisions, master plans and masters. But now they are coming back, sprouting up in the heart of our great cities, festering along the romanticized blue highways. Even a cornered rabbit fights. So too, apparently, do some Americans. As it happened Chorizo was not dusted by the nuclear test binge of the fifties. But it was a close thing. For more than a decade nuclear warheads were stored an hour away. A horse can cross the land in an easy day to the nearest abandoned Titan missile base. I have worried about Chorizo for years, but I finally believe it will survive the current plague. That is why I come here. It is safe from salvation.

(The woman in the photograph looks arrogant, rich, and full of city scorn with her black hair combed tight to her smug skull, her dark sunglasses, red polka dot dress and that damn shopping bag hanging from one cocked arm. A man with a tweed sport coat and fedora fills the frame beside her. I ask, "Who are these pricks?" She laughs and says, "That's me. It's Halloween and I'm a tourist visiting Chorizo.")

The woman I am talking with—her name is Jenny—was once in a play here and had to play a buxom woman, so she wore a bra stuffed with God knows what and looked like her breasts were about a 44-C. There is a picture of her in that brasierre contraption, an image of her bending over that she says someone keeps threatening to circulate—ah, she gives off another choked laugh—a record she cannot exterminate of that moment of pretending. The pretending is not the sole attraction of the place for me. I come for the failure. The West is full of schemers—every bare spot of ground a future city, every hill a mine, every desert a farm, every acre your dream home . . . here! . . . every immigrant beginning life anew—but Chorizo never manages to pull anything off successfully. The mines fail, the ranchers fail, the developers fail, and the tourists never seem to come here in more than dribs and drabs, and they leave very swiftly. There are two saloons, one general store, a cafe, a bakery, a feed store, and the current hot issue is to stop drunks from shitting on the two-block-long main street—a kind of anti-defecation league. All this in the oldest town site in the state, though the town site has never spawned a real town.

There are things the woman does not say and things I do not say. She never says she loves the place. I am also silent on this point. But we both love the place. What stops us from saying such a thing out loud? Is this thing called landscape not spectacular enough to give us the courage to admit our love? Why is it easier for most of us to say we love chocolate candy than to ever admit we love a piece of dirt? A fly lands on the face, the hand brushes it aside. But seldom the word *love*.

"Any killings?" I ask casually. She looks me over quickly because the question here is burdened with possible problems. This small community so close to the Mexico border lives in part off drugs. Stash houses, smuggling, the hills alive at night with strings of horses, men with packs, truckers running without headlights, the leaf springs splayed out flat with the load. Any killings?

Some men went out to the lake, down there in the trees, and they were drinking and there was an argument and one guy pulled out a gun and shot another man through the chest and the man died. A killing. Yes. When? God, years ago. Down by the lake, the bass noodling among the cattails, the catfish gorging on the bottom in the mud. She can't remember years, the names are vague too. It is one in the morning, and when I look at the window I cannot see out because the light is blinding me to the night.

Yeah, we're livin' on the border with the Border Patrol
And every one of them is a dumb asshole.
They got guns and dogs and a bad attitude
And one thing's for certain, they're gonna be rude.
If you're drivin' down the road, then they'll wanna know why.
They say they just protect us, but that's a big lie.
You came downtown just lookin' for some fun,
But you're lookin' at a cop and he's holdin' a gun.

Chorus:
We got drums, guitars, mikes and amps,
We're white guys on food stamps.
We ate too much garlic, got stomach cramps,
We're white guys on stamps.
                    —Mother Chorizo, "White Guys on Food Stamps"*

There's this old guy in Chorizo who has constructed a time line of the place going back into the deep tar pits of the past. He is good at keeping track of time. His ranch has a yellow Private Property/No Trespassing sign on the gate (the metal rectangle boasting a flag decal in one corner) and one more message: "NOTICE: Anyone found here at night will be found here in the morning." The ranch I stay at is more civilized with a polite sign advising, "Trespassers will be violated." I should mention that roads in Chorizo are not so good, nor are the roads into Chorizo. Local drunks regularly have head-on collisions with steers. People don't like the drive and this, naturally, keeps people out. For many residents, road improvements are an issue—they fight them. Some folks in the town publish a map for a walking tour of historical this-and-that, but there is this feeling in the air that Chorizo does not seek company. The hunters come during the season, and fishermen drop by at the small lake a few miles out of town, but if you go in the bars just about any hour you see the same faces there day after day. Maybe it's the bar fights, hard to say.

But there is plenty of time, centuries and centuries of time here, and all this time has left some tracks on the land, some scrawls on old pieces of paper. In the beginning was a dyke, a large dyke of stone reaching up toward the empty sky and trapping water and creating a lake (waves overlapping the town site of Chorizo), and the lake, well, maybe it festered and maybe it didn't, because all this seems to have happened long before people walked to and fro on this earth. Later, my kind came and dug in dry ground and they found bones.

(Imagine their camps, pith helmets on their heads, typewriters resting on rickety tables inside impossibly hot tents. I'm sure in the old photographs we can see spectacles on their sunburned noses and good stout boots laced up to the knees—the snakes! the snakes!—and off in the distance, perhaps almost fuzzy in these old photos, the flivers are tied up to the mesquites lest they drift off after good grass in the dark hours. And in the frame, looking very serious and worthy of the ponderous burden and responsibility of science, we behold the incredible monster hunters and the tamers of ancient and forgotten graves. Did they have women? And if they were women did they have men? Did they enjoy the flesh, back in those days and months they spent inventing the lives of long-dead souls they called beasts, creatures who had never passed an hour, I hope, without the sensation of some kind of lust? Then again, I suspect the finished lives speaking from the cold bones had no need of such a word as lust. Of course, I never have seen the photo I have just described, but I know it exists in some forgotten trunk, because it always does for them and for me. We are a people after all.) Some of these bones were very big and came from a long-dead type of elephantlike animal called a mammoth. And some of these bones were damned small and suggest a horse about three feet tall. Consider for a moment tiny vaqueros with lariats like shoelaces chasing Chihuahua-sized steers over the awesome Big Empty of the West. That is the barely known floor under the unknown present.

Other grave robbers found suggestions of our own kind. About 300 B.C. a tribe appears *(We do not know their own name for themselves, we do not know the sound of a single word in their language—we know next to nothing, but we continue confidently to ransack their abandoned homes and tell all about them. Imagine a group of future archaeologists explaining a vanished culture they have dubbed MADE IN USA and illustrating their theories by holding up fragments of Tupperware which they have artfully arranged in chronologies based on soil stratigraphy. Beer canisters also.)* which we call the Hohokam, and they persist in the area of Chorizo until about the year 1400. There are many debates in the journals and in the seminars about why they went away, but a big clue may be a lack of water, a drought that sweeps the entire region at the end of the thirteenth century and leaves in its wake many slain ideas about what the world means and what really matters in this particular valley where human beings watch kith and kin succumb to the powers of the planet.

After that . . . strangers come and they ride horses and the horses this time are more than three feet tall. These people carry lances, they fire guns and cannons, they speak of a carpenter who has nails driven through his palms and feet and asks his father for help and then watches an afternoon slide by while he writhes in agony. And three days after he dies, a large stone is rolled back from his tomb and his crypt is empty—and then he appears to people and ascends into the sky and leaves almost a vapor trail behind him which some people think spells out the word *love* and others see as letters with a different meaning. This is the story they come to tell, these people on horses, and they succeed and eventually almost everyone in Chorizo forgets any other stories concerning such serious matters. Though there are many arguments about details of the basic story.

Now dates appear. Father Eusebio Kino rides into Chorizo and marks the spot on his map of missions, and it is the year of our Lord sixteen hundred and ninety-five. Soon Chorizo is a *visita*, an outpost, where priests fly through like circuit-riding Methodists to minister to the tender and innocent souls of what they call Indians. Then in 1736 a man or a woman (or a child or a burro or an old hound dog) finds or scrapes a place in the earth a little bit south of Chorizo and silver gleams into the eye. The silver lies like thick T-bone steaks on the surface and can be harvested by anyone willing to bend over. This fact attracts notice (eventually the Americans will name an entire state after this strike, perhaps as part of their desire to announce who they are and what they are about) and people are sent north to look for more such bonanzas, and naturally some come to the bog and mosquitoes of Chorizo. Eventually the people who have long lived here disapprove of the people who have recently come, and in 1751 they rise up and slay many of the newcomers. A large battle in this conflict is fought near Chorizo. But, of course, the old settlers lose *(We can never imagine them winning, not for a second, because we are too committed to what we now are, to this computer flashing these words on a cathode tube as I pause briefly to bewail the slaughter of people denied the opportunity to be my ancestors. That is why we cherish this past, because we do not have to truly live with it.)*, their energies ebb, and they are overcome by the force of those whose hungers are greater. So great are these monstrous hungers that the newcomers must fling themselves outward into other places and other lives. We call them discoverers, explorers, and the like. Also, we make them into metal statues, although inevitably, after a few short months or years, these statues become invisible to everyone but the birds.

They're riding along, the three of them—here, pass me the bottle, I don't like this part—*when something happens*—Christ, I can't straighten this out, the stories vary, well, the two stories vary—*and the car pulls to the shoulder and after a while everybody is out of the car, and then the rock, and the swinging. The knife, ah, that seems later, five, ten, twenty shoves. And then there are two standing and one not standing.*

The sky is very blue. As expected.

A dull litany begins of expeditions and discoveries. In 1774 an experienced warrior of this ground named Juan de Anza mounts an expedition from a town nearby, and the group camps in Chorizo when outward bound on its voyage across the skin of earth to eventually found a colony named after Saint Francis, a beggar man said to have loved animals. Then in 1776 the new people think of founding a fort in Chorizo (they call it a *presidio*), but the sickness that springs from the bogs drives them elsewhere. A vast silence descends *(no one is listening, no one at all)* and there are no records until a real estate negotiation in 1853 called the Gadsden Purchase *(There is an old hotel named after this buy in a border town, and the staff insists it is haunted, and though it has a window of Tiffany glass, this feeling of a haunting is certain—I have talked to people who work there and visited the rooms where the spirit walks . . . a woman is bending over an ironing board deep in the basement surrounded by bare concrete walls and I ask the question and she raises her brown face and says yes, yes, and leads me onward into the gloom brooding past the reach of the bare bulb hanging over her work place, and she says, there, there is where the spirit appeared—and I carefully make notes in a small paper tablet brought just for the occasion)* which plops Chorizo into an entity caled the United States of America. Things began to happen at the same old rate but with more attention to what is happening, and this new sense of things, this keenness to detail, names, dates, and other facts is called history. Five years after Chorizo is bought from Mexicans who do not own it (at the time of the purchase there are but five thousand Mexicans in what becomes an entire state, and this population is almost completely clustered in one fifty-mile-long valley) and sold to Americans who are still trying to possess it, on one fine day in the year 1858, a strike of silver is found in the brown hills around the bog. This strike, this mine that drives men to shout and women to wear their best costumes, this very bonanza demonstrates why history is such a frail substitute for life. History is based on a crabbed and limited form of remembering; those who truly live seldom get remembered. For instance, we have no record of the men who found the mine or the women who celebrated or what they did that night after the drinking and how the sheets felt against their sweaty skin.

Mines have always had a way of getting lost in Chorizo. In 1763 some forgotten Jesuit pens the *Rudo Ensayo*, a kind of inventory of the region, and this black robe clucks how "there used to be near this place [Chorizo] one gold mine and silver mines which are now abandoned." Part of the problem for the mines lies in interpersonal relations: the local Indians have a vision of being differently abled and they keep killing off the miners. Then in 1812 one Augustin Ortiz buys up the whole area for about $750, puts in some cows, and then waits for the Indians to come and kill him and steal his herd. In a few years, naturally, he is gone. His heirs eventually peddle the land in 1856 to the Sonora Mining and Exploring Company, an outfit out of Cincinnati, Ohio. For a couple of years they play at being a business until they run into the same problems that have bedeviled everyone else in Chorizo and the outlying area: interpersonal relations.

(*"Our small party of five took turns in keeping watch and digging the graves. Burying the Papago in one grave, and the two Americans in the other, we wrote on a board—'Tarbox'; and under this: 'White man, unknown, killed by Apaches.' "*)

Samuel Colt of six-shooter fame bankrolls this venture and creates the first library in the territory so that boys swinging pick axes can improve their minds. The ranch that feeds and fattens the miners lists sixty-one people (nine of them black, a fact that, like most facts in Chorizo, will soon be forgotten.) But there is more to business, at least in Chorizo, than just business.

(. . .*"[H]earing that a wagon-load of watermelons had arrived at [Chorizo], and having lived on jerked beef and beans for nearly a year, I determined to go on with Poston. . . . About an hour and a half after these two men had left [Chorizo], they galloped back, showing in their faces that something awful had happened.*
'What is the matter?' asked Poston.
'There has been an accident at the mine, sir.'
'Nothing serious, I hope?'
'Well! yes, sir; it's very serious.'
'Is anyone injured—is my brother hurt?'
'Yes, sir, they're all hurt; and I'm afraid your brother won't recover.' . . .
Laying the bodies in a wagon just arrived from [Chorizo], we returned. . . . That evening we had another burial. . . . After this we . . . determined to leave the country by the nearest open route. The events of the past week, added to all that had gone before, began to tell on my nerves.")

After the Civil War ends cattlemen flood the territory, and the steers become the true explorers of this ground and wander up every canyon, find a way onto every mesa, seek out like lovers each blade of lonely grass. In 1887 Apaches kill a rancher and the ground shakes because of an earthquake. Also, a smallpox epidemic visits that year. Then in the early and mid-nineties the rains forget to come and the cattle die, and when their vast dying is over everyone notices that a lot of the earth is dead or dying also, and with time a word will come to spill from many lips, a long word, *overgrazing*. By 1895 Chorizo has 236 souls and everyone takes lots of quinine to keep the malaria at bay. Around 1912 a King 8, a Chalmers, a Ford and a Packard mosey into town. Four years later an army post is set up so that the troops can glare south at the revolution sweeping Mexico, and then in 1918 the influenza kills thirty locals. Another drought stops by in 1920 and 1921, and one guy sets up a bone yard and hauls away truckloads for processing into meal. Two years later, for lack of anything elso to do, a six-mile stretch of the road connecting Chorizo with the rest of the planet is graded. In the late thirties the state health department finally notices the persistent malaria in the area and tosses some mosquito-eating Gambusia fish into the bog. A real estate wheeler-dealer pops into Chorizo in 1948, announces the place would be perfect as an art colony, floats the idea of making a new Taos by the bog, peddles a hundred lots in a week and then leaves, and Chorizo goes back to sleep. Electric power straggles into Chorizo in 1956, and the locals begin to study "I Love Lucy." And then in 1972 eleven thousand acres of a big ranch that embraces Chorizo get busted up into forty-acre parcels, and new blood begins to seep into the old veins of the town.

And that's where the old rancher's time line peters out, because as he figures it, "The many new residents in the area as a result of available home sites together with the old residents of the town site will now be witness to a new chronology of events."

Oh, yes, and about that time a new group arrives in Chorizo.

Dope fiends.

Jenny holds the big, white scrapbook in her lap, the large pages splaying out like tongues eager to talk. Her finger caresses a set of sepia-toned images and she explains that this is Valentine Flat, a patch of low ground by a wild-looking river in western New York. The river looks cold, the rock cliff on the far side as ancient as God. Here, she points, is where the hippies gathered in the summer. The hills surrounding the river are where she was born and raised. Her eyes seem to sparkle as she speaks. Another photo looms up: They are sitting on the ground, the men have beards—"my brother, there's his wife, that's their kid . . ."—and the women look kindly, the hair hanging long, and it is a thousand or two thousand years ago and they are on Valentine Flat in the state of New York, and then—presto!—mesquite pokes up in the background of the next photo and mountains of rock grab at the horizon and there are tepees. Jenny's teeth are gleaming, her skin is glowing and it is the time before the dark time, that moment people call the sixties.

The explanation is simple but garbled as we stare at the photo book: There is a mining claim—"How did you hear of it?" "Someone bought it." "Who had the cash?"—and suddenly everyone in the photo taken at Valentine Flat is facing a camera at the Arroyo.

And others come. Everyone at that time seems to have very keen hearing. Everyone. And so people magically appear.

They are all smiling, the men bare chested, the sun pouring down like honey. In the foreground are tiny children, and if you press your nose close to the photograph the smell of marijuana comes almost within reach. Old songs lift off the page in the scrapbook, and words like *vibes* come to mind. Jenny picks out another face: the man is bearded and smiling, and on his head rests a cowboy hat with a flat crown and silver band. "He was violent," she notes evenly. "Liked to beat up women, and somehow they never seemed to hear about the ones before. Once I ran into him at a party and he said something and I talked right back and suddenly he threw me over his shoulder and ran off into the desert. He stopped after a little while and threw me on the ground and said, 'Just so you know what I can do to you if I want.' Beat the hell out of two women. And then he was living with a woman up in the city and beat her. She shot him dead.''

Night is coming down, there is that kind of soft, dying light above Chorizo, as the boys throw the body down the mine shaft—thud, thud, thud. That was easy, why didn't they tell us this in school? A faint breeze plays with the blue grama grass, the sounds of people come from down below.

The night will surely be fine now. Beer, girls, fun. To be sure, there will not be a lot of money, they guy only had a couple of bucks. But what the hell. There is the car . . . find some girls, life is roaring out ahead on the road.

Virgil stops by the ranch house every morning for one more early beer to help launch the day. In the past two or three weeks, he's knocked down twenty cases—of course that tally does not include his brews at the El Tonto. Also, he comes by each morning to leave off his dog, Baby, a small beast of two or three pounds. This is all because of thoughtfulness. His truck, parked for hours in front of the El Tonto saloon, would be too hot for Baby, and so he has a beer or two and then leaves the dog as he goes about his business in the liquid heart of Chorizo. He is a small man, I suspect in his early seventies. His manner is very deliberate, a slow, careful form of speech, an elaborate style of courtesy. He spent more than twenty years in the U.S. Army and is proud he left the service as he entered it, a private.

His past is frisky and has led him finally to this place—a common fate among many of the inhabitants. Chorizo sometimes is the last place a person can go. *(There is the whisper of a tale that about ten years ago, during the annual spring celebration, Chorizo Days, a motorcycle gang made a run from the city looking for a little fun in a hamlet seemly made for a new version of* The Wild One, *and then suddenly strange, scraggly looking armed guys poured out of hills and caves and God knows where and encircled the bikers. And they left.)* For many years he trapped the hills—he has tales of taking a half-dozen to a dozen bobcats out of a single canyon in a season—and one year when the price was good for pelts he cleared $12,000. Now he is past such work and lives on his Social Security, the government food program that periodically dumps cheese on Chorizo (cheese no one on earth seems willing to buy), and the profits of his penchant for the constant trading of horses and everything else. He is a collection of stories—riding the freights, working the oil fields, the army of course, but in the main kind of wandering about the Republic. Once he shed a shoe, pulled up a pant leg, skinned off his sock, and showed me the scars on his ankle from some bad weeks spent on a chain gang in Alabama. Virgil is the kind of person modern governments are determined to exterminate through various programs called aid or rehabilitation or retraining. He is the black hole in economic statistics, the insult to career ladders, the raw taste of that thing we increasingly find contemptible: freedom.

(Once I was in a ghost town in the desert of the Great Basin, and a man calling himself Silver Dollar Kirby had a saloon in one small room in the abandoned community—it was a proper ghost town, the table settings were still in place in the long-closed hotel—and his establishment consisted of one board, two sawhorses, a quart of whiskey and some shot glasses.

"How are you making out?"

"I'm doing okay," answered Silver Dollar Kirby.

And then he paused, as if considering whether his response was really honest, was truly forthcoming, and he slowly added, "I'm putting a little by.")

At one point Virgil had a saloon in Houston a few blocks off skid row and made a go of it for a while. He lived above the bar, slept on a cot, and augured a hole through the floor so he could constantly monitor his trade. He kept decorum by wielding a pool cue. He arrived in Chorizo courtesy of the legal notions of the American government. Some years back he had been in the large city that festers about an hour or so to the north and decided to enter a saloon for a cold one. As he walked in he noticed all the patrons were stretched out flat on the floor, and he caught a glimpse of two men squared off in a fight with pistols. The one he shot through the chest died almost instantly, the other one took a slug from a .380 square in the head right under the eye and, as Virgil says with a mixture of awe and contempt, "That was the son of a bitch that lived." They held him in jail for nine months trying to get a fix on the exact nature of his crime and finally released him into a ten-year probation. For a spell he hung around some small towns in the limbo of state supervision and then, with a wink and a nod, beat his way to Chorizo. He has never left. Of course, travel can be somewhat of a problem for him, what with a truck that has no registration, insurance, or plates and a wallet that has no driver's license.

He moves very deliberately and seems unruffled by what little happens in Chorizo. But his calm is not true of everyone here. I can remember sitting in the living room of this same ranch house and listening to the roar of the basic American debate about growth, change, tourists, money and ruin. Jenny was over and so was Molly who puts out the local monthly. They are in some ways very similar—two strong women who have tasted a lot of bumps in life but somehow managed not only to keep going but to keep learning.

(Jenny is living at the time—it's years and years ago—in a place just west of Chorizo, and things have been lean for a good long while when she suddenly comes into fifty dollars. So she piles the kids into the old car and drives to the general store and stocks up on all the good-tasting things they have not been able to buy and then drives home again. She backs the car up to the door—she's nine months pregnant that day and looking for every break she can find—to unload the groceries from the trunk, and she's standing there with her three- or four-year-old daughter when she suddenly catches a whiff of what smells like gasoline. Her house has no electricity so she goes in and gets the kerosene lantern, comes out on the porch and peers into the darkness and lights the lamp. The blast knocks her and her daughter over. Seems on the rutted climb back to her place a rock punctured the car's gas tank. Naturally, the machine's a total loss and all the groceries perish in the blaze. Her legs are seared, as is her face, and her eyebrows and some of the rest of her hair have vaporized. Her daughter is spooked—there will be nightmares—but unharmed.

She treats the burns with a salve she makes of aloe, and so long as she lies down with her legs propped up the pain is not so bad. Takes lots of vitamin E also. But she cannot stand. The child is born three weeks later. At home, of course, since Jenny has little use for doctors and their vile poisons and ideas. It's a boy. And that's the day of the big gasoline explosion. The car's still out there rusting away in the weeds.)

Now Jenny lives with her husband out in the country, raises goats, a big garden, keeps bees, has trained up four children, and hews to a simple way of life. Molly has raised up a crop of kids also but along with her husband has created on a knoll a large and beautiful house that never seems finished, a home that glows with her stained glass and tiles. They are both very alert women, with quick eyes and tongues, and between them seem to supply a lot of the civic fire power in Chorizo. The paper was originally started by Jenny and then taken over by Molly, just as the town walking tour was originally put out by Jenny and now is a project of Molly's. Anyway, as I sat there one afternoon they both drifted into a discussion of whether Chorizo should grow and what kind of folks if any should come here and whether tourists were a good thing or a curse, and it all sounded kind of familiar to me. Chorizo has been trying to bootleg itself into prosperity for decades and always fails. The tourists do come in trickles but they soon skitter out of town, and the real estate market has tiny fits of boom and long spells of bust. Basically, there seems little to do in Chorizo except drink, and there is no work—and I have a hunch this weight of boredom drives out all but the heartiest of souls. But such thoughts hardly bank the fires burning within the two women— Molly seeing tourism and growth as good for the town because they provide a living and Jenny seeing the same as an invasion. All this hard talk sounds wonderfully strange in a community where there seems to be about as many For Sale signs as trees.

After they finished going at it for a few rounds, Molly did not speak to Jenny for two solid months, a serious achievement in this microdot of a settlement. What struck me as odd was that since the earliest silver mines no one has ever really done too well at making Chorizo boom, and so growth as an issue seemed kind of a limited matter to me. But I was wrong. It no longer is an abstract subject in this country because everyone now has a sense of, well, of *them* breathing down their necks. We have become a nation of cornered rats. I've got a friend who just finished a place in an isolated section of the Rocky Mountains, and he told me with satisfaction, "I'm ready, I've got a three-hundred-foot well and six AKs." The West is no longer an open door but a wall bristling with armament.

Why does everyone in the West—the least populated region—argue about growth, about the possibility of more human beings moving onto the ground? There are only limited legal ways to keep people out, and there seems no sure way to make people pour into an area and boom the economy. The New Western Boot Hill is full of guys wearing white shoes who thought a billboard and a real estate office would make any subdivision thrive. There are some stubborn facts we all like to ignore. Tourism occurs because local people are anxious to sell out, to make a buck. So does sprawl, so does pollution, so does an invasion of strange folks from distant parts. *(Endless waves of Harvey girls beckoning the geeks; posses of studs with cowboy hats welcoming one and all to the dude ranches of our dreams.)* No one can stop people from coming. And no one has to sell out to them. Ah, you say you have been tricked? Well, then you were never likely to stick anyway. But don't feel bad, we've pretty much all sold out at one time or another. We hardly know anything else to do with ourselves. *(Albuquerque, Tucson, Phoenix, Santa Fe, Taos, Sedona, Tubac, Show Low, Pinetop, Lakeside, Greer, Moab, Durango, Prescott, Las Cruces, Truth or Consequences, Dolores, Telluride, every human community on the Front Range, Vail, Aspen, Steamboat Springs, Pagosa Springs, Flagstaff [there should be some special citation recognizing the zealous efforts of Flagstaff]—the roll call is very long and growing longer. The largest single industry on planet earth is now tourism. One out of every fifteen human beings is in the trade. Hugh Hefner was clearly on to something—we like to look.)* The people of the West love to see themselves as victims. (A curious unity exists between the whining of environmentalists and the whining of Sagebrush Rebellion warriors.) Never have so few asked for so many subsidies and acknowledged so little of this help. Chorizo itself might almost depopulate without food stamps, food handouts, and the national charity known as grazing permits on federal land. About the only serious sign of entrepreneurial spirit in the community is the drug traffic, and it also depends upon a federal program to drive up the price of the product, a program called The War on Drugs.

A young woman came to Chorizo around 1910 as the bride of a local rancher and she lived for over seventy more years. *(Jenny's husband, Jack, hands me an ancient photograph of the woman, his grandmother. Her face is hungry and lovely. She came as a school-*

teacher from Houston anxious to break out and see some Real West. His grandfather rode out to meet the stage and get first crack at a new white woman in the area. They moved in together— "Jack," *Jenny says,* "you don't want to say that to him; you don't want people to know that." *He smiles and says,* "Hell, everyone knows anyway. Besides, they did."—*and then they married and then the children started coming.*) In the 1930s she wrote a novel—mailed it as a blind submission to a New York publisher in December, held the printed copy in her hands the next April. She crafted her novel as part formula Western, part formula romance. She composed it in a nearby city, where she was living for a time while her children got some schooling. All this creativity came about within the fellowship of a local group called the Scribbler's Club. That April must have felt very fine to her. *(It is almost one in the morning, I am very tired but still the conversation keeps flowing, the bright light painting the window seems like some demon I cannot fathom how to extinguish. Jenny fishes out the book—the type on the binding is that thick, block style favored in the thirties, the pages are heavy, coarse paper, the whole thing gives off an aroma of age like a little, rectangular time machine.)* The local ground appears with faint disguise—Chorizo becoming Los Alamos, a big peak popping up as Squaw Tit, the bog a cool oasis. She had lots of experience to pack into the book: the days of riding the hills chasing the steers, the toil of cooking over a wood stove, of toting water from a spring, of struggling to keep her mind alive and her love alive. In her time Mexican bandits still crossed the line on brief errands of robbery and homicide, and she and her husband dealt with such forays. That is what is curious about her novel. *(I read it the very next day, sprawled out on the floor in the heat of the afternoon, and I never look up until I finish. It is clearly pulp fiction. I am completely seduced.)* The landscape is threatening and yet somehow physically faint; only the green trees and grasses around the bog seem alive and full of smells and textures and life. But the ground really only seems to exist when it decides to kill—the drought that downs and slowly chokes life from the herd, the violent storm that brings the arroyos up and almost drowns the heroine. And the Mexican-Americans periodically grace the pages as either, if men, simple and slow-witted fools *(feeding stock, saddling horses, sleeping out on the ground, going for the blind drunk in the cantina)* or, if women, as shimmering and predatory sexual threats *(singing love songs in the evening while they strum guitars, gleaming bridles of silver, bold eyes that do not turn shyly away, clothing that fails to disguise the generous curves of their bodies)*. Of course, it is easy to dismiss these features as products of that time, things to cluck our tongues over. But I am taken with other feelings when I read this early effort to capture Chorizo: that it is an honest account; that to an Anglo woman at the time of the First World War, the ground was unattractive and hostile (the nights are always beautiful in the book, what with the stars and the moon and scent of night-blooming cactus and the merciful fact that blackness hides the land from view); that to such a person household tasks were a drudgery and a form of mental debilitation; that for a proper young Miss from a more settled region, the open and eager sexuality of the Mexican-American women was terrifying and wet with desire. *(Jack hands me another photograph that has come down from his grandmother's days, one someone has identified in white ink as* "Spanish girl." *The woman in the image is on horseback, dressed as a charra, and on her fine-looking hip rides a holstered pistol. Her face has that traditional countenance of invitation mixed with scorn, a face seen at any fiesta in any town in Mexico as the night plows forward toward the hot and sensual hours.)*

I toy with getting the novel republished because I do not think it is past, not really. *(Jenny says there is a manuscript, a novel never published, and she seems almost embarrassed by its existence. It's like that crazy aunt proper Victorians seemed to always keep up in the attic—do you really want to bother other people with the raw facts of such an existence? But I have peculiar tastes and I want it. I know within its swirls of pulp obligations it will be fired by desires that cannot admit their own existence.)* It is just naked in its outlook. And naked is always a good thing. Better naked, the sun warming the skin, the smell of skin a drug, the absolute need to touch and caress, the hand reaching out. A far better thing than being correct. And I think the woman who wrote the novel understood that, since she spent—squandered?—a fortune during her long life tasting of life's pleasures. Her descendants have very little except for the best thing of all, an example.

The girls are easy to find, and the drive down the back roads feels fine. It is dark, down by the river, a good long way from Chorizo—ditch the fucking car, the party is over.
A clean thing.

The nights are very cold, and I roll up tightly in an old army blanket. I am up before first light, grab my rifle and drift into the darkness and toward the hills. The oaks brush my face, the rocks make me stumble, and the air remains cold. I can smell gun oil on my hands, and cartridges ride cool with their brass in my pocket. I follow an arroyo as it knifes into the hills and marches upward and then gouges a path into the mountains. Mexico stretches out a mile or two or three to the south, Chorizo snores by the bog a ways to the north. I am thirteen, fourteen, fifteen, and I want to kill a deer. Eventually, over time, I get my killing done but that is not what I remember. The gun—an ancient Enfield with a cheap scope and scarred military stock—was left behind in an attic on the East Coast in a move made years ago. Along with a sewing machine and a bootjack—life moves on without plan.

The smell is dry and dusty at midday, moist and cool in the evening. The deer move like shadows, the coatimundis roll along in a troop, all females as is their custom, and the mine shafts are scattered everywhere and gaping blindly up from the tall grass. I increasingly have trouble with words like *real estate* and *environment* and *ecology* and *lifestyle* and *tourism* and *back-to-the-land* and *conservation*. I find them ways to dodge the smells, the colors, the sweat on my back, the burn of the sun at noon, the way first my mind drifts and then my body seems to drift away also and I melt—eyes blinking, nose twitching, tongue licking my lips—but still I melt.

When I first start coming to Chorizo the big slab of ranch around the town site has not yet been subdivided into little ranchettes, the dope fiends have not yet migrated, and the road is still dirt—I remember coming down a hill in the rain, the clay soils sealed and the truck sliding like a sled hither-and-yon down the greased path—and, as always, the El Tonto saloon is open. So I have seen change and, for a spell, have given up on the town as a lost thing, something smothered by invaders and the greed of realtors. But I suspect this view is wrong. For there is more to changing a real place than change itself can ever accomplish.

(Virgil is talking in his low, patient way over his morning beer. He tells of an incident back when the new people came. A cowboy out riding in his truck got into some kind of a wrangle with a group of hippies. So he strode back to his pickup, sighted down the barrel of his .30/.30, levered in a cartridge, and blew the head off the ringleader. He went to prison for that one. And that's all that Virgil has to say about it.)

Wolves are slaughtered around Chorizo in the late forties. One lobo is seen feeding on a kill in 1956. Now not one howl in the night, not the faintest sign of a paw print in the dust. Gone. Dead. Destroyed. Mean, hard, cruel change. And yet Chorizo still perks along. Now coyotes flood the night with sound.

Out at the Arroyo things get a little lean at times. The leader of the outfit, a man with a beard in the old photograph taken at Valentine Flat in New York state, has survival skills worthy of being enshrined in a Green Beret manual. Everyone in the Arroyo is living in tepees or shacks, and there is no work or much desire for work. The leader always keeps a woman with a young child near at hand because he knows that the food stamp people are helpless in the face of a lactating female. And he sends the women into town from time to time for his grub—a case of hot dogs for him, oatmeal and beans for the woman and the child or children. There is also a friendly merchant who, out the back door, will take food stamps for beer. It is a complete and full life.

(Walking the ground, the rancher and his wife wade through the hip-high grass in the pasture and roll off the names of the gramas and other native species like calling up beloved children. The ground looks like a nature preserve—in fact, the nature preserve just over the fence doesn't look any better—and he quietly but firmly ticks off his expenses and how he pays taxes and how he produces meat for the nation and how . . . he pulls his own weight. And there are things left unsaid. And other things which cannot be said because there is no common language or even, perhaps, any mutual bedrock of desire. He does not go often to the El Tonto, just too much to do. He likes to rise before first light, saddle his horse, and be off on his land as the dawn comes on.)

Someday there will be people living on this earth who will look back at us and wonder about our obsession with a thing called the economy. They will study with amusement our various theological quarrels—communism, socialism, capitalism, fascism—and plot the course of this deadly illness through our lives. They will not understand us any more than we can grasp the values and feelings of a third-century anchorite. They will be baffled at our consistent determination to value money over love, pleasure, lust, food, the smile on a baby's face, the quality of light playing across a woman's body as she disrobes in the dusk. They will have many academic arguments about our passion for "fixing" the economy and our total disinterest in fixing ourselves. All our presidents will be blurs, a series of names without even as much flesh and character as the Caesars on those old Roman coins dug from ancient dirt. These people of the future will share my own interest in failure, though they will be much more advanced than I can ever hope to be, and they will use a different word for this same phenomenon. Places like Chorizo will be excavated and studied diligently, and there will be a constant hope among our descendants that some cache of Dead Sea–like scrolls will show up in these hills by the bog that will fill in the blanks about what really went on here. And no one living in this future time will know or use a certain phrase, *the West*. Because they will have moved beyond both a life and an understanding of living that is predicated on escape.

One day, two women living at the Arroyo look down at the ground and discover a five-dollar bill. They have been out there for two years feeding on oatmeal and beans, and they dream of raisins. They grab that five-dollar bill and start walking the twelve dirt miles into Chorizo. A bitch in heat hanging around the camp follows them, and nothing they say or do will make the little dog turn back. After walking for hours, the two women make it to the Chorizo general store, and as they shop inside for their dream of raisins, a cloud of local hounds gathers in front around the bitch in heat. This is long ago at a time when the word *hippie* was on people's lips instead of tucked away as a relic in the cobwebs of their memories. A lot of people in Chorizo who have been there awhile *("The many new residents, . . . together with the old residents of the town site, will now be witness to a new chronology of events.")* don't like the newcomers with the long hair, beards, and Indian tepees. When the two women come out and start up the road again, they are tailed by every male dog in Chorizo, and the boys drinking at the El Tonto see this sight and think, hell, these hippie broads have cast a spell on our canines, they must be witches. By now it is getting late in the day, and dusk is settling like a blanket over the valley. The women walk the dirt track, the Woodstock of love-struck beasts follows in their wake, and they look back at the tiny hamlet and suddenly see a pair of headlights, and then another, and soon it seems like a caravan is issuing from this speck of a community. The women think, my God, we may be raped out here in the dark and loneliness, and they take off cross country through the hills and canyons. They make it back to the Arroyo at daybreak, and they have their raisins. It has taken them a twenty-four-hour journey to bust free of a two-year oatmeal-and-bean dietary rut. And Chorizo now has in its history the day the witches came to town and voodooed the local dog population.

Some hunters saw them—there is no accounting for bad luck or good luck, just ask anybody, it can happen either way. And when they saw these two kids pitching a guy down the mine shaft, they skedaddled and called the cops, gave an ID on the machine's plates. Late that night the authorities fished the poor bastard out of the shaft.

The head was kind of messy from the pounding with the rocks. But after a day or two they figured out who he was from dental records.

The sign on the wall is a bit tricky with its claim that the El Tonto is the oldest bar in the oldest town site in the state. It is only after a case or two of beer that I notice it does not claim to be a very old bar at all, but simply the one with the longest record in this particular spot. But then time does not seem a keen issue in Chorizo. Virgil is here on his stool at the tip of the saloon's horseshoe bar, and across the way is Danny de Dios, a big man, with big arms, barrel chest, bald head, beard, and glasses through which he peers at the world with an almost childlike curiosity. The first time I met him he was peddling hoes he makes when he needs a little money, and the handles on his handiwork were of metal. I asked, "Don't these things kind of vibrate if you hit a stone when working the ground?" He looked at me with pity and answered, "I can tell by your question that you are not a gardener."

Danny is another basic Chorizo driver, his truck a bashed-up thing and his papers not in order. He has had, the locals say, hundreds of tickets for offenses of both man and machine. This is not a problem since he sees the county jail as a place of peace and quiet and decent food and free dental care. Also, Danny is a man of the faith, and when he is in jail he organizes prayer meetings and gets to preaching. In fact, jail is sometimes very attractive to him, and he has been known to call the sheriff's department from the pay phone in Chorizo and request that they come and haul him in. Increasingly, they decline. Recently, stunned by their feeble law enforcement, he hitched a ride to the jail, walked in and presented himself and his many offenses, and demanded incarceration. He was rejected.

They say that once upon a time he was a race car driver, and that once in support of his sport he had to do some deals, and that this landed him in prison for a stretch. This is possible. It is not unusual for the government to intervene when people try to make ends meet and to hurl their lives toward their dreams. And such people often tend to land in Chorizo. The most recent wave began in the late sixties when some immigrants the locals called hippies drifted into an old mining claim called the Arroyo. They stuck and are still here along with their children and soon their grandchildren. No one wanted to say it or admit it, but they represented the legend of the Old West, the lawless freedom—except that they did not look like John Wayne or act much like him. Jenny can remember the scorn in town when she first arrived, the sense of "us" and "them," but now she talks to people who once turned their backs at her approach. Somehow time has healed things—or maybe no one in Chorizo really has the energy to keep things going over a long haul. The newcomers have developed customs that enrich the local world—for example, a week-long party that blots out a chunk of early May. And they brought a new line of work here—or perhaps more accurately, rejuvenated an old one—drug smuggling. Stash houses began to dot the landscape and other odd matters occurred. But somehow this seems in good part to have been absorbed into the mores of Chorizo, tucked away like a child in bed with the soft blanket of local independence to protect against the night chill of outside interference, and most complaints seem to be against the Border Patrol and the various police agencies that prowl the area in ingenious and transparent disguises.

Perhaps for a place to be a real place, it has to be an idea squared off against other ideas: not the next Taos but the first Chorizo. I always wonder about this when I sit in the El Tonto, a kind of grazing ground for people who have rejected everything beyond the town and some of the things within it. Once Virgil got to explaining a guy who used to live by him in a trailer on the edge of Chorizo. This neighbor had a liking for the bottle, and eventually it got to him and the doctors told him he had to quit his boozing or he would surely die and die very soon at that. So when he got back to the town, he told Virgil he was going to have to dry out. Virgil looked at him—the man was jaundiced and yellow, and Virgil advised, "You might as well finish it." And the man thought about that and took Virgil's words to heart. He went back to drinking, and in a not very long period of time he was dead.

If that strikes your ear as a bad story or as a good story, then perhaps you are not right for Chorizo. That is a story. Given a hundred and thirty years to incorporate, the town has never gotten around to it. This is not an accident. Not every place is about destiny or progress or history. Some places are about things they cannot even figure out how to say, about just being a place. And whatever being a place means is something that is worked out day by day. Nights, also.

I'm driving a couple of miles down dirt roads with Virgil gently guiding—left here, a right there—and then we turn into the yard, the acres dotted with mesquite, and there in that big metal shed is where Plug works. He fixes the local cars and trucks and has been at it a good long time. He is somewhere around sixty. He is sitting in a lawn chair on the cool concrete, and three mangy dogs sleep sprawled out around him. He is from southern Mississippi, showed up here years ago after that ranch by Chorizo got busted into little pieces and now he has his acres, his shed, his trailer. His brother-in-law works with him, and his wife of forty years tends to the home. He hands out beers—there's four or five cases piled up, and on his tool chest sit three fifths of tequila. The flies buzz, it is just after noon, and he did a brake job that morning.

There is a lot of laughter, more beer, time slides by. Plug tells of when he worked on the river at Natchez and they had these gambling barges tied up midstream beyond and between the laws of Mississippi and Louisiana, and the oil crew he was part of went out there one day and lost everything. He says they were shuttled out in little boats and then couldn't leave until they'd been cleaned out. Well, after surrendering their paychecks they walked down the gangplank to the shuttle boat to be returned to shore, but at the last instant one guy in the crew leapt up and raced back onto the barge and grabbed a fire axe that was hanging on the ship's wall and raced fore and aft and cut the mooring lines. The barge drifted downstream, smashed into the supports of a big bridge spanning the Mississippi at Natchez and then peeled off and continued its journey toward the Gulf of Mexico.

I have never lived anywhere in my life where I have not known such moments—I stumble on situations and people and schemes, and in those sudden instants my eyes always flit here and there looking for the fire axe as I lunge toward the ropes.

Have a beer. The flies buzz, his brother-in-law is over there washing tools with gasoline, a lit cigarette in his mouth.

Some habits are not accepted in this country and not having a goal is one of them. Just getting by is frowned upon, and if you make a particular effort to just get by, you can be slapped down hard. The sky is overcast for the party but everyone comes anyway. There's fifty, a hundred people, maybe more; it is hard to count the turnout because everyone is spread out and sitting in circles on the ground having beers, eating some food, and the kids are running here and there and no one seems to pay much attention to their frolics. There's a bunch from the Arroyo here, and the men sport beards like biblical prophets, the women float past with clear eyes and tattoos. In the house on a table is a sign made from a piece torn off a cardboard box, and it explains that two kids born and reared in the Arroyo have been arrested for hauling a load and need money for their defense fund.

(Highballing a load through the night, one machine with a couple hundred pounds of marijuana, the other running blocker, roaring with lights off down the dirt road out of the oak hills toward the green mucky tongue lapping against Chorizo, the moon absent, stars out, cool feel in the air and then suddenly a Border Patrol truck slips out to bar the road and the kid driving blocker rams it and then you are caught. You are eighteen or nineteen and you have a plant that grows wild almost anywhere and you face ten, twenty, thirty years—hard to say, new mandatory guidelines, war on drugs, gotta protect ourselves. Do the crime, do the time. Drug lords. Corrupting our values. Enemy within. Gotta stop it. Don't inhale—this last item could be important later 'cause someone might ask questions, they increasingly do these days.)

Jake's at the party, he's the unofficial mayor of the Arroyo, and one of his kids is now facing serious time for that night ride. I've seen Jake in old news photos from the sixties—the hippie with the headband, long hair, and benign smile of chemical peace. Now he is gray headed, gray bearded, and near toothless but still smiling. *(Jenny turns a page in the white scrapbook and two little wwheauled kids maybe three or four years old stare up innocently from the page. They are the two villains captured on that night road running a load. One gets seven years, one nine. There is a system to things after all.)* A band is playing on a platform sited on the brow of the hill, and the core of their sound is a guy sitting on a carpet wailing at a sitar, and this droning sound floats out over the valley and against the green earth of the rainy season as a cloudburst walks across the slopes maybe five hundred yards behind him and his music. And then lightning streaks down from time to time, and I look at the big amps out in the weather and await an electrocution. Jenny's here, as are Molly and Danny de Dios and people of all ages and types. There doesn't seem to be an overwhelming pattern, just a grab bag of blood, an example of the diversity that sometimes is the boast of this nation.

After the sitar band finishes Mother Chorizo is slated to play, and I talk to them about their music. They all sport T-shirts that announce the Mother Chorizo World Tour and list the itinerary: Chorizo, Chorizo, Chorizo, Chorizo, Jones's Farm. That last venue is a prison camp in the East, where one of the band members has just spent a year or so after being caught with a load. This party is his homecoming. I ask the more-or-less head of the band just how big Mother Chorizo is, and he patiently explains that it is really six guys, but every time they get up to full playing strength they seem to lose someone, and so on any given day Mother Chorizo is really five strong. And then he smiles.

I get back to drinking a glass of wine and sitting on the brown earth and watching the rain move over the land. A friend of mine once came with his wife to Chorizo Days and set up a stand selling tortillas. It was a fine day, and then a big wind came on and my friend, who weighs two hundred pounds, was picked up and tossed ten feet by this sudden blast of air. And as he picked himself up he looked over and saw a small child being tumbled like a ball along the ground, and he raced over and grabbed hold of the child and stood there while the wind raked their hides. And that was the day the Hurricane came to Chorizo. Everyone remembers it, though no one can quite peg the year anymore. Including my friend.

As I sit looking at the window whited out by light, Jenny tells me that after she left the Arroyo she moved to another mining claim and spent about two years there and had two children. But mainly she read, just read and read and read. She is a fiend for reading. Once she went to the city for six months or a year to get some kind of degree, and this has helped her get work from time to time when the money is a little thin. Her biography is kind of scattered, like that of most of us, and the telling is a series of quick glimpses, the same way the need and word of God gets compressed into the feel of the beads as the rosary slides through the fingers. We are always careful when we first tell others of our life, because somewhere in our heads there is this template outlining what a life should be, and most of us know our own lives do not fit this pattern. We may all be like children at heart, but we have learned to be very careful children.

(Virgil has a kind of dream. He will have a truck that runs good, and a big horse trailer, the kind that has stalls fore and aft and in between squats a small cell with a bunk, and he will sally forth from Chorizo and wander from town to town buying horses here, selling horses there, talking with people, drinking beers in various saloons, living the life of a native trader, much like the first European wanderer of the West, Cabeza de Vaca. Virgil will see the country a bit, make a few dollars, maybe even get a driver's license. It is all clear in his head and vague in his speech, but somehow one image always comes to mind when he speaks of this dream—he is coming over a rise, the polished horse trailer in tow, a hand-rolled cigarette in his mouth, and it is morning and the air is fresh.)

We drift back to the time of the killing, when one man shot another man down by the lake and the bullet crashed through the tissue of a body and then death came. The murderer was sent up for a pretty good stretch, and then to everyone's surprise, when he got out he showed up back in Chorizo. The guys, Jenny explains, were down on him, real down and gave him a hard time. I do not ask what this entailed. But the guy did not leave, he hung on.

(There are so many variations on this matter of Chorizo homicide that it is a theme worthy of Bach and his student Goldberg. They talk of a man who lived west of town and he had a claim which others disputed and one night—these things always happen at night, the cover of darkness, the absence of the moon, the hand before the face and yet the eyes are blind—he exploded in a blast of dynamite. Not a clue. Dynamite man. Or there is the handless man. He got a piece of a mine or sold a piece of a mine—it all gets jumbled—and built a fine two-story house and then one day they found him in his new house with his hands cut off and his life gone. No one ever looked very hard for his killers, I'm told, because no one cared what happened to such a man.)

The man who got out of prison after the killing did hang on a while. And then he killed himself. After coming back, after the boys gave him a hard time, after a lot of things we will never know.

(I'm drinking with a rancher in the bar. He tells of the day he came down the canyon and sees this VW bus parked over by the bank. And when it's still there a day or two later, he decides to check. The windows are shut but for where a hose goes through, and there is tape around this opening. And the hose goes to the exhaust pipe. The man lies dead inside. I connect the two stories. Then disconnect. I have never asked.)

Ah, when? The dates do not come to mind. Nor does his name. He is a slowly eroding footnote to the life of Chorizo. A tiny detail. That's often all there is to a place, tiny details. And when there are bigger things, large moments, important movements, significant ideas, stuff worthy of statues and monuments and various memorials, then places are not so easy to locate. Then the ground ceases to have a particular and unique smell, the light does not feel special, and a place becomes a thing, I suspect.

So all I ever really wind up learning that night is that the guy came back.

And decided to never leave.

Turns out I knew one of the boys who murdered the guy and pitched him down the mine shaft. Met him once in the saloon when he bent my ear telling me this joke . . . you know the kind, about a black guy, a Jew, and a Catholic approaching St. Peter at those Pearly Gates. Can't remember the joke, quite. He seemed like a decent kid, though kind of slow—not retarded mind you, but just not real quick. A baseball cap was cocked on his head, and a faint mustache struggled above his lips and drooped around the edges of his mouth. All the time he was telling me the joke he had this yellow Sony Walkman clutched in his hand and the music plunging through the speakers clamped on his head.

The robbing-carjacking-killing turned out not to be such a good scheme. The guy who went down the mine shaft was low on change, and he'd just had to bum gas money off his old lady, a woman he was separated from. Of course, the car was only handy for a few hours before it was ditched in the mud by the river. About the girls, I can't say.

I spent a little time helping to find a decent lawyer—they were up on murder one. That's about it. Nobody in Chorizo talked much about it after the initial bust. By the next day the incident had vanished from conversation at the El Tonto like a ring of smoke melting in the calm of the saloon.

I asked Virgil what it all meant, and he drained his beer and allowed there was more killing needed thereabouts. Talked to the editor of the local paper and got the sense it was not indicative of the town. Must not be, since no mention of it ever ran. She's probably right. But then few things are ever indicative of a place. The bog is a part of it, the grasslands are a part of it, the bloody Marys downed with pistonlike regularity at the El Tonto, they're all a part of it. The hawks waiting in the cotton-woods, the man pitching down into the blackness of the shaft, the boys, hands on the knees of their girls, roaring down the road in the borrowed car. All of that and more. When The Case flashed on the evening news with footage of the cops staring into the shaft—the whole scene lit by floodlights—that never seemed a part of it but rather struck me as an artifact of something else from somewhere else.

At the time the killing went down, I was hiking in a stone canyon near Chorizo, wading across cold, smooth pools and waiting for rain which washed across the land later that night. I saw some Bewick's wrens.

Things happen. Everywhere.

It's what people make of a place that matters.

Maybe.

Once Jenny was driving down the main street when she saw a friend standing in front of the El Tonto pissing into the road. He looked up, saw her, and his face brightened. He waved with his free hand while continuing to void his bladder and said, "Hi, Jenny." Now when she thinks of what makes Chorizo special to her, she can see that guy waving.

I step out into the gray light of morning, a steaming mug of coffee in my hand, the dog worrying around my feet. The hills are still, and then I see gray forms flowing, bobbing and leaping through the yellow grass. Javelina, a piglike animal all the scientists say is not really a pig because of some way the bones lie when examined carefully on those cool, metal laboratory tables. Javelina have bristly hides, a scent gland that you can get a whiff of, if close, and miserable eyesight. They've been moving into this country for about a century now and seem entrenched.

The dog is not trained up to the country yet and takes off in a flash to confront this swarm of beasts. I watch her disappear over a knoll. In but a few seconds she comes flying back and roars up to stand close by me. I take another sip of coffee and feel light rain on my skin. The colors are coming on with the light, and under the heavy skies every leaf on the mesquites glows with green. That is it: the bitter taste of coffee on my tongue, the dog panting and rubbing against my leg, the gray forms sliding across the land in the early morning rain.

The pigs move on as if nothing has happened.

Probably nothing has.

Sometimes life is fine enough just to be; no troubling with being *about* something. And when that happens I stop moving, because there is nowhere to go and no reason to go there. These moments, alas, are not frequent. I am too addicted to some kind of rush to permit decent interludes. But at this instant I have surrendered to the gray sky, the faint colors, the steam off the coffee, the animals with their grace. Why don't I stay here? Why don't I begin again? Why don't I reach out on that table and take the offer? I own eight cookbooks, have excellent knives, sound pots and pans, a generous cutting board. I like slicing things, am never happier than when the stew is simmering. I should be home in my kitchen. I should make some kitchen my home.

I can see the pigs streaming silently across the hills. I can hear the rocks thudding into the man's head until his face is mush. The crack of a .30/.30, the headless body pitches forward into the dirt as an enormous silence settles. Kids fishing by the lake, the smell of homemade bread cooling on the counter, a couple dancing slowly to the music from the saloon jukebox, a blonde woman with a star tattoo just below her eye leans into me and says, "There's too many cops around here now," the gray forms bobbing as the light rain washes against the sunrise, a T-shirt emblazoned with an American flag and saying These Colors Don't Run, steam coming off my mug of coffee, the curls of smoke rising from the little households of Chorizo.

Come on, come on.

No Trespassing, the sign shouts.

Walking guide for historical buildings, the brochure whispers.

Saturday night, the heart murmurs.

No big words, please.

No words at all.

On a clear moonlit night when the wind is still you can still hear the Bill of Rights whispering in Chorizo.*

---

*Chorizo is, once again, an imaginary name, and its location is best kept a secret. Still, it can be found by anyone who goes somewhere and who then sticks and decides to hold that ground, whatever the cost. In this republic there will be many Chorizos as time stops, place begins, the beer keg is tapped and the dogs sleep through the heat of the afternoon. Such places cannot be planned. That has been tried and these efforts have failed. We have the records, almost endless records of such efforts. The people of Chorizo also exist, though the records, not surprisingly, do not often support this claim. There are very few places and very few people in the West, as the abundant census tracts clearly illustrate. But any optimist, and I count myself as one, can see that the future bodes well for places, just as it looks grim for transactions, V-8 engines, gun control, and poor strains of marijuana. And the people will come. Just as soon as they discover they actually exist, even if it takes forever. Which is the amount of time left on the game clock. . . .

CONTRIBUTORS:

BARBARA BABCOCK is a regents professor and director of the Program in Comparative Culture and Literary Studies at the University of Arizona. Her books include *The Pueblo Storyteller: Development of a Figurative Ceramic Tradition* and *Daughters of the Desert: Women Anthropologists and the Native American Southwest, 1880–1980*.

CHARLES BOWDEN has for many years been chronicling the growth and decay of the American Southwest, in periodicals ranging from *Buzzworm* to the *Los Angeles Times*, and in a series of books including *Frog Mountain Blues*, *Red Line*, *Desierto*, and most recently *Trust Me: The Extraordinary Adventures of Charles Keating*, published by Random House in 1993. He lives in Tucson, Arizona.

HARLAN C. CLIFFORD is a free-lance writer living in Aspen, Colorado. His first book, about the Aspen Mountain Rescue Team, will be published by HarperWest in 1995.

WILLIAM CORCORAN is an essayist and screenwriter living in Culver City, California.

LINDA HASSELSTROM is a rancher, poet, and essayist. Her books include *Going Over East* and *Land Circle*, for which she received a Mountains and Plains Regional Booksellers Award in 1992. She spends her time in South Dakota and Wyoming.

GLEN HUNTER has written for the *Arizona Republic*, the *Boston Phoenix*, and the *Los Angeles Times*, and he was associate editor of the *Santa Fe Reporter*. He currently lives in Albuquerque, where he is the editor of *New Mexico Business News*.

DEAN MacCANNELL currently teaches cultural analysis and criticism in the Department of Environmental Design and Landscape Architecture at the University of California at Davis. He is also adjunct professor of sociology and critical theory at the University of California at Irvine. He is the author of *The Tourist: A New Theory of the Leisure Class* and *Empty Meeting Grounds: The Tourist Papers*, published by Routledge in 1992.

RICHARD MANNING is an award-winning environmental reporter and writer whose work has appeared in numerous periodicals, including *Wilderness*, *Sierra*, and *Outside*. He is the author of *The Last Stand*, an exposé of the logging industry in the Northwest, and *A Good House: Building a Life on the Land*, published by Grove Press in 1993. He lives near Lolo, Montana.

ELLEN MELOY has written for *Northern Lights*, *Harper's*, *Outside*, *Travel and Leisure*, and other periodicals. Her book, *Raven's Exile: A Season on the Green River*, was published in 1994 by Henry Holt and Co. She lives in southern Utah and Montana.

MARK NEUMANN is an assistant professor in the Department of Communications at the University of South Florida in Tampa. He is currently writing a book on tourism at the Grand Canyon.

JOHN NICHOLS is a writer, photographer, and crusader for just and desperate causes living in Taos, New Mexico. His novels include *The Milagro Beanfield War*, *An Elegy for September* and, most recently, *Conjugal Bliss*. His recent works of photography and nonfiction include *The Sky's the Limit* and *Keep It Simple*.

SCOTT NORRIS is a graduate student in the Department of Biology at the University of New Mexico. He is the publisher of Stone Ladder Press.

EDUARDO PAZ-MARTINEZ is a wandering free-lance writer currently living in Fort Worth, Texas. He is a former Mexico City bureau chief for the *Houston Post* and has written for the *Santa Fe Reporter*, *The Boston Globe*, *New York Post*, and other papers.

C. L. RAWLINS combines outdoor work with a wild variety of writing, from scientific papers to poetry. He is the recipient of a Stegner Fellowship from Stanford University, is poetry editor for *High Country News*, and is the author of *Sky's Witness: A Year in the Wind River Range*, published by Henry Holt and Co. in 1993. He was born in the frozen, desolate state of Wyoming and still lives there.

RICHARD REINHART is a journalist who writes primarily about American cultural and social history. His work has appeared in *American Heritage*, *Wilderness*, and other periodicals, and he is the author of over a dozen books. He lives in San Francisco.

JIM ROBBINS has written about the American West for numerous newspapers and magazines, including *The New York Times*, *The Boston Globe*, *Audubon*, *Discover*, and *Smithsonian*. He is the author of *Last Refuge: The Environmental Showdown in Yellowstone and the American West*, published by William Morrow and Co. in 1993. He lives in Helena, Montana.

SYLVIA RODRIGUEZ is a professor of anthropology at the University of New Mexico. She is the author of a number of academic papers and a book on the matachines dance in northern New Mexico to be published by the University of New Mexico Press in 1995.

REG SANER is an award-winning poet and essayist and a professor of English at the University of Colorado. His most recent book, *The Four-Cornered Falcon: Essays on the Interior West and the Natural Scene*, was published in 1993 by Johns Hopkins University Press. He lives in Boulder.

DONALD SNOW edits *Northern Lights*, a regional journal based in Missoula, Montana, and is co-editor of a *Northern Lights* anthology to be published by Vintage Books in 1994. He is the author of *Inside of the Environmental Movement* and *Voices from the Environmental Movement*, both published by Island Press.

JIM STILES is a writer and editor of *The Canyon Country Zephyr* in Moab, Utah.

MARTA WEIGLE is a professor of anthropology and former chair of the Department of American Studies at the University of New Mexico. She is the author, co-author, or editor of a number of books, including *The Lore of New Mexico*, *Spiders and Spinsters: Women and Mythology*, and *Women of New Mexico: Depression Era Images*.

COURTNEY WHITE is a photographer whose work documents the changing landscapes of the American West. His book *In the Land of the Delight Makers* was published by the University of Utah Press in 1992. A collection of his photographs, *Unfinished Frontier: Life and Landscape in the Modern American West*, will be published by the University of Arizona Press in 1995. He lives in Santa Fe.

FLORENCE WILLIAMS is a Colorado writer specializing in environmental and planning issues. She is a frequent contributor to *High Country News* and *The Los Angeles Times*.

ALEXANDER WILSON is a journalist, horticulturalist, and author of *The Culture of Nature: North American Landscape from Disney to the Exxon Valdez*. He lives in Toronto.